LOSS AND REDEMPTION AT ST. VITH

LOSS AND REDEMPTION AT ST. VITH

The 7th Armored Division in the Battle of the Bulge

Gregory Fontenot
Colonel, US Army, Retired

UNIVERSITY OF MISSOURI PRESS
Columbia

Paperback ISBN: 9780826222220

Library of Congress Cataloging-in-Publication Data

Names: Fontenot, Gregory, 1949- author.
Title: Loss and redemption at St. Vith : the 7th Armored Division in the
    Battle of the Bulge / Gregory Fontenot.
Other titles: 7th Armored Division in the Battle of the Bulge
Description: Columbia : University of Missouri Press, [2019] | Series:
    American military experience | Includes bibliographical references and
    index.
Identifiers: LCCN 2019023568 (print) | LCCN 2019023569 (ebook) | ISBN
    9780826221926 (hardcover) | ISBN 9780826274359 (ebook)
Subjects: LCSH: Ardennes, Battle of the, 1944-1945. | World War,
    1939-1945--Campaigns--Belgium. | World War,
    1939-1945--Campaigns--Luxembourg. | United States. Army. Armored
    Division, 7th--History. | Germany. Heer--History--World War, 1939-1945.
Classification: LCC D756.5.A7 F66 2019 (print) | LCC D756.5.A7 (ebook) |
    DDC 940.54/219348--dc23
LC record available at https://lccn.loc.gov/2019023568
LC ebook record available at https://lccn.loc.gov/2019023569

Typefaces: Armalite Rifle, Acumin, and Minion

THE AMERICAN MILITARY EXPERIENCE SERIES
JOHN C. MCMANUS, SERIES EDITOR

The books in this series portray and analyze the experience of Americans in military service during war and peacetime from the onset of the twentieth century to the present. The series emphasizes the profound impact wars have had on nearly every aspect of recent American history and considers the significant effects of modern conflict on combatants and noncombatants alike. Titles in the series include accounts of battles, campaigns, and wars; unit histories; biographical and autobiographical narratives; investigations of technology and warfare; studies of the social and economic consequences of war; and in general, the best recent scholarship on Americans in the modern armed forces. The books in the series are written and designed for a diverse audience that encompasses nonspecialists as well as expert readers.

Selected titles from this series:

Military Realism: The Logic and Limits of Force and Innovation in the US Army
Peter Campbell

Omar Nelson Bradley: America's GI General, 1893–1981
Steven L. Ossad

The First Infantry Division and the US Army Transformed: Road to Victory in Desert Storm, 1970–1991
Gregory Fontenot

Bataan Survivor: A POW's Account of Japanese Captivity in World War II
Frank A. Blazich

Dick Cole's War: Doolittle Raider, Hump Pilot, Air Commando
Dennis R. Okerstrom

Contents

Foreword   ix

Author's Note on Equipment   xiii

Formation Symbols   xvii

Preface   xix

Acknowledgments   xxiii

INTRODUCTION   3

CHAPTER ONE   The Lucky Seventh Goes to War   7

CHAPTER TWO   Silesia Is Defended in the West   31

CHAPTER THREE   The Eve of Battle   55

CHAPTER FOUR   The Golden Lions at Bay   73

CHAPTER FIVE   The Lucky Seventh Goes to St. Vith   93

CHAPTER SIX   A Thin Olive Drab Line   117

CHAPTER SEVEN   Stand at St. Vith   145

CHAPTER EIGHT   Crisis at St. Vith   167

CHAPTER NINE   Decision at St. Vith   187

CHAPTER TEN   They Come Back With All Honor   209

CHAPTER ELEVEN   Reversal and Reconstitution   239

CHAPTER TWELVE   Redemption at St. Vith   263

viii   Contents

EPILOGUE   After the Battle   285

APPENDIX 1   Table of Ranks through Lieutenant Colonel   301

APPENDIX 2   Troop List—7th Armored Division   303

APPENDIX 3   German Units in Contact with
                7th Armored Division   307

Bibliography   311

Index   339

Foreword

General Frederick M. Franks, Jr.
General, US Army, Retired

I FIRST MET GREG FONTENOT during the thick of Operation Desert Storm, when he was a Lieutenant Colonel commanding TF 2-34, 1st Brigade, 1st infantry Division, "Big Red One," on 18 January 1991. Division Commander Major General Tom Rhame had assembled his chain of command on a patch of sand in his tactical assembly area to study just how to breach Iraqi defenses as part of our VII Corps attack. I wanted to see their efforts firsthand and to interact with the chain of command and senior NCOs there. Also present were assistant division commander for maneuver Brigadier General Bill Carter, First Brigade commander, Colonel Bert Maggart, and Greg's assault company commander, CPT Bob Burns. This was command face to face and up front, just as we all had practiced in VII Corps, the same way Brigadier General Bob Hasbrouck and his team had commanded the Lucky Seventh, the US 7th Armored Division, seventy-five years ago in defense of St. Vith in the Battle of the Bulge 1944–45.

In the ensuing assault, Greg commanded his task force with courage and distinction. After completing that mission, he moved TF 2-34 rapidly forward with 1st Brigade and the rest of the Big Red One more than 100 kilometers, then made forward passage of lines at night with 2nd ACR in enemy contact. Throughout that night and all the next day they fought elements of the Iraqi Republican Guards until mission complete, at the cease-fire, some 150 kilometers from that passage of lines.

After Desert Storm, Greg went on to continue a distinguished career as commander of 1st Brigade 1st Armored Division in the Implementation Force in Bosnia. He also served as director of the School of Advanced Military Studies (SAMS) at Ft. Leavenworth, Kansas. Prior to that I was fortunate when serving as TRADOC commander to have Greg as chief of my strategic planning group at our headquarters in a time of significant strategic change in the early 1990s.

Greg and I have become close and loyal friends based on shared combat service together, those face-to-face meetings, our continuing service together, and our mutual love of history. When it was my honor to present the VII Corps combat colors to Ft. Leavenworth and the School of Advanced Military Studies, it was Colonel Greg Fontenot who hosted the ceremony.

So when a tank battalion commander combat veteran writes a historic account with commentary of a World War II series of actions in and around St. Vith by the 7th Armored Division based on extensive research, personal interviews, and on the ground visits—in total research stretching from his undergrad days at Kansas State University to his graduate study at the University of North Carolina-Chapel Hill and at the School of Advanced Military Studies, we should all pay close attention. Pay attention because he is a combat veteran tank commander who has been in the middle of combat action. His commentary reflects those judgments and experiences. More important, pay attention because he is a distinguished historian who pays impeccable attention to details and personal accounts of combat all along the ranks, from enlisted soldier to senior commander. The result of Fontenot's long research and personal experience has in the pages that follow resulted in an enormously powerful book that is at once invaluable for historians, military veterans, military professionals looking to learn and grow in their ability to command in large-scale combat, or any reader wanting insights into the inspiring courage of American Soldiers and leaders in the borderline chaos that is close combat all arms battle.

When I deployed to Desert Storm I took with me five books to inform us of enduring truths of that kind of war: Clausewitz's *On War*; *Defeat Into Victory* by Field Marshal Slim; *Desert Generals* by Corelli Barnett; *On the Banks of the Suez* by Bren Adan; and *Rommel's War in North Africa* by Wolf Heckman. Had this book on the 7th Armored Division at St Vith in December and January 1944-45 existed then, I surely would have taken it, too. I was not looking for any recipe for our own situation many decades later but for enduring truths. I knew there were enduring truths about the operation we were about to undertake, even if there were also many things we would have to figure out for ourselves.

The central, perhaps most important, enduring truth is one that Greg Fontenot reminds us of again and again in this work. It is that soldiers, sergeants, and junior officers up through battalion level win battles and engagements.

It is their skill, courage, adaptability, and fierce will to win, even in severe conditions of weather and surprise enemy actions, and sacrifice that make victory possible. Furthermore he shows that a vital key to victory is that commanders be up front with those soldiers, making key decisions based on personal observation and listening to judgments made by subordinates face to face of current and rapidly changing situations. It is vital that these commanders ensure battle plans are flexible enough to allow for a variety of options, as so often well-laid plans give way to the realities of battle. Finally, and as Greg points out, adaptability was key in the WWII US Army, just as it was for us in 1991 during a sudden shift from defensive Cold War Germany to offensive large-scale all arms attack in the deserts of Iraq and Kuwait. Those mostly drafted soldiers in the 7th Armored Division and units attached in and around St Vith were innovative, able to quickly form teams out of fragments of units, overcome surprise while throwing in some surprises of their own for the attacking Germans, and display plain combat grit, something so necessary anywhere in the crucible that is close combat.

No one could write a history that lays all this out better than my friend and fellow Jayhawk VII Corps combat veteran Greg Fontenot. He has the heart of a warrior and the skill and attention to detail of a great historian.

Frederick M. Franks, Jr.
General, US Army, Retired

Author's Note on Equipment

In the interest of keeping the narrative flowing, I have not been specific in the text on just what types of equipment American and German units fought with during the battle but will do so here.

The Germans fielded many variants of trucks, prime movers, and combat vehicles. The 18th Volksgrenadier Division, for example, fielded two kinds of antitank guns. It had fourteen of the excellent fully tracked Sturmgeschütz Jagdpanzer 38(t) antitank guns familiarly known as Hetzers. Built in Czechoslovakia, the Hetzer proved itself effective in combat. The rest of the 1818th Anti-Tank Battalion fielded antitank guns towed by Raupenschlepper Ost, or RSO, tracked prime movers. The RSO was designed to enable the Germans to cope with conditions on the Russian front.

The Waffen Schutzstaffel (SS) divisions received the best equipment. During the Battle of the Bulge the SS antitank units fielded the Jagdpanzer IV and one battalion of the far more formidable Jagdpanther. Based on the Panzer IV chassis, the Jagdpanzer IV mounted a high-velocity seventy-five-millimeter gun. By contrast, the turretless Jagdpanther, built on the Panther tank chassis, had room for a larger, gun, the famed eighty-eight-millimeter cannon.

Three different kinds of German tanks saw action in the Ardennes Offensive: the Panzer Kampfwagen (PzKW) IV, V, and VI. The PzKW V and VI were known respectively as Panther and Tiger. The PzKW IV and the Panther were armed with seventy-five-millimeter cannons. The Panther had an improved .70-caliber cannon with higher muzzle velocity than the cannon on the PzKW IV, as well as better mobility and armor. The PzKW IV went through several upgrades and served well in the Bulge. Finally, the fearsome Tiger tank appeared in the Bulge, though in small numbers. Two Heavy Panzer Battalions, the 501st and 506th, fielded Tiger I and II tanks. The 653rd and 683rd Heavy Panzerjäger Battalions were equipped with the heavy tracked antitank system built on the chassis of a Tiger variant and fired an 88-millimeter cannon.

The Germans committed about 1,900 artillery systems to the fight, including both tubes and rockets. Howitzers and guns ran the gamut from seventy-seven millimeters to three hundred millimeters. The artillery included self-propelled, towed, and horse-drawn weapons. The German Nebelwerfer rocket artillery included both self-propelled and towed 150-, 210-, and 300-millimeter rocket launchers; the Americans called these systems screaming meemies.

The German infantry enjoyed one distinct advantage over its counterpart: it had more—and generally better—machine guns than the Americans carried. The armored infantry battalions assigned to the US 7th Armored Division (AD) even lacked the Browning automatic rifle or BAR carried by parachute and regular infantry units. The German MG 42s, with a rate of fire of 1,200 rounds per minute, set the standard in World War II; by 1944 there were plenty of them to go around, though it is likely that some units still had the earlier MG 34, which fired 850 rounds per minute; both had a rate of fire that far exceeded the six hundred rounds per minute of the standard M1919 .30-caliber Browning machine gun found in US infantry units.

American equipment is easier to track than the gear found in German units, but the US Army fielded a great many different systems as well. Most of the tracked vehicles in the 7th AD were built on the M4 Sherman chassis. The Lucky Seventh moved south on December 17, 1944, with two variants of the M4, one armed with a low-velocity seventy-five-millimeter cannon and the second with a much better high-velocity seventy-six-millimeter cannon. The armored division's self-propelled howitzer was known as the M7 Priest because its .50-caliber ring mount looked like a pulpit. The M32 tank recovery vehicle was another common variant. Finally, the M10 and M36 tank destroyers were built on the Sherman chassis; they were armed with three-inch and ninety-millimeter guns, respectively. The M18 tank destroyer fired a seventy-six-millimeter gun and was built on a different platform from that of the M10 and M36. Equipped with an early automatic transmission it was fast and maneuverable. The 7th AD's attached Tank Destroyer Battalion fielded M10 and M36 tank destroyers but had none of the M18s. Combat Command B of the 9th AD brought with it the similarly equipped 811th

Tank Destroyer Battalion, while the 820th Tank Destroyer Battalion of the 106th Infantry Division (ID) had towed three-inch guns.

The 7th AD's organic cavalry squadron depended on the agile but lightly armored and armed M8 armored car known as the Greyhound. Equipped with M5 Stuart light tanks and seventy-five-millimeter assault guns, the 87th Cavalry Reconnaissance Squadron was well equipped for both reconnaissance and security missions, including screening or guarding a flank.

Several kinds of artillery supported American units in the Battle of the Bulge. These ranged from towed seventy-five-millimeter howitzers found in the Parachute Field Artillery Battalions to the enormous 240-millimeter howitzer. All of the 106th ID's howitzers were towed. Corps artillery units included both towed and self-propelled variants. The US Army had a lot of artillery and used it effectively.

The 7th AD fielded a large fleet of half-tracks in a number of variants. Some were built to haul the armored infantry, and some as command and control vehicles; the 203rd Anti-Aircraft Artillery Battalion attached to the 7th AD had still more variants on which to mount antiaircraft weapons. The M16 motor gun carriage with quadruple mounted .50-caliber machine guns was the most common among these.

The 2.5-ton truck, or Deuce and a Half, was ubiquitous; it provided the platform for shop vans and ambulances, and it hauled every imaginable thing from people to food. It was reliable and could travel about anywhere; the Jeep, or quarter-ton truck, was nearly as numerous as the Deuce and a Half. Versions of the venerable Jeep served the US Army well into the 1980s.

For those who want the details on weapons systems by unit, there are several sources that satisfy. Much of what is in this note has stemmed from Jean-Paul Pallud's *Battle of the Bulge: Then and Now*, which is very good on the particulars of the German order of battle. Danny S. Parker is also a good source on German weapons and order of battle; his order of battle for the Ardennes for both sides can be found in Charles B. MacDonald's *A Time for Trumpets*.

Simon Forty's *American Armor* is more than adequate to see how the US Army organized its armored formations. Robert S. Cameron's *Mobility, Shock, and Firepower* is a good source for a look at how armor grew and the various iterations of organizational change.

Lieutenant Colonel Joseph R. Reeves's "Artillery in the Ardennes" is essential for those who want to understand the use and effect of artillery in the Battle of the Bulge. Boyd L. Bastrup's *King of Battle* is useful to understand the development of fire direction in the US Army and the technique for time on target. The Army introduced the proximity fuse in the Battle of the Bulge; artillery supporting the American counterattack in January 1945 used the new fuse to great effect.

Formation Symbols

Frequently Used Symbols

Echelon

I	Company	XX	Division
II	Battalion	XXX	Corps
III	Regiment	XXXX	Army
X	Brigade/Combat Command	XXXXX	Army Group

Formation

	Self-Propelled Antitank		Motorized Infantry
	Antiaircraft Artillery	HHC	Headquarters and Headquarters Company
	Armor / Panzer	QM	Quartermaster
	Armored Infantry / Panzergrenadiers	LOG	Logistics
	Armored Field Artillery		Medical
	Artillery		Maintenance
	Armored Reconnaisance	MP	Military Police
	Motorized Reconnaisance	BAND	Band
	Armored Engineer		Signal
	Engineer		Transportation
	Infantry		Modern US Army threat formation symbol

Preface

Wʜᴇɴ ɪ ᴡᴀs a child living in Fort Rucker, Alabama, my parents encouraged my interest in history and reading. For my ninth birthday my father,
a US Army sergeant and World War II submarine sailor, gave me Douglas
Southall Freeman's *Lee's Lieutenants*. I am compelled to admit I read only
the first of the three volumes. I really did not understand what Freeman was
trying to say until I reread volume 1 and then read the other two when I was
a student at the US Army Command and General Staff College. Despite my
dad's effort, it was my mother who really made history zing. She took me to
the post library often and indulged me to the point of arguing with librarians
who rightly thought I sometimes chose books that were beyond me. I happened one day on John Toland's *Battle: The Story of the Bulge*.

From that day to the present I have been captivated by Toland's book
and military history generally. Toland's account rings with an "I was there"
commentary that makes the story leap from the pages into my mind. As
a student at Kansas State University in the 1960s I had to cope with anti-
ROTC protests but relished military and naval history taught by the likes of
Stephen E. Ambrose, Edward M. Coffman, Kenneth J. Hagan, and Robin D.
S. Higham. They nurtured my love of researching and writing history using
original sources.

As a soldier I had the opportunity to pursue my interest in military history
in Europe and in the United States, visiting battlefields and studying warfare
as part of my own professional development. In 1984, I had the rare privilege
of joining the second class in the Army's Advanced Military Studies Program
at the School of Advanced Military Studies. There I researched and wrote
my second master's thesis, "The Lucky Seventh in the Bulge: A Case Study

for the AirLand Battle." The Army supported travel to do primary source research and to interview key leaders in the 7th Armored Division (AD).

Later in that year of study, Colonel Richard Hart Sinnreich and I organized and led staff rides in the Hürtgen Forest and in the Ardennes, where the Battle of the Bulge had played out. Walking the ground and seeing it for myself has been one of the highlights of my life. I have been back to the Hürtgen and the Siegfried Line since, leading officers of the brigade I commanded on a staff ride. These visits contributed to my continued interest in the Battle of the Bulge and to a determination that someday I would build on it. This book is the consequence of that interest and the pinnacle of my study but not, I hope, the end of it. The Battle of the Bulge and World War II will always be compelling to me.

The Battle of the Bulge is monumental in scope, scale, and complexity. Historians since the end of the war have written about various parts of it, including it in larger histories of the war in the west or focusing on the battle itself. There are regimental histories, such as Robert F. Phillips's *To Save Bastogne*, which tells the story of the 110th Infantry Regiment of the 28th Infantry Division (ID). Attacked by units from three German tank divisions and two infantry divisions, the 110th bought time to rush units in to defend Bastogne. John C. McManus's *Alamo in the Ardennes* builds on the story of the 28th ID to recount the bitter fight in the corridor forward of Bastogne. The 28th ID, the 10th AD, part of the 9th AD, and other units fought desperately and successfully to enable the defense of Bastogne. There are, of course, accounts of the stand of the 101st Airborne Division at Bastogne; Peter Schrijvers's *Those Who Hold Bastogne* is among the most recent.

Several good histories appeared soon after the war. Robert E. Merriam, who served as a combat historian with the 7 AD during the Battle of the Bulge, published *Dark December* in 1947, and R. Ernest Dupuy's *St. Vith: Lion in the Way* came out in 1949. Toland's very good popular history, *Battle: The Story of the Bulge*, reached bookstores in 1959.

The second tranche of histories appeared on the twentieth anniversary of the battle. The US Army official history by Hugh M. Cole, *The Ardennes: Battle of the Bulge*, appeared in 1965, and in 1969 John S. D. Eisenhower published his carefully researched *The Bitter Woods*. Both Eisenhower and Toland ably covered the battle from the highest-ranking officers to soldiers in foxholes. Toland set the standard for storytelling, while Eisenhower did the same for depth and accuracy. There are many other accounts that merit reading, but Charles B. MacDonald's *A Time for Trumpets*, published in

1985, forty years after the war, is the best written by a participant. MacDonald, well known for his personal narrative *Company Commander*, was one of the Army's official historians.

Charles Whiting, a British soldier who fought in the battle, found his calling writing novels and military history; he was, in particular, fascinated by the tragedy of the 106th Infantry Division. He wrote four books on the battle: *Death of a Division*, *Decision at St. Vith*, *The Last Assault*, and *Ghost Front*. Whiting did not annotate his work very well, but he told the story of soldiers with the advantage of understanding their lot, as did MacDonald. Peter Schrijvers's *The Unknown Dead* is an important addition to the historiography of the battle. Harold R. Winton, like MacDonald and Whiting, was a combat infantryman, albeit in a different war, and, like MacDonald, a trained historian. In 2007 Winton made a major contribution with *Corps Commanders of the Bulge*, in which he analyzed the leadership of J. Lawton Collins, VII Corps; Manton S. Eddy, XII Corps; Leonard Gerow, V Corps; Troy H. Middleton, VIII Corps; John Millikin, III Corps; and Matthew B. Ridgway, XVIII Airborne Corps. Winton's book is indispensable for those who seek to understand leadership at the highest tactical echelon in World War II. John Nelson Rickard, another soldier and trained historian, contributed to the understanding of leadership at the field army level with *Advance and Destroy* in 2011.

On the occasion of the sixtieth anniversary of the battle, Peter Caddick-Adams, a British soldier and combat veteran, published *Snow and Steel*. His is a first-rate scholarly work ably argued and well written. He writes his conclusions in two chapters: one that accounts for why things happened as they did, and one that reviews, in epilogue fashion, what became of some of the key characters in the story. Both chapters are magnificent.

This book is my attempt to share my fascination with the Battle of the Bulge and to examine a key part of the battle waged by a draftee armored division. That is my charge and my goal, and I believe there are insights from this narrative that are valid today.

.

Acknowledgments

This book is the realization of an effort that began nearly forty years ago. When I arrived at the Command General Staff College at Fort Leavenworth in the summer of 1983, I knew I wanted to tell the story of the 7th Armored Division. In part, I intended to confirm my view that Major General Matthew B. Ridgway had mismanaged the Division when it was assigned to his corps. During the academic year I learned I was wrong about Ridgway. The evidence would not support my bias, and in itself this was an important lesson. Go where the evidence takes you, not where you hope to go. My selection to remain at Fort Leavenworth for a second year to attend the School of Advanced Military Studies gave me an opportunity to turn an essay on the 7th Armored Division into a master's thesis.

I am most grateful to the veterans with whom I spoke or corresponded. I interviewed Major General Robert W. Hasbrouck, General Bruce C. Clarke, Major General A. J. Adams, Colonel Robert C. Erlenbusch, and Colonel Roy U. Clay. I corresponded with them as well, and with General William A. Knowlton, Colonel Marcus Griffin, Colonel John P. Wemple, and Colonel Charles E. Leydecker. Glenn Fackler, a 38th Armored Infantry Battalion combat veteran and president of the US 7th Armored Division Association in the mid-1980s, helped me locate veterans and enabled me to correspond with and/or visit them.

The US 7th Armored Division Association veterans held their last reunion in 2016, but their children and grandchildren maintain the association. They have digitized or transcribed thousands of pages of documents. To this day they work tirelessly to recover the remains of soldiers who remain missing. W. Wesley Johnston, the son of one of the veterans, has been the source of advice, data, and, through the excellent website he maintains, countless documents and photographs. My heartfelt thanks to Wes and the children and grandchildren of veterans who remain committed to the memory of the achievements of their fathers and grandfathers.

One of the great moments in this work came when I made a cold call to John Schaffner, president of the 106th Infantry Division. John is a hale and hearty survivor of the Schnee Eifel, Parker's Crossroads, and nearly six more months of fighting. He is a joy to speak with, and he helped me flesh out the 106th Infantry Division's part of this story.

Robert M. Epstein, who led my thesis committee, helped me navigate the process. Together with Colonel Richard H. Sinnreich, Bob and I walked the ground both in the Hürtgen Forest and in the Ardennes.

Mary Crow and Dan Doris at the Combined Arms Research Library at Fort Leavenworth unraveled the mystery of working with its extensive archives and with those of the National Archives and Records Administration. Just over thirty years later, Rusty Rafferty took over from Dan Doris as my guide and coconspirator, along with Elizabeth Dubbison and Susan Plotner. The Combined Arms Research Library is a wonderful place to work, supported by experts.

In the 1980s and since, my research has led me to the National Archives in Washington, DC, and Suitland, Maryland; the Military History Institute at Carlisle Barracks and its later, larger and even better iteration as the US Army Heritage and Education Center in Carlisle, Pennsylvania; and finally to the Dwight D. Eisenhower Presidential Library and Museum in Abilene, Kansas. In all of these archives the staff proved able, willing, and interested.

In particular, Marty Andreson, Rich Baker, and Lori Wheeler at the US Army Heritage and Education Center and Kevin Bailey at the Eisenhower Library and Museum helped me both on-site and remotely. The staff of the Center of Military History is as willing to support outside researchers as they are to sustain their own work; Sherry Dowdy supported my efforts to reproduce maps from the center's collection, and Carl Snyder searched for and provided photographs. Gordon Blaker at the US Army Field Artillery Museum at Fort Sill, Oklahoma; Robert Cogan at the US Army Armor Museum at Fort Benning, Georgia; and Bob Smith at the US Cavalry Museum at Fort Riley, Kansas, all helped find documents and or photographs. Congratulations to Jacob D. Turner, USMC, on his promotion to Staff Sergeant. Thanks, Jake also, for your volunteer work, including patiently scanning documents for me at the Field Artillery Museum—Semper Fi!

The library staffs at Columbia University, the George C. Marshall Foundation Library, the University of North Carolina, and the US Military Academy supported my work from afar; for their help I am truly grateful. The archivists at the Bundesarchiv in Koblenz, Germany, provided advice and scanned documents and/or photos. I am particularly indebted to Jasmin Brötz at the Bundesarchiv. It is wonderful to be able to do some of this work from home, and it would be impossible without librarians and archivists who genuinely care.

C. J. Kelly, author of *Red Legs of the Bulge*, provided sound counsel, photos, and maps. Carl Wouters shared with me his ideas on the work he is doing on the 106th Infantry Division. Carl lives in Belgium and routinely travels the battlefield, and is thus able to provide useful insights and images. Early on, I engaged Lieutenant Colonel Harold R. Winton, USA (Retired), my old seminar leader at the School of Advanced Military History, who wrote *Corps Commanders of the Bulge*. Hal moderated my tendency to critique generals at length and has always sharpened my thinking. Lieutenant Colonel Roger Cirillo, a proven historian of the Battle of the Bulge and the US Army, provided advice and leads. John McManus, author of (among many other things) *Alamo of the Ardennes*, lent an ear when I needed to talk about the book.

No one can edit his own work, or at least I am unable to do so. I therefore asked several old soldiers who happen also to be accomplished historians for help. Kevin Benson, Roger Cirillo, and David Mamaux read parts of the book, and Rick Swain read the whole thing. I am grateful to all of them for their candid criticism. Andrew Davidson edited my penultimate draft, and that is above and beyond the call of duty even for the editor in chief of the University of Missouri Press. Thank you.

Mark Osterholm has done maps and charts for me in three books. As always, he has done a great job, and remains a great friend.

The staff at the University of Missouri Press has been supportive both prior to accepting the book and once it cleared review. Brian Bendlin did the final edit; he is very good, and helped me correct mistakes and clean up syntax. Any mistakes that remain are my own, however.

Finally, I appreciate the support of the love of my life—Dana. Thank you.

Gregory Fontenot
Colonel, US Army, Retired
Lansing, Kansas
July 2019

LOSS AND REDEMPTION AT ST. VITH

Introduction

The aim of this book is to close a gap in the historiography of the Battle of the Bulge. The story of the 7th Armored Division (AD) has been told as part of the overarching story of the battle. Charles B. MacDonald, for one, did that ably in *A Time for Trumpets*. But no one has written the history of the 7th AD's fight from start to finish; this book will tell that story, from when the Division was alerted on December 16, 1944, through the stand at St. Vith, the withdrawal through the 82nd Airborne Division on December 23, the humiliation on Christmas Eve and Christmas Day, reconstitution, and the road back to St. Vith. On January 23, 1945, the Lucky Seventh, as the Division was called, recaptured St. Vith from the 18th Volksgrenadier Division, one month after the 7th AD had been forced to withdraw.

Setting context is necessary in recounting the saga of the 7th AD. The first four chapters do so by recalling the Lucky Seventh's introduction to battle and examining how both the Americans and the Germans organized, manned, and equipped their armies, with an emphasis on concepts, doctrine, and structure rather than equipment. The German Army had many variants of its own tanks, artillery, and infantry vehicles, and also made use of captured equipment of all kinds. Instead of coping with that confusion throughout the book, the Author's Note addresses combat equipment.

Both the Americans and the Germans had to confront a shortage of manpower in 1943 that grew worse in 1944. Both sides reduced the size of their divisions and the combat systems authorized. How each coped is part of the story. The Americans had a problem peculiar to them, based on assumptions made prior to the war. Originally the US Army planned to build two hundred divisions so that it could rotate units in and out of the fighting in order to provide time to rest, refit, and receive replacements. That decision played a key role when it became apparent that the United States would not be able to raise one hundred divisions, let alone two hundred. The US Army managed to raise eighty-nine divisions by the end of the war. Instead of rotating units to refit in the rear, the Army sent individual replacements forward through replacement depots, from which they were assigned to divisions. The Germans used their *Ersatzheer*, or replacement army, to manage replacements, and sent them forward in job lots organized as march battalions. On arrival in a US unit, a new soldier might or might not go through a local division school to assimilate; in many cases he went straight to a unit. The German army maintained a school unit in each division to train replacements.

With respect to concepts and doctrine, it is safe to say that the US Army relied more heavily on published doctrine than did the Germans. The German Army published doctrine but adjusted it by practice throughout the war. Its tactics and techniques reflected the experience gained over six years of fighting in Poland, the low countries, France, the Mediterranean, North Africa, and the Eastern Front, including the Balkan States. By the fall of 1944, even company-grade officers had come to share a common cultural view on how to fight. The US Army grew from insignificance in 1940 to eighty-nine divisions by 1945. To grow that quickly required how-to manuals for citizen soldiers and a great many young officers who rose rapidly as the Army expanded. This problem was not unique to the Americans. All of the belligerents experienced it, but the American response reflected the view that an army could organize to teach soldiering and do it quickly. Army field manuals did just that. In formulating doctrine the US Army borrowed heavily from what it saw the Germans doing during the war. It even published and distributed a translation of the basic German doctrine, assuming that the German Army depended on the written word, just as the US Army did.

US Army doctrine and several concepts from Carl von Clausewitz's classic treatise *On War* are essential parts to the analysis of operations in this narrative. How the two armies organized and how they planned to fight form principal questions that can be examined against how they actually did fight. Clausewitz addressed the influence of close terrain on command and the effects of battle on attacking and defending forces. He also considered the character of commanders and their will to overcome essential to what he described as "Genius." I have used ideas of his to judge the character of several of the men in this narrative.

The US Army encouraged initiative and believed when possible in issuing what Brigadier General (BG) Bruce C. Clarke called "mission-type orders." The essence of this approach was to tell subordinates what was to be achieved and not how it was to be done. BG Robert W. Hasbrouck is the central character in this context. To the extent possible, the narrative explores how he thought and why he did what he did. The same approach applies to the other Americans in the story, but less so to their German antagonists. This is not the Germans' story; their thinking builds context, but it is not the focus.

Twenty years after the battle, Clarke (who commanded Combat Command B), Hasbrouck, and several other soldiers who fought at St. Vith, including German general Hasso von Manteuffel, participated in a two-part US Army television documentary titled *The Battle of St. Vith*. In it Manteuffel described the battle as one in which the leadership and courage of the *kleine Leute* on both sides was central. He explained his meaning that in this instance *kleine Leute*, which literally translated as "little people," meant junior leaders and private soldiers whose initiative often proved decisive.

The Ardennes itself is a key part of the story. Thickly forested rolling hills cut by streams and ravines determined how units could fight. Massed formations of tanks could not operate in the Ardennes; attacks often occurred in small numbers on very narrow frontages because that is all the terrain afforded. Weather also played a central role: the winter of 1944–45 was purportedly the coldest and wettest in a century. Rain early in the month of December made the Hohes Venne, or High Fens, soft. Later, deep snow and ice inhibited maneuvers. For most of December and January, overcast skies relegated air power to a secondary role. That very fact dictated the time of the German counteroffensive and denied the Americans one of their singular advantages.

As veterans of the Battle of the Bulge grew older, they finally shared their experiences in the battle in short pieces on the Veterans of the Battle of the Bulge Association website, in published and unpublished memoirs, and in interviews done by the U.S. Army Heritage and Education Center, the Library of Congress, and the Texas Military Museum. Soldiers' stories are far more available now than at any time since the battle, and they are central to this narrative.

CHAPTER ONE

The Lucky Seventh Goes to War

The August battles have done it and the enemy in the West has had it.
> —Supreme Headquarters Allied Expeditionary Forces, G-2 summary,
> August 23, 1944

The Boche always come through the Ardennes.
> —Belgian civilian

In the early morning hours of Saturday, December 16, 1944, three German field armies comprising twenty-eight divisions, including nine Panzer divisions, attacked a thinly defended sector of the American lines in the Ardennes forest. Eventually two US field armies of twenty-nine divisions, including eight armored divisions, responded. A British corps of three divisions and three armored brigades backstopped the American effort. The German offensive aimed to seize Antwerp, thus cutting off the British-led 21st Army Group from its American allies. Success would protect the Ruhr industrial region and perhaps drive an irreparable wedge between the Americans and British. The German high command, or at least Adolf Hitler, believed doing so could lead to concluding the war in the west successfully.

Instead the Allies stopped the Germans short of the Meuse River and then drove them back. After six weeks of bitter fighting, Hitler's last significant operational reserve withdrew, much diminished, beyond its original line. By any measure this battle—the Battle of the Bulge—was the largest fought by the US Army during World War II. More than a half million Allied and German soldiers fought among the densely forested ridges of the Ardennes during the coldest winter in a century. More than two thousand tanks and tracked antitank guns fought along slippery roads and through small towns, supported by several thousand artillery pieces. The Luftwaffe took to the air in large numbers against the Allied air forces for the last time during the war. The US Army suffered nearly 80,000 combat casualties, including 8,607 killed in action, 47,139 wounded, and 21,144 captured or missing. German reckoning is less certain, but it appears the Germans had 12,652 killed, 38,600 wounded, and 30,582 captured or missing.[1] Trench foot, sickness, and nonbattle injuries claimed thousands more on both sides.

Peter Schrijvers's *The Unknown Dead* is the best source for the reckoning of the suffering among civilians. Many civilians fled, but whether they fled or not they suffered. Schrijvers reports "an estimated 2,500 civilians died in Belgium as a direct or indirect result of the Battle of the Bulge." Still more died in Luxembourg—as many as five hundred more. Sadly, Allied air raids killed roughly one-third of Belgian civilians who died. The horrendous destruction of homes, livestock, and infrastructure ensured that the misery extended beyond the end of the war.[2]

The Battle of the Bulge has transcendent explanatory power for the US Army in World War II, corresponding to that ascribed to the Battle of Gettysburg in the Civil War. Both battles took on mythic proportions in the history of the Army. The Battle of the Bulge remains memorable in scope, scale, and misery. For the US Army, the battle reflected strategic decisions taken as early as 1939 on equipment, leadership, and how to fight. For the German forces, the battle constituted Hitler's last gambler's throw, beyond which there was nothing but progressive and cumulative disaster.

The 7th Armored Division

American soldiers from private to general who served either in or alongside the 7th Armored Division (AD), the soldiers who fought to defend and then to retake St. Vith, are the chief protagonists in this saga of perseverance and adaptability in combat. The 7th AD joined the fight alongside the 106th Infantry Division (ID) and a part of the 9th AD on the second day of the battle, Sunday, December 17, 1944. Because the Germans had penetrated the defenses of VIII Corps, the troops of the 7th AD arrived amid mass confusion, in bitterly cold weather, and immediately entered a fight for their very survival. At the outset their commanders worked, as one said, "to keep the confusion from becoming disorganized." Though tired and scared, as well as confused, the American soldiers responded, according to the German general who commanded their antagonists, with "courage . . . of the highest order."[3] This is their story.

To comprehend their experience it is necessary to understand both the context of this battle and how the Army intended the 7th AD to fight. Not until after World War II did the United States maintain a large standing army in peacetime, something that neither the US Constitution nor the culture of the United States favored. During both world wars the Army grew rapidly—so rapidly that the number of citizen soldiers exceeded the number of experienced officers and noncommissioned officers available to train and lead them. Accordingly, the Army published doctrine that described how to fight and how to prepare to do so. Army field manuals and technical manuals of the era are remarkable for their scope and the speed with which they were published. Most of them were published after Pearl Harbor. They are richly illustrated self-help books à la *Plumbing for Dummies* (in this case, perhaps, *Fighting for Dummies*—or at least fighting for the hitherto innocent). These marvelous little books run the gamut from Field Manual (FM) 55-105, *Water Transportation: Oceangoing Vessels*, instructing the reader on the operations of the Army's quite large navy, to Technical Manual 9-759, *M4 Sherman Medium Tank Technical Manual*, which showed tank crews how to maintain their steeds.[4]

The structure of units and the Army's doctrine are the consequence of specific design concepts. The Army designed the Lucky Seventh and the other armored divisions to exploit penetration of enemy positions made by the infantry. According to FM 17-100, *Armored Command Field Manual: The Armored Division*, the "*primary role* [of the armored division] *is in offensive operations against hostile rear areas.*" FM 17-100, published on January 15, 1944, did not list defending a position among the thirteen missions imagined for armored divisions. Nevertheless, bowing to necessity, the manual did devote a chapter to defensive operations, specifying that armored divisions would assume the defense if forced or ordered to do so. Even then the doctrine required armored divisions to fight by active means, including counterattack. Accordingly, infantry and antitank units were to "occupy forward areas." Tanks, on the other hand, were to use their mobility and firepower in local counterattacks.[5]

The Army built armored divisions as balanced combined arms formations that included both infantry and tanks, but it did not equip or man them to fight extended defensive operations. Nor did the Army have the means to replace losses rapidly or to reconstitute units mauled in combat. The 7th AD fought desperately for six winter weeks in the Ardennes to defend and retain the important road junction at St. Vith. Eventually the Lucky Seventh withdrew under pressure and, for a brief period, it constituted the XVIII

Airborne Corps' reserve. During that time it reconstituted combat capability by assimilating replacements, replacing equipment lost in combat, and fielding some new equipment. The Division also trained both individual soldiers and small units to return to combat. Finally, supported by airborne infantry, the 7th AD resumed the offensive, retaking St. Vith a month after being forced to cede the town to General der Panzertruppe Hasso von Manteuffel's troops and thus concluding their part of the campaign. The 7th AD fought alongside other units, some of whom were formally attached, and others that joined on a commander's initiative or were dragooned by one the 7th AD's generals.

Armored and Infantry Division Organization

The organization of armored, infantry, and airborne divisions reflected both conceptual decisions and the reality that the United States had insufficient manpower to man its divisions as originally designed. The 7th Armored Division activated on March 1, 1942, at Camp Polk, Georgia, with Major General (MG) Lindsay McDonald Silvester in command. Formed around a cadre provided by the 3rd AD, the Lucky Seventh had little respite in the intervening two years before it landed in France in August 1944. The Division trained at Camp Polk and at Camp Coxcomb in the California desert. Finally the 7th AD participated in large-scale maneuvers in Louisiana and Texas before sailing with its equipment for the United Kingdom.[6]

In the midst of training and deploying units, manpower restrictions forced the Army to reduce the strength of its armored and infantry divisions. Even these cuts proved insufficient to address the manpower shortages. The Chief of Staff, General (GEN) George C. Marshall, then reduced the planned number of all types of divisions to ninety. After that decision the Army Ground Forces Reduction Board applied the knife to division structure, reducing the infantry divisions by nearly two thousand officers and men and the armored divisions by nearly four thousand. The Army reduced the number of tanks in armored divisions from 360 to 263. Finally, the expansion of ground forces that began in 1940 ended in August 1943, and no new divisions were activated after that time.[7] The Army made do with what it had. At the end of World War II it did not have a single division still in the continental United States; all eighty-nine divisions it finally fielded had deployed overseas by the end of the war in August 1945.

Beyond a shortage of manpower it is fair to say that neither the Army nor line infantry divisions received the cream of the crop. Until 1942, young men could avoid the draft by joining the Army Air Forces, the Marine Corps, or the Navy. The airborne infantry skimmed off more of the best and brightest soldiers, as did some of the specialty formations. The shortage of manpower reached its nadir in 1944. Soldiers had to be stripped from anti-aircraft artillery units and combat support and service support units to find infantry and armor replacements. Last but not least, replacements came from the Army Specialized Training Program designed to educate a cadre of bright young men in universities. Young men who had hoped to spend the war in college got a rifle instead of a degree and went to war—often without adequate training.[8] These young men were bright and for the most part highly motivated. They added high-quality troops to units in the field.

In any case, before deploying, the 7th AD reorganized from a "heavy" armored division of three robust regiments to a smaller combined arms division. The reduction and reorganization reflected not only manpower restrictions but also operational concepts and strategic decisions. First, building up air power took priority over ground troops. Second, Lieutenant General (LTG) Lesley J. McNair, the commander of the Army Ground Forces and the driving force of Army operational concepts, intended the armored divisions to exploit success, not attempt breakthroughs, which further justified their reduced numbers.[9]

The reorganized armored divisions fielded three tank and three armored infantry battalions. Two combat command headquarters, one commanded by a brigadier general, provided command and control of the maneuver battalions, which were attached to combat commands according to mission requirements. A third combat command reserve would control units rotated out of the line to rest and refit. In practice, the divisions used the combat command reserve as a third headquarters. In addition to six maneuver battalions (three tank battalions and three armored infantry battalions), a mechanized cavalry reconnaissance squadron supported the division, assuming economy of force and security missions. The armored divisions had combat support and service support formations similar to those in the infantry divisions. The combat support formations included three self-propelled 105-millimeter howitzer battalions. The armored divisions also had an organic armored engineer battalion. They usually had an attached antiaircraft artillery battalion and a tank destroyer battalion. The organic service support formations included an ordnance battalion and a medical battalion.

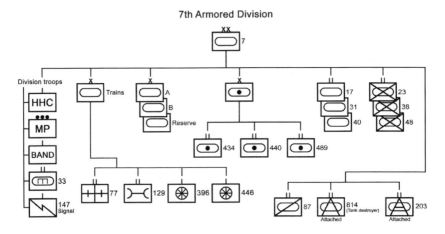

CHART 1. The organization of the 7th Armored Division reflected both the operational concept for armored division employment and manpower constraints. The Division was organized based on the 1943 Table of Organization and Equipment. That design reduced the armored division from six tank battalions organized in two tank regiments and three armored infantry battalions organized in a single infantry regiment to three tank and three armored infantry battalions. The 814th Tank Destroyer Battalion and the 203rd Anti-Aircraft Artillery Battalion (Automatic Weapons) were not assigned but remained attached from August 1944 until after the end of the war. The Division considered the two attachments "family" members.

Manpower shortages in late 1943 forced the Army to ravage units late on the deployment schedule to man those scheduled earlier. The 106th ID is perhaps the most poignant example. Activated on March 15, 1943, it suffered delay and disruption due to being "cadred." In the summer of 1944, after the 106th ID completed unit training, it lost 7,247 soldiers, or some 60 percent of its authorized strength. Plumped up just in time to deploy, the 106th ID arrived in Europe without the opportunity to train replacements adequately.[10] While the Division could be considered to have had two years of preparation, the majority of its soldiers enjoyed significantly less.

The 106th ID and the other infantry divisions organized with just over fourteen thousand soldiers. They remained robust, with three regiments of three infantry battalions. Each battalion consisted of nearly nine hundred soldiers, mostly riflemen. Infantry regiments also possessed an organic cannon company, normally of six towed short-barreled 105-millimeter howitzers to provide immediate fire support. Each infantry division fielded four artillery battalions commanded by a division artillery commander, normally a brigadier general. Three 105-millimeter howitzer battalions provided direct support to the regiments. A towed 155-millimeter howitzer battalion provided general support to the Division. The division artillery headquarters had the means to mass the fires of all four and integrate fires from reinforcing artillery. An engineer battalion rounded out organic combat support, and each infantry division also had a reconnaissance troop. Antiaircraft artillery, antitank battalions, and tank battalions attached from the field army routinely supported the infantry divisions. Transportation assets could be added to provide added mobility. Although numbered field armies provided the bulk of logistics support at supply points, the infantry division had some organic logistics organizations for transportation and distribution.[11]

A corps commander directed from two to as many as six divisions according to mission requirements. The corps echelon exercised tactical direction and coordination of attached divisions. The 1941 edition of FM 100-5, *Operations*, described the corps as "primarily a tactical unit."[12] Accordingly, it

106th Infantry Division

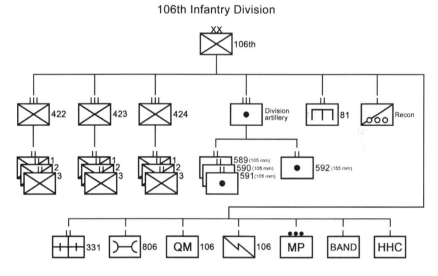

CHART 2. The 106th Infantry Division was organized, largely based on manpower constraints, in accord with the 1943 Table of Organization and Equipment. The 1943 division remained robust. By 1944 most infantry divisions had tank, antitank, and antiaircraft artillery battalions. At the outset of the Battle of the Bulge the 106th had several attachments. These included Combat Command B, the 9th Armored Division, the 14th Cavalry Group, the 820th Tank Destroyer Battalion (towed), the 440th Anti-Aircraft Artillery Battalion, the 634th Anti-Aircraft Artillery Battalion, and the 275th Armored Field Artillery Battalion. Combat Command B, 7th Armored Division also was attached briefly. The 106th was not fully reconstituted after the battle.

had almost no administrative responsibility for logistics or accounting for personnel and equipment. As such, corps headquarters had fewer than two hundred soldiers authorized. Depending on the assigned mission, a corps received various "pooled" units from its controlling field army. Typically it could expect cavalry, engineers, antiaircraft artillery, and field artillery to be assigned from the Army echelon. In turn the corps could retain or attach these to subordinate divisions to weight specific missions. Artillery was easily the most important combat support asset employed by the corps in support of operations.[13]

The Red Army was justifiably famous for barrages fired by artillery lined up hub to hub. What is not widely known is that only the Red Army had more artillery than the US Army. US artillery, however, demonstrated better agility and could mass fires from dispersed batteries using a technique called time on target, which required fire direction centers to coordinate direction of fire and time of flight for multiple artillery units. This technique enabled multiple battalions to deliver accurate bombardment with first rounds from as many as a hundred or more tubes of artillery striking simultaneously. On December 15, 1944, some twenty-three battalions of corps artillery and fourteen battalions of divisional artillery could support operations in the Ardennes stretch of the Allied line. Equally important, no artillery went to waste. The artillery that supported Americans in the Ardennes included two "provisional" battalions equipped with captured German 10.5-centimeter howitzers that were a close match to the US 105-millimeter howitzer. These were manned by reducing manning in several 155-millimeter battalions assigned to the VIII Corps artillery.[14] The US Army believed in and used artillery effectively.

The Breakout: Penetration, Exploitation, and Culmination

A brief review of events following the breakout after the Battle of St. Lo in July 1944 will set the context of the 7th AD's fight in the bulge. At the outset of the campaign in Normandy, British field marshal Bernard Law Montgomery led the Allied ground forces as commander of the 21st Army Group until late July, when LTG Omar N. Bradley activated the 12th Army Group, which was composed of First US Army, commanded by LTG Courtney H. Hodges, and Third US Army, commanded by LTG George S. Patton Jr. The Allies, led by US forces, exploited the breakout by repelling a heavy counterattack at Mortain and racing east and west, sending a corps to encircle the Port of Brest and the rest of Third Army around the southern flank of the German Army in Normandy. For a few weeks the Allies, and in particular the

US Army, demonstrated blitzkrieg to those who invented it. But the Americans and their allies did not demonstrate the level of expertise the Germans showed in 1939–41. After nearly encircling large German forces at Falaise, the Allies failed to close the gap because of difficulties coordinating forces from the converging 12th and 21st Army Groups attacking north and south, respectively.

As the Prussian military theorist Carl von Clausewitz observed, "the real fruits of victory are won only in pursuit."[15] More than two hundred years have passed since his widow published *On War*, yet that observation remains accurate. Clausewitz further argued that attacks, however strong at the outset, had limits. He showed that battles and engagements happen spasmodically because the combatants are never in equilibrium.[16]

After failing to close the encirclement at Falaise, the Allied forces pursued the escaping German forces to the Seine River, clearing the area north of the Loire River. Meanwhile, French and US forces landed in southern France and turned the remaining German forces in France out of position, making their withdrawal from France general. The British pursued the Germans into northern France and Belgium. The US forces, now organized in two field armies, raced toward the Rhine River. But the Allies outran their logistics system and, as Clausewitz theorized, culminated because it could not be sustained. In mid-September, although barely, the Germans won the race to the German border and occupied the rundown but still formidable defenses of the Siegfried Line.[17]

MG Leonard Gerow's V Corps reached the Siegfried Line in the Ardennes sector, literally on the heels of the Germans, on September 14, 1944. Short of fuel and ammunition, the V Corps attack in the Ardennes sputtered, along with the rest of the pursuit. At the end of the month, theater commander GEN Dwight D. Eisenhower had to admit to the Combined Chiefs of Staff that "the enemy has now succeeded in establishing a relatively stable and cohesive front."[18] Clausewitz explained this phenomenon as well when he argued that as an attack or pursuit continued, its strength diminished. Culmination occurred, he asserted, when the "attacker's superiority is exhausted"—in this case, logistically.[19]

A few days after reaching the Siegfried Line, Gerow left V Corps to return to Washington, DC, to testify at the congressional hearings on the Pearl Harbor attack. On his departure he sent a message to the Corps noting, "It is probable the war with Germany will be over before I am released to return to V Corps."[20] Gerow made his prediction without consulting the Germans, who were achieving what they called the miracle in the west. Mauled in France, they had nevertheless won the race to the Siegfried Line. Equally important, they had done so with many of their combat forces and nearly all of their tactical headquarters intact. The German Army did not disintegrate as it fled west, and the brains of the army—the tactical commanders and their staffs—survived to fight another day. Nearing the German frontier and their prepared defensive positions, the bedraggled Germans turned and fought. German resistance coupled with outstripped logistics brought the Allied pursuit to a halt.

To add further insult, German armor and infantry defeated British field marshal Bernard Law Montgomery's "airborne carpet," which was designed to enable his mechanized forces to establish a bridgehead on the Rhine at Arnhem. In doing so the Germans eviscerated the 1st British Airborne Division. Following the failure of Operation Market Garden in September 1944, Montgomery turned his attention to opening the Scheldt Estuary connecting the Port of Antwerp with the sea, a contributing factor to the logistics problems slowing the Allied advance. On Montgomery's right the Germans prevented the recently arrived Ninth US Army from closing on the Ruhr River. On Ninth Army's right, the Germans stopped First US Army in bloody fighting in the Hürtgen Forest. Third US Army ran out of steam just east of Metz, France. Attacking northward from the Mediterranean coast, LTG Jacob L. Devers's 6th Army Group, composed of Seventh US Army and French First Army cleared southern France. But the Germans stopped Devers's legions on the west bank of the Rhine at Colmar, France. Despite all of this, Gerow's cheery attitude prevailed among the Allies.

The Lucky Seventh at War: August–November 1944

The 7th AD landed in France shortly after the breakout, unloading August 10–14, 1944, at Omaha Beach. MG Silvester led the Division, as he had since activation. A World War I veteran awarded the Distinguished Service Cross in the 3rd Division, Silvester had found his way into armor as a commander of infantry tanks—not from either the World War I Tank Corps or the cavalry. His ideas reflected his infantry background, including the conviction that ground once taken must not be surrendered.[21]

The first units off the beach entered the fray immediately, motoring ninety miles to get into the fight. The Lucky Seventh fought hither and yon across France as part of Third US Army's XX Corps. As the pursuit lengthened, the 7th AD literally ran out of fuel at Verdun. There, the scene of horrific slaughter in World War I, the Division waited for fuel for several days before continuing onward. Constant fighting, particularly at Metz, drained the 7th AD. In September alone the Division lost fifty-five tanks, with 469 killed in action and another 737 wounded.[22] After hard fighting at Metz, the Division was ordered north to Holland to support British operations.

Losses continued unabated in Holland, where the British used the Lucky Seventh in ways McNair and the Army had neither intended, equipped, nor trained it to operate. Specifically, the British ordered the 7th AD into static defense. Worn out and fighting mostly roadbound, it did not perform well. The Division's performance in Holland proved to be the last straw for LTG Bradley, who commanded the US 12th Army Group. Bradley had been dissatisfied with MG Silvester since August. In his second autobiography Bradley described Silvester's performance in the latter stages of the pursuit as "inept." GEN George S. Patton did not care for Silvester either, having taken him to task in August for not doing well enough despite having thrown the green Division into combat literally as it unloaded.[23]

Bradley relieved Silvester on October 30 and replaced him with one of Silvester's subordinates, Brigadier General (BG) Robert W. Hasbrouck, who led Combat Command B. Hasbrouck took command in stride. The 7th AD continued to fight under British command until November 7. On that day it joined Ninth US Army to prepare for the planned attack on the Siegfried Line and then into in the heart of the Ruhr industrial center. Less than a month after assuming command, Hasbrouck led the 7th AD brilliantly under extraordinary conditions. In *The Struggle for Europe*, Chester Wilmot, critical of Allied and American leadership, called Hasbrouck "one of the great men of the Ardennes."[24]

Unlike the unfortunate Silvester, Hasbrouck came from the tank corps–cavalry school of thought. Hasbrouck graduated from the US Military Academy in 1917 with a commission in artillery and served in World War I, reaching the rank of captain. In April 1941 he assumed command of the 22nd Armored Field Artillery Battalion in the 4th AD. Subsequently he served as executive officer of the 4th AD artillery. He went overseas with the 1st AD as chief of staff, but returned to the United States to take command of a combat command of the 8th AD. In 1943 he went back overseas as deputy chief of staff of what became the 12th Army Group. Finally, in September 1944, he assumed leadership of Combat Command B, 7th AD. Hasbrouck had moved from battalion command to command of the 7th AD after "growing [up]" with the development of the armored forces.[25]

The Forest Primordial

By December, the war in the west settled into a war of attrition along a stabilized front as the Allies attempted to build up adequate supplies and combat power to breach the Rhine and renew the war of movement while, unbeknownst to them, Hitler readied his forces for a final throw of the dice. At Supreme Headquarters Allied Expeditionary Forces, Eisenhower planned to return to the offensive in mid-December, attacking both north and south of the Ardennes Forest, which bifurcated the Western Front. The Germans made no aggressive moves as they, too, sought to rebuild combat power. In the west neither side enjoyed clear superiority in numbers. In late 1944, despite their strategic weakness, the Germans enjoyed near parity on the ground with their enemies in the west.

In December the general trace of the Western Front extended more than five hundred miles. From its northern extremity at Arnhem the front ran generally south along the German frontier to Trier, then southeasterly toward Karlsruhe, and then south to the Swiss border. With fifty-four divisions ashore, Eisenhower could field roughly one division for every ten miles of front, or about twice the maximum ground the Army had designed its divisions to cover. To add to Eisenhower's burden, the US Army could no longer supply replacements, particularly infantrymen, in the numbers required. At war on a global scale, the United States had reached the bottom of its manpower barrel. In order to generate combat power to resume the offensive, Eisenhower had to concentrate forces. And to do that he had to assume risk somewhere; he and Bradley took that risk in the Ardennes.[26]

The Ardennes is itself an antagonist in this tale. Densely forested and hilly, the region is a significant obstacle to maneuver but not impenetrable, though many professional soldiers believed it so. Moreover, for a terrain obstacle to be effective it must be covered by observation and fire. Charles B. MacDonald, who commanded a rifle company in the battle, would later write *A Time for Trumpets*, but before that, just after the war, he worked as one of the Army's official historians; in the course of that work he wrote an article titled "The Neglected Ardennes." In his article MacDonald contended that any commander who "leaned too heavily on terrain obstacles to bar the enemy's way" risked defeat. "Never," he wrote, "has the error been so dramatically compounded as in the Ardennes region of Belgium and Luxembourg."[27] The Germans demonstrated MacDonald's thesis not once but four times—in 1870, 1914, 1940, and again in December 1944.

The forest has two components—one in Belgium and the other in Germany. East of the German border, the forest is known as the Schnee Eifel, while in Belgium and Luxembourg it is the Ardennes. MacDonald described it as "a big isosceles triangle with an 80-mile base along the frontiers [Belgium, Germany, and Luxembourg] from Aachen to the southeastern tip of Luxembourg. The length of the perpendicular from the base of the vertex west of the Meuse River is approximately 100 miles; yet so pronounced is the cut of the Meuse that the Ardennes can be said to end at the river roughly 60 miles from the German border."[28] Numerous streams cutting through a complex of ridges compartment the Ardennes. The highest elevation is more than 2,500 feet; it is "except for the Vosges Mountains in France [where Americans also fought] . . . the most rugged . . . of any terrain between the north sea and the Alps."[29]

The Ardennes is the kind of forest that evokes stories that frighten. It is beautiful but eerie to the point of dread. Quiet and cool even in high summer, it is deathly quiet, gloomy, bitterly cold, and alternately dripping or blanketed with snow in winter. The forebodingly named Schnee Eifel, or Snow Plateau, straddles the Belgian border with Germany and is densely wooded. In 1944, small towns and villages speckled the forest, nestled in vales alongside a good road network that generally followed streams. Where roads joined or crossed each other, towns with two to five thousand inhabitants had developed; Bastogne and St. Vith were two such towns. There were no cities except Arlon, Belgium, and the city of Luxembourg on the southern edge. With roughly four thousand and two thousand inhabitants, respectively, Bastogne and St. Vith were big towns in the Ardennes.[30]

The Ardennes is also compartmented in tactical terms. The trails, forest, and ridges precluded then and would today maneuver at scale for mounted forces. The consequence is that an attacker is unable to take advantage of greater numbers. Nowhere in the Schnee Eifel was there sufficient space for the maneuver of more than a dozen tanks or tracked vehicles, and there are very few such places in the Ardennes at large. In 1944–45 the terrain prompted fierce fighting to control crossroads and small villages. Often engagements between mounted forces occurred at close range, three hundred to four hundred yards. The compartments of the terrain and soft ground often reduced mounted forces to attacks literally along a narrow road or even a trail. The densely forested terrain also permitted dismounted infantry to infiltrate nearly at will.

The German Antagonists

Soldiers and commanders of Generalfeldmarschall Walther Model's Army Group B, especially those who served in the Fifth and Sixth Panzer Armies, are the antagonists in this story. Army Group B had borne the brunt of the

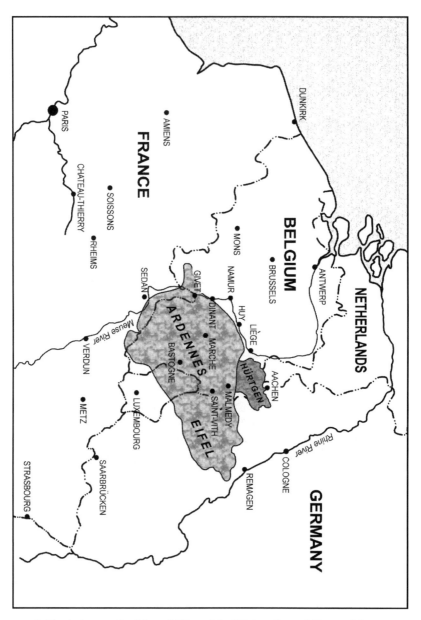

MAP 1. The Ardennes, the Schnee Eifel, and the Hürtgen Forest bifurcated the Western Front. British field marshal Bernard Law Montgomery's 21st Army Group operated north of the forests, while Lieutenant General Omar N. Bradley's 12th Army Group straddled them. Lieutenant General Jacob L. Devers's 6th Army Group operated on Bradley's right, or south. For a time during the battle, 21st Army Group directed the efforts of the First Canadian Army, Second British Army, and the First and Ninth US Armies. That left Bradley with only Third Army on the southern shoulder of the Bulge. Reproduced and edited from the original in Charles B. MacDonald, "The Neglected Ardennes," 77.

fighting since D-Day, and its units reflected the beating they took. The Fifth Panzer Army headquarters barely escaped being encircled in Normandy. Like many German units that made it back to the Siegfried Line, the Fifth Panzer Army and its surviving units arrived in tatters and with almost no equipment.

On September 7, 1944, Generalfeldmarschall Gerd von Rundstedt, who commanded the once powerful German forces in the west, reported to Oberkommando der Wehrmacht (OKW), the German Supreme Headquarters, that Army Group B had only one hundred operational tanks remaining of 1,552 available on June 6, 1944. Two of its assigned Panzer divisions had only two tanks each. He reported succinctly, "Our own forces are tied up in battle, and in part severely mauled. They are short artillery and anti-tank weapons. Reserves worthy of mention are not available. The numerical superiority of the enemy's tanks to ours is incontestable."[31] The Allied air forces also harried and destroyed Rundstedt's units. As he put it, the "enemy air force dominates the battle area and rear communications deep into rearward terrain."[32] His situation, which encompassed the entire Western Front, had improved by December 1944 but remained difficult.

Rundstedt's bleak assessment demonstrates that General Gerow and other Allied commanders had reason to believe the Germans were finished, or nearly so. But Hitler's cronies, generals, and soldiers had not given up. In his memoir *A Soldier's Story*, Bradley recalled that Rundstedt's units "had shown an astonishing capacity for recuperation."[33] The German Army demonstrated this trait throughout the war. In October the supreme commander of the Allies, General Eisenhower, wrote a friend to say he was "puzzled" that anyone could believe the battle was over or nearing its end. Further, he added, the Allies "have chased the Hun out of France, but he is fighting bitterly on his own frontiers and there is a lot of suffering and sacrificing for thousands of Americans and their allies before this thing is finally over."[34]

Hitler aimed to help Eisenhower realize his worst fears. In November 1943 Hitler's OKW issued Führer Directive 51, which explicitly shifted the main effort from the Russian Front to the Western Front because in the west Germany lacked strategic depth and Hitler wanted to generate forces to mount a counteroffensive. The German high command attempted to meet his requirements but did so within the exigencies of conditions in the east. Since defeating the Germans at Kursk in July 1943, the Russians had maintained the initiative and decimated German units as they advanced inexorably west. Moreover, German staff in the eastern theater indulged in the grand pastime of armies everywhere and throughout history: they dissembled, delayed, and even shanghaied units earmarked for the Western Front.[35]

Eisenhower's problems meeting his manpower and logistics requirements paled beside those of the Germans. Yet the Germans once again demonstrated the amazing recuperative powers Bradley had experienced in August 1944 when they managed their major counterattack at Mortain. However absurd it seems now, in the late summer of 1944 Hitler believed he could still defeat the Allies in the west. Afterward he could turn east and stop the Russians. As early as the failed effort at Mortain he imagined a counteroffensive in the west that, if successful, might force a peace with the Allies.

Hitler announced his intentions dramatically at his headquarters in East Prussia on September 16. He intervened in a briefing given by his chief of operations, Generaloberst Alfred Jodl, saying, "I have just made a momentous decision. I shall go over to the counter-attack." With that he pointed to the map on his conference table and said, "here out of the Ardennes, with the objective—Antwerp."[36] He went on to outline a concept that would envelop the northern group of the Allied field armies. To meet his intention the Reich had to create a reserve of some twenty-five divisions and husband air assets, fuel, and ammunition. Finally, Hitler wanted to launch the offensive on November 1.[37]

Finding the necessary troops and formations challenged German resources. The German Army reached a peak of 6,550,000 soldiers in 1943 but shrank to 5,300,000 by the end of the war. By comparison, US Army end strength rose to 8,000,000 in July 1944 and to 8,290,993 at war's end. To maintain units in the field and to generate additional divisions, the Germans resorted to desperate measures. They took healthy young men from protected industries, stripped the German Air Force and Navy, accepted volunteers from eastern European countries, found ways to use convalescing soldiers, and resorted to improvisations such as the so-called stomach battalions manned by limited-duty soldiers suffering from various stomach ailments. The German method proved effective. Those most fit served in the forward areas, and older recruits, wounded veterans, and those otherwise unfit replaced healthy troops in the rear areas, with the result that Hitler's minions found the means to man new and refitted divisions.[38]

Materiel proved more problematic. Despite heroic efforts and generally effective bombing, the Allied air campaign curbed but did not stop German industrial production. As they did in closing manpower gaps, the Germans found the means to recuperate. They improvised security for their industries by "dispersal and rationalization." For example, American bombers worked hard in 1943 to destroy ball bearing production and succeeded in reducing output by 66 percent. But by the fall of 1944 German ball bearing production rebounded and returned nearly to the levels achieved before the series of raids on Schweinfurt and other production sites. The manufacture of combat systems, including tanks, reached an all-time high in the fall of 1944. The bombing campaign and advancing Russian forces, on the other hand, materially affected fuel reserves. Coal, the essential ingredient in the German synthetic fuel industry, did remain plentiful and thus supported the continuing production of fuel. German improvisation and ruthless methods produced just enough to enable one last great effort.[39]

The End of the Siegfried Line Campaign

Dispersal, rationalization, and improvisation could not, however, generate combat power in the absence of time. And time had to be won on the battlefield. The Allies retained the initiative in the west even though their advance had momentarily stalled. For example, the 7th AD fought in Holland as part of Montgomery's 21st Army Group efforts to break into the Ruhr region. Bradley's 12th Army Group also mounted major operations in October and November. In three weeks of bloody and destructive fighting, the 1st ID, assigned to LTG Courtney H. Hodges's First Army, seized Aachen, the ancient capital of the Holy Roman Empire. After the battle one American soldier with a flair for metaphor observed, "The city is as dead as a Roman Ruin."[40] Indeed, the fighting reduced Aachen to ruins.

After Aachen, Hodges turned toward the Ruhr River dams, intending to take them in order to preclude the Germans from releasing water to cause flooding that would hamper the 21st Army Group's attack into the Ruhr north of the dams. This decision committed First Army to fighting in the Hürtgen Forest, the densely treed German twin to the Ardennes. The brutal fighting that followed began on October 6 with an ill-conceived attack by the 28th ID. First Army attacked unimaginatively throughout November, achieving little at a cost of twenty-three thousand casualties. Another eight thousand Americans "fell prey in the forest to combat exhaustion and the elements."[41]

Charles B. MacDonald, the author of the Army's official history of the fighting, concluded that the German Army "wrote the end to the Siegfried Line Campaign. . . . They had fought a large-scale delaying action with meager resources"[42] German units that fought in the Hürtgen Forest suffered badly, but their effort bought both time and space. Their commanders used that time and space to generate, train, and marshal the troops for the counteroffensive. On the Allied side the most damaged of the divisions that fought in the Hürtgen withdrew to the comparatively quiet sector of the line that ran north and south through the Ardennes.

The Nursery and Old Folks Home

On December 15, 1944, LTG Hodges's First Army exercised command of V, VII, and VIII Corps. Hodges's superior, Bradley, commanded the next higher echelon, the 12th Army Group. For a time during the Battle of the Bulge, Field Marshal Montgomery's 21st Army Group controlled the 1st and 9th Armies to compensate for the rupture of the 12th Army Group front.

Field army commanders shared logistics responsibility with the theater's Communications Zone (COMZ), a logistics organization commanded by LTG John C. H. Lee. The COMZ pushed supplies forward to field army supply distribution points positioned to the rear of the divisions, which drew what they needed from these caches. Withdrawal or destruction of supply points within the Bulge would prove to be a major challenge for the COMZ during the battle.

After V Corps arrived in the Ardennes in September various units moved in and out, but the sector remained quiet on both sides of the line. MG Troy H. Middleton's VIII Corps took over from V Corps in October. MacDonald, whose beat up and tired rifle company occupied a position in the VIII Corps line, famously described the sector as "at once the nursery and the old folks' home of the American Command."[43] Indeed it was. On October 20 the new and untested 9th AD joined the corps; the 14th Cavalry Group (CAV), with two cavalry squadrons, also arrived that day. On November 19 what remained of the 28th ID, battered in the Hürtgen Forest, took over a part of the VIII Corps line along the Our River near Ouren, Germany. The Germans had decimated all three of the 28th's regiments. Colonel (COL) Gustin M. Nelson's 112th Infantry Regiment arrived having lost more than 1,600 soldiers—more than half of its authorized troop strength. On December 7 the 4th ID, another tired division, relieved the 83rd ID. Finally, on December 11, the 106th ID "Golden Lions" took over from the 2nd ID, relieving it in place, meaning that they literally took the 2nd ID's place in the same foxholes and positions and used its cached ammunition and even some of its equipment.[44]

The Golden Lions disembarked at Le Havre, France, on December 6. The troops boarded trucks and crossed France to arrive cold and tired in assembly areas east of St. Vith, Belgium. Most of the 106th ID assembled near St. Vith on December 9. On December 11 the troops hiked up into the Schnee Eifel and just south of the plateau to relieve the 2nd ID. One of the Golden Lions' infantrymen remembered that he knew nothing about the Schnee Eifel other than he thought the name "stood for helluva lot of snow." The appearance of the arriving troops amazed the grizzled 2nd ID veterans of MacDonald's Company I, 23rd Infantry Regiment. He recalled, "They were equipped with the maze of equipment only replacements fresh from the states would have dared called their own. And horror of horrors, they were wearing neckties."[45] The troops of the 2nd ID believed they were leaving a quiet sector to move north and prepare to attack toward the Ruhr River. Accordingly, they greeted their relief with mixed emotions.

On arriving in St. Vith, John K. Kline of M Company, 3rd Battalion, 423rd Infantry recalled some of the troops in town providing them with advice traditionally given newcomers: "You'll be sorry." But the new arrivals also received some assurance, as some of the 2nd ID's infantrymen told them they had arrived in a "rest camp." The 2nd ID provided proof in the form of heated huts and/or covered dugouts that had kept them dry and reasonably warm in the snow-covered, dripping woods of the Schnee Eifel. COL Frank Boos, the outgoing regimental commander, advised his successor, COL Charles C. Cavender, "It has been very quiet up here and your men will learn the easy way."[46] Private Harry F. Martin Jr., an admittedly unenthusiastic rifleman, believed what the 2nd ID troops told him. He thought he would earn his Combat Infantryman's Badge in a quiet sector and might even enjoy periodic leaves in Paris. At that moment, he felt lucky to be in the Schnee Eifel.[47]

From north to south, MG Middleton's VIII Corps formations included the 14th CAV's 18th Cavalry Squadron Mechanized in the relatively open ground of the Losheim Gap. The 106th ID occupied the Schnee Eifel on their right. Next came the 28th ID, generally along the banks of the Our River. The 9th AD, less its Combat Command B, defended from Wallendorf on the Our River to the village of Berdorf. The 4th ID defended from Berdorf to east of the city of Luxembourg along the west bank of the Sauer River. Middleton's line amounted to a series of outposts with little depth.

Along the extended front line, often separated from the Americans only by a valley or the tank obstacles known as dragon's teeth, the antagonists lurked. Some German units had been there for nearly two months, while others had arrived only recently. But however long they had been there, the

troops of the 5th and 6th Panzer Armies now looked to last-minute preparations. In a matter of days they would spring forward along nearly ninety
miles of the First Army front from Aachen in the north to Trier in the south.
When they did so, Harry F. Martin Jr. would well and truly earn his Combat
Infantryman's Badge.

NOTES

1. Charles B. MacDonald's *A Time for Trumpets* is the best available source on orders of battle and casualties, as it also includes artillery and air orders of battle. The
Allies used more than four thousand aircraft. The Luftwaffe managed to mount an
effort of one thousand aircraft on a single day. On casualties, see *A Time for Trumpets*, 618, and for orders of battle for both sides, contributed by Danny S. Parker,
see 630–55. British XXX Corps lost 1,400 soldiers, including two hundred killed in
action. Because MacDonald's casualty numbers combined German totals, I have also
used Robert Merriam, *Dark December*, 212. See also Hugh M. Cole, *The Ardennes:
Battle of the Bulge*, 674–76. On numbers of aircraft employed, see Harold R. Winton,
Corps Commanders of the Bulge, xvi. Winton's study is the only work of its kind, and
invaluable. He worked carefully with US Army Air Force and Supreme Headquarters
Allied Expeditionary Force sources to document the important role that Allied air
power played.

2. Peter Schrijvers, *The Unknown Dead*, 359. Schrijvers's epilogue is an accounting
of the suffering that lasted until well after the end of the war.

3. General der Panzertruppe Hasso von Manteuffel to General Bruce C. Clarke,
August 1, 1964, General Bruce C. Clarke Papers. The first quotation is from Bruce
C. Clarke, who used this phrase frequently. From 1984 to 1986 the author corresponded with General Clarke. Clarke wrote frequently, often linking contemporary
military affairs to his experience as a combat commander in World War II, as a corps
commander in the Korean War, or as the commander of US Army Europe. He provided a copy of this letter and many other papers or extracts from articles he wrote
to make points either about fighting in the Bulge or how the Army might fight Soviet
Forces in Europe. The author has more than one hundred pages of documents, notes
or letters from that time, all of which are in the author's possession and cited herein
as General Bruce C. Clarke Papers. Manteuffel and Clarke seemed genuinely fond
of each other and collaborated at least twice to educate soldiers and others on the
battle. In 1964 they participated in a two-part *Big Picture* television production. See
US Army Pictorial Center, *The Battle of St. Vith*.

4. US War Department, *Water Transportation: Ocean Going Vessels*, FM 55-105;
US War Department, *M4 Sherman Medium Tank Technical Manual*, TM 9-759.
There are few sources that address the connection of combat effectiveness to doc-
trine; see Peter R. Mansoor, *The GI Offensive in Europe*; and John Sloan Brown,
Draftee Division.

5. US War Department, *Armored Command Field Manual: The Armored Division*, FM 17-100, 2–4, emphasis in the original.

6. US 7th Armored Division Association, *The Lucky Seventh*, 25, 38–39.

7. John B. Wilson, *Maneuver and Firepower*, 180–85, 227. The last two divisions formed in August 1943. At the end of World War II the Army fielded eighty-nine divisions, all of which deployed. All but one saw combat. See also Kent Roberts Greenfield, Robert R. Palmer, and Bell I. Wiley, *The Organization of Ground Combat Troops*, 210–35. Marshall's biographer, Forrest C. Pogue, devotes most of chapters 24 and 25 in his *George C. Marshall* to the problem.

8. Greenfield, Palmer, and Wiley, *The Organization of Ground Combat Troops*, 198–350, reviews the process, problems and solutions. See also Mansoor, *The GI Offensive*, 40, and chapter 2. On the 106th ID, see Colonel R. Ernest Dupuy, *St. Vith: Lion in the Way*, 7.

9. Greenfield, Palmer, and Wiley, *The Organization of Ground Combat Troops*, chapter V, "The Armored Division," 319–35. McNair firmly resisted any push back from the armored force, convinced as he was in his concept for the use of the armored division and because he thought the armored force leadership " 'Profligate,' 'luxurious,' and 'monstrous.' "

10. See Dupuy, *St. Vith: Lion in the Way*, 5–8.

11. Wilson, *Maneuver and Firepower*, 183, chart 19. On the general way that logistics functioned, see Roland G. Ruppenthal, *Logistical Support of the Armies*. The Army official history includes logistics and service support studies in its Technical Services series.

12. US War Department, *Field Service Regulations: Operations*, FM 100-5, 2.

13. George Forty, *U.S. Army Handbook, 1939–1945*, 31.

14. Lieutenant Colonel Joseph R. Reeves, "Artillery in the Ardennes," 138–42, 173–84. See also Victor Davis Hanson, *The Second World Wars*, 387–89. On general artillery tactics, see US War Department, *Field Artillery Field Manual: Tactics and Technique*, FM 6-20.

15. Carl von Clausewitz, *On War*, 531.

16. Clausewitz, *On War*, 216.

17. In 1944 the Siegfried Line was not particularly formidable. Some of the works had not been finished and others had not been well maintained, but it was defensible. See Matthew Cooper, *The German Army*, 517–18.

18. Joachim Ludewig, *Rückzug*, 281; the book is a German Bundeswehr official history. The official histories by the contemporary German Army are quite good. They are essential for those who want to understand the German perspective. See also Charles B. MacDonald, *The Siegfried Line Campaign*, 39–65.

19. Clausewitz, *On War*, 528.

20. MacDonald, *The Siegfried Line Campaign*, 65. Gerow served as chief of the Army's War Plans Division at the time of the attack on Pearl Harbor.

21. Hugh M. Cole, *The Lorraine Campaign*, 17; Robert W. Hasbrouck to Bruce C. Clarke, February 7, 1974, General Bruce C. Clarke Papers; Bruce C. Clarke to the author, July 6, 1984, General Bruce C. Clarke Papers.

22. Martin Blumenson, *Breakout and Pursuit*, 568–71; Cole, *The Lorraine Campaign*, 174. See also US 7th Armored Division Association, *The Lucky Seventh*, 25. Much of *The Lucky Seventh* is taken from the original history: 7th Armored Division, *From the Beaches to the Baltic*. The US 7th Armored Division Association survives under the efforts of descendants of those who served. Its website, http://www.7thArmdDiv.org, preserves many documents.

23. The Germans found the British use of the 7th AD puzzling, if not foolish. See MacDonald, *The Siegfried Line Campaign*, 240–41, where MacDonald quotes either a captured or intercepted German Army Group B intelligence assessment; on Silvester's relief, see 246–47; See also Omar N. Bradley and Clay Blair, *A General's Life*; and Martin Blumenson, *The Patton Papers*, 2:529.

24. Bradley and Clay, *A General's Life*, 309; MacDonald, *The Siegfried Line Campaign*, 247–48; Chester Wilmot, *The Struggle for Europe*, 584. Of the relief, Bradley said only that he had "lost confidence in Silvester." It is likely the British complained; otherwise, there is no explanation for why would Bradley have even known, given that the 7th AD was operating in the 21st Army Group.

25. Robert Wilson Hasbrouck, military biography, box 7, Charles B. MacDonald Papers; Major General Robert W. Hasbrouck (Ret.), interview with the author, Washington, DC, August 20, 1984.

26. Dwight D. Eisenhower, *Crusade in Europe*, 321–41; on risk, see 338. See also Stephen E. Ambrose, *The Supreme Commander*, 536–52. Ambrose was one of the editors of Eisenhower's papers. His *Supreme Commander* is a critical but favorable assessment of Eisenhower as commander. The discussion on risk between Bradley and Eisenhower did not occur until December 7. In his memoir, Eisenhower takes responsibility for the risk Bradley actually took.

27. Charles B. MacDonald, "The Neglected Ardennes," 74. See also MacDonald, *A Time for Trumpets*, 74.

28. MacDonald, "The Neglected Ardennes," 76.

29. MacDonald, "The Neglected Ardennes," 76.

30. On Bastogne, see The Siege of Bastogne Up Close and Personal," Yale University Press blog, December 3, 2014, http://blog.yalebooks.com/2014/12/03/siege-bastogne-close-personal/. On St. Vith, see Cole, *The Ardennes: Battle of the Bulge*, 42. Cole is not explicit, nor are other sources. Figures are seldom given, but the population range for St. Vith is 2,000–2,500.

31. Cooper, *The German Army*, 514. There are several good accounts of the fighting that summer and early fall; among them are Blumenson, *Breakout and Pursuit*; Wilmot, *The Struggle for Europe*; and Russell F. Weigley, *Eisenhower's Lieutenants*. During the exploitation and pursuit, the Allies exacted a great toll on the Germans. According to Weigley, 214, an incomplete count of German materiel losses included "220 tanks, 160 assault guns, 700 towed artillery pieces, 130 antiaircraft guns, 130 half tracks, 5,000 other motor vehicles and 2,000 wagons. There were also 1,800 dead horses." On the German perspective, see Ludewig, *Rückzug*. See also Hubert Meyer, *The 12th SS*. Meyer details the bitter fighting and claims atrocities on both sides. Given the 12th SS's reputation, his claims ring hollow. Rundstedt commanded

Oberbefehlshaber West; in September his order of battle included three army groups. Army Group B bore the lion's share of the fighting in the summer and fall of 1944.

32. Cooper, *The German Army*, 496, 514.

33. Omar N. Bradley, *A Soldier's Story*, 341.

34. Ambrose, *The Supreme Commander*, 539. Eisenhower's pessimism developed late given that in the same month he bet Montgomery the war would be over by Christmas 1944. See Harry C. Butcher, *My Three Years with Eisenhower*, 722.

35. Oberkommando der Wehrmacht, "Führer Directive 51," November 3, 1943. There is considerable evidence of competition for resources and bureaucratic wrangling. See General der Artillerie Walter Warilmont, "Reciprocal Influence of East and West Fronts," ETHINT-3, 4; Cole, *The Ardennes: Battle of the Bulge*, 13.

36. Cole, *The Ardennes: Battle of the Bulge*, 2.

37. Cole, *The Ardennes: Battle of the Bulge*, 10–12. Cole's description of Hitler's vision and the creation of the operational reserve to attempt the counteroffensive is clear and concise. His work, like all of that done by the Office of the Chief of Military History, underwent thorough vetting by peers and senior officer participants. That material can be found in John S. D. Eisenhower, Drafts and Other Materials from *The Bitter Woods*, Dwight D. Eisenhower Presidential Library and Museum.

38. On German manpower numbers, see Cooper, *The German Army*, 485. See also Cole, *The Ardennes: Battle of the Bulge*, 6–7. On US end strength, see Greenfield, Palmer, and Wiley, *The Organization of Ground Combat Troops*, 235, 253. See also Major Percy Ernst Schramm, "The Preparations for the German Offensive in the Ardennes."

39. Charles V. P. von Luttichau, *The Ardennes Offensive*, 43. Luttichau, as he put it, drew "heavily from the *United States Strategic Bombing Survey*." The bombing campaign did ultimately destroy the German economy, but that came after January 1945.

40. MacDonald, *The Siegfried Line Campaign*, 320; on Aachen, see chaps. 11–13.

41. MacDonald, *The Siegfried Line Campaign*, 493. The author has led staff rides and tours of both the Hürtgen Forest and the Ardennes. The terrain over which the 28th ID fought in the early days of October 1944 is even more difficult than the terrain in the Ardennes. Walking the ground over which they fought, it is difficult to fathom how the 112th Infantry Regiment got as far as it did.

42. MacDonald, *The Siegfried Line Campaign*, 615.

43. MacDonald, *The Siegfried Line Campaign*, 612. MacDonald commanded I and G Companies of the 23rd Infantry Regiment, 2nd ID. His account of his time in the Ardennes in the VIII and V Corps sectors can be found in Charles B. MacDonald, *Company Commander*.

44. MacDonald, *The Siegfried Line Campaign*, 612–15; Lieutenant General William F. Train, "My Memories of the Battle of the Bulge (16 Dec 1944–15 Jan 1945)," 2–3.

45. Gerald Astor, *A Blood-Dimmed Tide*, 35; MacDonald, *Company Commander*, 104.

46. John K. Kline, "The Service Diary of German War Prisoner #3151366." See also Dupuy, *St. Vith: Lion in the Way*, 16.

47. Astor, *A Blood-Dimmed* Tide, 11–12. See also Colonel Charles C. Cavender, "The 423 in the Bulge."

CHAPTER TWO

Silesia Is Defended in the West

One should never forget that the total amount of men employed on our side is still as large as that of our opponents.

—Adolf Hitler

The Germans have lost a million men in France and an enormous amount of equipment, yet there are no signs of collapse in morale and in the will to defend Germany.

—Captain Harry C. Butcher

As soon as Adolf Hitler reached his "momentous" decision, his staff began planning for the counteroffensive. The planning effort occurred in the strictest secrecy because Hitler surmised the Allies had access to accurate intelligence about his intentions and dispositions. Oddly, he retained absolute and absolutely unfounded confidence in the Enigma machines that encrypted his communications. In fact, the Allies had broken the Enigma code system and could read German military and diplomatic traffic. But instead of suspecting his communications as the source of leaks, Hitler believed they stemmed from disloyal officers in his own army.[1]

Accordingly, planning and preparation for the great counteroffensive took place behind a veil of secrecy aided by limiting the effort to a handful of senior officers. Because access was so limited, the planning staff did not use Enigma encrypted messages to communicate. This practically assured security of the planning effort, as the Allies relied on decrypted German message traffic known by the code name Ultra. Avoiding encrypted radio communications lulled the Allied command and reduced the chance of mishandled messages or rumor that might have revealed the plan. The Allies continued

31

to read Ultra communications between Germany and Japan, rail transportation communications, and other communications. Despite evidence of counteroffensive in those intercepts, no Allied leaders found the idea of a German counteroffensive plausible.[2]

Hugh Cole, the US Army's official historian of the Battle of the Bulge, claimed Hitler was "a fanatical believer in the Clausewitzian doctrine of the offensive as the purest and only decisive form of war."[3] Cole was right. Hitler intended his counteroffensive to defeat the Allies in the west in a decisive battle like those Carl von Clausewitz had witnessed. Doing so would enable Hitler to turn attention and resources back to the defeat of the relentless Red Army. Hitler's concept for the offensive envisaged attacking west through the Ardennes, then wheeling northwest to seize Antwerp. If the Germans retook Antwerp, they would cut off the northern group of armies led by British field marshal Bernard Law Montgomery. But why attack through the Ardennes, a dense, heavily wooded forest compartmented by rugged hills and cut by streams? Although a fairly good network of roads crossed the region, they were not really adequate for armor formations. Simply put, the Ardennes did not lend itself to rapid movement by mechanized forces such as those Hitler planned to employ.

Why the Ardennes?

Major Percy Schramm, the official diarist of the Oberkommando der Wehrmacht (OKW), or German Supreme Command, is the best source on Hitler's reasoning as well as that of his senior staff. Schramm recorded several reasons for attacking through the Ardennes. In the end the General Staff planners concluded that the axis Hitler proposed was best. Although it was not a factor at the outset, the Ardennes is where Lieutenant General (LTG) Omar N. Bradley accepted risk. His decision to defend a long line of complex terrain with a handful of worn-out and brand new (and therefore inexperienced) divisions, each covering more than twice their designed frontage, is the very definition of risk; that fact did not go unnoticed. The Germans also observed the movement into the Ardennes of three US divisions recently mauled in the Hürtgen Forest. According to Schramm, this development "was another indication of the scarcity of forces which was prevailing on the enemy side."[4] Attacking through the Ardennes had another advantage: the offensive aimed to split the Allied forces. Attacking to divide enemies is an old and honored tradition in making war. The Germans had nearly succeeded in doing so in the spring of 1918, and in 1940 they did succeed in driving a wedge between the British and the French.

Additionally, the total distance from the line of departure to the objective, though long, seemed manageable. Once the German mobile forces cleared the Ardennes forest, the terrain onward toward Antwerp permitted rapid movement. Liège and the Meuse River lay thirty miles west of the line of departure. Antwerp, the strategic prize, lay sixty miles farther west. The total distance also could be achieved within the available fuel reserves. Seizing Antwerp would cut off Montgomery's 21st Army Group and leave as many as two dozen Allied divisions entrapped. A defeat of that magnitude would threaten the Anglo-American alliance, or so Hitler believed.

Finally, in *Snow and Steel*, Peter Caddick-Adams offers a surprising reason. He suggests that the music of Richard Wagner, Bavarian forests, and German myths affected Hitler's choice of attack routes, Caddick-Adams believes that the notion of German forces attacking through and out of the gloomy, primordial forest played to the führer's fascination with German mythology.[5] Strange as this notion sounds, this explanation is plausible. Even more compelling, at least to the staff of the OKW, were Bradley's dispositions, which made it clear to the Germans that an attack through the Ardennes not only stood a good chance of achieving surprise but also success.

Assembling the Decisive Force

Clausewitz opined that superiority of numbers was "the most common element in victory" and a universal goal of generals. The Prussian theorist also believed that *"to take the enemy by surprise"* was just as important, for without the element of surprise, "superiority at the decisive point is hardly conceivable."[6] General der Panzertruppe Hasso von Manteuffel, whose Fifth Panzer Army played a central role in the counteroffensive, had read Clausewitz. Commissioned in the cavalry, Manteuffel was an early convert to armored warfare and a protégé of Heinz Guderian, perhaps the most famous advocate of tank warfare. Manteuffel understood that secrecy and deception were essential to achieving surprise. Surprise, he believed, would be "the chief factor for the Offensive's success." Secrecy, therefore, had to be maintained, even "if it rendered more difficult and even delayed the concentration of troops." Perhaps Manteuffel's chief of staff, Generalmajor Carl Wagner, said it best: "The best security [for the plan] was the improbability of the operation."[7]

The OKW, including the Oberkommando des Heeres (OKH), or Army High Command, did more than keep the secret. It developed and supported a story aimed at deceiving Allied intelligence. If produced as a staff college paper, the German deception plan would have earned high marks, as indeed it achieved high marks in the field that winter. The Americans and the British bought the deception story completely. Robert E. Merriam, who served as combat historian with the 7th Armored Division (AD) in the Bulge, got to the heart of the matter in his *Dark December*. The cover story worked, according to Merriam, "because it dovetailed so well with the Allied state of mind."[8]

Simply put, the deception portrayed the forces gathering near Cologne as defensive preparations for an Allied attack in the direction of Cologne and Bonn.[9] Even the code name chosen for the operation, Wacht am Rhein (Watch on the Rhine), conveyed a defensive orientation. Hitler chose the code name Herbstnebel (Autumn Mist) for the actual attack. Anyone who has walked in the Ardennes in the fall or winter will appreciate the choice. Finding a way through the forest in the fog, let alone seeing an approaching enemy, would prove difficult. Finally, the code name conveyed a passive condition like that obtained in the Ardennes since October.

As the Germans expected and intended, the Allies detected the concentration of the Sixth Panzer Army. Allied intelligence duly identified it as well as several other Panzer divisions forming west and southwest of Cologne. The Fifth Panzer Army, on the other hand, worked hard to mask its movement and largely succeeded in concealing its assembly areas. As one of the Fifth Panzer Army's corps commanders recalled, "great stress was laid on perfect camouflage."[10] That, too, was part of the plan: to show the bulk of the Sixth Panzer Army in a defensive posture and hide as much of the Fifth Panzer Army as possible.

Concentrating the attacking forces also required moving new and rebuilt divisions, as well as thousands of tons of equipment, ammunition, and fuel. Hugh Cole in *The Ardennes: Battle of the Bulge* reported that the Deutsche Reichsbahn, the German National Railway, both thoroughly militarized and efficient, moved the bulk of the troops, equipment, and stores. Originally built in the early twentieth century to support German war plans aimed at France, the rail network leading to the Belgian frontier served just as well in the fall of 1944. Equally important, the Reichsbahn proved surprisingly resilient despite effective bombing by the Allied air forces.[11]

In March 1945 Brigadier General (BG) George C. McDonald, the intelligence officer for US Strategic Air Forces Europe, issued a report titled "Allied Air Power and the Ardennes Offensive: 15 December 1944–16 January 1945." McDonald's report is a model effort to understand what happened and to examine critically the effect air power had on the outcome of the battle. The report proves conclusively that the Army Air Forces reported the concentration of German forces accurately, and attacked assembling units ferociously and often effectively, but did not prevent their concentration. Reports from aircrews and photoreconnaissance enabled accurate accounting of the number of trains the Germans used and the approximate locations where they unloaded. In what is surely an understatement, BG McDonald considered the Reichsbahn support of the concentration "a considerable achievement."[12]

That the Allied high command knew of the Germans' concentration of the Fifth and Sixth Panzer Armies is incontrovertible. It is equally accurate to say that the Allies senior leadership misread German intentions because it believed the Germans would behave as they would themselves behave. They succumbed to confirmation bias. General (GEN) Dwight D. Eisenhower and his subordinates perceived German actions in accordance with their estimate of the situation. Every report could be bent to confirm their bias rather than raise doubts.

To preserve secrecy, new German divisions formed and others refitted, largely in ignorance of the operation. Even the most senior officers learned of the operation as late as possible. Generalfeldmarschall Walther Model, the operational commander of the counteroffensive, and his superior, Generalfeldmarschall Gerd von Rundstedt, received their briefing on October 22. Model shared what he knew with his three army commanders, Erich Brandenberger, Sepp Dietrich, and Hasso von Manteuffel, on October 27. Model and his field commanders showed little enthusiasm for the plan, thinking it too ambitious given the troops available and the distance to the strategic objective. They, or rather Manteuffel, argued for envelopment short of Antwerp to cut off enemy troops, which Manteuffel called the Small Slam. Generaloberst Alfred Jodl, Hitler's factotum, pronounced the objective and thus the full plan "unalterable."[13] Although Model thought the concept had merit, he told his chief of staff, "If it succeeds it will be a miracle."[14]

German Operational Planning

Model and Army Group B owned the offensive in its entirety, and he drove the planning within the parameters left to him by the high command. In addition to the conventional infantry and armor forces, the high command organized a special operations unit under Otto Skorzeny, famous for freeing Benito Mussolini in a commando operation. Hitler brought Skorzeny into the mix in October. In a meeting at his eastern headquarters the führer told Skorzeny, "I am now going to give you the most important job of your life." He then proceeded to outline for Skorzeny Operation Greif. Formed of English speakers and equipped with captured American equipment and German gear modified to look like that used by the Americans, Skorzeny's 150th Panzer Brigade would attempt to get deep into the American rear to pave the way for the Sixth Panzer Army, spread confusion, and generate panic among the Americans. The high command also provided a parachute battalion under the command of Oberstleutnant Friedrich August Freiherr von der Heydte. Heydte's one thousand paratroopers were to jump in to seize high ground in the rear of the American lines in the Sixth Panzer Army zone of attack.[15]

Tactical details remained in the hands of the army, corps and—once included—division commanders. Despite reservations, Model thought success possible because "the enemy does not have a continuous main line of resistance."[16] The soldiers of the Fifth Panzer Army were the chief antagonists of the troops spread thinly along Major General (MG) Troy H. Middleton's VIII Corps sector. Understanding the planning and approach of the Fifth Panzer Army is central. The approach in the Fifth Panzer Army reflected the aggressive personalities of Manteuffel and Model; both men personally reconnoitered far forward to ascertain the character of the American defense. On the basis of his personal reconnaissance and the intelligence provided by Army Group B, Model developed a detailed and accurate assessment of American defenses and patterns of operation. Manteuffel, too, had carefully studied the opposition. He claimed that when the Fifth Panzer Army attacked on December 16 his commanders knew exactly what units they opposed and even the boundaries of their positions.[17]

German analysis of American habits suggested several things. Chief among these was that the German field commanders concluded that attacking just before sunrise would assure surprise. Model, Manteuffel, and others noticed that the Americans patrolled aggressively during daylight but seldom patrolled at night. Manteuffel noted the Americans remained alert during the hours of darkness until about 0400, when "their alertness and care decreased considerably." After midnight and before sunrise, American troops huddled in their holes. The Fifth Panzer Army's chief of staff concluded that American passivity at night would enable not only surprise but success since "night attack requires less skill, but higher morale than combat by day. It offers success, therefore, for troops who have not had the proper training."[18]

The very idea that a night attack is easier than attacking in daylight was and remains inconceivable to Americans. US Army doctrine described night attacks as characterized "by difficulty in movement, troop leading, and the maintenance of direction, cohesion and signal communication; and [here in confluence with German thought] by a more highly sensitive morale of the troops." German prewar doctrine closely matched the US Army's thinking, but combat experience altered that view. Oberstleutnant Dietrich Moll, operations officer of the 18th Volksgrenadier Division (VGD), noted with disdain the Americans had a "strong aversion to night fighting." According to him, the 18th VGD patrolled at night not only to reconnoiter but also to train in night combat. Moll believed that constant practice day and night "made the command channels operate smoothly." When the 106th Infantry Division (ID) arrived in December it did nothing to alter Moll's perception. Lieutenant Robert R. Wessels recalled that his 1st Battalion, 422nd Infantry patrolled "only in daytime."[19] The 106th ID and the 14th Cavalry Group (CAV) did not patrol aggressively and did not reconnoiter their antagonists' positions.

Doctrinally, German reconnaissance aimed to "produce a picture of the enemy situation as rapidly, completely and reliably as possible."[20] In the 18th VGD, patrolling helped train inexperienced infantry and enabled the Division to determine the position of its opponents with precision. Moll claimed accurately that his Division's patrols located American artillery that lay to rear of the frontline positions. In fact, the 18th VGD often penetrated two or more miles into the American rear. From prisoners taken by its patrols, the 18th VGD knew that the positions of the newly arrived 106th ID had not changed from those occupied by its predecessors.[21]

The 18th VGD designed patrols to assure the security of its own positions as well. Robust patrolling gave the relatively inexperienced Volksgrenadiers a distinct advantage. Other German units formed in the rear of the front line and thus had no chance to learn by doing. But because of 18th VGD's efforts and those of other units, both the Fifth Panzer Army and its subordinate corps could provide detailed intelligence to those less fortunate units. Ultimately, all of the attacking divisions planned the initial phase of the operations with accurate intelligence. They did not all have the opportunity to train thoroughly or gain experience in the line opposite where they would attack.

The corps commanders planned in parallel with their respective army commanders and conducted several map exercises to rehearse and refine their plans. General der Artillerie Walther Lucht, who commanded LXVI Corps, learned his mission and objective in late October or early November. Lucht's corps, composed of the 18th and 62nd VGDs, had to "take St. Vith and, in a deeply echeloned [divisions in column] formation make a thrust up to and across the Meuse." Furthermore, the Fifth Panzer Army ordered Lucht to bypass the two regiments of the 106th ID positioned in the Schnee Eifel. Lucht had also to seize the vital road junction at St. Vith on the first day.[22]

The Fifth Panzer Army planned to attack with three corps abreast. General der Panzertruppe Walter Krüger's LVIII Panzer Corps' 116th Panzer Division (PZ) and 560th VGD would attack on Lucht's left. On Krüger's left, General der Panzertruppe Heinrich von Lüttwitz's XXXXVII Panzer Corps would attack with the 2nd PZ, the 9th PZ, the Panzer Lehr, and the 26th VGD. Both Panzer corps planned to break through with their VGDs and exploit success with their Panzers. The two Panzer corps had to bridge the Our River en route to the Meuse. Accordingly, the attacking corps had to seize bridges intact and build additional tactical bridges on the first day. Manteuffel ordered the three corps to penetrate on narrow frontages. All three corps commanders planned to maneuver once they broke through the crust of US VIII Corps' defenses.[23]

The initial phase of planning occurred without participation by the divisions, which preserved secrecy but obviously affected planning. In Lucht's corps, the 18th VGD learned the ground over which they would attack. But the 62nd VGD had not been allowed forward either to reconnoiter or train. Therefore Lucht decided to execute a double envelopment of the two regiments positioned in the Schnee Eifel using only the 18th VGD. Planning did not address operations beyond the Meuse. Hugh Cole believed this serious oversight reflected the field commanders' resistance to the idea of seizing Antwerp rather than halting at the Meuse and destroying Allied units east of the river. In other words, they all favored the Small Slam. In another wrinkle, Oberstgruppenführer Sepp Dietrich, the Sixth Panzer Army commander, favored leading with his Panzers but Model overruled him. Army Group B directed achieving the breakthrough with infantry, as both US and German doctrine mandated.

The last chance for modifying the plan came at a meeting in Berlin on December 2, 1944. Model requested the meeting at Manteuffel's behest. It seemed that Manteuffel wanted another run at the Small Slam. Rundstedt chose not to attend, but did send his chief of staff. The army group delegation included Dietrich, Manteuffel, and Model; Hitler held all three in high regard. Rundstedt hoped that his three army commanders would be able to persuade the warlord to accept the Small Slam. They achieved little. Both Manteuffel and Model repeated their arguments. Hitler heard them out, and did so politely; he conceded that the decision of whether to go on to Antwerp could be made once they crossed the Meuse. Hitler did agree to some changes: he released several units from the strategic reserve, including the Führer Escort Brigade, a robust organization that was fully motorized and included a tank battalion. Hitler also agreed to Manteuffel's idea of attacking in darkness but did not authorize a genuine night attack. He set zero or null hour for 0530 on December 16, 1944.[24]

The Fifth Panzer Army's final order stressed the need to press on, no matter what. Manteuffel urged his unit to move forward "without looking right or left, across the Meuse towards Antwerp." He stipulated that every soldier in the Fifth Panzer Army should take this as his watchword. Manteuffel's concept for the operation required that "*armored units* survive the breakthrough in such a way that they retain combat capabilities for their original task, *operation in open terrain*, and that the armored units of the second echelon still mount their *attack on the first day of the offensive*."[25] Manteuffel's newly organized VGDs had to penetrate the American defenses quickly and seize crossings on the Our River, all within the first day.

German Organization, Training, and Planning

With the plan in place the curtain of secrecy rose. Moll recalled that the 18th VGD received the LXVI Corps operations order on December 1. With less than two weeks before execution, neither Moll nor his commander, the very able and highly decorated Oberst Günther Hoffman-Schönborn, complained about how little time they had. Oberst Friedrich Kittel, who commanded the 62nd VGD, did not assume command of his Division until November. His unit had no opportunity to rotate into the line, yet he, too, found he could manage with the time he had.[26] Today's US Army attempts to buy time for subordinate units by planning operations at multiple echelons in parallel—that is, subordinates are provided enough information to plan basic tasks. That is the essence of the method the Germans employed.

Rebuilding shattered units and forming new ones had gone on since September without reference to the details of the attack. Finding troops and equipment were no small tasks. Sixth Panzer Army commander Dietrich worried he would have to attack "with reformed divisions made up chiefly of kids and sick old men—and at Christmas!"[27] Nevertheless, to a remarkable extent the OKW made good on equipping and manning units. The German Army organized in ways similar to its enemies and, like them, had too few troops. The tale of the two VGDs assigned to the Fifth Panzer Army is emblematic of what the Germans achieved.

In a postwar paper, Dietrich Moll described the organization and training of the 18th VGD. The Division formed on September 9, 1944, composed of a mix of troops from the 18th Luftwaffe Division, other Luftwaffe units, and sailors from the Kriegsmarine. The Division filled out with five thousand "recruits" taken from protected industry and lower-priority units. Of the troops Moll observed that "Germany was in her sixth year of war, yet few men of this division had campaign ribbons or decorations."[28] They were, like their counterparts in the 106th ID, without experience. Yet the 18th VGD and the equally inexperienced 62nd VGD formed the striking arm of LXVI Corps essential to the Fifth Panzer Army's success.

Oberst Arthur Jüttner commanded one of the 62nd VGD's infantry regiments. Writing in a postwar veterans' journal, he recalled that the Division formed "from the remainders of the 62nd Division which had been liquidated in Russia, with most of its manpower coming from Silesia." Jüttner, an experienced and highly decorated officer, assessed the 62nd's combat value as "full for defense operations, limited for assault, not operational for breakthrough in uplands."[29] Yet that was exactly the task required of it. It is possible that these postwar assessments by German commanders understate their units' capabilities. German officers who participated in the US postwar studies compared their later war units unfavorably to those in which they served at the outset of the war. Later replacements simply did not, in their opinions, measure up to those who enlisted at the outset of the war. It is unlikely the newly raised units were as good as their predecessors, but it does not follow automatically that they were inferior to their opposition. In 1944 Germany had to dip deep in the barrel to find the manpower and equipment necessary for the offensive.

New and reorganized units had fewer than three months to equip and train. The 18th VGD and some other new units learned by doing. The 18th entered the line opposite the US 2nd ID in October. In the line, the troops gained experience by active patrolling and rotating units through the frontline positions. Some veteran units had less time because they had to be used elsewhere. For example, the 2nd Schutzstaffel (SS) PZ remained in the line until the second week of October. In late October the 9th PZ, also slated for the counteroffensive, mounted a counterattack against the 7th AD in Holland.[30] Withdrawn at the end of October, the 9th PZ had about six weeks to refit and train. Despite everything, morale remained relatively high. According to Dietrich Moll, the troops in the 18th VGD "still believed that the war might have a favorable outcome."[31] In November, the 62nd VGD entrained for the front. The troops chalked slogans on their rail cars; "Silesia Is Defended in the West" appeared among them. The 62nd's soldiers may have lacked experience, but they remained willing to fight.[32]

Just as the Americans reduced the size of divisions to accommodate a shortage of manpower, so too did the Germans. The Germans, however, suffered even graver materiel problems. As a result, the tables of organization for German formations proved aspirational rather that actual. Some of these could not be solved. As a consequence, the VGDs had few vehicles, and the Volksgrenadiers moved on foot. The "standard" infantry division organized with three infantry regiments, but the VGDs had only two. Each VGD had a powerful, albeit horse-drawn, artillery regiment. The 18th VGD's 1818th Artillery Regiment had three battalions of horse-drawn artillery, including a battalion each of 75-, 105-, and 150-millimeter howitzers. Some fifty-four pieces provided adequate fire support. An antitank battalion and reconnaissance battalion rounded out combat support. Among other weapons, both the 18th and 62nd VGD fielded fourteen of the reliable and effective Hetzer seventy-five-millimeter tracked antitank guns. The VGDs also boasted a fusilier battalion mounted on bicycles. The 18th VGD had twelve thousand troops, the 62nd eleven thousand.[33] In contrast, a full-strength US infantry division formed with three regiments of three battalions each boasted more than fourteen thousand soldiers.

The Panzer divisions had also declined in strength. The 1944 Panzer division organized with one tank regiment and two Panzergrenadier regiments authorized half-tracked infantry carriers. The 116th PZ illustrates how the regular army Panzer divisions organized. Its Panzer regiment had two battalions, as did each of its two Panzergrenadier regiments. An assault gun battalion, a reconnaissance battalion, an artillery regiment, an antiaircraft artillery battalion, an engineer battalion, and a signal battalion provided combat support. The Division also had limited logistics support. The 116th PZ fought the 28th ID in the Hürtgen Forest and like the 28th ID did so understrength. When they came, replacements arrived in swarms that threatened to overwhelm the Division's ability to accept them. On December 7 the 116th PZ replacement battalion had 1,800 officers and men. It received 1,800 more replacements the next day. Heavy equipment arrived as well; by December 10 the 116th had sixty-nine operational tanks (two in maintenance) and thirty assault guns. On December 16 the 116th PZ had nearly sixteen thousand soldiers assigned.[34]

18th Volksgrendier Division

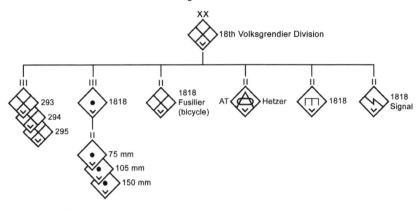

CHART 3. The 18th Volksgrenadier Division organization reflects the manpower and equipment constraints that plagued the Germans in the later years of the war. The Volksgrenadier Divisions retained three infantry regiments, but these regiments had only two battalions each. The Volksgrenadier Divisions had sufficient artillery, but all of it was towed. The 18th's Anti-Tank Battalion was robust, fielding both the Hetzer and towed antitank guns. Although it is not shown here, the Division also had some limited supply capability using horse-drawn supply vehicles. The 18th had some twelve thousand soldiers assigned, while the similarly organized 62nd Volksgrenadier Division had eleven thousand.

The SS and regular army Panzer divisions varied in strength and equipment but shared the same basic organization. Hitler cherished his SS divisions, so they fielded the best equipment and more of it. For example, the 116th PZ had 103 tanks authorized but only sixty-nine tanks and thirty assault guns assigned on December 16. The 116th had none of the King Tiger tanks armed with the justifiably feared 88-millimeter gun. Dietrich's 1st SS PZ, by contrast, had 134 tanks, including fifteen King Tigers. The 1st SS also had twenty-six assault guns. Another of Dietrich's divisions, the 2nd SS PZ, attacked with eighty-six tanks and twenty-eight assault guns.[35]

The Stage Is Set

Generalfeldmarschall Model's Army Group B, composed of three field armies, fought in the battle, but only two of them are antagonists here. Manteuffel's Fifth Panzer Army attacked with three corps: two Panzer corps and one infantry. General der Artillerie Walther Lucht's LXVI Corps' 18th and 62nd VGDs were key actors, as were the 116th PZ and the 560th VGD of General der Panzertruppe Walter Krüger's LVIII Panzer Corps. Oberst

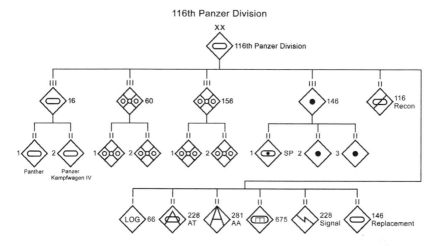

CHART 4. The 116th Panzer Division was organized as a "1944" Panzer Division. All of the Panzer Divisions that fought in the Battle of the Bulge organized on the same pattern, but with variations in equipment and assigned strength. The 116th Panzer Division included a Panther battalion and a battalion of the less capable but excellent Panzer Kampfwagen IV. Of the four Panzergrenadier battalions, only the 1st Battalion of the 60th Panzergrenadier Regiment had the Sonderkraftfahrzeug Sd.Kfz 9 half-track. The Sd.Kfz 9 lacked front-wheel drive, and was thus less mobile than the US Army half-track on rough terrain or soft ground. The remaining Panzergrenadier battalions traveled on a variety of trucks.

Otto-Ernst Remer's large and well-equipped Führer Escort Brigade was an essential player as well. The Sixth Panzer Army attacked with two SS Panzer corps and one infantry corps. The 1st SS PZ, 2nd SS PZ, and 9th SS PZ of the Sixth Panzer Army all fought against the 7th AD.[36]

In November 1944 Klaus Ritter, an antitank gunner in the 18th VGD, moved into a dugout on the line with the seven other *Landsers* in his squad. (*Landser* is the German equivalent of the honorifics "GI" or "doughboy" that were applied to American soldiers in World War II.) Ritter's antitank squad oriented itself on a ridge opposing one occupied by troops from the 106th ID's 423rd Infantry Regiment. The Germans' position was near the village of Sellerich, less than three miles east of Bleialf and across the valley from the Americans. The *Landsers* had "raised an earth-work of semicircular shape" to shield their towed seventy-five-millimeter antitank gun.[37]

Ritter was an *alter Hase* (old hare), or veteran soldier. Earlier that fall he had returned from Russia on emergency leave. A native of Windsheim, a village not three miles east of Sellerich, he sought and received a transfer to the 18th VGD. That is how he found himself manning a gun pointed at the Schnee Eifel a few miles from his hometown. Ritter knew a good thing when he saw it. He and his colleagues lived comfortably in a dugout heated by a woodstove. They ate well, hunting denizens of the forest or killing farm animals abandoned during the fighting in September and October. Once a week Ritter went to the battery headquarters, where he drew rations for his squad and enjoyed a hot bath. The old hare managed to make that his task alone rather than sharing this pleasant interlude away from the squad's dugout. In *Ghost Front*, Charles Whiting quotes Ritter as saying that his time in the line before the attack amounted to a "time out" from the war. Unlike their American counterparts, Ritter and the men of the 18th VGD patrolled aggressively. In addition to learning the ground, patrolling enabled them to loot more creature comforts from farms and or enemy dead.[38] In December, however, Ritter could see that the "time out" was coming to an end as movement of mobile forces picked up; he could smell an operation but knew not what it was.[39]

By sunset on Tuesday, December 12, 1944, the conditions were in place for Hitler's great gamble. That evening at his forward headquarters near Zeigenberg, Germany, the führer harangued field commanders, including the division commanders, about what he wanted them to achieve. He wandered far afield, but he did highlight several key points. Among these were several injunctions: not a moment could be wasted, the enemy must be made to realize that Germany would not capitulate, and no defeatist talk would be tolerated. Hitler even took a moment to compare himself to Frederick the Great. He noted with satisfaction that Germany confronted a coalition the likes of which no one had ever encountered. Britain, he said, was "a dying empire," the United States "a colony striving for independence." He continued, "There is friction between these states [including the Soviet Union] even today about their future goals." Hitler believed that if "a few more very hard blows are delivered . . . this artificially-supported common front will collapse with one tremendous clap of thunder."[40]

Two nights later a patrol from the 18th VGD discovered a gap of nearly two miles between the 14th CAV's 18th Cavalry Squadron and the American infantry on the Schnee Eifel. On December 15 Oberst Günther Hoffmann-Schönborn conferred with Lucht, his corps commander, recommending that the 18th VGD leave only two hundred or so troops from the Division's school battalion in the line opposite the 422nd Infantry Regiment to maintain the illusion that the lines remained manned. The rest of them Hoffman-Schönborn proposed to withdraw that day and assemble for the attack.

Furthermore, he proposed to lead personally the 294th and 295th Volks-grenadier Regiments and Klaus Ritter's 1818th Anti-Tank Battalion through the gap and around the flank of the 106th ID. General Lucht thought this a capital idea, and he toasted the 18th VGD's commander with a traditional German soldiers' exhortation, "Hals und Beinbruch, mein Lieber," which amounted to "Break a leg."[41]

A Failure of Command Portrayed as Failure of Intelligence

In his magisterial account of American corps commanders in the Bulge, combat veteran soldier and historian Harold R. Winton described Hasso von Manteuffel as "one of the Wehrmacht's most savvy tacticians." Winton's as-sessment is entirely accurate. A cavalry officer and skilled equestrian, Man-teuffel performed well in World War I and brilliantly in World War II.

MG Troy H. Middleton, in command of VIII Corps, was also an able sol-dier. During World War I, Middleton rose rapidly on the basis of success in combat. In October 1917, at the age of twenty-nine, he took command of the 4th ID's 39th Infantry Regiment and led it in an attack the following day. He was the youngest colonel and youngest regimental commander in the American Expeditionary Force. During the interwar years he served on the faculty of the infantry school and graduated near the top of his class at the Command and General Staff College at Fort Leavenworth, Kansas. In fact, Middleton graduated well ahead of his classmate, George S. Patton Jr. Upon graduation Middleton joined the faculty at Fort Leavenworth, where he taught, among others, "Dwight Eisenhower; Jacob Devers, six army com-manders . . . ten corps commanders." He was, as Winton asserts, "next to [George C.] Marshall, the consummate American infantryman of the inter-war period."[42]

Like his adversary, Middleton excelled in World War II as well. He com-manded the 45th ID brilliantly in Sicily and at Salerno. He took command of VIII Corps in England in March 1944. In August of that year Middleton led the Corps successfully, fighting in the Cotentin Peninsula and the breakout at Avranches that launched LTG Patton around the German south flank. Middleton and VIII Corps drew the unglamorous but essential task of tak-ing the Brittany ports. After concluding operations in Brittany, VIII Corps relieved V Corps in the Ardennes.[43]

Middleton had fewer illusions than most about the predicament of VIII Corps in the Ardennes. In *The Bitter Woods*, John S. D. Eisenhower reports a conversation between Middleton and his army group commander. Of the possibility that the Germans might attack the weak line Middleton held,

LTG Bradley remarked, "Don't worry, Troy. They won't come through here." Middleton responded, "Maybe not, Brad, but they've come through this area before." And indeed they had—three times, to be precise.[44]

If the American senior commanders knew that the Germans had attacked through the Ardennes before and recognized the potential for such an attack now, how is it that the Germans achieved surprise? And this, according to Hugh Cole in *The Ardennes: Battle of the Bulge*, was a surprise on the order of Pearl Harbor. It is equally certain that some future disaster will merit addition to the list of horrific surprise attacks inflicted on US forces or US cities. As long as intelligence requires assessment and decision, surprise is possible and even likely.

These "surprises" are often described as intelligence failures. But even when intelligence officers and analysts get it wrong, they are never the ones to decide what to do about what is known or unknown about an enemy. That is the business of commanders. In December 1944 no Allied commander or intelligence officer, with the exception of Colonel (COL) Oscar W. Koch, believed a German counteroffensive in the Ardennes or anywhere on the Western Front likely enough to merit doing anything about it.[45] Koch, Patton's intelligence officer, divined the massing of German units opposite VIII Corps largely from tracking rail movement, for which the Army Air Force provided much of the data. He briefed Patton and the Third Army staff on December 9, 1944, to the effect that the Germans had massed what amounted to nine divisions opposite VIII Corps just north of the 1st and 3rd Armies' boundary. Koch believed the Germans could mount a limited attack with at least a two-to-one advantage over VIII Corps.[46]

Patton and his staff decided that this information should not interfere with their planned offensive. Nevertheless, Patton had the Army staff do some preliminary contingency planning. Patton made no mention of this briefing or his guidance in his own diary. Days earlier he wrote, "I believe that the enemy has nearly reached his breaking point. As a matter of fact, we are stretched pretty thin ourselves."[47] It is hard to credit Patton or anyone else with prescience in the matter of German intentions. The decision to do contingency planning was well taken, but neither Patton nor Koch thought it necessary to call First Army or the 12th Army Group and compare notes. In his autobiography Koch took care to explain, "Too much overexpansion of subordinate headquarters' interest is viewed askance in intelligence circles."[48] In plain English, COL Koch believed that neither the 12th Army Group nor First Army would be likely to accept his estimate or be happy to hear from him.

Therein lies the heart of the American intelligence failure and, for that matter, the Allied intelligence failure. The intelligence apparatus of the various American units involved did not work well together. This was a failure of command rather than intelligence. Hugh Cole's description of the debate over blame remains valid today and includes "public polemic, personal vituperation, and ex parte vindication." All of this and wrangling over phrases in estimates and messages to "fix blame and secure absolution."[49] Intelligence officers in the 12th Army Group tended to squabble rather than collaborate. In that respect they reflected their commanders. Powerful men with tender egos are unlikely collaborators, and tender egos abounded among the Americans and Western Allies in 1944. Vituperation occurred rather more frequently than teamwork in the competition for resources and laurels.

This is not unusual in human affairs, but it is obviously not helpful in the quest to understand enemy capabilities and intentions. Developing intelligence is painstaking and difficult. It requires analysis of information stemming from disparate sources, and the number and reliability of sources is essential to estimating what an enemy is likely to do. Intelligence officers on the Western Front enjoyed nearly the same suite of sources as exist today, less satellite images. They had access to electronic intelligence, though it was not on the scope and scale that is today.

During the late fall of 1944 three things confounded commanders and intelligence officers and led to the "intelligence" failure. First and foremost, they suffered from "confirmation bias"—that is, they saw what they expected to see and fit their observations to suit their intuitive conclusion, as MG Leonard Gerow had done when he left V Corps for the United States. After the beating the Germans took following the breakout, few Allied planners really believed they could yet again rebound. Moreover, an attack through the Ardennes made little sense to them, and they therefore assumed the Germans had reached the same conclusion. Second, as noted, the key players in this drama did not work well together. Finally, VIII Corps, including Middleton and his command, were complacent to the point of indolence. Having said his piece to Bradley, there is little evidence that Middleton and his staff sought additional reconnaissance or visited units to see what was being done to improve defenses or to assure adequate patrolling.

The idea that the Germans could not and/or would not mount a counteroffensive was pervasive from GEN Eisenhower's headquarters down. BG Edwin L. Sibert, Bradley's intelligence officer, issued his G-2 Summary No. 18 on December 12, 1944. It shows how strongly this view prevailed. His estimate condescended to explain, "It is now certain that attrition is steadily sapping the strength of German forces on the western front," and continued with condescension: "the crust is thinner, more brittle and more vulnerable than it appears on G-2 maps or to the troops on the line."[50] Charles B. MacDonald, in *A Time for Trumpets*, shows that Sibert was not alone in his view. Field Marshal Montgomery's 21st Army Group estimate reported that the Germans "cannot stage a major offensive."[51]

In the postwar debate over whom to blame and whom to praise, COL Benjamin A. "Monk" Dickson often gets credit for "getting it right." Dickson issued the First Army's *G-2 Estimate No. 37* on December 10, 1944. In the conclusion of his estimate Dickson cited three enemy capabilities. One of them, capability number 2, noted that "the enemy is capable of a concentrated counterattack with air, armor, infantry and secret weapons at a selected focal point at a time of his own choosing." But the estimate went on to add that counterattack "is to be expected when our major ground forces have crossed the Roer River."[52] It is true that Dickson considered the Germans having the capability to counterattack or even mount a counteroffensive. On December 14 he slapped the First Army G-2 situation map and announced, "It's the Ardennes," then he went on leave to Paris, "stating later that he needed the rest and was confident that he had done all he could."[53] If he was sure it was the Ardennes, how did he feel comfortable with going on leave? Clearly he did not expect an attack soon, or at least not while he took his leave. After reading Dickson's estimate, Eisenhower's intelligence officer, BG Kenneth Strong, telephoned Sibert to complain that Dickson's estimate was unduly pessimistic. That call may have produced the tone in Sibert's *Intelligence Summary No. 18*. There is little reason to accept Dickson's postwar claim of prescience.

There is no evidence that LTG Courtney H. Hodges, Dickson's boss, paid much attention to *Estimate 37*. His war diarist, Major (MAJ) William C. Sylvan, reports only that Hodges met with Dickson that evening. No mention is made either of a possible German counterattack or counteroffensive in the following days. The diary reflects where Hodges's mind was—the Ruhr River. He visited V and VII Corps, both of which were earmarked for the attack, but not the quiet sector where VIII Corps defended. In the entry for December 13, 1944, MAJ Sylvan reported the beginning of Hodges's attack toward the Ruhr River dams. Hodges thought the attack had caught the Germans "off-base" and that "the V Corps sector was merely an extension of the quiet VIII Corps zone."[54]

At VIII Corps, COL Andrew R. Reeves issued his estimate on December 9, the day before Dickson's *Estimate No. 37*. Reeves concluded that the pattern of the enemy's operations "indicates his desire to have this sector of the front remain quiet and inactive."[55] Despite that assurance, MG Walter M. Robertson, commanding the 2nd ID, spoke with Middleton on the December 10 about enemy activity and the sound of vehicular traffic reported by his forward units. Middleton told Robertson, "Go back to sleep, Robbie. You've been having a bad dream."[56] This is the same Robertson who would tell MG Alan W. Jones on his arrival, "Take it easy, General. The Krauts won't attack even if they were ordered to."[57] Furthermore, the exchange supports the idea of complacency and/or indolence in VIII Corps.

Although the leadership and intelligence officers at Eisenhower's Supreme Headquarters, in both army groups, and in the concerned field armies tracked the German concentration, it did not alter their conviction that the Germans were unlikely to attack. At the 12th Army Group Bradley and his three Army commanders focused on their planned offensives toward the Ruhr River dams north of the Ardennes and toward Frankfurt south of the forest. What they saw confirmed their bias. Nor did they seek evidence that might overturn their view. Photoreconnaissance might have helped, but the VIII Corps sector had a lower priority than those areas where the field armies planned their offensives. An oblique view taken over the 28th ID's 112th Infantry on November 25 was the last photoreconnaissance mission in the VIII Corps sector prior to the offensive. Yet on December 10, when Robertson asked for a reconnaissance mission, Middleton turned him down.[58]

Units in contact are nearly always the best source of tactical information. This is true if they observe their enemy's habits and conduct security and reconnaissance patrols. Patrolling enables units to capture enemy troops or accept the surrender of deserters. The troops in the line in VIII Corps did little to help themselves. Robertson's 2nd ID occupied the same positions in the line for two months. During that time the Division never issued the doctrinally mandated G-2 *Estimate of the Enemy Situation*. The 2nd ID did patrol. In his well-known book *Company Commander*, Charles B. MacDonald discussed both contact patrols and the far more dangerous reconnaissance patrols. His suspicion that little use was made of these was well founded based on his own experience and postwar study.[59] Even worse, patrol reports and information that did not fit current assumptions did not receive close attention. The units in Middleton's VIII Corps did not patrol aggressively, nor is there any evidence to suggest he encouraged them to do more. Patrolling may produce prisoners if patrols cross the enemy's lines. From December 1 through December 15, 1944, VIII Corps units captured only thirty-one prisoners, and the 2nd ID captured none. Two rookie units, the 9th AD and the 106th ID, captured two and five, respectively. The 28th ID captured seven and the 4th ID seventeen.[60] Most American patrols failed to cross into the enemy's positions.

Aces and Eights: Dead Man's Hand

Whether it patrolled aggressively or not, the 106th ID drew a bad hand. First the US Army stripped it of troops for higher priority units. After filling the Division with raw replacements, the Army deployed it without time to re-train. Soon after arriving in the United Kingdom, the 106th's troops boarded landing ship tank amphibious vessels and a conventional transport to cross the English Channel. At sea, a storm kept them from landing so they bobbed about helplessly in the channel, many of them seasick for several days. When they got ashore many of them spent their first night in an open field in the rain. Then they rode in cold 2.5-ton trucks across France and Belgium to get to their sector. Arriving, cold, wet, and tired, the infantrymen trudged into positions they took over from the 2nd ID.

Perhaps because of their misery the 106th ID set about improving on sur-prisingly good living conditions rather than preparing for combat. There were exceptions to those caught up in that unfortunate trend. BG Leo T. McMahon, the division artillery commander, was one of them. He was ac-tive and aggressive. The Division arrived without its basic load of ammuni-tion, but McMahon solved that problem by driving his team hard and going where he needed to go to get ammunition so the division artillery had what it needed by December 14. Elsewhere aggression and drive were less evi-dent. Although small arms ammunition was not in short supply, some offi-cers chose not to issue any at all, while others issued what to their soldiers seemed a paltry amount compared to what the combat veterans they re-placed had carried. Junior officers at the company level had not yet made the mental transition from peace to war. There are all kinds of reasons for this lack of focused effort. The troops were cold, and many of them suffered from the early symptoms of trench foot, but the priority in combat is to deal with what will kill you first and then deal with what *might* kill you later. The first priority in those first days in the dugouts and huts should have been learning the sector and preparing for combat, not making sure the huts were dry and heated and that everyone had galoshes.[61]

Some historians have defended the relative passivity of the 106th ID as natural given its inexperience and the complacency at VIII Corps. The reac-tion of disorientation and confusion given the environment is understand-able but indefensible. General McMahon demonstrated the urgency combat requires, as did the Division's logistics team. They did as they should have, and went from supply point to supply point in order to find ammunition, overshoes, and other essential items. Leadership in combat requires difficult decisions and iron determination of the kind Clausewitz described as essential for commanders. Sadly, the 106th ID lacked that kind of leadership.

Arriving in a combat zone is disorienting regardless of the conditions. Nothing is familiar, and everything is hard—much harder than was experienced or even imagined in training. If something takes a half hour in training it will easily take an hour in a combat zone. COL R. Ernest Dupuy, in *St. Vith: Lion in the Way*, wrote a spirited defense against what he believed constituted unreasonable and unfair criticisms of the Division. Dupuy's argument resonates, and indeed it is right; the 106th ID deserved better than it got. Yet his description of the Division's actions on arrival is also right: "And so they drifted for a few days while it snowed, and rained, and life in general was miserable."[62]

The VIII Corps did little to help other than provide Lieutenant Colonel W. M. Slayden, the assistant corps intelligence officer, to help the 106th ID find its way. On Thursday, December 14, the 106th ID senior leadership met for an intelligence conference and to discuss counterattack planning based on an VIII Corps directive received that day. None of the commanders liked the positions they had been forced to occupy. The enemy was several thousand yards east of its position, and the Division had no contact with it. Accordingly, the Division intelligence officer rightly urged the regiments to patrol "deeper to find the enemy, plot his minefields and capture prisoners." The very next day one of the forward units captured two soldiers from the 18th VGD who reported an attack imminent.[63] It was too little too late. Overcoming complacency that came from the top down and from the bottom up was beyond the newly arrived Division.

NOTES

1. Charles B. MacDonald, *A Time for Trumpets*, 40. British code breakers solved the puzzle of the Enigma encryption machine; under the code name Ultra, the Allies read Hitler's "mail."

2. See Charles Whiting, *The Last Assault*. Because the allies still had access to diplomatic and other German governmental communications, Whiting argues that Eisenhower knew the Germans were massing for an attack. He did nothing, according to Whiting, because he wanted the Germans to come out from behind their fortifications so he could destroy them. Whiting is prolific and useful, but his speculation misses the mark. This is not the kind of secret that governments are able to keep.

3. Hugh M. Cole, *The Ardennes: Battle of the Bulge*, 11.

4. Percy Schramm was a professor of medieval and modern history at the University of Göttingen and an Army reservist. He joined the high command staff in March 1943 and kept a war diary until the end of the war. He did two major manuscripts for the European Command during his captivity. I have read these documents, but use here the excerpt that appears in Danny S. Parker, ed., *The Battle of the Bulge: The German View*, 45, 87.

5. Peter Caddick-Adams, *Snow and Steel*, 125–34.

6. Carl von Clausewitz, *On War*, 194, 198, emphasis in the original.

7. General der Panzertruppe Hasso von Manteuffel, "An Interview with Gen Pz Hasso von Manteuffel," ETHINT-45, 4; Generalmajor Carl Gustav Wagener, "Fifth Panzer Army (2 Nov 44–16 Jan 45)," 10. Born in a military family, Manteuffel began his professional education at age eleven, and it concluded when he served as commandant of an officer training school just before World War II. See Donald Grey Brownlow, *Panzer Baron*, 39.

8. Robert E. Merriam, *Dark December*, 17. First published in 1947, *Dark December* remains a standard among books on the Bulge.

9. Merriam, *Dark December*, 17.

10. General der Artillerie Walther Lucht, "LXVI Infantry Corps," 4.

11. Cole, *The Ardennes: Battle of the Bulge*, 64–74.

12. Brigadier General George C. McDonald, "Allied Air Power and the Ardennes Offensive," 45.

13. MacDonald, *A Time for Trumpets*, 36.

14. Samuel W. Mitcham Jr., *Panzers in Winter*, 45.

15. John Toland, *Battle: The Story of the Bulge*, 13–14, 15.

16. Charles Whiting, *Ghost Front*, 100. Whiting served with the British Army in World War II. He became fascinated with the Bulge.

17. Manteuffel, ETHINT-45; John S. D. Eisenhower, notes from interview with General der Panzertruppe Hasso von Manteuffel, October 12, 1966, box 6, Charles B. MacDonald Papers. On Manteuffel knowing the opposition and boundaries, see General der Panzertruppe Hasso von Manteuffel, "Fifth Panzer Army Ardennes Offensive," 65. See also Whiting, *Ghost Front*, 100.

18. Manteuffel, "Fifth Panzer Army Ardennes Offensive," 67. Generalmajor Carl Gustav Wagener, "Fifth Panzer Army—Ardennes (Special Questions)."

19. US War Department, *Field Service Regulations: Operations*, FM 100-5, 179; Oberstleutnant Dietrich Moll, "18th Volks Grenadier Division," 8; First Lieutenant Robert R. Wessels to Colonel S. L. A. Marshall, August 24, 1945; Bruce Condell and David T. Zabecki, eds., *On the German Art of War*, 104.

20. Condell and Zabecki, *On the German Art of War*, 39.

21. Moll, "18th Volks Grenadier Division," 12–13.

22. Lucht, "LXVI Infantry Corps," 1. It is difficult to determine exactly when various field commanders received their initial briefing. Lucht says he knew in late October. Moll is explicit, saying the 18th VGD received its order on December 1. It is likely that commanders from the Division up knew the outline of the plan in November.

23. Parker, *The Battle of the Bulge: The German View*, 149, emphasis in the original.

24. Parker, *The Battle of the Bulge: The German View*, 37–38. See also Brownlow, *Panzer Baron*, 124–25.

25. Heinz Günther Guderian, *From Normandy to the Ruhr*, 514. The Fifth Panzer Army field order is appendix 16 in Guderian's history of the division, with which he served from its organization in the spring of 1944 until its collapse in April.

26. See Moll, "18th Volks Grenadier Division"; and Generalmajor Friedrich Kittel, "62nd Volks Grenadier Division." The author has been unable to find any interviews of Hoffmann-Schönborn.

27. MacDonald, *A Time for Trumpets*, 37.

28. Moll, "18th Volks Grenadier Division," 1.

29. Oberst Arthur Jüttner, "Report by Colonel Jüttner of the 62nd VGD in the Battle of the Bulge," 2.

30. Merriam, *Dark December*, 26. See also Charles B. MacDonald, *The Siegfried Line Campaign*, 242–47; and Michael Reynolds, *Sons of the Reich*, 183. The 9th Panzer Division generally served in the Fifth Panzer Army, but in this narrative it was serving in the Sixth Panzer Army.

31. Moll, "18th Volks Grenadier Division," 19.

32. Friedrich Kittel, "A New 62nd Inf. Div.—the 62nd VGD."

33. See Moll, "18th Volks Grenadier Division." There are a number of sources for general data on German units; see, e.g., Matthew Cooper, *The German Army 1933–1945*, chap. 29, "Military Demise," for gross numbers of troops and key equipment; Jean-Paul Pallud, *Battle of the Bulge*, 34–56; and Christer Bergstrom, *The Ardennes 1944–1945*, 70–71, for division end strengths, key equipment lists, and numbers. Pallud is the best source for availability versus assigned strength. George F. Nafziger, the author of several detailed German orders of battle, is a reliable source for unit designations; here I have used Nafziger, *German Army: Battle of the Bulge*.

34. Brigadier General Siegfried von Waldenburg, "Commitment of the 116th Panzer Division in the Ardennes 1944/45"; Bergstrom, *The Ardennes 1944–1945*, 71; Pallud, *Then and Now*, 49. See also Guderian, *From Normandy to the Ruhr*, 290–91.

35. Bergstrom, *The Ardennes 1944–1945*, 70–71; Pallud, *Then and Now*, 49, and on the 1st SS PZ, 43. These numbers do not reflect available rates. On December 10, the 1st SS PZ had eighty-six tanks operational, with thirty King Tigers en route. Pallud believes that at least half of them reached the front, as the Division reported thirty on hand on December 17. See also Reynolds, *Sons of the Reich*, 183.

36. German units essential to the story are derived from US after action reports and do not include ancillary contact but only those with whom the 7th AD and its attached and supporting units fought.

37. Klaus Ritter, statements, box 10, Charles B. MacDonald Papers, pt. 1. Ritter's squad was assigned to the 1818th Anti-Tank Battalion. While in the line, the Battalion supported the 293rd Volksgrenadier Regiment of the 18th VGD. Just how old Ritter was in 1944 is uncertain; Whiting claims in *Ghost Front* that he was twenty-two, but Heino Brandt, the translator of Ritter's statements, wrote that he was eighteen.

38. Whiting, *Ghost Front*, 69–72.

39. Whiting, *Ghost Front*, 71–72.

40. Parker, *The Battle of the Bulge: The German View*, 8.

41. Charles Whiting, *Death of a Division*, 16–17.

42. See Harold R. Winton, *Corps Commanders of the Bulge*, on Manteuffel, 139, and on Middleton, 35–39. The six US Army commanders were LTG Courtney H. Hodges (First Army), LTG Alexander Patch (Seventh Army), BG Robert L. Eichelberger (Eighth Army), GEN William H. Simpson (Ninth Army), LTG Simon Bolivar Buckner (Tenth Army), and MG Leonard Gerow (Fifteenth Army). LTG Jacob L. Devers commanded the 6th Army Group. See also Brownlow, *Panzer Baron*.

43. Winton, *Corps Commanders*, 39.

44. John S. D. Eisenhower, *The Bitter Woods*, 100.

45. Whiting, *Ghost Front*, 185. See also Brigadier General Oscar W. Koch with Robert G. Hays, *G-2: Intelligence for Patton*, 92–103.

46. Koch, *G-2*, 95.

47. Martin Blumenson, *The Patton Papers*, 587.

48. Koch, *G-2*, 93.

49. Cole, *The Ardennes: Battle of the Bulge*, 56.

50. MacDonald, *A Time for Trumpets*, 53. MacDonald devotes two tightly written chapters to the German deception effort and the allied intelligence. His discussion is the best on the matter.

51. MacDonald, *A Time for Trumpets*, 53.

52. Headquarters, First United States Army, *G-2 Estimate No. 37*, 4.

53. Whiting, *Ghost Front*, 187. See also David W. Hogan Jr., *A Command Post at War*, 207.

54. Major William C. Sylvan and Captain Francis G. Smith Jr., *Normandy to Victory*, 202, 205.

55. MacDonald, *A Time for Trumpets*, 74.

56. MacDonald, *A Time for Trumpets*, 75.

57. Whiting, *The Last Assault*, 12.

58. Whiting, *The Last Assault*, 12. See also Royce L. Thompson, *American Intelligence on the German Counteroffensive*.

59. MacDonald, *Company Commander*, 99.

60. Thompson, *American Intelligence*, 1:4–5. Two different sets of prisoners were captured by the 4th ID and the 106th ID on December 15, 1944. Two of the prisoners came from the 18th VGD. One reported the German Army would attack between December 17 and 25. The 4th ID captured two German deserters from a fortress unit. They reported hearing of an attack involving a Panzer division and two infantry divisions.

61. See Colonel R. Ernest Dupuy, *St. Vith: Lion in the Way*, on ammunition shortage, 15, and on trench foot, 19. On living conditions, see Peter Elstob, *Hitler's Last Offensive*, 41–42. The weather was abysmal, but the huts and dugouts the 2nd ID built were reasonably comfortable, according to soldier interviews. On the small arms ammunition complaint, see John Davis with Anne Riffenburg, *Up Close*, 38.

62. Dupuy, *St. Vith: Lion in the Way*, 19. Dupuy makes a compelling case on the atmosphere in the Corps.

63. Dupuy, *St. Vith: Lion in the Way*, 18.

CHAPTER THREE

The Eve of Battle

On the nights of 12–13 and 14–15 December vehicular movement was heard all along the front.

—VIII Corps after action report, December 1944

Tomorrow brings the beginning of a new chapter in the Campaign in the West.

—Oberbefehlshaber West war diary, December 15, 1944

December 15, 1944

THE SUN ROSE at 0823 on Friday, December 15, 1944, providing little warmth or light to an overcast winter day. In reserve to XIII Corps, Brigadier General (BG) Robert W. Hasbrouck's 7th Armored Division (AD) lay astride the border between Holland and Germany, with part of the Division near Heerlen, Holland, and the rest near Geilenkirchen, Germany. Two of his combat commands spent the day rehearsing for an attack designed to clear the west bank of the Ruhr, preliminary to Ninth Army's drive on the river. The division artillery occupied forward positions to reinforce the fires of the 84th Infantry Division (ID). At 1030 hours the Lucky Seventh's artillery fired a massed time-on-target mission in support of the 84th ID, and it fired a second later that afternoon. Otherwise the 7th AD passed a quiet day.[1]

Some seventy miles south, the day began peacefully enough for Major General (MG) Alan W. Jones's Golden Lions of the 106th ID. They occupied defensive positions that meandered from the Losheim Gap generally along or near the Siegfried Line south to the village of Lützkampen, near the triborder area of Belgium, Germany, and Luxembourg. In addition to his three rifle regiments, Jones had the 820th Tank Destroyer (TD) Battalion and the 14th Cavalry Group (CAV) attached. Even so, with about twenty-two miles of difficult ground to cover, he had too few troops to defend the heavily wooded Schnee Eifel in the density required.

Accordingly, his front or, in doctrinal terms, main line of resistance, constituted a line only in so far as a line connects two points. The Army defined the term as, "a line joining the forward edge of the most advanced organized defense areas"[2] In fact, the "line" of the 106th ID consisted of small-unit positions separated often by hundreds of yards. The troops occupied holes, dugouts, Siegfried Line pillboxes, some buildings, and a few road-blocks along and on both sides of the meandering frontier between Belgium and Germany.

The Schnee Eifel and the positions inherited from the 2nd ID made its defense problematic because it included a vulnerable salient that extended into Germany. Army doctrine mandated that commanders choose defensive positions based on analysis of the terrain. But no one had done a terrain analysis of the Schnee Eifel and chosen positions on that basis. No one had drawn the "line"; rather, it happened where the pursuit figuratively and literally ran out of gas. The 4th ID created the salient in September when it attacked through St. Vith and penetrated the Siegfried Line. When the front stabilized, no American general seriously considered withdrawing or making any adjustments that could be seen as giving up ground.[3]

American commanders proved nearly as reluctant to give up ground as Adolf Hitler was. When MG Walter M. Robertson moved the 2nd ID into the line in early November he concluded that the salient put his troops at risk. He asked MG Troy H. Middleton for permission to withdraw from the salient. Middleton agreed, but both Lieutenant General (LTG) Courtney H. Hodges at First Army and LTG Omar N. Bradley at the 12th Army Group refused to give up the ground, as it might be used to launch an attack through the gaps created in the Siegfried Line.[4] British field marshal Bernard Law Montgomery commented on the American penchant for fighting to hold ground in a postwar letter to John S. D. Eisenhower, accurately noting that US commanders had an "emotional attitude toward giving up terrain."[5]

The Ardennes is rugged throughout, but the Schnee Eifel sets the standard. Parallel ridges running from northeast to southwest dominate the plateau. It averages fifty or more inches of snow and rain per annum and fifteen days or more of rain or snow each and every month. All of that water and snowmelt flows downhill on either side of the ridges, creating creeks and ravines. Near St. Vith the Our River and its right-hand tributaries drain the Eifel. Several

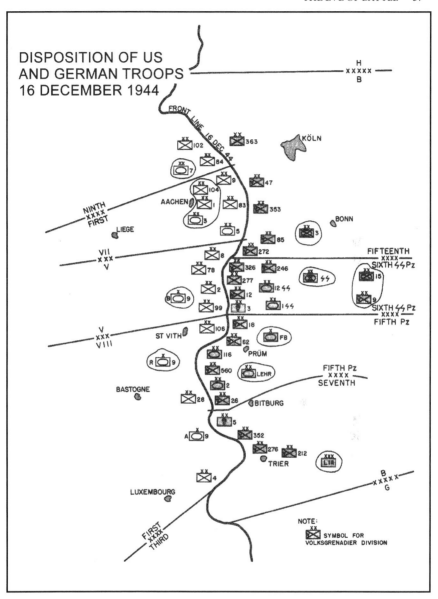

DISPOSITION OF US
AND GERMAN TROOPS
16 DECEMBER 1944

MAP 2. The positions as shown are indicative rather than exact. For example, the 62nd Volksgrenadier Division and the 116th Panzer Division had not yet closed when the fighting began. German units are shaded to differentiate them from Allied units. This map used the World War II convention on tactical symbols; all, including the enemy units, are shown as rectangles. Reproduced from the US Army Armor School publication *The Battle at St. Vith*.

of these streams cut through the valleys and ravines of the plateau. East-west movement is difficult, as it requires surmounting the ridges in turn, but decent roads run through the Losheim Gap and along many of the streams. The one referred to by Americans as the Skyline Drive runs from Diekirch generally north and northwest along the ridges and over the top of several. It was then and remains today the most important north-south artery in the area. The Losheim Gap at the northern end of the line genuinely merits its title. It runs from northeast to southwest with a ridge to the north and the Schnee Eifel to the south and southeast.

German place names tell the terrain story as well. The German word for stream is *Bach*. Many towns and villages take their names from nearby streams, so their names end in *-bach*. Town names ending in *-schied* denote crossroads or in some cases nearby ravines. The suffix *-feld* denotes a field or pasture, and there are several towns advertising open fields or ravines in their names. The names of the local towns and terrain features remind the reader that the Ardennes itself is a character in this story. Two of the Our's left tributaries, the Auw and Ihren, flow west and then south on western slopes of the Eifel. Both of those streams and the Our flowed south in the rear of much of the 106th ID's positions and forward of friendly lines in the 28th ID sector. The terrain generally favored the defense, the Schnee Eifel impeded movement, and the streams that flowed off the slopes cut the routes running west and south, also interfering with movement.[6]

Defending ground that offers both cover from fire and concealment from observation has advantages, but these may be forfeited if not developed. Carl von Clausewitz described this problem two hundred years ago, and conclud-ed that if a defender has too few troops to assure adequate coverage of the ground, then he must "place additional reliance on mobility, active defense, and even offensive measures."[7] The doctrine the 106th ID's officers learned in their professional education echoed Clausewitz's thinking. "The conduct of the defense must be aggressive," according to the Army's operations manual, which went on to assert that, "the counterattack is the decisive element of defensive action. It is seldom feasible to hold a defensive position by passive resistance only."[8]

It is in this context that the actions of the 106th and those of the 7th AD and other units that joined the defense must be examined. Simply put, how did VIII Corps, the 106th ID, the 7th AD, and the other units that fought in the St. Vith sector respond to the German counteroffensive that began on December 16, 1944? The VIII Corps directed the 106th ID to mount an "ag-gressive defense" without specifying what that meant, though presumably it meant more than passive resistance.⁹ Did the 106th fight as its organization and doctrine designed it to fight? When it arrived, did the 7th AD fight "aggressively"? Did unit commanders make sound decisions within the frameworks of their organization, doctrine, and orders? Similarly, how did their enemies from the Fifth and Sixth Panzer Armies operate? What effect did their choices have on the outcome? And finally, what outcomes did the belligerents achieve?

106th ID and 112th Infantry Dispositions

The VIII Corps boundary with V Corps ran just north of the Losheim Gap and then meandered south, following the trace left at the end of the pursuit operation in late summer. The 14th CAV led by Colonel (COL) Mark A. Devine defended the Losheim Gap on the boundary with the 99th ID of V Corps. On Devine's right, or south, Jones's three infantry regiments defended abreast, the 422nd, 423rd, and 424th positioned from north to south. COLs George L. Descheneaux, Charles C. Cavender, and Alexander D. Reid commanded the three regiments, respectively. The 422nd and a battalion of the 423rd occupied a salient that extended nearly two miles deeper into the Eifel and east of the Siegfried Line bunkers and tank obstacles. These units occupied some of the Siegfried Line pillboxes, or at least slept in them. Obviously the Germans knew just where to find them. The 423rd's main line of resistance bent sharply back west toward the town of Bleialf. From there the line ran south to the boundary with the 424th. The 424th had a smaller salient that extended southeast about a mile. A provisional battalion formed under the command of the 424th's antitank company commander defended the southernmost part of the line. The provisional battalion included the antitank company; B Troop, 18th CAV; one platoon from the regimental cannon company; and a platoon of infantry.

MG Jones retained two battalions of infantry as the 106th ID's reserve. The 2nd Battalion, 423rd Infantry (INF) was at Born, Belgium, about six miles north of St. Vith and "nine miles to the rear" of the forward line of troops. The 1st Battalion, 424th INF occupied an assembly area around the German village of Steinebrück (literally, "stone bridge") on the Our River some three miles from the line but closer than the troops in Born. The 106th's artillery located its battalions just to the rear of the forward troops. These included the 275th Armored Field Artillery (AFA) in direct support of the 14th CAV, the 589th Field Artillery (FA) as support to the 422nd INF, the 590th FA to the 423rd INF, and the 591st FA to the 424th INF. The 106th ID's general support battalion, the 592nd FA, positioned its 155-millimeter howitzers to fire across the Division's entire front. Quite a few other units were in the 106th's sector to support operations. These included the 820th TD Battalion, the 440th Anti-Aircraft Artillery (AAA) Battalion Automatic Weapons (which was a VIII Corps unit positioned forward to shoot at V-1 buzz bombs, a primitive ancestor of the cruise missile), the 634th AAA, and eight corps artillery battalions organized in two artillery groups. Logistics troops manned a ration supply point and the rail yard at Gouvy, Belgium.[10]

The boundary between the 106th ID and the 99th ID of V Corps ran through a valley or gap just north of the Losheim Gap. COL Devine's 14th CAV defended with the 18th CAV forward in the gap. The 18th CAV gave up its B Troop in return for a "detachment of towed TD (tank destroyer) guns and two recon platoons of the 820th TD battalion." Lieutenant Colonel (LTC) William F. Damon's 18th CAV manned "eight garrison strong points" in small villages supported by a few roadblocks.[11] The term "strong points" may have inspired confidence, but in reality they lacked strength. Hugh Cole, official historian of the battle, described them with precision as "small islands of resistance, manned usually in platoon strength."[12] The squadron's sector lay down slope from the Schnee Eifel, with the tank obstacles known as dragon's teeth and the pillboxes of the Siegfried Line also looking down on them. A Company, 820th TD, with two reconnaissance platoons, manned outposts and roadblocks in three small villages. The 14th CAV's second squadron, the 32nd CAV, under the command of LTC Paul Ridge, remained in Vielsalm, Belgium, in reserve and doing much needed maintenance on its light tanks. Ridge's squadron was attached to the group on December 10. COL Devine planned to rotate the 32nd into the gap to relieve the 18th on December 20. LTC Roy U. Clay's 275th AFA provided fire support.[13]

In Lanzerath, a village on the boundary with V Corps, three three-inch (seventy-six-millimeter) antitank guns assigned to the 820th TD supported by forward observers from the 275th AFA constituted the garrison. The Intelligence and Reconnaissance (I and R) Platoon of the 394th INF overlooked the village from a tree line just south of the corps boundary. On December 10, Major (MAJ) Robert Kriz, the regimental intelligence officer of the 394th INF, ordered the I and R Platoon across the boundary to assure tight security along the vulnerable division and corps boundary and to support the tank destroyers. Lieutenant (LT) Lyle Bouck led the 394th's scout platoon. The I and R Platoon took over holes dug by the 2nd ID but had improved upon them. Its job was to maintain contact with the 18th CAV—in this case, with the tank destroyer section in Lanzerath.[14] The 18th CAV ran contact patrols south to the 422nd INF.

COL Descheneaux's 422nd INF defended the northwestern part of the Schnee Eifel from Kobscheid, the boundary with the 14th CAV, south to his boundary with the 423rd. That boundary ran westward from the front line through the town of Oberlascheid. Descheneaux's regiment manned the salient east of the Siegfried Line. The Ihrenbach River flowed south to the rear of his defensive positions. Several *Bachen*, or streams, cut ravines leading south and west to drain into the Our River flowing south from its source in Manderfeld.

The 422nd had its main command post in the village of Laudesfeld. The regiment's direct support artillery, the 589th, occupied positions near Auw. The regiment's three battalions defended abreast, the 2nd, 1st, and 3rd positioned from north to south, respectively.[15] The woods in the 422nd's sector were so dense that visibility "was restricted in places to 40–50 feet." On December 14, MG Jones visited the 422nd command post. Descheneaux asked him, "What will we do if we get an attack?" Jones responded, "All we can do is hold at any cost."[16] Holding ground was a shibboleth in the US Army.

COL Charles C. Cavender's 423rd INF defended roughly from the village of Bleialf south to the boundary with the 424th Infantry at Grosslangenfeld. Cavender's 2nd Battalion formed part of the Division's reserve and was situated in the towns of Born and Medell. The 423rd did not defend as far to the east as the 422nd. With only two battalions, COL Cavender used attachments and makeshift solutions to cover the nearly eight miles of front he had to defend. Jones attached B Troop, 18th CAV and C Company, 820th TD to help. The 590th FA provided direct support to the regiment with positions to its rear.[17]

The 423rd defended with the 3rd Battalion in the north in the salient with the 422nd. The 1st Battalion defended in the center, bending or refusing the line sharply westward toward Bleialf. To coordinate the attached units, Cavender formed a provisional battalion commanded by his antitank company commander. The antitank company rounded out with an infantry platoon and a platoon from the cannon company combined with B Troop, 18th CAV and C Company, 820th TD constituted his third battalion. The provisional battalion defended from just east of Winterscheid south to the boundary with the 424th just north of Grosslangenfeld, leaving a gap of two thousand yards between it and the 1st Battalion. In direct support, the 589th FA occupied marshy ground in the meadows created by the Ihrenbach.

COL Reid's 424th extended the line to the boundary with the 28th ID's 112th INF running west from the town of Lützkampen. To cover six miles of undulating front, Reid had only his 2nd and 3rd Battalions, as his 1st

Battalion formed part of the Division's reserve at Steinebrück. With the Our River to his rear and north, Reid's position was difficult to defend. The regiment lay astride the major highway running northwest from Bitburg, Germany, through St. Vith and onward. The regiment's direct support artillery, the 591st FA, positioned more or less in the center of the regiment's sector just to the rear of the 3rd Battalion.

COL Gustin M. Nelson defended on Reid's right. Nelson had literally rebuilt his 112th INF after it was mauled in the Hürtgen Forest. His line, like that of the Golden Lions, had gaps. To compound the difficulty he had a high-speed avenue of approach to defend. The road that ran from Lützkampen on the border and zigged and zagged through Troisvierges, Gouvy, Houffalize, and farther west was vital to the Fifth Panzer Army.

German Assessment and Intentions

Because forest and obstacles constrained avenues of approach, the Fifth and Sixth Panzer Armies generally attacked along roadways. These were not maneuver corridors but instead narrow roadbound routes traveling along through valleys or along ridges. Of the avenues of approach heading westward on either side of the Schnee Eifel, those emanating from the Losheim Gap were best. The northernmost of these ran westward to the region known as the Hohes Venn, or High Fens. The second extended from Losheim southwest through Manderfeld, then to Schönberg and finally St. Vith. A major road junction, St. Vith had five radials branching out to the north, northwest, west, southwest, and south. Additionally, a rail line ran north and south through St. Vith. The third extended from Roth in the Losheim Gap through Auw and then cross-country to Schönberg or by road to Bleialf. The fourth avenue originated in Prüm and went west through Bleialf, where it joined the third avenue, and then cross-country to Steinebrück or via Winterspelt to St. Vith. The final route crossed the Siegfried Line near Lützkampen and ran westward to Troisvierges. There were two major roads north toward St. Vith: one from Gouvy and the other from Houffalize. Heading west from Houffalize, the terrain opened up.[18]

The Sixth Panzer Army, making Model's Army Group B the main effort in the north, would attack along designated routes, or Rollbahns, for its armored formations. These were labeled alphabetically from north to south, A–E. The two southernmost routes, D and E, impinged on the boundary, with the Fifth Panzer Army attacking to seize the vital road junction at St. Vith. Route E ran southwest from Manderfeld and deep into the Fifth Panzer

Army sector before turning back north. The two southern routes originated in the Losheim Gap and cut through the defense of the US 14th CAV.

General der Panzertruppe Hasso von Manteuffel's Fifth Panzer Army would attack on the Sixth Panzer Army's left. Manteuffel intended to bypass the regiments in the Schnee Eifel in order to take the crossroads at St. Vith on the first day of the offensive. Doing so would enable the Fifth Panzer Army to stay well clear of the southern Rollbahn of the Sixth Panzer Army and assure access to the routes running westward to the Meuse.

Moving into final positions was all that remained to be done. To coordinate movement forward and assure secrecy, Army Group B defined phase lines beyond which units could move only when given an order to do so. Most of the assault divisions not already in the line advanced to the first phase line by December 12. That phase line stretched "between Gemund (a town about 10 miles east of Monschau) and Bitburg, about 12 miles behind the front." The next day the divisions moved another six miles, to the final phase line. On the night of December 14–15, 1944, most of the attackers moved into their final assembly areas.[19]

Oberstleutnant Heinz Günther Guderian, the son of the famous German tank general Heinz Guderian, served as operations officer of the 116th Panzer Division (PZ). As part of the security measures, Guderian and his commander, Siegfried von Waldenburg, worked out the details of their part of the attack without involving battalion commanders. The 116th PZ repositioned units forward. Finally, on December 14, battalion commanders received their orders. In his book *From Normandy to the Ruhr*, Guderian quoted the 2nd Battalion of the 16th Panzer Regiment journal for the 14th: "0730 hours, the battalion commander drives to the front for a reconnaissance. 0900 hours, the regimental scout platoons drive out to reconnoiter march routes and preparation areas."[20] The battalion commanders had very little time.

Officially the battalion commanders may have been ignorant of the attack plan, but clearly, like Klaus Ritter, they were *alten Hasen* (old hares); they knew something was afoot, and several divined the intent. The 116th PZ had been withdrawn from the defensive battles in the Hürtgen Forest and east of Aachen at the end of November in order to replace heavy losses in soldiers and equipment. The 116th PZ began moving forward by rail on December 4. The division commander, Generalmajor Waldenburg, showed excitement the next day when he wrote in his pocket calendar, "God willing, all things planned will work out."[21] Major Fritz Vogelsang, the adjutant of the 116th

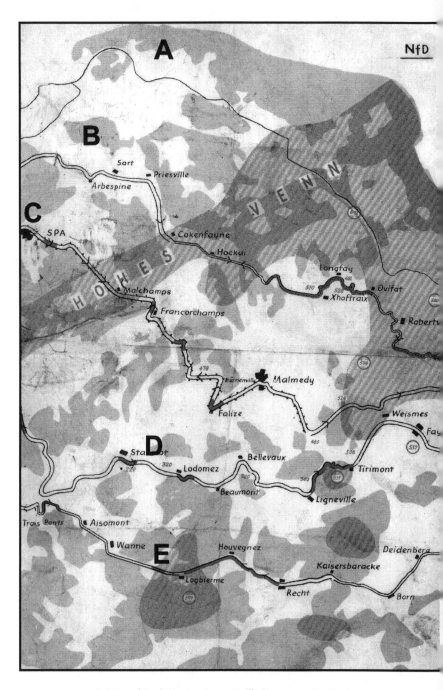

MAP 3. Map of Sixth Panzer Army Rollbahn routes. Setting letters that identified the routes in bold is the only change made to the original. The shading illustrates altitude, forests, and moors. The Hohes Venn (High Fens) is a region of upland peat bogs. Marshy ground, found throughout the Ardennes, is also shown. The altitude varies from 400 meters in the valleys to as high as 646 meters near

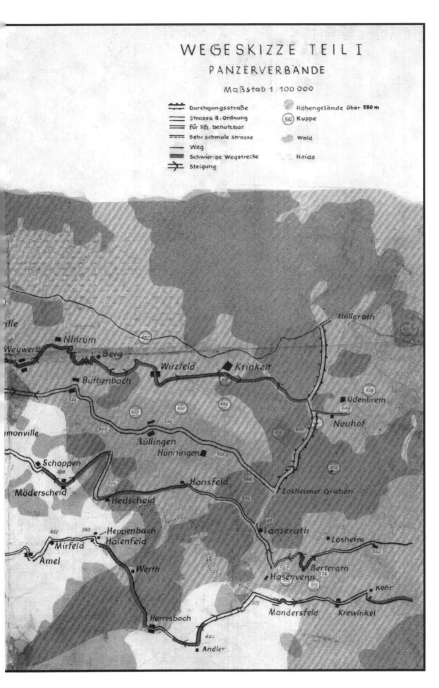

Krinkelt at the eastern end of Route B. The terrain is fairly rugged in places but rolling hills are everywhere. The route sketch is detailed as to slope, suitability of the road net, and obstacles. None of these routes supported rapid transit by tanks and half-tracks. Reproduced from the original, captured early in the fighting, which is in the Dwight D. Eisenhower Library and Museum.

MAP 4. The 1st SS Panzer Division's thrust against the 14th Cavalry Group and the 99th Division is the northernmost attack pertinent to this narrative, while the attack of the 116th Panzer Division against the 28th Infantry Division is the southernmost. The attack of LXVI Corps on the 106th ID is shown in the center. Reproduced from maps 2 and 3 in Hugh Cole, The Ardennes: Battle of the Bulge, with thanks to Sherry Dowdy and the staff of the of the US Army Center of Military History.

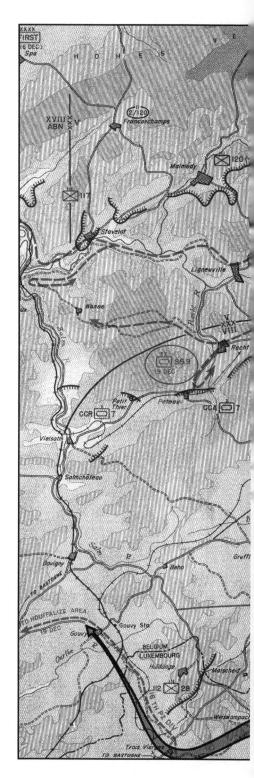

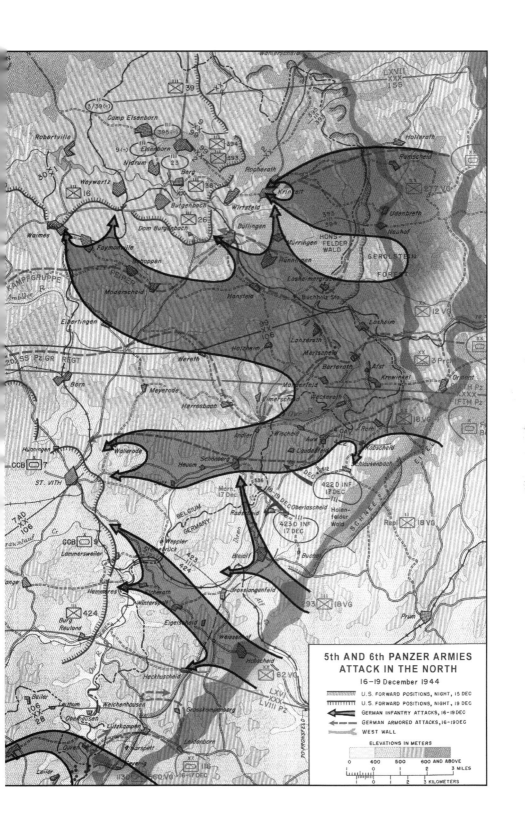

**5th AND 6th PANZER ARMIES
ATTACK IN THE NORTH**

16–19 December 1944

ⲚⲚⲚⲚⲚⲚⲚⲚ	U.S. FORWARD POSITIONS, NIGHT, 15 DEC
▬▬▬▬▬▬	U.S. FORWARD POSITIONS, NIGHT, 19 DEC
◀━━━━	GERMAN INFANTRY ATTACKS, 16–19 DEC
◀┅┅┅	GERMAN ARMORED ATTACKS, 16–19 DEC
⇜⇜⇜	WEST WALL

ELEVATIONS IN METERS

400	500	600 AND ABOVE

0   1   2   3 MILES

0   1   2   3 KILOMETERS

PZ, maintained a meticulous diary that reflected his optimism and energy. On December 7 he reported in his diary, "Activity everywhere, like in a bee-hive. Army and Waffen-SS vehicles with the most varied division insignias are buzzing all over the place on the roads."[22] On December 14 General Man-teuffel and General der Panzertruppe Walter Krüger, the LVIII Panzer Corps commander, visited Waldenburg, who told them, "Fuel and essential parts of the Division are still missing."[23]

But no changes could be made and no further delays would be permitted. That very day the effervescent Vogelsgang wrote, "Everything is rolling! We almost feel the way we did during the offensive in France in 1940, weeks that seem an eternity ago." Despite his continued optimism, Vogelsgang added a concern: "If only we had enough fuel."[24] Although considerable quantities of fuel had been found for the offensive, much of it remained east of the Rhine River. Manteuffel had wanted five units of fuel (a unit is a full tank) but received less than two. According to Manteuffel, fuel reserves remained east of the river for two reasons: "first, because the railroad system west of the Rhine was almost completely smashed; and, second, because it was con-sidered safer there."[25]

The Stage Is Set

Despite implacable complacency, the movement forward of the assault forc-es did not go unnoticed, nor did it go unrecorded. The Golden Lions had settled in and finally had become more active in patrolling—at least in lateral patrolling. Private Harry F. Martin Jr., serving with L Company, 3rd Battal-ion, 424th INF, typified the new unit's experience. He had grown used to German harassing fire, parachute flares, and the fearful Nebelwerfer rocket launchers. He knew his regiment had "huge gaps in our line."[26] He also re-called patrolling the gaps at night but not attempting to penetrate the Ger-man positions. The 106th ID and other units also perceived that German patrols had penetrated their positions. Clarence L. Buckman, assigned to the 106th ID headquarters, awakened on his first morning in the sector near St. Vith to a note left on his pup tent by a German patrol that read, "Welcome 106th to the front."[27] In the 99th ID, MAJ Kriz, the intelligence officer of the 394th INF, found positive evidence in the form of ski tracks that passed through the 394th's lines along the boundary it shared with the 14th CAV. German reconnaissance patrols penetrated the American lines routinely.[28]

The 106th ID and other units on the line heard movement and passed what they heard up the chain. John W. Morse, a rifleman in the 422nd, and members of his squad reported hearing motor movement. His lieutenant took action and organized a patrol to investigate. The patrol did not get far before it was driven off by enemy fire.[29] Reports duly went up from the 106th ID to VIII Corps. Martin believed the 106th's concerns were dismissed as the "front line jitters of the newly arrived division."[30] Multiple German V-1 buzz bombs overflew the 106th on the nights of December 13–14 and December 14–15, and during the night of December the 15–16, German aircraft flew parallel to the line.[31] There is no evidence that any of these reports found fertile ground, regardless of the source. Reports of activity consistent with an attack in the offing had gone up all along the VIII Corps line and part of the V Corps line to the north without evoking a response from either of the two corps or First Army.

Although the 106th ID was learning, the two regiments in the Schnee Eifel still did not patrol aggressively. On the evening of the December 15, the 18th Volksgrenadier Division (VGD) withdrew the two regiments opposite Cavender and Descheneaux and replaced them with the Division's school battalion of two hundred or so soldiers.[32] In the absence of combat patrols, neither the 422nd nor the 423rd detected the relief.

Despite unease and several alarms, the 106th ID and 14th CAV spent December 15 in comparative peace, "acclimating" in their quiet sector. That afternoon "fog [came] creeping along the valley" between the 106th ID and the 18th VGD.[33] Visibility had dropped to no more than fifty meters when the order came for the final assembly of the 18th VGD. Antitank gunner Klaus Ritter and his *Landser* colleagues received the order to move to an assembly area, still unaware of the coming attack. Ritter was unhappy to see his "time out" end. He recalled thinking, "Gone our dreams all of sudden!" Ritter's squad humped their ammunition down the reverse slope to their prime mover and prepared to tow their antitank gun.[34]

Once loaded, the members of the squad trundled off, sitting on ammunition boxes aboard their prime mover, already regretting the loss of their warm dugout. That night around 2100 hours they arrived at the 1818th Anti-Tank Battalion assembly area. There the battalion commander briefed them on the plan of attack. First they would move farther forward to position on the Siegfried Line, itself astride the road to Bleialf. On the morning of December 16, after a short bombardment, they would attack to seize Bleialf and hold the road open. Following a patriotic harangue they had what Ritter described as a "comparatively opulent" supper with a bottle of wine for every two men and twenty cigarettes apiece. With more than a little of his tongue in his cheek, Ritter recalled, "We younger people are soon getting euphoric, just as if we would actually be in Paris within four weeks—just a trip."[35] Enthusiasm percolated even in the old hare.

After supper the Battalion moved on with its headlights off (traveling in what soldiers call "blackout") to a ruined village near the Siegfried Line. Ritter's squad arrived at the bunker assigned to it at about midnight on December 15–16. The troops parked their guns and, after allocating sentries, waited for morning. Ritter stretched out his "tired bones on the cold concrete floor" of the bunker but found that, "Dog-tired as I am—I find no rest."[36] Other German soldiers, just as cold and tired as Ritter and his mates, were on the move that night. Most of the 116th PZ rolled all night, only reaching their start line after the attack had begun the next morning. Though the 116th PZ attempted some reconnaissance on December 15, it achieved little. Guderian wrote that the Division's attack "had to be started in uncertainty."[37]

Navy Captain Harry C. Butcher, an aide to General Dwight D. Eisenhower and a committed diarist, made no diary entry for December 15. Eisenhower himself remained concerned that his headquarters and those below had lost track of the Sixth Panzer Army. He was worried about V and VII Corps of LTG Hodges's First Army. The two corps had begun an attack on December 13 to reach the Ruhr. The Sixth Panzer Army remained "the strongest and most efficient mobile reserve remaining to the enemy." At First Army, Hodges's diarist MAJ William C. Sylvan's entry for December 15 reported in detail on V and VII Corps' attack. With respect to VIII Corps he noted only that it reported no change except that "increased artillery fire was received."[38]

NOTES

1. Donald P Boyer Jr., *St. Vith: The 7th Armored Division in the Battle of the Bulge*, 2. See also 7th Armored Division, Tactical headquarters journal, December 1944, entry for December 15, 1944. A cavalryman, Boyer served as the S-3, or operations officer, of the 38th Armored Infantry Battalion. After the war, while assigned to the US Army Armor School, he wrote the narrative cited here and the unattributed study *The Battle at St. Vith Belgium*.

2. US War Department, *Infantry Field Manual: Rifle Regiment*, FM 7-40, 150. Determining the length of the 106th ID front is a matter of estimation. Some authors claim it was as long as twenty-seven miles. I have used Google Maps, Colonel R. Ernest Dupuy's *St. Vith: Lion in the Way*, and several combat interviews to arrive at twenty-one miles.

3. Charles B. MacDonald, *The Siegfried Line Campaign*, 49–56.

4. Charles B. MacDonald, *A Time for Trumpets*, 115.

5. John S. D. Eisenhower, Drafts and Other Materials from *The Bitter Woods*, Dwight D. Eisenhower Presidential Library and Museum, box 2, contains detailed notes from an interview with Montgomery. Bruce C. Clarke, who commanded CCB, 7th AD, made the same complaint on more than one occasion. Once ground was taken, US commanders loathed giving it up.

6. The tributary listings and the length of the Our River and its tributaries can be found on a number of websites, including various sites written in French. Although the author does not suggest considering Wikipedia an authoritative source, its entry for the Our River seems as accurate as the Duchy of Luxembourg site, and it is in English; see "Our (River)," Wikipedia, https://en.wikipedia.org/wiki/Our_(river).

7. Carl von Clausewitz, *On War*, 507.

8. US War Department, *Field Service Regulations: Operations*, FM 100-5, 152.

9. Colonel R. Ernest Dupuy, *St. Vith: Lion in the Way*, 11.

10. For "aggressive defense," see Dupuy, *St. Vith: Lion in the Way*, 9. There were surely other VIII Corps troops in the sector that are not listed here. General support units such as the military police and communications units were likely in the area but not shown on overlays. Hugh M. Cole, *The Ardennes: Battle of the Bulge*, is the best source on unit orders of battle and locations; on the corps artillery and rations supply point, see 141, 286. For all other units, see Dupuy, *St. Vith: Lion in the Way*.

11. Lieutenant Jack T. Shea, "Fourteenth Cavalry Group," 2. LT Shea served as combat historian assigned to the 2nd Information and Historical Service.

12. Cole, *The Ardennes: Battle of the Bulge*, 138.

13. Shea, "Fourteenth Cavalry Group," 2–8. The 18th CAV arrived in the Losheim Gap in November 1944.

14. Alex Kershaw, *The Longest Winter*, 57–63.

15. Lt. Col. Joseph C. Matthews, interview by Capt. William J. Dunkerley, 1–2. Descheneaux was not interviewed, as he had contracted tuberculosis while held as a prisoner of war. Oberstleutnant Dietrich Moll, "18th Volks Grenadier Division," 24.

16. Matthews interview, 5. See also Dupuy, *St. Vith: Lion in the Way*, 24, map.

17. Colonel Charles C. Cavender, "The 423 in the Bulge," 88. See also Captain Allan W. Jones Jr., "The Operations of the 423rd Infantry."

18. Cole, *The Ardennes: Battle of the Bulge*, 141. All of the roads are extant today and can be seen on satellite images. Seeing them conveys the importance of St. Vith as a crossroads.

19. Samuel W. Mitcham Jr., *Panzers in Winter*, 49.

20. Heinz Günther Guderian, *From Normandy to the Ruhr*, 296.

21. Guderian, *From Normandy to the Ruhr*, 293.

22. Guderian, *From Normandy to the Ruhr*, 293.

23. Guderian, *From Normandy to the Ruhr*, 296.

24. Guderian, *From Normandy to the Ruhr*, 296.

25. General der Panzertruppe Hasso von Manteuffel, "An Interview with Gen Pz Hasso von Manteuffel," ETHINT-46, 3.

26. Harry F. Martin Jr., *I Was No Hero in the Battle of the Bulge*, 123.

27. Veterans of the Battle of the Bulge, Inc., *The Battle of the Bulge: True Stories of the Men and Women Who Survived*, 59–60.

28. Kershaw, *The Longest Winter*, 69. See also Moll, "18th Volks Grenadier Division."

29. John W. Morse, *The Sitting Duck Division*, 66–67.

30. Morse, *The Sitting Duck Division*, 126.

31. Forty-one American prisoners of war from the 106th ID, attached units, the 28th ID, and a single soldier from the 99th ID, group, interview by Lieutenant Jack Shea, casern at Erfurt, Germany, May 10, 1945, 9.

32. Moll, "18th Volks Grenadier Division," 30.

33. John Schaffner, telephone interview with the author, December 3, 2017. There are very good weather records for December 16, 1944–January 16, 1945, but eye-witnesses are the best sources for weather outside that period. See also Klaus Ritter, statements, box 10, Charles B. MacDonald Papers.

34. Ritter, statements, pt. 1, pp. 2–3.

35. Ritter, statements, pt. 1, p. 4. Ritter's squad traveled on the Raupenschlepper Ost, a tracked truck designed for service on the Eastern Front. The Germans built a great many of these and used them as prime movers.

36. Ritter, statements, pt. 1, p. 5.

37. Guderian, *From Normandy to the Ruhr*, 299–300.

38. Dwight D. Eisenhower, *Crusade in Europe*, 341. See also Major William C. Sylvan and Captain Francis G. Smith Jr., *Normandy to Victory*, 211–12.

CHAPTER FOUR

The Golden Lions at Bay

The American soldiers of the 106th stuck it out and put up a fine performance.
—Field Marshal Bernard Law Montgomery

The enemy, in skillful operations, made use of tanks, anti-tank units and engineers. They were brave blokes whose resistance could only be broken by fire.
—Oberst Friedrich Kittel

At 0510 ON the morning of Saturday, December 16, 1944, antitank gunner Klaus Ritter and his mates waited impatiently and nervously for the promised artillery preparation to begin. It was cold, several degrees below freezing, with nearly a foot of snow on the ground. The sky was overcast and fog hung low. When the barrage began, Ritter thought, "The end of the world begins! We hear the muffled thunder of the firing guns behind us, then a hundredfold howling and whizzing above us, and then we see the fiery hands of uncountable detonations in front of us—like a wide luminescent band."[1] Searchlights lit the low overcast, the light reflecting from clouds and snowy ground and providing artificial moonlight for the attackers, though not enough to compensate fully for the dense fog, and "flares—red, green, amber and white—flickered over treetops."[2] Some Americans experienced the first rounds of the barrage as a spectacular light show produced by German artillery muzzle flashes in the distance. A few German aircraft joined in the attack, bombing the cavalry in the Losheim Gap.[3]

Theory and Practice

Doctrine, courage, and character all played a role in what followed after the German bombardment that Saturday long ago. The two sides had similar doctrine. New and veteran units on both sides suffered from too little training, and everyone had to contend with miserable weather. At the beginning the Germans outnumbered their American counterparts, but the Americans had fuel and ammunition to burn, and when the skies cleared they enjoyed a pronounced advantage in the air.

Men on both sides confronted the environment of war described by Carl von Clausewitz more than one hundred years earlier. Soldiers and officers passed through a realm of physical exertion, suffering, and uncertainty. Success, and often survival, depended largely on what Clausewitz called "the play of courage and talent . . . in the realm of probability and chance," which depended, he wrote, "on the particular character of the commander and the army." Determination and sheer bloody will remain necessary in war, in both leaders and the led. In December some surmounted the challenges. Others did not.[4]

Opening Shots

The intense and frightening barrage fired by the Germans jolted American soldiers into adrenaline-fueled alertness. Eugene Morell, an artilleryman in C Battery, 591st Field Artillery (FA), was called out with his howitzer crew to fire a mission just as the barrage began. "Of course we had the urge to find cover but kept following orders for aiming and loading for what seemed like an eternity," he would later recall.[5] Morell's dilemma is easily understood by anyone who has experienced artillery fire. In the presence of incoming rounds, one can think of nothing else. North of the Losheim Gap, James R. McIlroy, an infantryman in the 99th Division could see that "the sky was almost light from heavy mortar and artillery fire and from the Germans beaming spotlights against the clouds. This was on our right."[6] From the Losheim Gap south across the front of VIII Corps and all the way to Echternach, Luxembourg, General der Panzertruppe Hasso von Manteuffel's artillery banged away with everything from fourteen-inch guns to the three-hundred-millimeter Nebelwerfer rocket launcher known as the screaming meemie for the noise it made.

As suddenly as the barrage began, it stopped or shifted. An eerie quiet fell over parts of the front while artillery continued to land in the rear of the main line of resistance. Flares and searchlights cast shadows over the snow-covered ground, illuminating the night. At the edge of the Losheim Gap, the tanks of the 1st Schutzstaffel (SS) Panzer Division (PZ) had lined up, ready to follow on the heels of the paratroopers of the 3rd Fallschirmjäger Division. One German tank commander waved at one of his lieutenants and promised, "See you in America."[7]

As mentioned, the boundary between the Fifth and Sixth Panzer Armies ran through the Losheim Gap. The LXVI Corps mounted the northernmost attack of the Fifth Panzer Army. On their right, the 1st SS Panzer Corps attacked on a narrow axis in the Losheim Gap and to the north. In the gap the 3rd Fallschirmjäger Division's 9th Fallschirmjäger Regiment (FJR) had the task of breaking through the crust of the American defenses so that the 1st SS Panzer Corps' tanks could race for the Meuse River. Specifically, this meant the 1st SS PZ Division, known by its title Liebstandarte Adolf Hitler (Adolf Hitler's Lifeguards). The 1st SS needed to get on Rollbahn Routes D and E and head west. The 14th Cavalry Group (CAV) and 99th Infantry Division (ID) stood in its way.

Kampfgruppe Peiper, the 1st SS spearhead, stood behind the 3rd Fallschirmjäger Division paratroopers, waiting for them to achieve the penetration and open the way west. Led by Obersturmbahnführer Joachim Peiper, the battle group comprised "117 tanks, 149 half-tracks, eighteen 105 mm and six 150 mm howitzers." Fully motorized and supported by air defense and logistics, Peiper commanded 4,800 men. His battle group was powerful, fielding more tanks than the 116th PZ Division attacking farther south.[8] And it was unwieldy: Peiper's column stretched ten or twelve miles in length and depended on narrow forest roads.

The 294th and 295th Volksgrenadier Regiments (VGRs) of the 18th Volksgrenadier Division (VGD) moved out to flank the Schnee Eifel from the north through a gap that patrols had discovered between the 18th CAV and the 422nd Infantry (INF). Bypassing the Schnee Eifel's dense forest toward Manderfeld would enable the two regiments to descend south along the Our River. The 18th VGD's commander, Oberst Günter Hoffmann-Schönborn, spelled out the mission and his intent: the Division "will attack with the point of the main effort on the right wing. Forward elements will cross the main line of resistance and advance on both sides of the Schnee-Eifel. The initial objective will be the crossing of the Our River at Schönberg, after which the division will advance with all mobile forces along the Our River road towards St. Vith, which will be taken by surprise assault."[9]

The 293rd VGR formed the southern wing of the 18th VGD. It assembled near Brandscheid on the night before the attack. When the barrage lifted, the 293rd skirted the southern edge of the Schnee Eifel, attacking to seize the crossroads at Bleialf. From there roads led to Schönberg, Winterspelt, and, ultimately, to St. Vith. Once west of the Schnee Eifel the two wings would join, effecting the isolation of the two regiments of the 106th ID on the Schnee Eifel. One bicycle mounted battalion and the bulk of the antitank battalion followed two Volksgrenadier regiments making the main effort. Hoffman-Schönborn intended to use his limited mobile capability to exploit success.[10]

The 62nd VGD, the other division assigned to General der Artillerie Walther Lucht's LXVI Corps, formed the left or southern wing of the Corps. The 62nd's zone of action extended from Grosslangenfeld generally northwest toward Winterspelt, Steinebrück, and then St. Vith. The 62nd VGD aimed to envelop the Schnee Eifel from the south. South of the 62nd, LVIII Panzer Corps attacked with the 116th PZ, and the 560th VGD both against Colonel (COL) Gustin M. Nelson's 112th INF. South of LVIII Panzer Corps, XXXXVII Panzer Corps' three Panzer divisions and one Volksgrenadier division landed on the remainder of the 28th ID.[11]

The German attack encountered difficulty from the outset. Hoffmann-Schönborn led his 295th VGR on the intended route. But the 294th led by Oberstleutnant Wilhelm Drueke got lost in the fog and thus fell behind. The 62nd VGD also had trouble. At 7:00 Oberst Arthur Jüttner, in command of the 164th VGR supported by the "mobile battalion" mounted on bicycles, waited expectantly for information. What he felt was "complete uncertainty, but order given to advance party for assembly." Nothing happened as he had hoped. First the bicycles had to be pushed, and then "Nothing to be seen—fog." The 62nd VGD groped its way toward Winterspelt against spirited resistance from the 424th INF. The 560th VGD attacking south of LXII Corps had even more serious problems. It attacked that morning with two regiments, as its third regiment still had not arrived. To add to the 560th's misery, its engineer battalion and antitank battalion had not arrived either. Adding insult to injury, one of the two attacking regiments wandered around disoriented by the fog.[12]

The 14th Cavalry Group in the Losheim Gap

The 14th CAV arrived in the Losheim Gap in October, but with only the 18th CAV assigned. The 2nd ID used the 18th CAV to defend VIII Corps' flank. COL Mark A. Devine did not have a second squadron until the 32nd CAV arrived in December. Even then, the 32nd went into reserve to rest and perform maintenance. Using the 18th CAV to screen a flank was one thing, but assigning it a defensive mission was another.

The 18th CAV lacked the numbers and heavy weapons of an infantry battalion. As a result, between Lanzerath and Afst to the southeast the "islands of defense" were merely roadblocks established by ten towed antitank guns from the 820th Tank Destroyer Battalion (TD). With less than six hundred soldiers, Lieutenant Colonel (LTC) William F. Damon's 18th CAV confronted three German regiments supported by tanks, assault guns, and antitank guns. The so-called strongpoints in Lanzerath, just west of the Losheim Gap, and in smaller villages extending east to Afst, then south to Roth, and finally to Kobscheid, could not support each other. The cavalrymen referred to these positions as sugar bowls: because the villages were all on crossroads or roads located in valleys, these positions were "sugar" to any attackers.[13] During their short time in the gap, Damon's troopers improved their positions. They dug trenches and tunnels connecting positions and deployed automatic weapons to their advantage. They emplaced defensive mines and wire covered by fire. Equally important, LTC Roy U. Clay's 275th Armored Field Artillery (AFA) observers planned and adjusted some two hundred artillery concentrations. Nevertheless, the Germans held the winning hand, outnumbering the 18th CAV on the order of six to one.[14]

At 0600 the Germans lifted fire from forward positions and shifted west to impact on the cavalry group command post in Manderfeld. German artillery "continued to harass" the cavalry the rest of the day. German aircraft also dropped a few bombs on Kobscheid and a single bomb on Manderfeld. The German ground attack did not begin immediately on the heels of the barrage except at Roth. Troopers there repulsed elements of the 294th VGR with direct fire and concentrations fired by the 275th AFA.[15]

Not until after daylight did enemy ground troops appear throughout the sector. In the north they attacked at 0730, but not particularly effectively. Some German infantry wearing snow capes, probably from the 9th FJR, "approached the positions in mass formations, singing, shouting and generally acting as though influenced by strong stimulants."[16] A Company, 820th TD, with one of its tank destroyer platoons and one of the Battalion's reconnaissance platoons, manned a roadblock among the handful of buildings that formed Lanzerath. Together the two platoons had just over thirty men. The tank destroyer platoon had four very effective three-inch or seventy-six-millimeter antitank guns, all towed by half-tracks. The reconnaissance platoon brought one scout car armed with a thirty-seven-millimeter canon and five Jeeps, each armed with a .30-caliber machine gun. Without infantry they stood little chance. The roadblock delayed but did not stop the enemy. Around 0940 they withdrew west toward Manderfeld, having lost one gun.[17]

As the German infantry moved out of Lanzerath it took devastating fire from Lieutenant (LT) Lyle J. Bouck's intelligence and reconnaissance platoon from the 394th INF of the 99th ID. The platoon occupied a position on a ridge overlooking Lanzerath. Bouck had selected the position for the eighteen soldiers he led and they dug in. His troops oriented south, thus enfilading the German paratroopers as they came out of town. The platoon devastated the paratroops, killing and wounding perhaps a hundred. Later that afternoon the 9th FJR finally overran and captured Bouck's platoon. None of his eighteen soldiers were killed, and they turned in quite a record on their first and only day in combat. Historian and soldier Peter Caddick-Adams argues that this rookie platoon "validated the infantry training of the American divisions," yet "Bouck's personal leadership and clear decision-making" cannot be discounted.[18] Some units lacked the caliber of leadership Lyle Bouck demonstrated in the Losheim Gap.

By 0800 the Germans had come to grips with all of the 18th CAV's strongpoints. During the course of the morning they overwhelmed the lightly manned posts in the northern part of the Losheim Gap and began to unravel the 18th CAV's defense. The tank destroyer detachments lost seven of their ten guns, at least five of which were turned against the Cavalry by its antagonists. The garrisons at Afst and farther south fared better but had to withdraw when the Germans broke through in the north. LT Kenneth C. Farrens commanded at Krewinkel. His command included his platoon from C Troop and a tank destroyer reconnaissance platoon from the 820th TD. At first light Farrens saw "a column of Volksgrenadiers, marching four or five abreast, and in parade formation."[19] The Krewinkel garrison "blazed away with all weapons," obliterating the leading enemy troops. The grenadiers of the 295th VGR reacted quickly and managed to reach the village, but Farrens's platoon and the tank destroyer troops stopped them cold. The 295th withdrew, but as they were leaving, one of them shouted, "Take a ten minute break, soldier. We'll be back." Farrens responded, "And we'll be waiting you son of bitch."[20]

During the "break" LT Aubrey L. Mills, the C Troop executive officer, arrived in Krewinkel with much needed ammunition. He delivered the ammunition, then left to deliver ammunition to another strongpoint, but he failed to make his next delivery, as an enemy sniper killed him. Although pummeled by self-propelled antitank and artillery fire, the small garrison at Krewinkel held the 295th until ordered to withdraw, at about 1100 hours. Overloaded with equipment and wounded, Farrens and his cavalrymen withdrew in good order. About a mile north of Krewinkel, LT Max Crawford and his cavalry platoon fought it out in the tiny crossroads village of Afst. Crawford's handful of troops, equipped with two M8 scout cars, two sixty-millimeter mortars, rifles, and a few light machine guns, shot up the 295th VGR until ordered to withdraw. The enemy pressed the platoon as it attempted to leave. Crawford personally delayed them long enough to escape by stopping a Hetzer 38(t) self-propelled antitank gun with a bazooka rocket.[21]

A Troop, 18th CAV manned the two strongpoints south of Krewinkel at Roth and Auw. In January 1945 LT Jack Shea, an army military historian, wrote an important narrative of the 14th CAV's fight in the Ardennes. Shea could not report the story of Roth fully because he wasn't able to speak to anyone who fought there. Private First Class (PFC) Dante Archimede, the only survivor of the garrison, lived only because he missed the fight. Archimede left Roth to pick up ammunition just before the Germans overcame the defenders. Captain (CPT) Stanley E. Porché and A Troop got hit hard. Porché had only his headquarters, his 2nd Platoon, and two towed antitank guns from the 820th TD. Part of the 295th VGR supported by Hetzers hit Roth while other units of the regiment bypassed the village, threatening to isolate the garrison. Porché held out as long as he could. He made his last radio transmission at 0430, saying, "Tanks 75 yards from CP. Firing direct fire out." He attempted to lead his troops to safety, on foot, but was compelled to surrender soon after his last message.[22]

Ill equipped for static defense and hugely outnumbered, LTC Damon's 18th CAV fought on December 16 with good effect—with the exception of the lightly defended northern outposts. Strange things occurred in the 14th CAV that day and the next. COL Devine, the group commander, made puzzling decisions. Those decisions and his behavior have been questioned ever since, and he remains an enigmatic figure. An ambitious spit-and-polish soldier, Devine created an environment both of fear and respect. His relationship with his subordinates can best be described as difficult. Devine and Damon, in particular, did not work well together.[23]

Devine recognized the 18th CAV could not hold the gap against the sizable attack underway. At 0600 he alerted LTC Paul A. Ridge to get his 32nd CAV ready to move on order. The 32nd, Devine's reserve, was in the rear at Vielsalm. Devine knew it would be some time before Ridge could move but he needed the 32nd. At 0640 Devine asked the 106th ID to let him bring the 32nd forward to Manderfeld, where it could thicken the defense. Jones agreed. At 0932 the 32nd CAV, less its light tank company, headed northeast from Vielsalm. F Company had its engines on the ground for maintenance, so it did not move with the squadron. By 1200 hours that day CPT Horace N. Blair had his light tanks back together, minus one key system. He moved without intercom.[24]

After giving Ridge his orders, Devine went forward to see what he could of the fighting. He returned to his command post at 1100, just as the 32nd began to arrive. Devine personally chose positions for the 32nd CAV to occupy. He placed two troops in and around Manderfeld, while B Troop remained in reserve in Andler, a small village on the road to St. Vith. Now the first of several command problems emerged. LTC Ridge, who appeared to those around him agitated and in "a highly nervous state," turned over command of the squadron to Major (MAJ) John L. Kracke, the executive officer. Ridge announced he would go get more ammunition for the squadron and departed for the rear.[25]

It is fair to say that Devine suffered from intense pressure not to cede any ground. He, like other American officers, understood the culture—once taken, ground was to be held. Moreover, he knew that if he held Manderfeld, the 18th CAV could withdraw through the 32nd. Finally, holding Manderfeld prevented the envelopment of the Schnee Eifel from the north. As the 32nd established positions without its squadron commander, Devine ordered MAJ James Mayes, the 32nd's operations officer, to counterattack to retake the Losheim Gap and Krewinkel. Doing so would restore contact with the 99th ID and protect the northern flank of the 106th ID's infantry regiments.[26] The Cavalry was poorly suited to attack anyone, especially along the roads.

Nevertheless, Mayes moved out with C Troop supported by E Troop, the squadron's seventy-five-millimeter assault gun troop. German paratroopers backed up by assault guns and captured US antitank guns stopped Mayes's counterattack before it really got underway. Devine concluded he had no alternative but to withdraw, so he ordered Mayes to fight to delay the enemy. Covered a little by Mayes, Devine withdrew the 14th CAV, without orders, at around 1600 hours. Devine then decamped to the 106th ID headquarters without issuing any further orders. He remained there until morning. By nightfall, after a hard day's fighting, the Germans had cleared the Losheim Gap and arrived at the headwaters of the Our. A reflection of how hard the

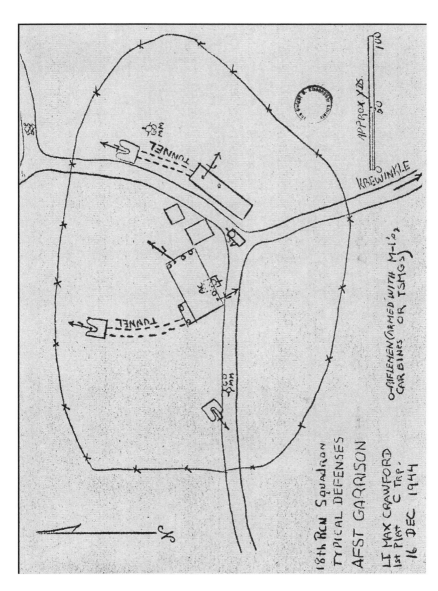

MAP 5. The cavalry's "strong points" were small and manned usually by a platoon. The sketch shows sixty-millimeter mortars oriented east and north. Four machine gun positions (symbol is an arrow with a bar) and nine rifle positions are shown. Only two M8 cavalry vehicles are shown: one appears to be backed into a building or garage, and the other is in the intersection. Each had a thirty-seven-millimeter cannon, a .50-caliber machine gun, and a .30-caliber coaxial machine gun. Reproduced from Lt J. T. Shea, "Fourteenth Cavalry Group (MECZ) and Its work in the Counter Offensive 16-31 Dec 1944."

Cavalry fought is borne out by the 275th AFA. LTC Clay's battalion nearly ran out of ammunition after firing what amounted to two basic loads. The 14th CAV's isolated units had fought well, but showed signs of cracking.[27]

The Golden Lions

Reports flooded into Major General (MG) Alan W. Jones's command post on his first day in serious combat. In *Guns at Last Light*, Rick Atkinson artfully describes Jones as having "brilliantine hair and a Clark Gable moustache."[28] Jones looked like a division commander but now had to act the part. Leading up to this moment neither the Army nor his corps commander had served him well. The reports he sent up that morning elicited little help, and those he received provided little useful information. To say that reporting in combat is difficult is to do injustice to the idea of difficulty. Accurate reports are hard to come by and suffer from the problematic nature of eyewitness reports—that is, they are limited to what those who report are able to see. Worse still, they often come secondhand. Jones experienced the same uncertainty that was reported on the other side of the field by Arthur Jüttner, who claimed he could not "see" the battlefield.

That morning Jones knew for certain only that artillery seemed to be falling everywhere, including fourteen-inch shells landing near his headquarters. After the war he noted, "When they begin to drop 14-inch shells it's the real thing."[29] However serious the attack, it seemed limited to the Losheim Gap north of the Schnee Eifel and south of the densely forested plateau. Within the first hour Jones released the 32nd CAV at Devine's request. Doing so suggests he understood the danger in the gap. Soon after, Jones ordered LTC Joseph F. Puett, commanding the 3rd Battalion, 423rd INF, to prepare for movement. Unlike MG Walter M. Robertson in the 2nd ID, Jones had positioned neither of his reserve battalions where they could influence the Losheim Gap or readily interdict the Skyline Drive. To compound matters, what happened during the course of the day challenged Jones's ability to see the battlefield, and he failed to demonstrate the intellect Clausewitz described—which, "even in the darkest hour, retains some faint glimmering inner light"—and follow it where it led. If Alan Jones perceived the light, he had to decide whether to follow it. That required courage in the face of great difficulty.[30]

Poor communications further complicated Jones's ability to "see" or "sense" the battlefield. German patrols and artillery cut telephone wires. The Germans jammed US radio frequencies and even goaded the Americans on their command nets. Even the weather seemed against Jones as dense fog added to the "fog of war." Other officers struggled to understand the battle. MAJ John C. Hollinger, operations officer of the 422nd INF, noted activity in the Losheim Gap and a penetration in the 423rd INF that resulted in the loss of the village of Bleialf. Otherwise the "front remained quiet."[31] MAJ Frederic W. Oseth, executive officer of the 3rd Battalion in the 422nd INF, echoed Hollinger, noting "only minimal activity" in his sector.[32] Nothing much was happening to the units in the Schnee Eifel, but what did that mean?

The ability to see the battlefield did not improve with distance from the front. At VIII Corps, MG Troy H. Middleton was aware of the threat in the Losheim Gap and knew that Germans had attacked all along his front. The scale of the attack alarmed him sufficiently that he asked Lieutenant General (LTG) Courtney H. Hodges at First Army to release Combat Command B (CCB) of the 9th Armored Division (AD) from its role as a reserve to V Corps. Despite believing the Germans had mounted only a spoiling attack, Hodges agreed. Middleton then told Jones he would get CCB but could not commit the unit without permission. Located at Faymonville, Belgium, twelve miles north of Jones's command post at St. Vith, CCB could come quickly. Middleton also attached the 168th Engineer Battalion immediately. By the end of December 16, Middleton had given Jones what he could.[33]

The southern wing of the 18th VGD struck COL Charles C. Cavender's 423rd INF. According to Cavender, "A wedge was immediately driven between Troop B [of the 18th CAV, attached to the 423rd INF] on the extreme right and the AT [antitank] company." The 293rd VGR penetrated the 423rd's main line of resistance and seized Bleialf at about 0800. Cavender responded by organizing a scratch force to retake the town.[34] The division commander's son, LT Allan W. Jones Jr., served in the regiment. The younger Jones believed the counterattack succeeded by dint of a "bitter house to house struggle" that lasted from 1200 until 1500 hours. Once driven from Bleialf, the 293rd's men dug in just out of rifle shot. Despite hard fighting at Bleialf, LT Jones described the action elsewhere in regiment's front as "minor enemy attacks."[35]

Soon after the bombardment ended, all three regiments of the 62nd VGD struck COL Alexander D. Reid's 424th INF. To add to Reid's troubles, both the 560th VGD and the 116th PZ attacked along the boundary he shared with COL Nelson's 112th INF of the 28th ID. Units from both hit a glancing blow to Reid's southern flank. At 0550, before the bombardment ended, Reid's K Company, 3rd Battalion, 424th INF saw enemy infantry advancing on its positions. The 62nd came fast, driving hard against the 3rd Battalion.

Reid realized early that his regiment was in trouble. If the 62nd VGD and the units attacking Nelson's regiment took Winterspelt, they would cut off the regiment. To solve the problem he had to "rob both Peter and Paul to pay Winterspelt."[36] Reid asked the Division to release his 1st Battalion, which Jones had held in reserve. The assistant division commander, Brigadier General (BG) Herbert T. Perrin, was on the scene. He apparently let Reid have one company of the Battalion: Company C, which Reid rushed to Winterspelt. Ultimately MG Jones released the 1st Battalion. Reid moved the Battalion to Winterspelt just in time to hang on to the town.[37]

The 62nd VGD pressed the attack throughout the day. Right after the bombardment, CPT Lee Berwick, operations officer of the 3rd Battalion, 424th INF, set off to join the battalion reserve. He was en route in the company of LT William V. Shakespeare's weapons platoon. Suddenly he heard the lieutenant yell "Halt!" To Berwick's surprise, Shakespeare captured a German captain and three soldiers from the 116th PZ. The captain had with him orders and maps, including the orders for Otto Skorzeny's special operations troops disguised as Americans. When Berwick and his party continued on, they took fire from a group of three houses that lay between them and the reserve company. Berwick organized an attack supported by a borrowed infantry platoon and compelled the surrender of 107 German soldiers deep in the regiment's defensive sector.[38] Berwick's achievement was a bright moment in an otherwise dark and hard day.

The day ended with the 106th ID in serious trouble. At sunset Reid retained a tenuous hold on Winterspelt on his southern flank but had lost contact with the 423rd and was thus threatened on both flanks. During the day MG Jones had used all of his reserves, and he released the 32nd CAV to Devine. He had given Reid the requested 1st Battalion. At midday Jones ordered LTC Puett to move his 3rd Battalion, 423rd INF to new positions near Schönberg and prepare a position there in the event the Germans broke through. Puett dug his troops in astride the main road that ran northwest to Manderfeld. Jones had no uncommitted troops. He did have a promissory note from VIII Corps. First Army released CCB, 9th AD to VIII Corps at around 1200 hours. Middleton, in turn, assigned CCB to Jones for use only with Middleton's approval. At sunset it was apparent that Germans had succeeded in isolating COL George L. Descheneaux's 422nd INF and Cavender's 423rd INF, and the situation deteriorated during the evening.

The situation to the south of the 106th ID was no better. Soon after the fight began that morning, Sergeant Paul G. Oxford, a communications sergeant in

F Company, 2nd Battalion, 424th INF, received bad news. He was scanning the frequencies on his radio when he heard "someone from the 28th Division say they were being overrun."[39] The Germans indeed had overrun units in the 28th ID. PFC Earl T. Chamness, one of Oxford's counterparts in the 112th INF, responded to a call on his switchboard. When he answered, a German was on the line.[40] The 28th fought that day against six different divisions, four from the Fifth Panzer Army and two from Seventh Army.

By 0845, the 112th INF, already fighting the 560th VGD, learned that the 116th PZ was also in the area. Nelson's regiment fought ably throughout the day. His junior leaders and battalion staffs showed their experience by reporting efficiently and with reasonable accuracy. Nevertheless, he was concerned about the wedge the 62nd VGD had driven between the 424th INF and his regiment.[41] Otherwise the 112th was in good shape, having prevented or reduced enemy penetrations. The regiment had captured two hundred prisoners and identified its immediate opposition. COL Nelson found the 560th's tactics puzzling because at "several points the enemy had attempted to move against our positions in what was almost close order formation. As a result, they were easily 'wiped out' by machine gun fire from our positions."[42]

Allied Perceptions and Confusion

Tremors of the attack rippled out and up rapidly. The news reached First Army via VIII Corps by 0700, and Supreme Headquarters Allied Expeditionary Forces (SHAEF) at Versailles by around 1200 hours.[43] LTG Omar N. Bradley happened to be at Versailles, having driven there that morning to discuss the shortage of infantry replacements with General (GEN) Dwight D. Eisenhower. As the reports came in, Eisenhower quickly realized the bill had come due for the risk he and Bradley had assumed in the Ardennes. In *Supreme Commander*, Stephen Ambrose notes that "despite his mistakes Eisenhower was the first important Allied general to grasp the full import of the attack" and to realize the opportunity the counteroffensive afforded and to adjust accordingly.[44]

In *Crusade in Europe*, Eisenhower claimed, "I was immediately convinced this was no local attack." Whatever shortcomings he had, the decisions Eisenhower made that Saturday illustrate competence as supreme commander. At first Bradley believed the attack was local and designed to spoil his intended offensive. Eisenhower, on the other hand, recognized this was no spoiling attack but instead a counteroffensive. He huddled with Bradley and the SHAEF staff to find units to stem the tide and to determine what must be done over time. The problem was not trivial, as Eisenhower had no operational reserves. SHAEF had XVIII Corps, and the 82nd and 101st Airborne Divisions near Paris in the theater reserve, but little else. The best that could be done was to identify units not actually in contact. In the north, they found the 7th AD in Ninth Army. It was out of contact, preparing to join Ninth Army's attack on the Ruhr River. In Third Army, the 10th AD was as yet uncommitted. Orders went out to get the 7th AD headed south and the 10th AD headed north. They identified units still in Britain and a corps in Field Marshal Bernard Law Montgomery's British Second Army that could be used if necessary.[45]

At First Army in Spa, Belgium, LTG Hodges, although concerned, still looked at the German effort as a spoiling attack aimed at disrupting his own attack toward the Ruhr. Indeed, Hodges's war diary quotes him as saying exactly that. Yet First Army identified seven Volksgrenadier and two Panzer divisions attacking all of VIII Corps and part of V Corps. In *A Time for Trumpets*, Charles B. MacDonald asserts that Hodges demonstrated uncertainty. The evidence supports MacDonald. Hodges, like Middleton and Jones, found the situation ambiguous. He left it to GEN Leonard Gerow at V Corps to decide whether to call off the 2nd ID's attack. Nevertheless, he alerted the 1st ID, in reserve near Aachen, and ordered VII Corps to prepare CCB, 3rd AD for movement. In a conversation with Bradley, Hodges learned he would receive the 7th AD, and he had released CCB, 9th AD to VIII Corps. Whatever he believed, Hodges began assembling forces to react to the German attack.[46]

By nightfall, at VIII Corps in Bastogne, Middleton knew that the 106th ID had serious problems, but no one had reported that the Germans had cleared the Losheim Gap and a path west. Peiper was on the move, but as yet undetected by the Corps. Middleton, however, fully understood that the two US regiments in the Schnee Eifel were in danger given the attacks both north and south of the plateau. To that end he called the 106th ID to suggest that Jones withdraw the 422nd and 423rd from the Schnee Eifel. Jones demurred, saying he thought they could hold. He believed that once Middleton released CCB, the 9th AD he would be all right.[47] Middleton acceded to Jones's point of view with respect to the regiments on the Eifel. It does not appear that either Jones or Middleton discussed the Losheim Gap.

Shortly before 1800 hours Middleton told BG William M. Hoge, who commanded CCB, that he would be attached to the 106th ID. He told Hoge to plan on arriving with his command before dawn on Sunday, December 17. Hoge alerted his troops for the move and then drove to St. Vith, arriving a half hour later. There he met with MG Jones, whom he found "jittery" and unable to tell him much other than that he wanted his unit in Manderfeld at dawn, prepared to counterattack. Right after Hoge left Jones's office, Middleton called. He told Jones that a combat command of the 7th AD would arrive at 0700 the next morning to join the defense.[48]

The situation with the regiments on Schnee Eifel had deteriorated since the conversation Jones had had with Middleton about them. Shortly before 2100 hours, General Jones concluded that he should withdraw the two regiments. He called Middleton but was diffident, asking, "Now about my people. Don't you think I should call them out?" Because the connection was so bad, Middleton apparently did not hear the second part of the communication—the question—and thus responded, "You know how things are up there better than I do, but don't you think your troops should be withdrawn?" Jones decided that since Middleton had not actually ordered him to withdraw the regiment he must have meant them to stay.[49] When the phone call ended the two regiments remained on the Schnee Eifel, as yet not surrounded.

Neither officer made sure he was understood. A crackling, noisy, bad connection on a military telephone should have come as no surprise to either of them. The Army had protocols to work around bad connections, but it is not apparent that either of them employed those techniques. Furthermore, the call occurred at about 2200. Yet not quite an hour earlier Middleton had issued a fragmentary order that among other things directed that "troops will be withdrawn from present positions only repeat only if positions become completely untenable." Further, the order required the high ground west of the Our River to be held "at all costs."[50] Given that Jones's regiments were east of the Our, he should have asked questions. Middleton's order lends credence to Jones's belief that he was to leave his regiments in place. Orders should clarify; this one did not.

General Jones failed to act on his own and failed to be sure he understood what Middleton intended. His diffidence likely stemmed from inexperience. Given the order issued at 2100, Jones's reluctance to act, while damning in light of subsequent events, is not surprising. That Middleton trusted Jones's judgment rather than his own is harder to understand. It is equally unfortunate that Middleton failed to make his intent clear.

In any case, Middleton believed Jones was going to withdraw the two beleaguered regiments, and Jones thought they were to stay. In his brilliant book *Battle: The Story of the Bulge*, John Toland reported what transpired next: "With a sigh Jones looked up at Colonel Malin Craig, one of his artillery officers. 'Well that's it!' He said tightly. 'Middleton says we should leave them in. Get General Hoge.'"[51] When Middleton hung up, he announced to one of his staff officers, "I told him to pull his regiments off the Schnee Eifel."[52]

Middleton exacerbated the confusion when he told Jones to expect the first combat command of the 7th AD at 0700 the next morning. LTC William M. Slayden, the VIII Corps assistant intelligence officer who had been with the 106th since it arrived, knew this to be unlikely. In fact, he thought, "It was impossible, and I should have said so, but that would have put me in the position of calling the Corps commander a liar."[53] In light of the news that the 7th AD would arrive at 0700 on December 17, Jones revised his thinking. Around midnight on December 16–17 he decided to have Hoge attack toward Winterspelt to confound the 293rd VGR and the 62nd VGD attacking south of the Schnee Eifel. CCB, the first unit of the 7th AD to arrive, would go to Manderfeld to restore the northern flank.[54]

German Perceptions

For Klaus Ritter and his *Landser* comrades the day had not gone well. Ritter's platoon followed the 293rd VGR toward Bleialf. Taken under fire first by American mortars and then by machine guns, they made little headway. The Americans wounded one soldier when "deadly strings of the tracer ammunition found their way to us." Because they had no field ambulances, Ritter and three others bore the wounded man toward the rear. They were too slow; their comrade bled to death before they could get him to an aid station. American machine guns from Cavender's 423rd INF put "an end to the idea of a rambling tour of Paris" for at least one *Landser*. Ritter ended the day back where he began, wondering, "Who had ever imagined that the Yanks were capable of doing so well!"[55]

The situation looked better from Hasso von Manteuffel's perspective. First the day's fighting seemed to validate his decision to attack on a broad front with all three of his corps. Lucht's LXVI Corps had nearly completed the encirclement of the Schnee Eifel and seemed poised to take St. Vith the next day. General der Panzertruppe Walter Krüger's LVIII Corps had struggled but managed a bridgehead across the Our River. On Krüger's left, General der Panzertruppe Heinrich von Lüttwitz's LVII Corps had savaged the 28th ID but had not achieved a breakthrough. At the 18th VGD, Oberstleutnant Dietrich Moll found the inaction of the two regiments in the Schnee Eifel puzzling. He and his commander thought they might have withdrawn. So in the afternoon they sent combat patrols forward from their deception effort opposite the Schnee Eifel and discovered to their satisfaction that the two regiments remained in place.

Believing they had penetrated the crust of the defense, the Germans planned to complete the job the next day by seizing St. Vith. To do so, Manteuffel planned to resume the attack at daybreak, not only to seize St. Vith but also to gain crossings over the Our and open the way to the Meuse through Bastogne. He anticipated success, as he "expected local tactical reserves of the enemy would be committed at the same time." Furthermore, he "did not think the Americans would be able to defend St. Vith."[56] His expectation was not unreasonable given that the 18th VGD had accounted for the 106th ID's reserves. Manteuffel's chief of staff, Generalmajor Carl Wagener, went further: "We counted upon finding no enemy operational reserves in the area of the attack."[57]

NOTES

1. Klaus Ritter, statements, box 10, Charles B. MacDonald Papers, pt. 1, p. 5.

2. Colonel R. Ernest Dupuy, *St. Vith: Lion in the Way*, 21.

3. Charles B. MacDonald, *A Time for Trumpets*, 104–5. See also Lieutenant Jack Shea, "After Action Report of the 14th Cavalry Group Mechanized." Shea's report appears in several iterations, and draws heavily on eyewitness reports and sketches contemporary to the fight. See also Marvin D. Kays, *Weather Effects during the Battle of the Bulge and the Normandy Invasion*.

4. Carl von Clausewitz, *On War*, 101–2, 89.

5. Veterans of the Battle of the Bulge, Inc., *The Battle of the Bulge: True Stories of the Men and Women Who Survived*, 303.

6. Sergeant James R. McIlroy, "A Soldier's Story . . . Krinkelt, 1944.".

7. John Toland, *Battle: The Story of the Bulge*, 21.

8. Peter Caddick-Adams, *Snow and Steel*, 348.

9. Oberstleutnant Dietrich Moll, "18th Volks Grenadier Division," 23, 28.

10. Moll, "18th Volks Grenadier Division," 28–29.

11. The general outline of Army Group B's attack is illustrated in Hugh M. Cole, *The Ardennes: Battle of the Bulge*, maps 1–6. The 110th Infantry Regiment absorbed the largest attack on the first day. The imposed delay helped buy time to establish the defense of Bastogne.

12. Moll, "18th Volks Grenadier Division," 36. Oberst Arthur Jüttner, "Report by Colonel Jüttner of the 62nd VGD in the Battle of the Bulge," 4.

13. Lieutenant Jack T. Shea, "Fourteenth Cavalry Group," 3.

14. Shea, "Fourteenth Cavalry Group," 4.

15. Shea, "Fourteenth Cavalry Group," 8–11.

16. Shea, "Fourteenth Cavalry Group," 12.

17. 820th Tank Destroyer Battalion, "After Action Report," 2–3; Company A, 820th Tank Destroyer Battalion, "After Battle Report," 1–2.

18. Caddick-Adams, *Snow and Steel*, 347; see also 345–46.

19. Shea, "Fourteenth Cavalry Group," 17.

20. Shea, "Fourteenth Cavalry Group," 18. The exchange between Farrens and the unknown German is deservedly quoted in nearly every book on the Bulge. Shea spelled Farrens with an *a*, but Charles MacDonald spelled it with an *e* in *A Time for Trumpets*, 106.

21. Shea, "Fourteenth Cavalry Group," 19. Shea did not identify the armored vehicle that Crawford hit with a rocket, but the German vehicle almost certainly belonged to the 1818th Anti-Tank Battalion—likely a Hetzer Jagdpanzer 38(t) armed with a seventy-five-millimeter cannon. "Jagdpanzer" translates literally as "tank hunter."

22. Shea, "Fourteenth Cavalry Group," 14–15. See also MacDonald, *A Time for Trumpets*, 105–6. It is unlikely that A Troop confronted tanks. The tanks Porché reported were probably Hetzer 38(t) antitank guns, though at dusk they could have looked like tanks.

23. Toland, *Battle: The Story of the Bulge*, 28, 32, 54, 63; Charles Whiting, *Decision at St. Vith*, 70–71; Robert E. Merriam, *Dark December*, 109; Roy U. Clay, "Tinstaafl: Autobiography of Roy U. Clay," 86. See Shea's comment on the command in "Fourteenth Cavalry Group," 12. Merriam served during the war as a military historian. Although assigned to the Ninth Army History Detachment he elected to travel with the 7th AD when it received orders to go south. He stayed with the 7th AD through the fighting, interviewing many of the Division's soldiers and some from the 14th CAV, so was familiar personally with these combat actions. Ralph Hill, a civil affairs captain in Büllingen, undertook to salvage Colonel Devine's reputation. The author is in possession of some of Hill's correspondence that defames others in the support of Devine. Hill became belligerent with those who disagreed, but his correspondence sheds light on the confusion in the 14th CAV.

24. Shea, "Fourteenth Cavalry Group," 12, 20.

25. Dupuy, *St. Vith: Lion in the Way*, 25–31. Ridge was eventually relieved of his command.

26. Shea, "Fourteenth Cavalry Group," 20–22. Shea called this section of his narrative "The Stand at Manderfeld." It did not last long, with nearly three enemy infantry regiments supported by assault guns and, in the north, by tanks. See also Dupuy, *St. Vith: Lion in the Way*, 29–31.

27. Shea, "Fourteenth Cavalry Group," 20–22. See also Rick Atkinson, *The Guns at Last Light*, 432–33; and Colonel D. J. Judge, "Cavalry in the Defense Dec. 16–18 1944."

28. Atkinson, *The Guns at Last Light*, 434.

29. Dupuy, *St. Vith: Lion in the Way*, 21.

30. Carl von Clausewitz, *On War*, 102.

31. Major John C. Hollinger, "The Operations of the 422nd Infantry Regiment."

32. Major Frederick W. Oseth, interview by Major J. F. O'Sullivan.

33. Harold R. Winton, *Corps Commanders of the Bulge*, 144–45. See also MacDonald, *A Time for Trumpets*, 125.

34. Colonel Charles C. Cavender, "The 423 in the Bulge."

35. Captain Alan W. Jones Jr., "The Operations of the 423rd Infantry," 13, 14. Jones and Hollinger appear to have been classmates in the same course, for which they wrote their essays.

36. Colonel A. D. Reid, interview by Captain K. W. Hechler. The tension in that interview is palpable. Reid clearly believed MG Jones had erred in not committing the 1st Battalion earlier in the battle. Hechler notes that Reid stared at him for minutes when he asked Reid whether there was difficulty in getting the reserve released. Across more than seven decades Reid's frustration is crystal clear.

37. Reid interview, 1.

38. Captain Lee Berwick, interview by Captain K. W. Hechler.

39. Sergeant Paul G. Oxford, "Excerpts from a Letter."

40. Earl T. Chamness, " 'HQ' Company, 112th Infantry Regiment, 28th I.D."

41. Headquarters, 112th Infantry Regiment, periodic reports, December 1944; Headquarters, 112th Infantry Regiment, S-2 Journal December 16, 1944, 1.

42. Colonel Gustin M. Nelson and Major Justin C. Brainard, interviewer not identified, January 14, 1945.

43. Major William C. Sylvan and Captain Francis G. Smith Jr., *Normandy to Victory*, 213; on Hodges's assessment of the operation as a spoiling attack, see 214.

44. Stephen E. Ambrose, *The Supreme Commander*, 556.

45. Dwight D. Eisenhower, *Crusade in Europe*, 343; on staff assessments, see 343–45. See also Ambrose, *The Supreme Commander*, 556. Ambrose reviews the staff work and decisions taken that day. His account supports General Eisenhower's recollections. Omar N. Bradley, in *A Soldier's Story*, 445, admits he believed the German operation to be a spoiling attack rather than a counteroffensive. Hodges did not immediately understand the import of the attack. Patton, too, believed the ongoing operation to be a spoiling attack. See Martin Blumenson, *The Patton Papers*, 595. See also David W. Hogan Jr., *A Command Post at War*, 209.

46. MacDonald, *A Time for Trumpets*, 261. See also Sylvan and Smith, *Normandy to Victory*, 214; and Hogan, *Command Post at War*, 209.

47. Toland, *Battle: The Story of the Bulge*, 35; MacDonald, *A Time for Trumpets*, 125.

48. On the Hoge senior officer debriefing, see MacDonald, *A Time for Trumpets*, 126. Dupuy, *St. Vith: Lion in the Way*, 23, specifies Combat Command B.

49. Caddick-Adams, *Snow and Steel*, 332. See also MacDonald, *A Time for Trumpets*, 128–29.

50. Winton, *Corps Commanders*, 145–46.

51. Toland, *Battle: The Story of the Bulge*, 32–33. It is not clear that Hoge was still in the command post. Toland says he was not.

52. MacDonald, *A Time for Trumpets*, 129.

53. Dupuy, *St. Vith: Lion in the Way*, 25. The copy of Dupuy's book in the author's possession was signed and annotated by LTC Slayden, who bought the book for a friend. Slayden is often quoted in accounts from the time. It is remarkable that he kept his counsel knowing that Middleton was mistaken on when Combat Command B, 7th AD could arrive.

54. Cole, *The Ardennes: Battle of the Bulge*, 158.

55. Klaus Ritter, statements, pt. 1, p. 7.

56. General der Panzertruppe Hasso von Manteuffel, "An Interview with Gen Pz Hasso von Manteuffel," ETHINT-45; General der Panzertruppe Hasso von Manteuffel, "An Interview with Gen Pz Hasso von Manteuffel," ETHINT-46, 5.

57. Generalmajor Carl Gustav Wagener, "Results of the Ardennes Offensive," 5. See also MacDonald, *A Time for Trumpets*, 261–64.

CHAPTER FIVE

The Lucky Seventh Goes to St. Vith

My first ride as newly promoted Sergeant Tank Commander was into battle.
—Sergeant Howard Moore

In the history of every unit there is a time when certain events overshadow all else that has or will take place.
—7th Armored Division, Artillery After Action Report, December 1944

I wanted to take St Vith on 16 Dec 44.
—General der Panzertruppe Hasso von Manteuffel

A Quiet Day

Saturday, December 16, 1944, passed much as the day before had for Brigadier General (BG) Robert W. Hasbrouck and the troops of the 7th Armored Division (AD), who were in reserve to XII Corps. He expected to be committed in support of the XII Corps attack on the Ruhr River. The division artillery and a tank battalion were already in action. Nevertheless, Hasbrouck recalled, "It was a quiet day, but along about 5:30 PM I received a very laconic message from Ninth Army which read 'Prepare your command for movement to Century.'"[1] Century was the code word for VIII Corps at Bastogne. However laconic the message, Hasbrouck acted with alacrity. He called in Lieutenant Colonel (LTC) Everett W. Murray, his intelligence officer, for an update on VIII Corps' sector. Murray could tell him very little other than that the sector was reputedly quiet. Later that evening, LTC Murray returned to report a German attack was underway but he had no information as to its scale or scope.[2]

Within minutes of reading the message Hasbrouck issued a warning order to his units. Meanwhile, his staff tried to determine what was going on and to arrange for road clearance and routes. Even during a war, especially during a war, units don't just move. The road net and the authority to use it belonged to the field armies within their boundaries. Their traffic regulators issued clearances and assigned routes. At about 2100 hours Hasbrouck called BG Bruce C. Clarke, his Combat Command B (CCB) commander. According to Clarke, Hasbrouck told him "there had been some trouble in VIII Corps area, and that I should go to Bastogne and contact the Corps Commander (Middleton) and find out the situation." The Division would follow. In addition to Clarke's party, a small Division advance party also went south.[3]

Clarke took with him his operations officer, Captain (CPT) Owen E. Woodruff; a staff officer from the Division; and a "radio" Jeep so he could communicate. By 2200 he was on his way. Clarke and his party arrived in Bastogne at about 0400 on December 17. On arriving he met with Major General (MG) Troy H. Middleton, who was awake and reading in his "sleep van." Middleton briefed Clarke on the situation and told him that he intended to use the 7th AD in support of the 106th Infantry Division (ID). He advised Clarke to get a few hours' sleep and head to St. Vith to meet with MG Alan W. Jones later in the morning. After sleeping a few hours, Clarke made a radio call to Hasbrouck and gave him an update. Specifically, he made sure Hasbrouck understood the Division was not to go to Bastogne but to St. Vith. Clarke recommended the town of Vielsalm, a few miles west of St. Vith, as an assembly area. Hasbrouck advised that because of trouble getting road clearance, the Division had only gotten underway at 0430. Clarke's CCB, though in the lead, would not reach the area until that afternoon.[4]

In part because of ambiguity about the situation, inertia, and the required coordination between First and Ninth Armies, the 7th AD had not received its routes and clearance until the early morning hours. Although assigned to Ninth Army, the 7th AD would be traveling through First Army's sector, so First Army provided routes and clearances. Additionally, because the march was administrative, the Division organized in formations by battalion rather than task organized. Moreover, the Lucky Seventh's units occupied disparate assembly areas convenient to supporting the XII Corps attack on the Ruhr rather than a move south. They thus had to move from these assembly areas to reach the initial point on the authorized routes. The XII Corps also had to relieve the 17th Tank Battalion (TB) from attachment to the 84th ID. Forming pure formations and organizing two parallel columns took time.[5]

Ninth Army issued the order for the Lucky Seventh to move at 2345 hours, quite soon given that the reinforcement had only been ordered late that afternoon. The order required the Division to move at the "earliest practical date" to Vielsalm on the Salm River in Belgium. Additionally, it required 7th AD to send an advance party to Bastogne to coordinate with VIII Corps, to whom it was going to be assigned. Within hours, First Army traffic regulators issued road clearance and routes, but then delayed the start time. All of this led to a mostly sleepless night for the 7th AD and its attached units. At 0130 the Division received an order reassigning it from Ninth Army to First Army. Too little time remained to post guides and distribute route overlays at the company level. As a result, "many company commanders did not know their destination until they arrived in the St. Vith–Vielsalm area." In any case, the first unit to move, the 87th Cavalry Reconnaissance Squadron (87th RCN), did not cross the initial point on the western route until 0430, and then was ordered to halt by the side of the road and wait for an hour. Combat Command Reserve (CCR), leading the way on the eastern route, crossed the initial point at 0800.[6]

First Army assigned two parallel routes. One route originated at Heerlen, Netherlands, and went west to Heer, near Mastricht, where it turned and ran more or less south to Vielsalm. The eastern route originated in Geilenkirchen, Germany, and ran south through the ruins of Aachen, then into Belgium at Eupen, through Malmedy to Ligneuville, and finally to Vielsalm. The 87th RCN led the western column. The units in that column included CCB with the 23rd Armored Infantry Battalion (AIB); the 31st TB, Combat Command A (CCA) with the 40th TB and 48th AIB; the 814th Tank Destroyer Battalion (TD); the 7th AD main command post; the 33rd Engineer Battalion (EN); and the Division trains. In the east, CCR with the 17th TB and 38th AIB led, trailed by the 7th AD tactical command post; four battalions of division artillery; the 203rd Anti-Aircraft Artillery Battalion (AAA); and B Company, 129th Ordnance Battalion. First Army estimated arrival at 1400 hours on December 17, and closure at 0200 the next morning, contradicting an earlier estimate of 0700 and 1700 on December 17 and negating what Middleton had told Jones the prior evening.[7]

In his magnum opus, Carl von Clausewitz devoted three chapters to marches, which he called "a mere transition from one position to another," but he did not consider these transitions trivial. Clausewitz believed marches should be devised in accordance with the plan of employment and cited as mistakes certain instances when that did not occur. The Prussian theorist

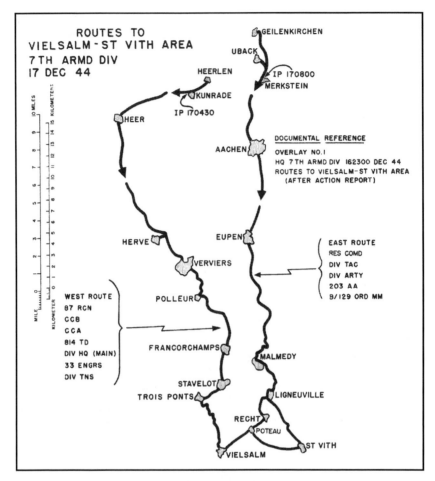

MAP 6. Both routes were west of the original forward position of friendly troops. In the early afternoon of December 17, the 1st SS Panzer Division cut the eastern route and soon thereafter massacred most of Battery B, 285th Field Artillery Observation Battalion. Reproduced from the US Army Armor School publication *The Battle at St. Vith*.

would have found much to criticize in the 7th AD's march south. The Lucky Seventh moved in an administrative road march unrelated to a scheme of employment, and much later than presumed at the outset.[8] The ensuing friction would not have surprised Clausewitz.

First Army acted without a clear understanding of conditions along the main line of resistance. Thus, it assigned routes that required the 7th AD to move perpendicular to the front and the spearheads of the attacking Sixth Panzer Army. In fact, the assigned route in the west crossed all five

Rollbahn routes assigned to the Sixth Panzer Army, while the eastern route crossed four of the five routes. The routes assigned and the Division plan for movement nevertheless met the concepts embodied in doctrine for an armored division. Doctrinally mandated rates of march, intervals between vehicles, and control measures all enabled rapid planning for march units and groupings of units called serials, determining pass time and the length of the column—or, in this case, columns. Moving at the doctrinal rate of twenty miles per hour with a doctrinal interval of fifty yards, each combat command covered about twenty miles of roadway and took just over an hour to pass any point along the way. Moving south to Vielsalm was no trivial matter.[9] Achieving doctrinal rates of march proved impossible. Assigning routes without regard to the developing enemy situation turned out, to say the least, ill advised. First Army, too, did not "see" the battlefield. The consequences played out at Malmedy.

March, Countermarch, and Confusion

Just getting in position for the march proved uncomfortable. Morphis A. Jamiel, an infantryman in B Company 38th AIB, described how it went: "Everyone was tired . . . but we managed to crawl into our half-tracks [8 or 9 soldiers crammed in the 'box like' infantry compartment] and try to get some sleep. It was so cold outside and inside of the halftrack felt like a refrigerator car."[10] The expression "cold-soaked" accurately describes sleeping or traveling in an unheated armored vehicle. Tanks, half-tracks, trucks, and Jeeps absorb warmth like sponges. Metal floors and interiors suck the warmth from those riding inside. Depending on their location in the assembly area, the 7th AD units had to travel seventy to eighty miles to reach St. Vith. That assured the march would be long, cold, and tiring, as any soldier who has ever ridden in a combat vehicle on a winter's day can attest. Sergeant (SGT) Donald Hondorp, a tanker, described the ride as "long, cold, and miserable" and "the necessary air intake through the open hatches" as bitter. At the end of a long cold day, Hondorp arrived in an equally cold "muddy field."[11] The arrival times estimated by First Army assumed standard march rates and accounted for rest stops and maintenance. Their estimate assumed an average rate of less than ten miles per hour. Even that proved wildly optimistic.

The order to move south caught several officers and soldiers on leave or in the hospital. Most of the men who found themselves in these situations tried to return to their units. Colonel (COL) John L. Ryan Jr., commander of CCR; LTC Vincent L. Boylan, commander of the 87th RCN; and LTC Robert B. Jones, commander of the 814th TD were on leave in Paris when they heard the news. They immediately set out to find their units. Heading north they saw 7th AD tanks in column. According to Boylan, "We huddled—decided to follow the column." Traveling in their dress uniforms of "pinks and greens" they found the Division command post, where they met BG Hasbrouck. Boylan recalled Hasbrouck "was delighted to see us."[12] Soldiers and officers made their way back as they could. Lieutenant (LT) William A. Knowlton, recovering from a wound, "left the hospital with my papers (slightly illegally), got a carbine and a truck [full] of gasoline . . . and started into the Bulge to find the 87th."[13]

Still in assembly areas around Faymonville, Belgium, BG William M. Hoge's CCB, 9th AD received orders to move just after midnight on December 16–17. CCB—composed of the 14th TB, 27th AIB, 16th Armored Field Artillery (AFA), and D Troop, 89th Cavalry (CAV), each with a platoon of light assault guns and light tanks; B Company, 9th Armored EN; A Company, 811 TD Self-Propelled (SP); and B Battery, 482nd AAA (Automatic Weapons)—moved out at 0400 "to seize and hold the high ground south of the Our River at Steinebruk [sic] and to be prepared for a further attack to seize and hold Winterspelt on division order [106th ID]."[14] For the time being, CCB's logistics units remained in their original positions at Ligneuville, placing them astride Kampfgruppe Peiper's zone of advance.

Unlike those under BG Hasbrouck, none of the German units enjoyed a quiet day on December 16. In the north, the Sixth Panzer Army took longer than planned to break through the Americans defending the Losheim Gap and the ridges north of it. At Losheimergraben, a German town on the Belgian frontier, German engineers had blown up the bridge that passed over a railway when they retreated in the fall. Now the 1st Schutzstaffel (SS) Panzer Division (PZ), or at least Obersturmbahnführer Joachim Peiper, intended either to use the overpass or close the gap so tanks could cross over the railway.

Unable to maneuver or even move freely, Kampfgruppe Peiper and the rest of the 1st SS slept no more than their protagonists. The Kampfgruppe struggled forward after the 9th Fallschirmjäger Regiment (FJR) and the 18th Volksgrenadier Division (VGD) cleared the entrance to the Losheim Gap. The 1st SS had two routes assigned—Rollbahns D and E. Peiper's Kampfgruppe, the main effort, had Rollbahn D. Nevertheless, he intended to open up Rollbahn C at Losheimergraben. Because he was the main effort for the 1st SS PZ, Peiper was indifferent to who actually had priority on Rollbahn C. The 2nd SS Panzergrenadier Regiment would make the 1st SS supporting effort on Rollbahn E. Army Group B assigned routes and drew boundaries without much regard to the facts on the ground. Rollbahn E, for example, dipped south of the Sixth Panzer Army boundary with Fifth Panzer Army. Repairing the overpass at Losheimergraben proved impossible, so Peiper's engineers filled in the gap; that operation took until 1930 hours. Someone either at the corps or army level ordered the 12th VGD's horse-drawn artillery forward, so "it clogged up the roads." Furious but helpless, Peiper did what he could to manage traffic while his tanks and half-tracks burned fuel he could ill afford to waste.[15]

The lead tank battalion of the 1st SS did not reach the Belgian frontier until about 2000 hours on December 16. Peiper's second tank battalion closed at 2200. Just getting through the Losheim Gap cost Peiper five tanks and five other armored vehicles to a combination of German and American mines. His spearhead finally reached Lanzerath at midnight, having moved all of three miles in four hours.[16] The Sixth Panzer Army's main body stacked up behind him in what German drivers today know as a *Stau*, or traffic jam. Bad roads, mines, and sheer numbers of troops on the move produced a *Stau* of biblical proportion. Peiper's orders required him to move rapidly, ignore his flanks, and ignore leaving garrisons in captured towns, all of which he could do except move rapidly.

Oberstleutnant Friedrich August Freiherr von der Heydte had an even more difficult time. In a forlorn hope, he led some 870 paratroopers in a parachute assault in the early hours of December 17. The operation demonstrated just how far the German Air Force and its once vaunted airborne units had declined. Heydte's drop literally scattered to the four winds. He eventually managed to gather about three hundred of the paratroopers in the forest near Baraque Michel, seven miles north of Malmedy in the Sixth Panzer Army zone. Too few to do anything else, Heydte's handful of paratroopers huddled together for three days waiting for the linkup the Sixth Panzer Army estimated would occur within twenty-four hours. Although it achieved little else, Heydte's forlorn hope spread fear and confusion among the Americans, who imagined that the paratroopers had landed in many more places than they actually had.[17] Otto Skorzeny's troops disguised as Americans generated even more chaos. Soldiers unknown to other Americans they encountered found themselves answering increasingly obscure trivia questions at the point of gun.

General der Artillerie Walther Lucht's LXVI Corps worked like a well-oiled machine in comparison to Heydte's operation. During the night the 18th VGD prepared to attack down the Our River valley toward Schönberg and from south of the Schnee Eifel toward Schönberg to complete the encircling of the 422nd and 423rd Infantry (INF) regiments. The Division commander, Oberst Günter Hoffmann-Schönborn, brought forward his "mobile" bicycle battalion to follow the 294th Volksgrenadier Regiment (VGR) to exploit any success. He also had his tracked antitank battalion to take advantage of any breakthrough. The 18th VGD remained in good shape, having suffered what Oberstleutnant Dietrich Moll described as "reasonable" casualties. Moll did complain about conditions on the roads, noting that "many German vehicles had bogged down."[18] Nevertheless, the 18th VGD renewed the attack at first light.

The 62nd VGD renewed its attack at first light as well. According to Oberst Friedrich Kittel, the 62nd's commander, COL Alexander D. Reid's 424th INF continued to resist "tenaciously."[19] The corps commander, General Lucht, assessed the US effort in the north to be fairly weak by comparison to the fight the Americans put up in the southern part of his zone.

General der Panzertruppe Walter Krüger's LVIII Panzer Corps had not fared as well as Lucht's Corps. But it, too, renewed the attack at first light. Oberst Rudolph Langhäuser's 560th VGD suffered heavy losses on December 16, amounting to nearly a thousand killed, wounded, or missing. Some of the missing turned up the next day. But the 560th attacked with two understrength battle groups, which together fielded fewer than a thousand infantrymen supported by Division troops and an armored reconnaissance battalion. To compound Langhäuser's problems he had two grenadier battalions that still had not reached the battle area.[20]

On the first day of the offensive, COL Gustin M. Nelson's 112th INF fought off both the 560th VGD and the 116th PZ. The 116th PZ had been unable to cross the Our River on December 16 as planned and lost eight tanks and three hundred soldiers in hard fighting. The 116th renewed the attack with the 16th Panzer Regiment and the 156th Panzergrenadiers Regiment (PZGR) reinforced by the 2nd Battalion, 60th PZGR. They attacked northwest from Lutzkampen.[21] General Krüger needed the 116th PZ to cross the Our River on December 17.

The Golden Lions' Crisis

On December 17, MG Alan W. Jones confronted disaster. During the night his intelligence analysts concluded, "The enemy is capable of pinching off the Schnee Eifel area by employing one VG Division plus armor from the 14th CAV sector and one VG Division plus from the 423rd Infantry sector at any time."[22] They had it right. The battered remnants of COL Mark Devine's 14th

CAV had withdrawn west of Manderfeld in confusion. Doing so opened the route southward from the headwaters of the Our River at Manderfeld toward Schönberg at the rear of the Schnee Eifel. CPT Franklin P. Lindsey's B Troop, 32nd CAV remained at Andler, southwest of Manderfeld; otherwise Schönberg was ripe for the taking.

The 422nd and 423rd INF remained moribund on the Schnee Eifel, at serious risk without really having fought. The evening before, MG Middleton, the corps commander, had released BG Hoge's CCB, 9th AD to the 106th ID. Jones first intended to use Hoge's troops to restore the line in the north and thus his left flank. Later Middleton promised Jones a combat command of the 7th AD and further stipulated it would arrive by 0700. Accordingly, Jones decided to use Hoge's combat command differently than originally planned. He ordered Hoge to attack on the morning of December 17 to "destroy enemy forces in vicinity of Winterspelt. Extend the left flank of 424th Infantry to the railroad [in the Ihren Valley]." Afterward Jones wanted Hoge to withdraw west of the Our River and prepare to counterattack as required.[23]

Exacerbating Jones's problem, enemy penetrations of the main line of resistance exposed the 106th ID's artillery to being overrun. The 589th Field Artillery (FA) in direct support of the 422nd INF and the 592nd FA, the Division's general support battalion, occupied positions on the reverse slope of the Schnee Eifel. The Skyline Drive ran through the 106th sector from Bleialf along the ridge to the village of Auw. The 18th VGD took Auw on December 16. If the 18th VGD took Bleialf it could overrun both artillery battalions and the nearby 590th FA. The 589th, in particular, was at risk, as its guns were in the marshy ground along the Ihrenbach River.[24]

On the first day of the battle the Germans made it clear they knew the locations of all three batteries of the 589th. The LXVI Corps artillery banged away at the 589th with counterbattery fire all day. Late that day, A Battery fought off part of the 18th VGD's antitank battalion. By nightfall it was clear the Golden Lions' artillery was in extremis. BG Leo T. McMahon, the division artillery commander, decided to withdraw the 589th and the 592nd. McMahon determined that once these two battalions had displaced, the 590th would follow. The 592nd FA withdrew at 2300 but had to abandon a mired howitzer. The division artillery ordered the 589th FA to withdraw at 0400. By then it was too late for C Battery. The 589th reported shortly after getting the order, "No further direct communication was heard from this portion of the battalion [C battery, the battalion commander, and part of the battalion staff]."[25]

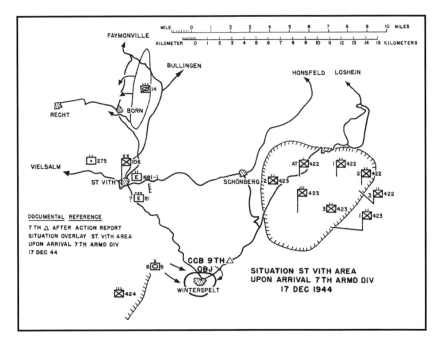

MAP 7. The 422nd and 423rd Infantry Regiments are shown east of St. Vith on the Schnee Eifel. Major General Allan Jones has positioned part of his organic 81st Engineer Battalion and all of the 168th Engineer Battalion from VIII Corps on the Prümerberg. Reproduced from the US Army Armor School publication *The Battle at St. Vith*.

Although the day dawned cold and overcast, visibility improved. American and German aircraft appeared over the battlefield, though neither side succeeded in seriously hampering the operations of the other. Regardless of air activity, effective or not, the 106th ID seemed to be unraveling. Neither Middleton nor Jones could "see" the battlefield. Their orders suggest two things. First, enemy actions came more quickly than they could respond to, and second, their system for understanding reports and combat information generated from multiple sources proved inadequate. The situation, already grim, deteriorated rapidly. At 0636 the 423rd INF lost Bleialf to the 293rd VGR, the southern wing of the 18th VGD. The 293rd, supported by part of the 18th's supporting tracked antitank battalion, overran five howitzers of the 589th FA as it attempted to withdraw. In the end, only three of the twelve howitzers assigned to the 589th escaped the Schnee Eifel. Of the 590th FA, the direct support battalion to the 423rd, only the service battery escaped.[26]

At midnight on December 16–17 only three troops of the 14th CAV remained anywhere in position to protect the northern flank. LT Robert P. Reppa's A Troop and Headquarters Troop, 32nd CAV occupied positions in and around Herresbach, the woods to the west, and the village of Holzheim. Lindsey's troop defended Andler to the south. The Cavalry's situation was, to say the least, tenuous. In predawn darkness an A Troop Greyhound armored car commander in the center of Herresbach, a SGT Creel, "saw a figure with a flashlight guiding a tank" by his vehicle. "As the tank came abreast of the A/C [armored car] Creel saw a large swastika on the side of the tank." Creel could not get his thirty-seven millimeter cannon on the enemy tank, as a trailer hitched to his Greyhound blocked his line of sight after the tank passed him. Enemy tanks began firing into the troop command post. Creel's crew and the crews of three other Greyhounds fled. They joined with another platoon and withdrew to Manderfeld. Tank destroyers from the 820th TD withdrew with A Troop. The squadron command post issued a warning and then headed west as well. The squadron withdrew C and E Troops along with F Company of light tanks through part of Herresbach just ahead of German tanks. The 1st SS had arrived.[27]

At about 0830, Tiger tanks assigned to the 1st SS 506th Heavy Panzer Battalion appeared at Andler. The Tigers, justifiably fearsome, came south from Rollbahn D looking for a road that would bear their weight. CPT Lindsey's lightly armed cavalry was no match for Tigers so he withdrew B Troop south through Schönberg and then west to Heum. Hoffmann-Schönborn's grenadiers capitalized on the largess of the Tigers and seized Schönberg at 0845. The Tigers, damage done, apparently drifted back north and out of the Cavalry's sector. The 32nd CAV command post lay a few kilometers north of Andler at Herresbach, with the remainder of its troops east of the road leading from Andler. Once B Troop withdrew, the rest of the squadron retired to the west. As they withdrew they felled trees to help delay the enemy and recovered equipment, people, and vehicles along the way.[28]

At sunup on December 17, COL Reid had reason to fear encirclement of his 424th INF. He had no communication with COL Nelson's 112th INF on his right, so he did not know that Nelson's infantry had fended off both the 560th VGD and the 116th PZ. At first light Oberst Arthur Jüttner's 164th VGR drove Reid's 1st Battalion out of the little town of Winterspelt, opening the way toward Steinebrück on the Our River.[29] Reid's outfit fought stubbornly, preventing the 62nd from exploiting its success at Winterspelt, but had suffered penetration both north and south.

Reid needed to hang on in order to support Hoge's CCB, 9th AD's passage forward so it could retake Winterspelt. Hoge's effort was stillborn. CCB drove through St. Vith toward Winterspelt. On the way, it encountered one of Jüttner's infantry battalions west of the Our River near Steinebrück. Hoge's 27th AIB, supported by tanks, drove the Volksgrenadiers back across the Our around noon. Shortly afterward Jones sent word that Hoge could continue the attack to Winterspelt but then must withdraw. Hoge expressed his frustration succinctly: "What the hell is the use of that; we are losing men all the time. . . . To hell with that, we are going to quit right now, and we are going to draw back during daylight."[30]

With what little Jones had left, he ordered LTC Thomas J. Riggs Jr. to man a roadblock on the Prümerberg, a ridge just over a mile east of St. Vith. Riggs's roadblock provided the nucleus around which BG Bruce C. Clarke, CCB, 7th AD, would form the defense of St. Vith. The road in question linked the Skyline Drive and the roads south from the Losheim Gap to Schönberg. From Schönberg a single road ran straight west through the village of Prümerberg, over the ridge itself, and then to St. Vith. To block the road Riggs had one understrength company from his 81st EN and two companies from the 168th EN of VII Corps commanded by LTC W. L. Nungesser. A towed tank destroyer platoon and the 592nd FA's ten remaining howitzers rounded out the defense. Riggs disposed roughly 375 combat engineers astride the road. They did good work from the outset. Supported by LT George Stafford and LT Alonzo A. Neese, observing from a light observation aircraft, Riggs's artillery destroyed the lead tracked antitank vehicle of an approaching German column at about noon.[31]

Friction

The ability to see the battlefield, to sense what is happening—what Clausewitz described as "glimmerings of inner light"—was in short supply on December 17. Struggles reduced to blue and red arrows on a map to illustrate the flow of the battle could not be seen that cold morning. As the attackers, the Germans enjoyed the advantage of initiative. At 0400 Peiper resumed his attack. Unsatisfied with the 9th FJR's performance, he took personal command of the spearhead. At 0600 the paratroopers and Panzers seized

Honsfeld without firing a shot and captured scores of troopers from the 32nd CAV and dozens of vehicles. The Tiger tanks that ran CPT Lindsey's B Troop out of Andler opened both Rollbahns D and E. Neither route was adequate for heavy traffic. Mines, bad roads, and the 32nd's efforts to delay continued to irritate, but at last the 1st SS could move.[32]

With the Sixth Panzer Army using a route that cut into the Fifth Panzer Army zone, traffic built up on the fragile Belgian roads. The right wing of the 18th VGD, personally led by the division commander, Oberst Hoffmann-Schönborn, attacked south through Andler on the heels of Lindsey's troop. At about noon on December 17, the Volksgrenadiers took Schönberg—capturing, intact, the bridge over the Our. The 293rd, comprising the 18th VGD's southern wing, attacked north from Bleialf, closing on Schönberg early that afternoon.[33]

The 18th VGD did not advance without having to fight both traffic and Americans. Klaus Ritter, the *alter Hase* (old hare) from the antitank battalion, and his mates moved slowly: "Long columns are jammed on the road to Schönberg. Vehicles move ahead for a few hundred meters, come to a halt for half an hour or even more then move again another 500 meters in the direction of the first Belgian Village. A Belgian Village with a German name!"[34] Ritter knew that there was nothing ironic about Schönberg's name. The village had been ceded to Belgium in 1919 as part of the Treaty of Versailles. According to Ritter, "People at Schönberg talk my native dialect. To me this is no enemy country."[35]

The slow-moving column reached Schönberg around noon. Ritter and most of his squad were ordered to clear the nearby woods. They found no live "Yanks" but instead a "deserted column of [American] vehicles." Ritter and his *Landser* buddies looted the abandoned American equipment: "Chocolate, cigarettes, and tins, tins, and tins again are filling haversacks and pockets."[36] After a few drags on a liberated cigarette, an officer ordered them on. Disappointed, the *Landsers* gave up most of their loot and returned to their gun. The column moved on. The 18th VGD had completed isolating the 422nd and 423rd infantry regiments.

The 62nd VGD struggled, as it had on December 16. At 0900 Jüttner's 164th managed to get through Winterspelt and drive toward Steinebrück, but against stiff resistance. As Jüttner recalled, "Surprise fire strikes were carried out by the American artillery on our spearhead and we encountered a counter attack from the road on the right of our advance."[37] When that occurred he passed forward the regiment's second battalion and continued the attack. As it moved out of Winterspelt the 164th captured a ration dump where it looted "tinned sausages, tinned bacon, [and] cigarettes."[38] For the moment, at least, life seemed good.

Clarke Prepares to Defend St. Vith

After radioing both Hasbrouck and his combat command, BG Clarke made his way to St. Vith, arriving at 1030 on December 17. There he met with MG Jones. Jones, apparently believing CCB had arrived with Clarke, told him that the 422nd and 423rd INF were isolated on the Schnee Eifel and that the 14th CAV was in rocky shape. He concluded by saying, "I want you, Clarke, to take your combat command and counterattack toward Schönberg about seven miles to the east of us, and break that ring that these people have closed around the Schnee Eifel." Clarke had to tell him, "General I have no idea when my troops will arrive." Clarke explained his combat command had not left until nearly 0500. Jones and his staff were shocked by the news, as they had expected Clarke to arrive with his command hours earlier.[39]

Although "fit to be tied," the two generals could do nothing but wait. According to Clarke, four hours into their vigil, "A Cavalry Colonel [the 14th CAV's COL Mark A. Devine] burst into Jones's office and said, 'We got to run. I was chased into this building by a Tiger Tank.'" Clarke believed Devine had gone off the rails. He suggested that they "send Colonel Devine back to Bastogne. Maybe he could give General Middleton a first-hand account of the conditions up here."[40] Jones neither relieved Devine nor ordered him to Bastogne. Instead Devine returned to the 14th CAV command post. Not long thereafter he ordered his troops to withdraw, without orders, farther west.

Later, after learning that Devine had withdrawn the 14th CAV without authorization, Jones ordered him back to St. Vith to explain himself. On Devine's arrival Jones told him he wanted the 14th CAV back in position on the line from Born south to Wallerode. Devine left after nightfall to carry out his orders. Because he had ordered the group to withdraw, his cavalrymen jammed the road from St. Vith to Poteau and from Born west. German troops intermingled with the retreating Cavalry attacked Devine and the small group of staff traveling with him. He survived the ambush, but effectively he was hors de combat.[41]

During his vigil at the 106th ID, Clarke observed that Jones varied between apprehensive and optimistic. He perceived that Jones was stressed because his son was on the Schnee Eifel. About the time that Devine burst in, Jones took a call from Middleton, during which he seemed optimistic, saying to the corps commander, "We'll be in good shape. Clarke's troops will be here soon." Although puzzled by Jones's equanimity, Middleton accepted his judgment.[42] Soon after, Jones and Clarke heard small arms fire in the east. The two went to the third floor of the building. From there they thought they could see German troops two miles away. Jones turned to Clarke and said, "I've thrown in my last chips. I haven't got much, but your combat command is the one that will defend this position. You take over command of St.-Vith right now." Clarke agreed, but wondered aloud, "I will. I'll take over but with what?" In less than forty-eight hours the 106th ID had collapsed. Jones, now gloomy, concluded that he "had lost a division quicker than any other Division Commander."[43]

Apprised of Riggs's patched-together effort, Clarke headed east to "take over command."[44] He had sent his operations officer CPT Woodruff forward earlier to stop westbound traffic and be on the lookout for the 87th CAV. On the way to meet Riggs he found Woodruff by the side of the road, jammed with westbound prime movers from a Corps artillery battalion. Woodruff reported that an VIII Corps Artillery lieutenant colonel had forced him off the road. What neither Clarke nor Woodruff knew was that BG John McMahon, commander of the VIII Corps artillery, had ordered all of the Corps artillery, less the 275th AFA, to withdraw. Clarke had sharp words with the unfortunate lieutenant colonel and began "to prevent the confusion from becoming disorganized."[45]

As Clarke noted, "The confusion was so great that I can't describe it."[46] Luckily, he had Riggs, a very talented officer, already in place, and Riggs soon had the ball rolling. His makeshift task force had already fought off the advancing 18th VGD and destroyed one or more tanks or Hetzer antitank guns. Riggs used the 592nd FA and at least one flight of P-47 fighters to keep the Germans at bay. Clarke also had the good fortune of having another talented officer join the fragile defense of St. Vith. Earlier that day LTC Roy U. Clay, commanding the 275th AFA, had become frustrated with COL Devine.

On the first day of the German offensive Clarke's 275th fired nearly all of its ammunition in support of the 14th CAV. But on December 17, unsure of where his units were, Devine forbade Clay to shoot. Despite assurances that the 275th would not shoot unobserved missions, Devine remained adamant. This frustrated Clay, who thought the battlefield unreasonably quiet—too quiet. In fact the battlefield seemed quiet because the 14th CAV had broken contact with the enemy. That morning Clay felt unsettled, believing "there is something that the 275th Armored Field Artillery Battalion should be doing and we weren't doing it."[47] He went to 106th ID Division Artillery Fire Direction Center to complain and ask for missions. There he learned from an VIII Corps artillery liaison officer that he would be supporting the 7th AD. Although Clay did not find Bruce Clarke that day, his forward observers met Clarke's units as they arrived and went to work.[48]

Accretion of the Defense at St. Vith

At noon on December 17, MG Hasbrouck arrived in Bastogne, where he met with MG Middleton. Middleton gave a quick briefing and ordered Hasbrouck to get to St. Vith and "cooperate" with MG Jones. Hasbrouck set out for St. Vith via Vielsalm while his division marched south, unaware that "Panzer columns of two German Panzer Armies had crashed through the American lines and were racing westward."[49] The Lucky Seventh's units following the 87th CAV south on the western route made good time as far as Vielsalm. The 87th motored east through Vielsalm around 1030, pausing long enough to refuel. Once they left Vielsalm they and the rest of the Division struggled against a tide of Corps artillery moving west under orders, if not under control. Intermingled with the artillery, Devine's Cavalry streamed west and south along with corps and army units of all descriptions. It took four or more hours for Hasbrouck's western column to move fourteen miles from Vielsalm to St. Vith.[50]

The troops "still did not know of the critical situation into which they were advancing." As LT Richard A. Hardin, in command of B Company, 17th TB, asserted, "Nobody in the company knew where it was going or what was in store for it." According to B Company tanker Frank A. Swantack, "there were all sorts of rumors floating around. Nobody knew anything about the breakthrough, and the report got around that the outfit was being pulled back and was going to be sent home and then to the Pacific."[51] Ignorant or not, the 7th AD trundled on toward St. Vith and destiny.

In *The Ardennes*, historian Hugh Cole described the traffic problem. No doctrine, no systems for planning a road march, "could give a formula for the coefficient of 'friction' in war, in this case the mass of jeeps, prime movers, guns, and trucks which jammed the roads."[52] The conditions proved even worse on the eastern route. Major (MAJ) Donald P. Boyer, operations officer of the 38th AIB, described what he found at Poteau, near the terminus of the eastern route. Traveling ahead of his battalion, Boyer reached the road junction at Poteau at 1230: "As we [Boyer and his driver, Private First Class Alfred Falter] arrived at the road junction, we were hit by a sight that we could not comprehend at first, a constant stream of traffic hurtling to the rear (to the west) and nothing going to the front (to the east). We realized that this was not a convoy moving to the rear; it was a case of 'every dog for himself'; it was a retreat, a rout."[53]

Ordered to withdraw, VIII Corps artillery accounted for much of the westbound traffic. Boyer's assessment was nevertheless accurate. Corps units withdrawing included antiaircraft artillery positioned to shoot at V-1 buzz bombs and various logistics units responsible for supply points. Orders or not, many of these units succumbed to panic. Still others, including the 14th CAV, withdrew on their commander's accord and not with orders—or in an orderly way.

B Troop, 87th CAV, the first 7th AD unit to reach St. Vith, arrived around 1600. Clarke sent B Troop east on the road to Schönberg, telling the troop commander, "Keep going down this road. You'll run into this great big lieutenant colonel named Riggs. Tell him you're attached to him, and he'll tell you what to do."[54] Riggs positioned them on the north side of the road from St. Vith to Schönberg. Clarke grabbed units as they arrived and sent them east to Riggs, who assigned positions. According to Clarke, "No tactics applied; I just got units down the road to the east of St. Vith."[55]

A Company, 31st TB arrived next. The company commander, CPT Robert Foster, and LT John J. Dunn, 3rd Platoon Leader, moved on foot off the Schönberg road north along the Prümerberg to select positions for their tanks. As they crested the ridge they could see at least three enemy tanks. When Dunn returned with his tank platoon, they were fired on by one of these tanks. Dunn's tankers destroyed it, and his three tanks took up positions on the left of the growing line.[56]

Everything happened extemporaneously. On arriving at the 106th command post, MAJ Boyer met with Clarke, who had a 1:25,000 map of the sector. With both of them looking at the map he instructed Boyer, "Go in town [St. Vith] and get 'B' Co of the 23rd which you will find on the main street. Have them take up positions here (pointing at the southeastern approaches to St. Vith)." When Boyer asked about the positions of other units Clarke answered, "We don't know about the right; CC-B of the 9th is there somewhere. On the left, some Eng[inee]rs; further to the left, a recon troop from the 87th." With that Boyer found CPT D. J. Britton, commander of B Company, 23rd AIB, and passed the orders. Britton moved out and got his troops in position.[57]

CCR, led by its executive officer, LTC Fred M. Warren, traveled on the eastern route and crossed both Rollbahn C at Malmedy and Rollbahn D at Ligneuville without incident. CCR's lead unit, the 38th AIB, arrived in its assembly area near Recht at 1230, only four hours after crossing the initial point. CCR's last unit, the 17th TB, closed at 1500.[58] CCR was the last unit to cross without incident the routes the Germans planned to use. Kampfgruppe Peiper determined the timetable for those who followed. Joachim Peiper's column used Rollbahn C long enough to seize fuel from a US supply point at Büllingen. On the lookout for better roads, he zigged south to Rollbahn D, his assigned route, and then back to Baugnez on C, then south again to Ligneuville, and then west on his assigned route. Along the way he spread fear and confusion among units supporting the rear area, including the 47th Field Hospital at Waimes, which evacuated just ahead of Peiper's troops.

Battery B, 285th Field Artillery Observation Battalion did not escape. Battery B was a sound and flash target acquisition unit equipped and trained to support counterbattery fire. Although not assigned to the 7th AD, CPT Leon T. Scarborough arranged to move his thirty-three vehicles with the eastern column. The Battery trailed CCR by a few minutes, as planned. Because Scarborough had gone ahead to arrange positions for the Battery, his executive officer, CPT Roger B. Mills, led the column.[59]

LTC David E. Pergrin, commanding the 291st EN, stopped Mills. Pergrin explained to Mills that the Germans had broken through at Bütgenbach. Alerted to the 7th AD convoys, Pergrin recommended that Mills alter his route and go west, then south on the western convoy route. Mills considered Pergrin's suggestion but decided to continue on. Mills led the convoy uphill toward the intersection of five roads at Baugnez, where he encountered Peiper's troops. There in a field beside the road Peiper's SS men accepted the surrender of the men of Battery B and then committed the infamous Malmedy Massacre, murdering at least eighty-six of them. There is some debate about how the massacre began, but no debate about who was responsible.[60]

LTC Pergrin soon posted a sign reporting the road under fire. The rest of the eastern column had to reroute and take the west route. At Ligneuville, Peiper's troops shot up the trail party of Hoge's 14th TB. An upgunned Sherman traveling with the trail party managed to knock out a Panther tank with its high-velocity seventy-six-millimeter cannon, enabling the survivors to escape south. The 14th TB service troops forced Peiper to commit his Panzergrenadiers to clear the town. After helping himself to American rations, Peiper went on his way with his spearhead—or as he termed it, his *Spitze*, or point. Afterward, Belgian civilians witnessed a German noncommissioned officer shoot eight prisoners in the head. Miraculously, one survived.[61]

Arriving near Recht, six miles northwest of St. Vith, LTC Warren had no orders and no contact as yet with the Division. Around 1530 a CCR soldier reported "that 'he heard' that the Germans had occupied Ligneuville about 30 minutes after our column had cleared."[62] Warren and MAJ Fred C. Sweat, the operations officer, reconnoitered toward Ligneuville, where military police on the south side of the town verified German occupancy. Warren and Sweat then went to St. Vith, looking for General Clarke. When they found him, Clarke took the 38th AIB and added it to the defenses east of St. Vith. He told them what he could. Warren and Sweat returned to Recht. After study of "the road net and terrain," Warren decided to defend Recht, at least for the night. LTC John P. Wemple's 17th TB established roadblocks.

Hasbrouck, like Clarke, traveled first to Bastogne to get briefing and instructions from Middleton. On arrival he observed that "people were retiring double banks down the roads." Hasbrouck did not believe that anyone at VIII Corps understood what was happening. In Bastogne he "received no direction at all. What they [the Corps] told me about the situation was very sketchy. I finally decided I was wasting time."[63] The 7th AD, used to relying on radios, could communicate effectively, so Hasbrouck headed for St. Vith, where he knew Clarke and Jones could be found. He arrived around 1600.[64] What he learned worried him.

Hasbrouck knew nothing about the fighting in the 28th ID sector. He learned what he could of the fighting around St. Vith. He knew that south of St. Vith COL Reid's 424th Infantry held positions centered on the town of Burg-Reuland. Hasbrouck knew Hoge had established positions on the Our River opposite Winterspelt, and Riggs's pickup team occupied the Prümerberg, supported by three companies from Clarke's CCB. Hasbrouck knew also that the 106th had two regiments cut off on the Schnee Eifel. He knew that there were Germans all along the northern flank. On the basis of this, Hasbrouck made two important decisions. Although Middleton had authorized him only to commit two of his three combat commands in support of the 106th ID, Hasbrouck decided to commit all of the Division to the fight at St. Vith. He believed that if he did not, the Germans would roll up the Corps from north to south. He also confirmed Warren's choice to defend Recht. COL Ryan, CCR's commander, had caught up and went on to Recht to resume his command.[65] That evening COL Dwight A. Rosebaum's CCA assembled in Beho. Hasbrouck had the night to consider what to do next.

In the meantime, there was plenty to do to prevent "the confusion from becoming disorganized." The defense of St. Vith and its environs grew by accretion. Units from three divisions, VIII Corps, and First Army cooperated and made do without clear command relationships. Intermingling of units prevented the formation of a coherent front line. LTC William L. Nungesser of the 168th EN, understated the problem when he observed that "it was difficult to find the responsible officer for the heterogeneous elements in the line."[66] Much moving about occurred that night, some of it planned and some of it not as officers at all levels sought to restore orders while fending off German probes. At midnight on December 17–18 Hasbrouck ordered Rosebaum to report to the command post in St. Vith for orders at 0700 December 18.

Hasbrouck received more bad news that evening that demonstrated his division's vulnerability. At 2045 COL Church Matthews's Jeep driver arrived at CCR's command post "on foot and very winded. . . . He and Colonel Matthews had been ambushed by a German tank on the road east of Recht. They had both dismounted and had become separated."[67] Matthews never turned up. While his driver went back the way they had come, Matthews had gone up a nearby hill. He was killed near the ambush site. Hasbrouck had served with him previously and brought him to the Lucky Seventh to be his chief of staff less than a month earlier. For Church Matthews and many others, duty with the Lucky Seventh that winter proved most unlucky.

Model and Manteuffel Direct Traffic

Twenty years after the Battle of the Bulge, the US Army aired a television documentary on the Battle of St. Vith. Many of the soldiers mentioned here participated. Two of them, the German general Hasso von Manteuffel and the American brigadier general Bruce C. Clarke, dominated. They knew each other well by then, having met more than once. Together they led the narrative of the action over the piece of ground where they had fought. At one point they recalled that both had functioned as traffic police on December 17.[68] They were not alone. Generalfeldmarschall Walther Model, who commanded Army Group B, met Manteuffel on the road to Schönberg. Manteuffel was on his way to goad the 18th VGD into moving more aggressively, as he wanted St. Vith taken the next day. Model, on a similar mission, met his Fifth Panzer Army commander after nightfall.

Both were on foot, as the traffic jam Klaus Ritter observed that morning had not dissipated. Neither of them, despite their august stations, could get the German *Stau* unjammed. Model asked Manteuffel how it was going. Manteuffel described his situation as "Mostly Good," to which Model responded, "So? I got the impression you were lagging, especially in the St. Vith sector." Manteuffel admitted as much but asserted, "We'll take it tomorrow." Model stipulated, "I expect you to and so you'll take it quicker, tomorrow I'm letting you use the 'Führer Begleit Brigade' [Führer Escort Brigade]."⁶⁹ Like Bruce Clarke in CCB and Fred Warren in CCR, these two German officers went forward to see for the conditions on the ground for themselves.

NOTES

1. Army Pictorial Center, *The Battle of St. Vith*, pt. 1.

2. Hugh M. Cole, *The Ardennes: Battle of the* Bulge, 274.

3. Brigadier General Bruce C. Clarke, "The Hour by Hour Journal of Activities, Conferences and Directions of Brigadier General Bruce C. Clarke and CCB, 7th Armored Division," General Bruce C. Clarke Papers; the parenthetical name is in the original; the corps commander was MG Troy H. Middleton. On the warning to units, see 7th Armored Division, G-3 journal, entry 19, 1745 hours. The 203rd Anti-Aircraft Artillery, the last unit that acknowledged receipt, did so at 1815 hours. On staff officers, see W. Wesley Johnston, *Combat Interviews of the 7th Armored Division Headquarters*, 38. Just who went south and by what route is unclear. At least two officers departed the 7th AD command post at 2130 on December 16. Major Werner J. Moeller, assistant G-3, and Major Charles New, assistant G-2, 7th AD, left together and arrived at the 106th ID command post before Bruce C. Clarke; see 38–39 and 43–44. The two determined to separate, with New remaining at St. Vith and Moeller going to Vielsalm to meet the Division as it arrived. See also US Army Armor School, *The Battle at St. Vith Belgium*, in which Clarke reports taking the call from Hasbrouck at 2100.

4. Charles B. MacDonald, *A Time for Trumpets*, 322–23. See also Donald P. Boyer Jr., *St. Vith: The 7th Armored Division in the Battle of the Bulge*. Boyer's study became the basis for US Army Armor School, *The Battle at St. Vith Belgium*.

5. 7th Armored Division, G-3 journal, December 16, 1944; on the 17th TB, see the entry at 1959 hours.

6. Boyer, *St. Vith: The 7th Armored Division in the Battle of the Bulge*, 3; 7th Armored Division, G-3 journal, December 16, 1944, entries at 1145, 1330, and 1530 hours; Cole, *The Ardennes: Battle of the Bulge*, 274. Cole reports that Ninth Army received notice of the start times for the two routes "shortly after midnight." See also Dwight D. Eisenhower, *Crusade in Europe*, 343–44.

7. Cole, *The Ardennes: Battle of the Bulge*, 274–77.

8. Carl von Clausewitz, *On War*, 314; see also 316–18.

9. US War Department, *Armored Force Field Manual*, FM-17, 12–15.

10. Veterans of the Battle of the Bulge, Inc., *The Battle of the Bulge: True Stories of the Men and Women Who Survived*, 207, brackets in the original.

11. George J. Winter, "The Capture of Poteau," 3. On arrival in the muddy field, however, Hondorp and his buddies found shelter in nearby homes.

12. Vincent L. Boylan, interviewer not identified [probably John Toland], n.d., box 33, John Toland Papers.

13. Lieutenant William A. Knowlton to John Toland, n.d., box 1, Knowlton file, John Toland Papers.

14. Combat Command B, 9th Armored Division, "Action South of St. Vith 17–23 Dec 1944." On the troop list, see Combat Command B, 9th Armored Division, "After Action Report for the Period 1–31 December 1944."

15. Obersturmbannführer Joachim Peiper, "An Interview with Obst. Joachim Peiper," ETHINT-10, 13–14. MacDonald, *A Time for Trumpets*, 323, claims three routes for Peiper, which would include Rollbahn Route C, but Peiper in this interview says the route, at least west of Losheimergraben, belonged to the 12th SS PZ.

16. Obersturmbannführer Joachim Peiper, "Kampfgruppe Peiper," 14; MacDonald, *A Time for Trumpets*, 323.

17. Peter Caddick-Adams, *Snow and Steel*, 353–56.

18. Oberstleutnant Dietrich Moll, "18th Volks Grenadier Division," B-688, 39. Moll does not specify the mission of the bicycle battalion. I have inferred the mission from the context.

19. Generalmajor Friedrich Kittel, "62nd Volksgrenadier Division," 2, 30. Kittel expressed surprise at the level of resistance he encountered.

20. Generalmajor Rudolph Langhäuser, "560 Volks Grenadier Division" and "12 Volks Grenadier Division," 9–11. Langhäuser could not recall the unit identification of the armored reconnaissance battalion but believed that it came from either the 2nd PZ or the Panzer Lehr Division.

21. Heinz Günther Guderian, *From Normandy to the Ruhr*, 306–7.

22. Cole, *The Ardennes: Battle of the Bulge*, 157.

23. Colonel R. Ernest Dupuy, *St. Vith: Lion in the Way*, 64, brackets in the original; MacDonald, *A Time for Trumpets*, 310–11. See also Cole, *The Ardennes: Battle of the Bulge*, 156–61.

24. It is difficult to pin down just when MacMahon decided to withdraw the threatened artillery. The author relied on after action reports for the artillery battalions and the division artillery. See Dupuy, *St. Vith: Lion in the Way*, 78–86. See also MacDonald, *A Time for Trumpets*, 313; MacDonald mistakenly identified the 589th FA as the 598th FA.

25. 589th Field Artillery, "After Action Report," 5.

26. Dupuy, *St. Vith: Lion in the Way*, 65; Moll, "18th Volks Grenadier Division," 40; Division Artillery, 7th Armored Division, "After Action Report, Month of December 1944." See also 592nd Field Artillery Battalion, "History—592nd FA Battalion," 9, which asserts that they were ordered to withdraw at 2000 hours. This contradicts Division Artillery, "After Action Report," but is likely. The 106th ID reported tanks in several places early on December 17. These must have been Hetzer antitank guns. LXVI Corps had no tanks in contact on December 17.

27. Lieutenant Jack T. Shea, "Fourteenth Cavalry Group," 28–29. Shea's narrative does not identify the tanks as coming from the 1st SS PZ; that is this author's inference.

28. MacDonald, *A Time for Trumpets*, 314; Shea, "Fourteenth Cavalry Group," 29.

29. Cole, *The Ardennes: Battle of the Bulge*, 159. See also Oberst Arthur Jüttner, "Report by Colonel Jüttner of the 62nd VGD in the Battle of the Bulge," 6.

30. General William M. Hoge, *Engineer Memoirs*, 133–34.

31. MacDonald, *A Time for Trumpets*, 320–21. See also US Army Pictorial Center, "Battle of St. Vith," pt. 1.

32. Peiper, ETHINT-10, 15.

33. Moll, "18th Volks Grenadier Division," 40.

34. Klaus Ritter, statements, box 10, Charles B. MacDonald Papers, pt. 2, p. 2.

35. Ritter, statements, pt. 2, p. 2.

36. Ritter, statements, pt. 2, p. 2.

37. Oberst Arthur Jüttner, "With the Same Efficiency as the Panzers!," 4.

38. Jüttner, "With the Same Efficiency as the Panzers!," 4.

39. John S. D. Eisenhower, *The Bitter Woods*, 228–29. There are numerous accounts of this conversation, and nearly all of them depend on Clarke's recollection. Eisenhower's account is the best documented. Bruce C. Clarke told his story a great many times, and I have several versions in my possession. With small variations, it remained consistent and is borne out by Eisenhower's account.

40. General Bruce C. Clarke to the Chief of Military History, May 20, 1986, General Bruce C. Clarke Papers.

41. Shea, "14th Cavalry Group," 30–31. See also Dupuy, *St. Vith: Lion in the Way*, 69–70. At about 1300 hours Devine ordered the group to withdraw to a line ran from Born south to Wallerode on his own initiative. Ultimately that led to more confusion and jammed roads. Roger Cirillo, author of *Ardennes-Alsace*, in a telephone conversation with the author, April 5, 2019, explained that he believes a near miss from artillery on December 16 may have concussed Devine. That could explain Devine's behavior.

42. Eisenhower, *The Bitter Woods*, 229.

43. Clarke to Chief of Military History, May 20, 1986, 3. See also Eisenhower, *The Bitter Woods*, 229.

44. Eisenhower, *The Bitter Woods*, 229–30. In his 1986 letter to the chief of military history Clarke wrote that he ordered Riggs into position. That is mistaken. He did, however, meet Riggs and confirmed Riggs's command on the Prümerberg.

45. Clarke, "The Hour by Hour Journal."

46. General Bruce C. Clarke (Ret.), interview with the author, McLean, VA, August 20, 1984, General Bruce C. Clarke Papers. Clarke repeatedly used this phrase in short articles and speeches that he gave.

47. Colonel Roy U. Clay (Ret.), interview with the author, Carlisle, PA, August 28, 1984. Clay met with Devine at 0330 and again at 0900 asking for permission to fire. Devine denied permission each time. See Roy U. Clay, *Curbstone: The History of the 275th Field Artillery Battalion in World War II*, 12–13. On leave in Paris when the 14th CAV assumed responsibility for the sector, Clay had not met Devine. On hearing of the attack, Clay made his way from Paris back to the sector, meeting Devine for the first time in the early hours of December 17.

48. Roy U. Clay, "Tinstaafl: Autobiography of Roy U. Clay," 88.

49. Boyer, *St. Vith: The 7th Armored Division in the Battle of the Bulge*, 6–7.

50. Boyer, *St. Vith: The 7th Armored Division in the Battle of the Bulge*, 5–8; Cole, *The Ardennes: Battle of the Bulge*, 275. Exactly how long is difficult to calculate. The

division journal notes that the bulk of the Division closed at 2150; see 7th Armored Division, G-3 tactical journal, December 1944, entry 7. B Troop 87th Cavalry Reconnaissance Squadron arrived first about 1600.

51. Boyer, *St. Vith: The 7th Armored Division in the Battle of the Bulge*, 6; W. Wesley Johnston, *17th Tank Battalion*, 50.

52. Cole, *The Ardennes: Battle of the Bulge*, 275.

53. US Army Armor School, *The Battle at St. Vith Belgium*, 7.

54. MacDonald, *A Time for Trumpets*, 328.

55. Clarke interview, August 20, 1984. See also W. Wesley Johnston, *Combat Interviews of the 87th Cavalry Reconnaissance Squadron*, 28, and 32, sketch.

56. W. Wesley Johnston, *Combat Interviews of the 31st Tank Battalion*, 30.

57. Boyer, *St. Vith: The 7th Armored Division in the Battle of the Bulge*, 161–62.

58. Combat Command R, 7th Armored Division, "After Action Report, Month of December 1944," 7; MacDonald, *A Time for Trumpets*, 208–18. See also William C. C. Cavanagh and Karl Cavanagh, *A Tour of the Bulge Battlefields*, 78–79, map.

59. MacDonald, *A Time for Trumpets*, 213.

60. MacDonald, *A Time for Trumpets*, 213–21; Cole, *The Ardennes: Battle of the Bulge*, 260, 261–64. Cole, 262, estimates that Peiper's troops "murdered approximately 350 American prisoners of war and at least 100 unarmed civilians."

61. MacDonald, *A Time for Trumpets*, 228–29.

62. Combat Command R, 7th Armored Division. "After Action Report, Month of December 1944," 7.

63. W. Wesley Johnston, *Combat Interviews of the 7th Armored Division Headquarters*, 16.

64. Boyer, *St. Vith: The 7th Armored Division in the Battle of the Bulge*, 8–10.

65. US Army Armor School, *The Battle at St. Vith Belgium*, 7. Major General Robert W. Hasbrouck (Ret.), interview with the author, Washington, DC, August 20, 1984. Clarke did have all of his combat command by nightfall on December 17.

66. Lieutenant Colonel W. L. Nungesser, Major Harry W. Brennan, and Lieutenant Harry Balch, interview by Captain K. W. Hechler.

67. Boyer, *St. Vith: The 7th Armored Division in the Battle of the Bulge*, 12. See also "Matthews, Church M." (obituary), USMA Association of Graduations, https://www.fieldsofhonor-database.com/index.php/en/american-war-cemetery-henri-chapelle-m/47668-matthews-church-m.

68. US Army Pictorial Center, "Battle of St. Vith," pt. 1.

69. MacDonald, *A Time for Trumpets*, 327.

CHAPTER SIX

A Thin Olive Drab Line

The second phase of the defense was to deny the vital road nets to the enemy by building strong defenses in front of St. Vith, Houffalize, Bastogne and Luxembourg as rapidly as possible.

—VIII Corps after action report, April 6, 1945

The last ounce of strength Germany still possessed was expended.

— Oberstgruppenführer Sepp Dietrich

The 7th which has joined up with the one regiment of the 106th Div not cut off is doing a magnificent job in holding firm at St. Vith against tremendous pressure.

— Major William C. Sylvan and Captain Francis G. Smith Jr., First
Army war diary

UNDERSTANDING WHAT HAPPENED, when, and why, during the early days of the German offensive of December 1944 is difficult. Reconstructing events from reports made during the battle and related in after action reports, interviews, and historical accounts reflect the confusion of battle complicated by subsequent interpretation. In some ways the confusion is greater now than then, as the agendas of the participants are blended with those who reported the story. Who killed Colonel (COL) Church Matthews and why COL Mark A. Devine behaved as he did are questions for which categorical answers are unlikely. Despite the passage of time, clarity has not emerged. The late evening hours of Sunday, December 17, 1944, and the early morning hours of December 18 were as confusing as any in combat. Chaos reigned that night and during the days that followed.

Contact at Recht

The actions at Recht in the early morning hours on December 18 and later in the day at Stavelot exemplify the confusion among the Americans and Germans. At 1530 on December 17, COL Devine ordered the 14th Cavalry (CAV) to withdraw, doing so without authorization. When the Cavalry withdrew, they opened the way for the two Kampfgruppen of the 1st Schutzstaffel (SS) Panzer Division (PZ). Now Kampfgruppe Peiper on Rollbahn D and Kampfgruppe Hansen on Rollbahn E advanced largely unopposed. That night Obersturmbahnführer Joachim Peiper's spearhead groped its way forward at "little better than a walking pace" on narrow icy roads. His *Spitze*, or advanced guard, reached a hill above Stavelot around midnight, and stopped not far from the tail end of the 7th Armored Division (AD) convoys stalled on the Division's western route. Obersturmbahnführer Max Hansen's unit also kept moving west. But instead of exploiting the opening created by the 14th CAV's withdrawal, the 1st SS PZ ordered Hansen to occupy the village of Recht and await the arrival of the 9th SS PZ.[1] Only then could Kampfgruppe Hansen continue westward.

West of Hansen's column, Combat Command Reserve (CCR), 7th AD passed through Ligneuville. CCR's infantry continued on to St. Vith and joined the line of resistance forming there. At around 1500 hours CCR learned the enemy had taken Ligneuville. Lieutenant Colonel (LTC) John P. Wemple, commanding the 17th Tank Battalion (TB), dropped off a tank company just south of Ligneuville to secure his "rear." The rest of the Battalion continued through the village of Recht and occupied high ground about one thousand yards south of the village. Wemple chose his positions without knowing either friendly positions or those of the enemy. At 1530 an equally ignorant CCR established its command post in Recht. Wemple sent his C Company to provide local security. The Company moved into the village at dusk.[2]

Sometime around midnight, dismounted Panzergrenadiers from Kampfgruppe Hansen entered Recht. Accounts vary as to precisely when this occurred and how serious the infiltration was. Some suggest the action took place prior to midnight, while others assert it began no sooner than 0200 on December 18. When the 1st SS finally ordered Hansen to mount an attack to take Recht, Wemple's tankers stopped him. Lieutenant (LT) Irving Goodman recalled that at midnight, "The Germans were just starting to infiltrate into the northeastern end of the town." C Company perceived the German effort as combat patrols rather than a general attack. But without infantry, C Company was vulnerable. Tanks unsupported by friendly infantry do not fare well against determined and well-armed enemy infantry, especially in the dark of night. A firefight ensued, with the Germans employing "mortar, machine gun, and small arms fire and a few flares." LTC Fred M. Warren, in command of CCR, moved his command post forthwith. Warren moved southwest along the highway to the village of Poteau while C Company dueled with Hansen's Panzergrenadiers.[3]

After CCR left, so did C Company. It withdrew "between 0300 and 0400" along the road that led to Nieder-Emmels and, ultimately, St. Vith. The Company joined the bulk of the 17th TB on a ridge overlooking Recht. C Company took positions south of a railway track that ran in a gentle arc from the east curving southward toward St. Vith. The tank crews oriented their tanks back in the direction they had come. Not long after that, some Panzergrenadiers moved into positions along the railway embankment south of Recht. At around 0500 a single German tank emerged from the town heading southeast through the highway underpass at the railroad. Inexplicably the C Company tankers believed the tank might be American until it fired four rounds. The fusillade destroyed a Sherman and wounded two of its crewmen. Satisfied, the German vehicle retraced its steps. Chastened, C Company withdrew further along the road to positions that afforded better fields of fire. Kampfgruppe Hansen, intent on heading west, made no probes after daylight.[4] Neither side sought to prosecute the action to conclusion. Tactically the Germans retained the initiative.

German Assessments and Orders

Both sides missed opportunities during the first two days of the German offensive. Tactical performance and decision-making in the 106th Infantry Division (ID) and the 14th CAV reflected no great credit on either unit. Their performance may even have added to the myth of German tactical excellence. Nevertheless, there is ample evidence that German commanders showed far less initiative and excellence than their admirers claim. Among those who compare the Americans unfavorably to the Germans are Trevor N. Dupuy in *A Genius for War* and Martin van Creveld in *Fighting Power*. Both rely heavily on casualty counts and quantitative analysis. The contemporary US Army explicitly accepts the notion of German excellence, particularly in initiative. The Army claims its notion of "mission command" stems from the excellence of German method as Americans imagined it to be. That method or approach is called mission orders. The Germans used the term *Auftragstaktik* (literally, "task tactics"). The historians of the Bundeswehr, the successors to the Wehrmacht, are not as sanguine about German excellence as Dupuy and Van Creveld are, and they make far less of *Auftragstaktik* than Americans have. Karl Heinz Frieser, in *The Blitzkrieg Legend*, and Gerhard P. Gross, in *The Myth and Reality of German Warfare*, writing for the Bundeswehr Center of Military History and Social Science, provide balance.[5] In short, the German Army of 1944, and perhaps from the outset of the war, may not have merited its reputation. It is readily apparent that whatever edge it enjoyed in 1940 did not manifest itself in December 1944.

Obviously the German Army had the advantage of experience bought at great cost in six years at war. Yet at the same time the US Army showed amazing capacity to learn, led for the most part by able and energetic officers and supported by rapid production and reasonably efficient dissemination of lessons learned. Well equipped and operating with air superiority, the US Army was more than a match for its antagonists. Even without generous air support the Army showed resilience and skill at all levels during the Battle of the Bulge.

By sundown that Sunday, December 17, 1944, American soldiers had irrevocably upset the German timetable. The Sixth Panzer Army, composed almost entirely of the vaunted SS, struggled against weak defenses in the Losheim Gap. The parachute drop designed to secure the ridges to the rear of the American main line of resistance failed miserably. In the 106th ID the 424th Infantry (INF) fought effectively against regiments of two divisions. From the beginning the raw material in even the newest American tactical formations proved to be at least as good as that of their antagonists. Notably, the 18th Volksgrenadier Division (VGD), poorly equipped and manned by a menagerie of airmen, old men, and youngsters, performed better than either the purportedly elite Fallschirmjäger or the SS, and without committing war crimes. Apologists for the German Army claim that the excellence of 1940 had eroded. Certainly that is true, but most of the Americans fighting in World War II had no more experience than most of their German counterparts—and in many cases far less.

In any case, the missteps taken at the outset of the offensive had not gone unnoticed in the German high command. The Army Group B commander, Generalfeldmarschall Walther Model, had not plodded down the line of German vehicles outside of Schönberg out of idle curiosity. He needed to kick the offensive into gear but realized that the Sixth Panzer Army had for the moment failed. According to Wehrmacht war diarist Percy E. Schramm, "not only did 6 Panzer Army threaten to bog down, but also the enemy made counter thrusts against the flanks."[6] Generaloberst Alfred Jodl spoke more plainly, noting that "in the sector of the Sixth Army, where we had the most armor and expected the quickest breakthrough we achieved the least."[7] In a postwar interview Generalfeldmarschall Gerd von Rundstedt complained, "Allied countermovements were made more quickly than expected by OKW [Oberkommando der Wehrmacht, or German Supreme Headquarters]." It is fair to also say that Rundstedt took no responsibility for any of what had gone wrong.[8]

General der Panzertruppe Hasso von Manteuffel understood what Model required: it fell to the Fifth Panzer Army to take St. Vith and open the vital road and rail network. In arriving at his estimate of the situation Manteuffel enjoyed a reasonably clear vision of the battle based on information from American prisoners, his visit forward, and "intercepted messages of traffic control points."[9] He, too, had gone forward to push his troops. Even the well-led 18th VGD missed opportunities on December 17. The 18th VGD and the rest of the Fifth Panzer Army had to do better—much better. Manteuffel believed that for them to do so, leaders from small units to the corps level had to exhibit obduracy. In the short, bitter days of December—and, for that matter, throughout the war—Manteuffel maintained that "the power of personality on the battlefield has not diminished, despite the higher effect of the weapons."[10] The diminutive general sought to bend the Fifth Panzer Army to his will.

That night Model released Oberst Otto-Ernst Remer's Führer Escort Brigade (FEB) for the Fifth Panzer Army's use. He directed Manteuffel to use the FEB to take St. Vith—and to get it done soon. A powerful all-arms formation was equipped with both field and antiaircraft artillery regiments; Remer's brigade fielded twenty-three tanks, forty-eight antitank guns, and three battalions of infantry, two of them motorized and one on bicycles.[11] Remer's troops boosted General der Artillerie Walther Lucht's LXVI Corps significantly, so the Corps planned to take St. Vith on December 18. Lucht's orders required the 18th VGD to envelope St. Vith from the north while its southern wing pressed westward alongside the 62nd VGD attacking from the south. Lucht wanted the FEB to follow the right wing of the Corps. For the attack to succeed, LXVI Corps' two divisions and the FEB would have to get their heavy weapons and artillery forward over the same roads that the Corps' few mobile units had jammed on December 17. According to the 18th VGD operations officer, the chief determinant to success would be whether the Americans could "concentrate strong forces in and around St.

Vith to prevent the attacking force from crossing the hills east and north east of the town."[12] That, of course, was the goal of the arriving 7th AD.

On Lucht's left, General der Panzertruppe Walter Krüger's LVIII Panzer Corps' two divisions needed to get unstuck from the stubborn 112th INF. Late on December 17, the 116th PZ forced a crossing over the Our River at Kalborn, about seven miles south of the crossing at Steinebrück. Division commander Generalmajor Siegfried von Waldenburg, moving with his spearhead, exulted in his radio report to Krüger, "Attack in full swing, can no longer be stopped."[13] Krüger ordered the 116th to attack northwest with the 560th VGD on its right. The Corps objective was to secure a crossing on the Ourthe River, some twenty miles distant. Krüger's order included an exhortation from Rundstedt that "no commander will be found in a house tonight."[14] At sunup, only COL Gustin M. Nelson's 112th INF stood in the way.

American Assessments and Orders

General (GEN) Dwight D. Eisenhower's decision on December 16 set in motion the rapid countermovements that confounded Rundstedt and his senior commanders. The 7th AD and 10th AD arrived in the VIII Corps sector the very next day. Other reinforcements, including XVIII Corps' 82nd and 101st Airborne Divisions (ABNs), were on their way. Late on the night of December 17, Major General (MG) James M. Gavin, the acting forward commander of XVIII Airborne Corps and commander of the 82nd ABN, headed north from Rheims to reconnoiter and get orders. Finally, Eisenhower ordered the theater services of supply, ordinarily concerned exclusively with logistics, to prepare to defend the crossings of the Meuse River.[15] The supreme commander had done what he could. Eisenhower's perception of the battle—his ability to see the battlefield in those early days—belies the criticism of his acumen as supreme commander.

On December 18 Captain (CPT) Harry C. Butcher, Eisenhower's naval aide, visited the 12th Army Group. There he found "an atmosphere around the 12th Army Group Headquarters which reminded me of the Kasserine."[16] Butcher's comparison to the Kasserine Pass disaster suggests surprise and even fear at the 12th Army Group. Major (MAJ) Chester Hansen, Lieutenant General (LTG) Omar N. Bradley's diarist, reported that Bradley was worried but that the general claimed he worried now "less than in Tunisia," during the Kasserine Pass incident.[17] That Bradley drew the same analogy as Butcher is instructive.

The mood at First Army was no better. On December 18, MAJ William C. Sylvan, who kept a diary for First Army's LTG Courtney H. Hodges, wrote,

"The situation is rapidly deteriorating and the position of the enemy is uncertain."[18] Hodges was sick with the flu and depressed. COL Samuel L. Meyers, his deputy chief of staff, later confided that Hodges felt "very badly about what had happened." In any case, LTG Hodges was not at his best on December 17 and 18. Nevertheless, he met with Gavin and others.[19]

The First Army staff continued to coordinate the movement of reinforcements into the area with its subordinate corps and with Ninth Army for additional resources, including trucks and the 30th ID. Unlike LTG George S. Patton Jr. at Third Army, Ninth Army commander GEN William H. Simpson pitched in without complaint. On December 18, First Army assigned routes and clearances for twenty-two convoys. Some 7,440 vehicles moved the 30th ID and supporting units south toward the battle. The following day the 3rd AD moved 2,026 vehicles in ten convoys.[20] Both the 30th ID and 3rd AD were moving toward Werbomont, north of the German penetration, to extend the shoulder forming along the flank of Model's Army Group B. First Army's commander may well have been sick but his staff moved troops rapidly.

In *Corps Commanders of the Bulge*, Harold R. Winton aptly titles a section in his narrative on VIII Corps, "Trading Lives for Time, 18–19 December." Middleton still had trouble seeing across the VIII Corps sector, but he knew the Germans had penetrated both the 106th and 28th. With the arrival of the 7th AD, the Corps could defend St. Vith and conceivably stymie both the Fifth and Sixth Panzer Armies and therefore Army Group B. Middleton focused next on the trouble in the center of the VIII Corps sector—the 28th ID's positions. He shoved units into the fray east of Bastogne as he could find them. These included CCR, 9th AD and small task forces from Combat Command B (CCB), 10th AD. These units and the badly battered 28th ID bought time for the 101st, the 82nd, and other reinforcements to arrive.

At the outset of the battle, Middleton's reactions seemed slow to the point of indolence, at least as he dealt with MG Alan W. Jones. There is evidence to support that view. But historian and combat veteran soldier Jerry D. Morelock offers a more generous assessment of Middleton. In *Generals of the Bulge*, what some, including this author, take for complacency, Morelock perceives as calm and collected resoluteness. That the decisions Middleton made after the first two days proved sound and effective lend credence to Morelock's view.[21]

Middleton's decision not to decide who would command at St. Vith produced less confusion than it might have. Jones turned over defense of St. Vith to Brigadier General (BG) Bruce C. Clarke. Clarke's mandate did not include BG William M. Hoge's CCB, 9th AD; COL Alexander D. Reid's 424th INF; or the two regiments on the Schnee Eifel. With the arrival of the 7th AD, BG Robert W. Hasbrouck fielded the most combat power, but he had no authority to assume command of the sector. Indeed, Middleton told him to collaborate with Jones, and so he did; but in the course of doing so Hasbrouck himself, as he put it, "gradually assumed command."[22]

Despite the lack of a clear chain of command, Hasbrouck effectively commanded the defense of the sector and made decisions he thought necessary—and with increasing confidence as Jones acquiesced. Hasbrouck, like Clarke, believed Jones was "out on his feet." Despite a lack of clear lines of command, Clarke, Hoge, and Reid worked together effectively in the early stages of the fight. Clarke and Hoge worked particularly well together. According to Hoge, "Clarke was a damned good fighter. We played it just by mutual conferences."[23] Despite accepting command of the defense of St. Vith, Clarke never thought he worked for anyone other than his own division commander. Hasbrouck confirmed Clarke's early decision and took responsibility for developing a wider defense; how much wider he did not yet understand.[24]

Hasbrouck Builds a Horseshoe

BG Hasbrouck set about organizing the defense as units arrived, while at the same time planning for the arrival of his artillery and supporting units still stuck on the road. Although Jones wanted very much for him to mount an attack to relieve the two regiments on the Schnee Eifel, it could not be done. German pressure required Hasbrouck to focus first on establishing a coherent defense. At 0300 on December 18 Hasbrouck issued a fragmentary order. In it he assigned defensive sectors and contact points between units. He ordered CCR to defend the northern flank of the Division and CCB to defend the sector east of St. Vith, centered on the Prümerberg. The order formally confirmed Clarke's decision to accept responsibility for St. Vith from MG Jones. Finally, Hasbrouck designated Combat Command A (CCA) as the Division reserve.[25] He issued no orders to Hoge, as CCB, 9th AD remained attached to the 106th ID. Nevertheless, Clarke, Hasbrouck, and Hoge functioned smoothly together from the outset. In part this was so because all of them took the armored force approach to combat operations.

Armored divisions were not organized, equipped, or designed to fight a static defense. Armored force doctrine specified that when in the defense the armored division should "occupy the forward areas with the armored infantry, antitank guns, engineers and some tanks for local counterattack purposes." Doctrine further specified that the armored division "retain the bulk of the tanks in division reserve as a general counterattacking force."[26]

Clarke, Hasbrouck, and Hoge were plank holders in the recently formed armored force. Hasbrouck organized the first armored field artillery battalion. Clarke came to the armored force in 1940 when he joined the experimental 7th Cavalry Brigade (Mechanized) at Fort Knox. He commanded CCB, 4th AD during the breakout from Normandy and pursuit in the summer and fall of 1944. Hoge, an accomplished engineer, built much of the famed Alaska–Canada Highway and then helped organize the 9th AD. He was pulled from that task to organize and command special engineer formations in support of the invasion of Normandy. He returned to the 9th AD to command CCB in November 1944.[27]

The three senior armor soldiers on the scene understood armored force doctrine because they participated in developing and practicing it. According to Hoge, when forming the 9th AD the troops and their officers "were learning together."[28] Tankers and armored infantry came to see terrain differently than did their infantry colleagues. Unlike most infantrymen these officers saw little benefit in holding ground just for the sake of holding ground. When BG Hasbrouck joined the 7th AD he found MG Lindsay McDonald Silvester had instructed that "they [the Division] must never give ground." He believed that sacrificing mobility to hold ground was "silly."[29] Clarke, who arrived at the 7th AD soon after Hasbrouck took command, shared this view. Clarke thought the 7th AD, as Silvester had employed it, inflexible. Silvester organized and operated his combat commands as fixed formations similar to the triangular infantry division and "normally engaged in the classic 'two up, one back' formation."[30]

In the end, Hasbrouck fought his units; CCB, 9th AD; and disparate units from Army, Corps, the 28th ID, and the 106th ID actively. Flexible task organization characterized his approach along with manning forward positions with combined arms formations supported by mobile reserves designed to counterattack or reinforce as necessary. He strove to take advantage of the mobility afforded by his tanks and half-tracks.[31]

During the course of the night of December 17–18, Hasbrouck, to paraphrase Clarke, sought to "organize" the confusion and gain control over the accretion of the defense around St. Vith. Anchored on the work LTC Thomas J. Riggs Jr. had begun on the Prümerberg, the main line of resistance came to resemble an elongated horseshoe. Hasbrouck directed the reorganization of CCR to return part of the 38th Armored Infantry Battalion (AIB) so CCR could fight with infantry support. CCR sought to gain control of traffic of the road from Rodt southwest to Poteau, jammed full with retreating 14th CAV, Corps, and Army units. Hasbrouck's operations officer LTC Charles E. Leydecker and the division staff prepared orders for their own units, which were stuck in traffic jams overnight. Those stuck at nightfall on December 17 continued to fight horrific traffic but moved as they could. Company A, 814th Tank Destroyer (TD) Battalion, moving with one of the Battalion's reconnaissance platoons, finally reached Vielsalm at 0100 on December 18. There they refueled and continued on to St. Vith to join the defense. The remainder of the Battalion assembled three miles west of St. Vith.[32]

The arriving 7th AD troops shared Clarke's perception of incredible confusion. On the way to make contact with the 106th ID and 9th AD, Sergeant (SGT) Howard Watson, a tank destroyer reconnaissance section leader, found "abandoned vehicles all along the way but no personnel. The vehicles would run, but no one around. We finally got to a village, which turned out to be a supply depot. There wasn't a living soul in the village. We loaded up with bacon, coffee, hams and canned goods."[33] Watson and his troops shared an eerie parallel experience with their counterparts in Klaus Ritter's 18th VGD antitank crew—that is, they looted US supply points. CPT Wilbur S. East led his armored infantry company into Vielsalm on Sunday, December 17, but then could not move on. Ordered to Rodt, a distance of less than ten miles, East complained, "Every damned vehicle of the 106th seemed to be on the road, together with plenty of vehicles from other outfits. It took us from 1500 on Sunday to 0400 Monday to go from Vielsalm to Rodt."[34]

Threatened with isolation, Hasbrouck focused on stabilizing his northern flank, particularly from Recht southwest to Poteau. Several discrete events helped. First, after leaving Recht, CCR's command post moved to Poteau, where it could better cope with both traffic and the enemy. LTC Warren used his staff to gain control of the traffic problem at Poteau, as he lacked the means to do little else. CCR had too few forces to hold Recht, and none that it could position at Poteau. The 17th TB defended along a ridge straddling the road south of Recht. From there it could engage enemy forces moving from Recht toward Poteau or to the south and prevent them from descending on St. Vith. CCR received help from an unexpected source—the 14th CAV. In less than twenty-four hours, command of the collapsing cavalry group had passed from COL Mark A. Devine to LTC William F. Damon to LTC Paul A. Ridge, who absented himself on December 16. Early on December 18, LTC Augustine D. Dugan, the 14th CAV executive officer who had survived the ambush with Devine and evaded capture, returned to take command of what remained of the 14th CAV. At that point the group had lost nearly half its combat strength. Dugan immediately took on the 14th CAV with energy. In *A Time for Trumpets*, Charles B. MacDonald described Dugan's energy, writing that he "was here, there and everywhere."[35]

The Last Stand of the 14th Cavalry Group

Dugan intended to carry out the last order MG Jones had issued COL Devine: reestablish the Born-Wallerode line. He began by stopping the disorganized retreat of the 14th CAV and turning his units around. His efforts and those of CCR staff proved mutually supportive. Clearing the mess at Poteau enabled Dugan to organize a task force composed of headquarters soldiers and two cavalry troops—one each from the 18th CAV and 32nd CAV. He assigned command to MAJ Walter J. Mayes, the 32nd's operations officer, and directed him to reoccupy Recht. Mayes moved out at 0700 on December 18 in dense fog, heading northeast on the road toward Recht, unaware that Kampfgruppe Hansen's Panzergrenadiers had taken the town hours before. After the skirmish at Recht, the Panzergrenadiers regrouped and were moving slowly down the same road.[36] In the meantime, CCR established its command post in Petit-Thier, west of Poteau.

Mayes's column traveled no more than two hundred yards before Hansen's Panzergrenadiers hit it with Panzerfausts (rocket launchers) and small arms fire. The Germans knocked out the light tank leading the column and several scout cars. The ersatz squadron fled into Poteau, abandoning several scout cars and Jeeps. Dugan and Mayes rallied the survivors and established a hasty defense of the village before the Panzergrenadiers went over on the attack. Dugan positioned light tanks on the ridge north of Poteau, where they raked the Panzergrenadiers with machine gun fire. Other cavalrymen extended the line to the south. Under LTC Dugan's leadership the survivors of the ambush fought effectively against Hansen's regiment-size Kampfgruppe for the rest of the morning.[37]

At one point the Panzergrenadiers broke contact. Dugan or one of his subordinates ordered a combat patrol forward to learn whether Hansen's troops were regrouping to renew the attack. The patrol also sought to discover if any of the enemy combatants were wearing American uniforms. The often embellished story of Otto Skorzeny's troops masquerading as Americans was common knowledge by December 18. Practically every American in the Ardennes believed that Germans, disguised as Americans, were everywhere. With that in mind, SGT John C. Meyers led a patrol of five other soldiers back up the road from Poteau.[38]

At the point where Hansen's Panzergrenadiers ambushed Mayes's task force, Meyers could see a group of soldiers wearing American gear gathered around an M8 scout car. Meyers called out to them, inquiring whether they were Americans. One of them responded affirmatively, so Meyers continued toward them. At twenty yards he recognized these troops were armed with German weapons. Simultaneously, MAJ James W. Farris, watching from the edge of town, yelled, "Look out! They're wearing German boots." The patrol dropped to the ground and exchanged fire with the Germans. One of the cavalry's mortarmen scored a "one-in-a-million" hit, dropping a mortar round in the open turret of the captured M8, ending the firefight and enabling Meyers's patrol to get back to Poteau.[39]

At around noon the SS Panzergrenadiers renewed the assault supported by seventy-five-millimeter Jagdpanzer IV assault guns. In short order the assault guns ended the defense of Poteau. Dugan withdrew the remnant of two cavalry troops to Petit-Thier, a mile west. Only a single light tank, three scout cars, and a Jeep got out. A few cavalrymen escaped on foot. The fight at Poteau effectively completed the destruction of the 14th CAV. The VIII Corps, having already relieved Devine and Ridge, relieved Dugan that afternoon and attached what was left of the Cavalry to 7th AD. Hasbrouck ordered LTC Damon to reorganize the remnants of the 14th CAV into a single squadron to be prepared to return to combat on December 19. Damon did not have much to work with, as the two squadrons suffered 28 percent casualties and lost 35 percent of their equipment. Many of those reported missing turned up later, but without their equipment. Damon proved able to produce nearly a complete cavalry squadron from the remains.[40]

Task Force Navajo

The sad end of the 14th CAV accomplished two important things. First, Dugan's troops extended the fight in the north long enough for CCR's command post to escape to Petit-Thier. More important, the fight at Recht and Poteau delayed Kampfgruppe Hansen and thus the Sixth Panzer Army. The delay afforded time for personal initiative and a bit of serendipity to play a role in the defense of St. Vith. On December 18, LT Joseph V. Whiteman demonstrated the kind of leadership the Army described in its doctrine. Field Manual (FM) 100-5, *Field Service Regulations: Operations*, included a chapter on leadership. The manual intoned, "In spite of the advance of technology, the worth of the individual man is decisive." Soldiers and officers should, according to the manual, "exploit a situation with energy and boldness." Further, the manual asserted that effective leaders should exhibit "will power, self-confidence and disregard of self."[41]

It is unlikely that Joe Whiteman ever read FM 100-5, but he and many other young officers and soldiers behaved as though they had not only read the manual but taken it to heart. One of eleven siblings, Whiteman was born in New Mexico, literally across the road from the Navajo Nation reservation. He supposedly worked his way through college selling Navajo blankets; it was a story that earned him the sobriquet Navajo. Whiteman was well known in the 7th AD. Assigned as executive officer of B Company, 23rd AIB, he was the acting battalion motor officer when the 7th AD moved south. Leading the trail party and recovering broken-down vehicles, Navajo went through Vielsalm and reached Petit-Thier after dark on December 17. There the traffic snarl ended the march.[42]

The next morning, as Whiteman prepared to get his group underway, he noticed "all hell break loose up the valley toward Poteau." He could see tracers and hear gunfire from the ambush of Task Force Mayes. He decided, "If Jerry was going to be stopped, he'd have to be stopped some place, and it might as well be right there." In addition to maintenance vehicles, Whiteman had a seventy-five-millimeter antitank gun mounted on a half-track and two machine gun squads with a half-track each. He positioned his antitank gun where it could fire up the road supported by his two machine gun squads.[43]

Looking for help, Navajo encountered a lieutenant from the 31st TB who had with him three or four Sherman tanks and two 105-millimeter assault guns. Whiteman asked for help. The lieutenant agreed and moved his tanks to support the roadblock. LTC James G. Dubuisson, commanding the 434th Armored Field Artillery Battalion (AFA), met Whiteman at about 0900. Dubuisson supported Whitman's action. Apparently Navajo was as good at selling admission to a fight as he was at selling blankets. He stopped a small convoy of six trucks coming through Petit-Thier. The convoy, led by a lieutenant, was carrying eighty-four infantrymen from the 424th INF. That worthy told Navajo that he was "out of ammunition, out of chow and out of orders." Whiteman gave him and his troops all three, and the infantrymen joined the defense. At 1000 hours, thanks to Dubuisson, forward observers from all three of the Division's artillery battalions arrived. Whiteman put them to work building fire plans to support the defense.[44]

At 1030 one of the artillery forward observers passed a message from BG Hasbrouck, received on the artillery radio net, confirming Navajo in command of the defense at Petit-Thier. By nightfall what began with a handful of half-tracks had grown to about six hundred troops from ten different units supported by seven M36 ninety-millimeter tank destroyers from the 814th TD and as many as nine tanks and assault guns. Late that day C Company, 33rd Engineers (ENG) joined, so command passed to CPT Edgar J. Albrick until he was wounded on December 20.[45]

Late Arrivals

Peiper's intervention at Malmedy forced the 7th AD's artillery, part of the 814th TD, the 203rd Anti-Aircraft Artillery (AAA), and several logistics units to alter course and travel on the western route. Most of these units managed to get through Stavelot but eventually could get no farther. Stopped by the enormous traffic jam, the column spent the night stretched along the road as far back as Stavelot. The 203rd AAA attached to the 7th AD formed the trail unit. The troops spent the night doing their best to stay warm, but were on the move again before first light.[46]

Peiper's spearhead had halted for the night on a ridge overlooking Stavelot. When the 7th AD column began to move, Peiper's troops took it under fire with at least one eighty-eight-millimeter cannon, machine guns, and mortar fire. CPT Henry A. Eaton ordered his D Battery, 203rd AAA into action. Eaton deployed his half-track mounted automatic weapons teams to cover the artillery. Firing all out with a combination of quadruple-mounted .50-caliber machine guns and thirty-seven-millimeter cannon, D Battery kept Peiper's troops at bay long enough for the artillery to escape to the south.[47]

Eaton's problems did not end when the artillery moved south, as he was caught on the north side of a railway overpass the Germans were shelling. He believed they were trying to trap him north of the railway, so he kept the fire up while turning the Battery around one vehicle at time. Finally Eaton broke contact and headed back north to find a way around the advancing Germans. D Battery found its way to the Division the next day. CPT Eaton lost a single half-track and had a few wounded, but he denied Peiper's troops another massacre.[48] The Division's three battalions of self-propelled howitzers closed into the sector by noon on December 18. By midday Hasbrouck had his entire Division and was employing it to build the defense of St. Vith.

Forward of St. Vith

On the Prümerberg, LTC Rigg's main line of resistance had grown thanks to Clarke sending 7th AD troops east as they became available. At dawn on December 18, in addition to Rigg's task force, Clarke had the bulk of the 87th

CAV; LTC William H. G. Fuller's 38th AIB, with two of its companies and one from the 23rd AIB; and A Company, 31st TB in the line. The remainder of the 31st TB, commanded by LTC Robert C. Erlenbusch, and the remainder of LTC Robert L. Rhea's 23rd AIB occupied high ground west of St. Vith from which they could counterattack or plug holes as necessary.[49]

At sunrise BG Hoge's CCB, 9th AD defended west of the Our River but was yet not in physical contact with Clarke's troops. Hoge retained the bulk of his tanks and armored infantry in reserve to use in counterattacks. The bridge at Steinebrück remained intact, but Hoge's troops defended the near side of the bridge and rigged it for demolition. COL Reid's 424th INF defended on Hoge's right, with their main line of resistance east of Burg-Reuland, Belgium.[50]

Reid focused his efforts on holding open the road through Burg-Reuland to afford CCB, 9th AD the means to counterattack to relieve the two regiments

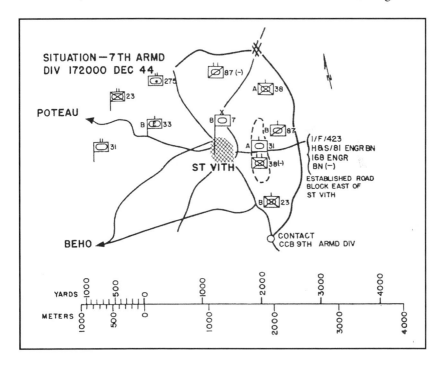

MAP 8. Combat Command B, 7th AD has established the defense of east of St. Vith with the rest of the Division closing. The defense is not yet coherent. Combat Command B, 9th Armored Division defended on the right in contact with the 424th Infantry Regiment on its right. Reproduced from the US Army Armor School publication *The Battle at St. Vith.*

on the Schnee Eifel. Reid's direct support artillery battalion, the 591st, remained available to him. He still had no clear idea of what had become of COL Nelson's 112th INF. Reid's 2nd Battalion had adopted a company of the 112th that had been driven north. During the day Reid sent patrols both north and south to make contact with his counterparts. He made tenuous contact with CCB, 9th AD that morning and with the 112th at 1800 hours.[51]

During the first two days of fighting Nelson's troops did more than hold their own. However, by the afternoon of December 17 enemy penetrations had deprived Nelson of contact with either of the units on his flank. The regiment had also suffered penetrations of its sector. The Germans, in fact, had reached the Our, and were literally across the river from his command post. At 1600 hours Nelson sent his executive officer, LTC William F. Train, to the 28th ID command post located at Wiltz to brief the commanding general on the deteriorating situation. Train met with MG Norman D. (Dutch) Cota, who gave Train a shot of whiskey and told him that he had already ordered Nelson to withdraw the regiment west of the Our. Train returned in time to support the withdrawal of the regiment and the regimental command post. At one point Train shouldered a bazooka and, supported by a soldier to load for him, prepared to defend the command post personally.[52] COL Nelson observed, "So close was the enemy, that when a radio operator walked out of the door of the CP [command post] he was 'burp-gunned' and killed."[53] Nelson and his headquarters troops barely got out.

The 112th spent much of December 18 reorganizing their defense around the town of Weiswampach, Luxembourg, oriented south and east. The regiment's direct support artillery broke up several desultory attacks that morning. In the afternoon, however, a more serious threat developed. The forward observers operating from the top of the 112th's command post building called LTC Train upstairs, where, he later recalled, they "directed my attention to the BC [battery commander's] scope. As far as I could see along the Luxembourg Ridge road, there were German tanks appearing bumper to bumper." A tank destroyer from the attached 630th TD disabled two of the tanks, at which point the German tank column turned around and went back in the direction they had come.[54]

These tanks probably belonged to the 116th PZ. The road they had been on led northwest rather than west, so it is possible the German armor simply took a wrong turn. Whatever the Germans meant to do, the tank destroyer crew let them know that moving perpendicular to a well-positioned antitank gun was a bad idea. South of Weiswampach these same tanks or others from the 116th PZ attacked E Company, 2nd Battalion, 112th INF. F Company, extending the 2nd Battalion's line to the Our River, fought off enemy infantrymen from the 560th VGD. At 1500, the 28th ID ordered Nelson's 112th to withdraw yet again, this time southwest toward Troisvierges, Luxembourg. From there Cota wanted Nelson to fight a delaying action toward Bastogne. Nelson knew German armor had bypassed him heading west. He estimated there were as many as three Panzer divisions moving in that direction. With only towed tank destroyers and howitzers, he concluded that "to fall back on it [Troisvierges] would have been suicide."[55] Instead he reported to Cota that the regiment would move early on December 19, bypass Troisvierges to the north, and attempt to get ahead of the German advance.[56]

On the Schnee Eifel, COL George L. Descheneaux Jr. of the 422nd INF and COL Charles C. Cavender of the 423rd INF continued to demonstrate their inexperience. Both were good men thrust too soon into a desperate situation. They knew the positions they had been required to occupy were dangerously exposed, but LTG Hodges insisted the salient in the Siegfried Line must be held. Middleton demurred, but to no avail. When Jones expressed his concern to MG Walter M. Robertson, his predecessor in the line, Robertson asserted, "Take it easy, General. The Krauts won't attack even if they were ordered to."[57] In turn, when Descheneaux complained, Jones told him they had to hold. Descheneaux told his staff, "There'll be no retreating for the 422nd."[58] At an VIII Corps intelligence conference just before the assault Jones mentioned to Middleton that his troops heard "heavy armored movement." One of Middleton's staff officers advised, "Don't be so jumpy. The Krauts are just playing phonograph records to scare you newcomers."[59]

The bill for inexperience in the new men combined with the hubris among the old-timers, and their insistence on holding ground regardless of the situation, would soon come due. Cavender, Descheneaux, and Jones ran up the bill by not insisting that their views be heard. Their predecessors who commanded regiments in the 2nd ID helped create the debt, as did Bradley at the 12th Army Group, Hodges at First Army, and Middleton at VIII Corps. Now the troops in the Schnee Eifel would pay.

After the 18th VGD encircled the two regiments and cut their telephone cables, neither could communicate effectively with the rest of the 106th ID or each other. The Germans jammed their radio frequencies so effectively that the 422nd and 423rd had only sporadic contact on the Division command net or Division artillery net. Assured that help was on the way, the two regiments remained passive. Just after midnight on the morning of December

18, Cavender passed on to Descheneaux the twelve-hour-old message ordering the two regiments to retire west of the Our River. Since both had radioed they could hold if resupplied by air, they "agreed to disregard this now superannuated order."[60]

At 0730 Cavender received an order from the 106th ordering the two regiments to mount an attack on "Panzer Reg[imen]t[a]l CT [combat team] on the Schönberg–St. Vith road." The order promised an airdrop of supplies and further required the two regiments to "move to St. Vith–Wallerode–Wepler. Organize and move west."[61] Descheneaux received the message about a half hour later, to which he remarked, "My poor men—they'll be cut to pieces."[62] The effort constituted a forlorn hope. With very little planning between them other than deciding they would advance abreast, the two regiments started west at 1000 hours, more or less together. Cavender's 2nd Battalion, 423rd INF encountered Germans just east of Bleialf and began driving them to the west. But in the midst of this burgeoning success Jones ordered Cavender to orient northward on Schönberg. By the end of the short winter day, confusion and the enemy overcame the poorly coordinated attack. Cavender sought to set his regiment up to attack Schönberg from the southeast, but neither regiment did little else the night of December 18.[63]

Combat Command A Attacks at Poteau

At sunup on December 18, COL Dwight A. Rosebaum's CCA occupied an assembly area near Beho, about 7 miles south west of St. Vith and five miles south of Poteau, ready to move on thirty minutes' notice. Rosebaum had two battalions organized as combined arms task forces. As ordered, the night before the attack Rosebaum drove from Beho to meet Hasbrouck in St. Vith. To get there Rosebaum drove via Vielsalm, Poteau, and Recht in a big loop, passing through Poteau just before the Germans attacked. Traffic remained difficult, so it was 0830 before he reached St. Vith, where he learned that Hasbrouck had gone to Vielsalm. Rosebaum then made his way to Vielsalm via yet another looping route, this time to the south. On arriving, he and Hasbrouck considered how to employ CCA. With the attack on Poteau, the answer seemed obvious to both. Hasbrouck ordered Rosebaum to take Poteau. They agreed also to leave D Company, 40th TB's Stuart tanks and A Company, 33rd ENG in Beho as the division reserve.[64]

At 1010, CCA moved out organized to fight a meeting engagement. According to FM 17-33, *The Armored Battalion, Light and Medium*, meeting engagements may occur when the "situation is obscure." FM 17-42, *The Armored*

Infantry Battalion, asserted "A meeting engagement is an unexpected meeting of hostile forces, neither being fully disposed for combat."[65] CCA duly organized to fight a meeting engagement. LTC John C. Brown of the 40th TB led the advance guard, composed of his C Company and C Company of the AIB. Rosebaum and a small command group followed the advance guard with the remainder of the 40th TB behind them; LTC Richard D. Chappuis's 48th AIB brought up the rear. CCA moved northward from Beho through St. Vith, where it took mortar fire, through Rodt, and on to Poteau.[66]

CPT Roy "Big Moose" Nelson commanded C Company, with LT Gerald E. Reeves's 1st platoon leading the way. SGT Truman Luther Van Tine led the platoon in his tank. Tanks commanded by SGT Milan K. Alpeter, LT Reeves, and LT Gayle H. Spencer followed. Van Tine, who worked well with his tank crew, often reminded them at the end of a day, "See, we made it through another one. It wasn't that bad was it? We're one day closer to the end."[67] The road to Poteau was lined with trees and thus subject to ambush. At about 1300 hours Van Tine cleared a tree line less than a thousand yards from Poteau. Ahead the tankers could see the remains of the cavalry's equipment destroyed earlier, along with eight abandoned American eight-inch howitzers. Van Tine also understood very well that a clearing is a great place to get killed, so he and his wingman, SGT Alpeter, sprinted their tanks across it. Although fired on by assault guns, both managed to reach the edge of the village. Rosebaum came forward to see the situation for himself while Brown deployed his tanks and dismounted his armored infantry.[68]

Poteau was a tiny village of five houses at the intersection of the road from Recht that went on west to Petit-Thier. Three more houses were located two hundred yards south, at the bend in the road from Rodt that intersected with a farm road running south. A deep railway cut that ran east to west ruled out maneuvering mounted. LTC Brown crossed the clearing and brought up the infantry from C Company, 48th AIB to join the developing hasty attack. As Reeves's tanks and the infantry moved into town they continued to take fire from both the village and a hill to the north. German artillery joined in damaging Rosebaum's command half-track. Nevertheless, the hasty attack made headway. LT Spencer, traveling with 1st Platoon, and SGT Van Tine led the way into Poteau. As they came into town, a Panzergrenadier launched a Panzerfaust at Van Tine's tank, but missed. Van Tine clambered out of the turret to man his .50-caliber machine gun. When he did, a German shot him in the head. His gunner, Corporal (CPL) Gerald Nelson, effectively suppressed the enemy when he "put a round in each of three buildings."[69]

The infantry followed the tanks in and got a toehold in the first house by 1320. The "doughs," as the tankers called the infantry, cleared two more houses that enabled them to control the southern road junction and fire into Poteau proper.[70] Van Tine's crew withdrew to evacuate their fatally wounded tank commander, leaving LT Spencer in a "tight spot" until LT Reeves and SGT Alpeter could join him. But CCA held only the edge of the town, and that just barely. CPT "Big Moose" Nelson forced several more tanks into town but could not overwhelm the defenders. At 1600 hours, Hasbrouck sent a terse message to Rosebaum: "Imperative you seize POTEAU and hold it!" CCA renewed the attack after dark. Van Tine's tank crew returned. CPL Nelson avenged his tank commander's death by destroying three enemy tanks. The infantry renewed their attack, illuminated by burning German tanks and "cleared out the enemy, house by house." The Germans "did not surrender, nor did they run—they stayed and fought it out until they were killed or blown up."[71]

LTC Chappuis's A Company, 48th AIB cleared the woods east of the town while his C Company cleared the road to the west of it. Fighting at Poteau died down during the evening but never stopped altogether. Neither side could force the other out of direct fire range of the intersection. Rosebaum brought up more troops, enabling him to control the main intersection and the ground east and west of the town south of the railway embankment. For the time being, at least, CCA held the better hand. During the course of the evening Rosebaum stabilized his position and prepared to clear the ground north of Poteau on December 19.

At St. Vith, Clarke reported that he and Hoge would "concentrate." Clarke reported "no news of Reg[imen]ts fighting way back will make plans for delaying positions." To this Hasbrouck responded, "Reference delaying action decision as to necessity yours as to time mine." He amplified his guidance by saying, "Corps desire[s] we hold if possible."[72] Lastly, Hasbrouck ordered Rosebaum to prepare two contingency plans. First he wanted a plan to attack Recht joined by the 17th TB, and then a second plan "to withdraw via Petit Thier–Vielsalm to Pos[itio]n W. of River LOURTHE.[73]

Securing the Southern Flank

LTC Robert O. Stone commanded the 440th AAA (Automatic Weapons). Equipped with a combination of quadruple-mounted .50-caliber machine guns and forty-millimeter antiaircraft cannons, the 440th had been positioned in the Losheim Gap to shoot at V-1 buzz bombs. Withdrawn from the gap and attached to the 106th ID, the antiaircraft batteries were parceled out to support the remnants of the 106th ID, the 275th AFA, and arriving artillery from the 7th AD. On December 18 Stone led this head-quarters battery through Gouvy toward the railhead at the Gouvy station. At 1300 the column stopped near the rail yard, where Stone waited for his re-connaissance party to show him and his troops where to establish the battal-ion command post. Three German Panther tanks, probably from the 116th PZ, came through Gouvy, shooting up the town and Stone's column. They set some vehicles afire and shot up a ration dump, then turned on their heels and left. A burning air compressor truck that blocked the road may be all that saved Stone's troops from worse.[74]

Stone was furious. He took command of the situation and acted contrary to his orders, saying, "By God, others may run but I'm staying here and will hold at all cost!"[75] The railway station, the rations dump, and the crossroads had obvious value. Stone's "command" included the 89th Quartermaster Railhead Company; the 92nd Ordnance Company (sixty-five troops); six light tanks and the mortar platoon of the 40th TB; C Battery, 965th Field Ar-tillery Battalion (with towed 155-millimeter howitzers); his own headquar-ters battery; and stragglers from the 110th INF, 112th INF, and 106th ID. The tanks belonging to D Company, 40th TB were M5 Stuart light tanks com-manded by CPT Walter J. Hughes. Hughes had platoons on outpost in the nearby villages of Ourthe and Deiffelt. LTC Stone, like Navajo Whiteman, was creating order from chaos and providing Hasbrouck with at least a sem-blance of a flank.[76]

On December 18, General Hasbrouck and his troops began to restore or-der in and around St. Vith. They established a coherent if tenuous defense. Their line took the shape of a horseshoe, albeit one with gaps. In the nar-rative written to accompany the packet for a Distinguished Unit Citation, MAJ Donald P. Boyer Jr. described what the Division achieved that day: "By midnight of the 18th/19th the 7th AD found itself covering almost 52 miles of front," or nearly as wide a sector as VIII Corps had on December 16. The line extended east from Poteau and then in an arc to a point a mile east of St. Vith. Then it curved south and then west through the positions held by CCB, 9th AD and the 106th ID's 424th Infantry. From the 424th's right rear a gap of several miles existed, with two companies at Beho and a few roadblocks manned by the 7th AD trains.[77] The 7th AD's cobbled-together positions stuck like a bone in the throat of Model's Army Group B.

NOTES

1. Michael Reynolds, *The Devil's Adjutant*, 112–13. Reynolds argues that Hansen had an open road, if only he had been allowed to use it. Michael Reynolds, *Sons of the Reich*, 192, asserts that Kampfgruppe Hansen reached Recht at "last light" on December 17. CCR, 7th AD passed through Recht at 1500 and the command post set up in the village without interference until after midnight. Hansen did not reach Recht on December 17. See also Lieutenant Jack T. Shea, "Fourteenth Cavalry Group," 29.

2. 17th Tank Battalion, "After Action Report, Month of December 1944," 8. The report claims that C Company moved into the town at 0100 in response to reports of German movement. Combat interviews suggest that C Company moved in at dusk; see W. Wesley Johnston, *17th Tank Battalion, 7th Armored Division*, 64–65.

3. 17th Tank Battalion, "After Action Report, Month of December 1944," 8–9. On general confusion on timelines, see Johnston, *17th Tank Battalion, 7th Armored Division*, 65. See also Charles B. MacDonald, *A Time for Trumpets*, 333. MacDonald argues that the fighting began at 0200 and lasted for about forty-five minutes.

4. MacDonald claims that LTC Warren ordered C Company out of town, but there is no documented evidence contemporary to the time that supports that conclusion. The combat interviews do not clarify times and who ordered what and when. The best account is that of LT Irving Goodman, C Company, in Johnston, *17th Tank Battalion, 7th Armored Division*, 65–66; the unit after action report for December is also bound with the combat interviews, 109–25. Times cited in the after action report do not match those in any of the interviews. In 7th Armored Division, G-2 journal, CCR is cites as reporting the contact at 0245. That time is generally consistent with the combat interviews. The entry specifically says that the Germans did not use mortars. After action reports were written from daily journals, and recollections; Major General Robert W. Hasbrouck (Ret.), in an interview with the author, Washington, DC, August 20, 1984, urged the author not to rely on them. They are, however, far less likely to reflect poor or negotiated memory years after the fact. The confusion in the reports and interviews is a reflection of the conditions of battle.

5. See Martin van Creveld, *Fighting Power; and* Trevor N. Dupuy, *A Genius for War*. Both van Creveld and Dupuy, especially, focused on combat operations during which the Germans had the advantage of defending. The comparison of casualties stemming from examining Germans defending is less than compelling. There is insufficient effort to examine context or US operations versus those of the US allies. Their analysis has merit, but their conclusions overreach. Karl Heinz Frieser with John T. Greenwood, *The Blitzkrieg Legend*, and Gerhard P. Gross, *The Myth and Reality of German Warfare*, offer ample reason to doubt the overarching myth of German operational brilliance and tactical excellence.

6. Major Percy Ernst Schramm, "The Course of Events of the German Offensive in the Ardennes," 3.

7. Generaloberst Alfred Jodl, "An Interview with Genobst Alfred Jodl: 'Planning the Ardennes Offensive,'" ETHINT-50.

8. Generalfeldmarschall Gerd von Rundstedt, "An Interview with Genfldm Gerd von Rundstedt," ETHINT-47, 11.

9. General der Panzertruppe Hasso von Manteuffel, "An Interview with Gen Pz Hasso von Manteuffel," ETHINT-45, 14. The German Army had robust electronic warfare capabilities, including both jamming and radio intercept. Manteuffel and others have commented on tracking US movement by intercepting military police and movement control networks. See Albert Praun, "German Radio Intelligence," 141. Praun ended the war as a general der Nachrichttruppen (Signal Corps) in command of all radio troops of the German Army and Armed Forces. During the battle in the Ardennes the Germans claimed "all established rules were violated" by First Army military police.

10. General der Panzertruppe Hasso von Manteuffel, "Fifth Panzer Army (Ardennes Offensive Preparations)," 140.

11. Jean-Paul Pallud, *Battle of the Bulge: Then and Now*, 34–35. To reach the battle Remer's brigade had to travel from Prüm to Bleialf and then Schönberg—no easy feat given the congestion produced by the supporting formations and artillery on the road on December 18.

12. Oberstleutnant Dietrich Moll, "18th Volks Grenadier Division," 41.

13. Heinz Günther Guderian, *From Normandy to the Ruhr*, 309.

14. Guderian, *From Normandy to the Ruhr*, 310.

15. Dwight D. Eisenhower, *Crusade in Europe*, 348. See also Stephen E. Ambrose, *The Supreme Commander*, 558–59. Eisenhower believed denying the Germans access to US fuel depots essential to winning the defensive phase of the battle. Thus, holding the east of the Meuse was, as Ambrose, 559, puts it, "the *sine qua non* of Eisenhower's plan." James M. Gavin, in *On to Berlin*, expresses strong but well-supported opinions. MG Matthew D. Ridgway, who commanded XVIII Airborne Corps, was in England with his main command post training the 17th ABN. Gavin had the forward command post when the Corps moved. See Matthew B. Ridgway, *Soldier: The Memoirs of Matthew B. Ridgway*, 112. Ridgway flew to the Continent at dawn on December 18.

16. Harry C. Butcher, *My Three Years with Eisenhower*, 723.

17. Chester B. Hansen, diary, entry for December 18, 1944, 1.

18. Major William C. Sylvan and Captain Francis G. Smith Jr., *Normandy to Victory*, 220.

19. David W. Hogan Jr., *A Command Post at War*, 212. Hogan's work is well done. Much of what happened at First Army headquarters in the early days of the offensive is in dispute. Hogan lays out the argument on both sides, but leaves it to the reader to decide. Sylvan, Hodges's diarist and aide-de-camp, says nothing about his general's conduct but it is clear Hodges was barely able to function.

20. Convoy statistics appear in the annexes in First US Army, "After Action Report: 1–31 December 1944."

21. Harold R. Winton, *Corps Commanders of the Bulge*, 153; the section appears in chap. 7, "VIII Corps Slows the Flood." See also Jerry D. Morelock, *Generals of the Bulge*, 161–71.

22. Major General Robert W. Hasbrouck (Ret.), interview with the author, Washington, DC, August 20, 1984.

23. General William M. Hoge, *Engineer Memoirs*, 135.

24. Clarke's performance as commander of CCB, 4th AD and CCB, 7th AD earned him a premier place in the pantheon of US tank commanders in World War II. Frankly, he worked hard the rest of his life to burnish that well-earned reputation, arguably at Hasbrouck's expense, but he faithfully claimed in the written and spoken word that he worked for Hasbrouck. Brigadier General Bruce C. Clarke, "The Hour by Hour Journal of Activities, Conferences and Direction of Brigadier General Bruce C. Clarke and C. C. 'B.' 7th Armored Division," General Bruce C. Clarke Papers. Clarke sent many versions of this memorandum to many people over the years, and I am in possession of several different copies. The version cited here was attached to a letter from Clarke to MG Ronald L. Watts, May 28, 1986. I was the plans officer for Watts's 1st Infantry Division (Mechanized), and Watts passed the memorandum on to me.

25. 7th Armored Division, "Battle of St. Vith: 17–23 December," 3.

26. US War Department, *Armored Command Field Manual: The Armored Division*, FM 17-100, 76.

27. Hasbrouck interview, August 20, 1984; Morelock, *Generals of the Bulge*, 183; Hoge, *Engineer Memoirs*, 104–29.

28. Hoge, *Engineer Memoirs*, 106.

29. Hasbrouck interview, August 20, 1984.

30. Morelock, *Generals of the Bulge*, 188. In fact, Clarke did not serve in the 7th AD with Silvester. Clarke replaced Hasbrouck at CCB in November when Hasbrouck took command of the Division. Clarke's view is an ex post facto assessment reflecting attitudes in the division.

31. In multiple postcombat and later postwar interviews, Clarke and Hasbrouck, in particular, are on record claiming that infantrymen, including Hodges and Ridgeway, did not understand how to use armor and wanted to hold on to ground unnecessarily.

32. 814th Tank Destroyer Battalion, "After Action Report December 1944," 1. See also Calvin C. Boykin Jr., *Gare la Bête*, 73–74.

33. Boykin, *Gare la Bête*, 73.

34. W. Wesley Johnston, *Combat Interviews of the 38th Armored Infantry Battalion*. 15.

35. MacDonald, *A Time for Trumpets*, 333; Donald P. Boyer Jr., *St. Vith: The 7th Armored Division in the Battle of the Bulge*, 15. The record is not definitive on whether Warren was in command at this point. COL Ryan, the assigned commander, replaced COL Matthews as chief of staff of the Division, but just when is uncertain. The author believes Warren was again acting commander of CCR at daybreak on December 18. See also Lieutenant Jack T. Shea, "Fourteenth Cavalry Group." The three command changes stemmed from confusion caused by a Corps order requiring the 14th CAV group commander to report to Bastogne. Apparently, Middleton wanted

Devine to report to Bastogne so he could relieve him. Since Devine had passed command to Damon, that officer headed off to Bastogne. Ridge then assumed command until Dugan turned up. Both Ridge and Devine were relieved of their respective command of the 32nd CAV and the 14th CAV Group. There is some confusion in the accounts as to when Ridge left. LT Shea's narrative suggests Ridge did not leave until the afternoon of December 17. Whether he remained or not, Dugan was running the remnants of the group.

36. Shea, "Fourteenth Cavalry Group," 32–35.

37. Shea, "Fourteenth Cavalry Group," 32–35. The Panzergrenadiers obliterated the lead unit of Mayes's small task force. It is hard to nail down exactly what Mayes's losses were, but they included a half dozen scout cars, several Jeeps, and a light tank. German cinematographers, accompanied and supported by still photographers, filmed the detritus of the aftermath and staged some scenes to suggest they were filming actual combat. The best account of that effort is in Pallud, *Battle of the Bulge: Then and Now*, 208–23.

38. Shea, "Fourteenth CAV," 35.

39. Shea, "Fourteenth Cavalry Group," 35.

40. Shea, "Fourteenth Cavalry Group," 36–39.

41. US War Department, *Field Service Regulations:* Operations, FM 100-5, 18–19.

42. W. Wesley Johnston, *Combat Interviews of the 23rd Armored Infantry Battalion*, 83. See also MacDonald, *A Time for Trumpets*, 335. Family information is drawn from the 1940 US census.

43. Johnston, *Combat Interviews of the 23rd Armored Infantry Battalion*, 84.

44. Johnston, *Combat Interviews of the 23rd Armored Infantry Battalion*, 84.

45. Johnston, *Combat Interviews of the 23rd Armored Infantry Battalion*, 85. Albrick is mistakenly identified as Albright in several sources, including both Boyer and MacDonald. Johnston, working with the US 7th Armored Division Association, has corrected the record.

46. The conditions on the march were miserable. Cold, icy roads, as well as rumor and ambiguity, combined to make it truly awful. The best account of the road march is Boykin, *Gare la Bête*, 71–72.

47. Boyer, *St. Vith: The 7th Armored Division in the Battle of the Bulge*, 23. See also 203rd Anti-Aircraft Artillery Battalion, *203 AAA*, 26; this is small bound pamphlet-size unit history published at the end of the war. The battalion after action review for December 1944 is two pages long and of little use; it makes no mention of D Battery's fight at Stavelot. D battery fielded M15 and M16 antiaircraft tracks. The M15 had a single thirty-seven-millimeter cannon and a coaxially mounted .50-caliber machine gun. The M16 had quadruple mounted .50-caliber machine guns. D Battery had impressive automatic weapons capability.

48. Captain Henry A. Eaton, "Interview with Captain Henry A. Eaton, 203rd AAA."

49. US Army Armor School, *The Battle at St. Vith Belgium*, 10.

50. Boyer, *St. Vith: The 7th Armored Division in the Battle of the Bulge*, 14. See also Colonel Ernest R. Dupuy, *St. Vith: Lion in the Way*, 115–21.

51. Dupuy, *St. Vith: Lion in the Way*, 119–20.

52. Lieutenant General William F. Train, "My Memories of the Battle of the Bulge."

53. Combat Interview, Colonel Gustin M. Nelson and Major Justin C. Brainard, interviewer not identified, January 14, 1945, 3.

54. Train, "My Memories," 11. See also Nelson and Brainard interview, 6.

55. Lt Col Joseph L. Macsalka, Captain William G. McLaughlin, 1st Lt Walton Fitch, 2d Lt Edwin B. Cline, and S/SGT Owen A. Paul, interviewer not identified, January 22, 1945. See also Col. Gustin M. Nelson to his father, May 1945, box 3, Charles B. MacDonald Papers.

56. MacDonald, *A Time for Trumpets*, 268.

57. Charles Whiting, *Ghost Front*, 190.

58. Charles Whiting, *Decision at St. Vith*, 7.

59. Whiting, *Decision at St. Vith*, 11.

60. Dupuy, *St. Vith: Lion in the Way*, 121.

61. Hugh M. Cole, *The Ardennes: Battle of the Bulge*, 166.

62. Dupuy, *St. Vith: Lion in the Way*, 121.

63. Cole, *The Ardennes: Battle of the Bulge*, 167–68.

64. Combat Command A, 7th Armored Division, "After Action Report, December 1944," 8; W. Wesley Johnston, *Combat Interviews of the 7th Armored Division Combat Commands*, 11–12, interview of COL Dwight A. Rosebaum. I have inferred the return route. To get to Vielsalm without going through Poteau, the logical route is St. Vith back to Beho and then north through the village of Commanster to Vielsalm.

65. US War Department, *Armored Force Field Manual: The Armored Battalion, Light and Medium*, FM 17-33, 81. See also US War Department, *Armored Infantry Battalion*, FM 17-42, 71.

66. Combat Command A, "After Action Report, December 1944," 8.

67. George J. Winter, "The Capture of Poteau."

68. Winter, "The Capture of Poteau," 6.

69. Winter, "The Capture of Poteau," 7.

70. 7th Armored Division, G-3 journal, December 1944, entry 52. See also W. Wesley Johnston, *Combat Interviews of the 48th Armored Infantry Battalion*, 54–59, interview of LT Richard T. Johnson and SGT Keith G. Brock.

71. Winter, "The Capture of Poteau," 8–10. See also Boyer, *St. Vith: The 7th Armored Division in the Battle of the Bulge*, 19.

72. 7th Armored Division, G-3 journal, December 1944, entries 82 and 90.

73. 7th Armored Division, G-3 journal, December 1944, entry 91.

74. Cole, *The Ardennes: Battle of the Bulge*, 286–87. See also George C. Meyer, *Mud, Dust, and Five Stars*, 22–23. There is some confusion on the date of this contact. Boyer, *St. Vith: The 7th Armored Division in the Battle of the Bulge*, claims that D Company, 40th TB arrived on December 19 and fought off an infantry attack. Most sources report D Company arriving on December 18. Either way, D Company formed part of Task Force Stone.

75. 7th Armored Division, "Battle of St. Vith: 17–23 December," 8.

76. 440th Anti-Aircraft Artillery Battalion, "After Action Report, December 1944," 5–6. See also George C. Meyer, *Mud, Dust, and Five Stars*; and Cole, *The Ardennes: Battle of the Bulge*, 286–87.

77. Boyer, *St. Vith: The 7th Armored Division in the Battle of the Bulge*, 23b.

CHAPTER SEVEN

Stand at St. Vith

You are doing a grand job. Hold your positions and we will do the same.

—Major General Troy H. Middleton to Brigadier General Robert W. Hasbrouck, December 19, 1944

You didn't know when the crisis that was out there all around three sides of the area that 7th Armored was clinging to would come home to you as an individual.

—Major Carl McArn Corbin

Brigadier general (bg) Robert W. Hasbrouck earned Chester Wilmot's accolade as "one of the great men of the Ardennes."[1] If nothing else, he deserved it for his ability to make effective decisions on the basis of little information. Hasbrouck's level of tolerance for ambiguity is one for the record books. He issued clear orders, underwrote initiative where he found it, and reacted rapidly but never lost sight of his obligation to plan ahead. Most of his subordinates also showed amazing tolerance for ambiguity and had the courage to act as they thought best in the absence of orders or with little more than clearly expressed intention. Seven decades later most of us are decidedly less tolerant of ambiguity. There is little necessity to accept not knowing where we are or having to decide on the basis of sketchy information. Nevertheless, it is as difficult now to penetrate the "fog of war" that obtained in 1944. Judgment about what happened is required.

After two horrendously difficult days, the night of December 18–19 passed comparatively quietly in St. Vith and on the Schnee Eifel. Hasbrouck's makeshift defense held up. The fact that German units were passing westward both north and south of St. Vith required Hasbrouck to defend in depth with too few resources. Accordingly, roadblocks manned often by no more than a platoon accounted for much of the 7th Armored Division's "defense." The 7th Armored Division (AD) trains, including maintenance medical and supply units, manned roadblocks as far west as Samrée and La Roche-en-Ardenne. The trains' position illustrates just how tenuous the situation remained in Hasbrouck's "horseshoe." On December 18 Colonel (COL) Andrew J. Adams, who commanded the trains, established twelve roadblocks in order to secure the Division's rear area. Located more than ten miles west of St. Vith and about fifteen miles north of Bastogne, the trains were farther back than desirable but could not safely be established nearer to the front. That first day, Adams's troops managed to clear the roads of retreating Americans, establish their supply points, and fight off a reconnaissance patrol from an advancing German unit.[2]

During the night of December 18–19 Hasbrouck's units patrolled actively and remained on high alert, both at his behest and as a consequence of their own fears. Negative reports from patrols and units on the line characterized the early evening hours of December 18. Yet at 2140 hours the 87th Cavalry Reconnaissance Squadron (CAV) reported a "T[an]k at[tac]k," although the Germans failed to press. The cavalrymen endured some desultory fire from German armor supported by infantry. Subsequently, they could hear tanks moving to their front. For the rest of the night the 87th CAV and 17th Tank Battalion (TB), both subordinated to Combat Command B (CCB), 7th AD, reported enemy activity. The enemy did little more than maneuver, shoot flares, and occasionally fire at the troops on the Prümerberg.[3] At 0525 CCB reported twelve enemy tanks to their front. At 0712 CCB reported, "All quiet except for indications of En[emy] forming along road north east of town."[4] Clearly BG Bruce C. Clarke's CCB could expect an attack sometime after the sun rose at 0840.

The German Estimate of the Situation

On December 19, Generalfeldmarschall Gerd von Rundstedt, never very enthusiastic about the offensive, concluded it could not succeed. He believed the Germans "should abandon the offensive and prepare to defend the area we have gained." He continued with a succinct description of the German position: "Sepp Dietrich's forces are held up between Monschau and Malmedy. St. Vith has not been taken. We have only just reached Bastogne, which ought to have been taken on D plus 1 [December 17, one day after the attack began]."[5] Generalfeldmarschall Walther Model did not agree, as he believed the offensive might still make useful gains. He understood as well as

Rundstedt that the offensive was sputtering. However, General der Panzer-truppe Hasso von Manteuffel's Fifth Panzer Army had broken through the 28th Infantry Division (ID) in the center of the VIII Corps sector. Model believed if he reallocated forces from the Sixth Panzer Army to exploit Man-teuffel's success, much could still be achieved.

During a roadside encounter on the evening of December 18 Model effectively shifted the main effort to Hasso von Manteuffel. If the offensive were to succeed, it would do so only in the Fifth Panzer Army zone of attack. The Sixth Panzer Army had failed to achieve the necessary breakthrough. Obersturmbahnführer Joachim Peiper's column was a thin reed, with the remainder of the 1st Schutzstaffel (SS) Panzer Division (PZ) and the 9th SS PZ stacked up and bumping along the northern flank of Hasbrouck's horse-shoe. North of the 1st SS, the 12th SS PZ, the infamous Hitler Youth Division, operated in difficult terrain and made little progress against stubborn American resistance.[6]

Because General der Artillerie Walther Lucht's LXVI Corps failed to take St. Vith on December 17, it would take a deliberate attack to reduce the defenses. On December 18 Model assigned the Führer Escort Brigade (FEB) to the Fifth Panzer Army for that purpose. In turn, Manteuffel subordinated FEB to LXVI Corps and told Lucht to get on with it and take St. Vith. With the Volksgrenadier Divisions (VGDs) attacking from the east and southeast and the FEB from the north and northeast, Manteuffel believed that LXVI Corps would overwhelm the defenders of St. Vith. The FEB, he felt sure, would make the difference, as he "had the greatest respect for the fighting ability of these men, because most of them came from the Gross Deutsch-land Division which I had once commanded."[7]

Lucht's 18th and 62nd VGDs had closed on St. Vith, but the roads behind them remained clogged with their artillery and logistics units. As a consequence, the FEB struggled to get forward. Moreover, the Corps had to reduce the pocket on the Schnee Eifel. By the morning of December 19 the road network in LXVI Corps had become nearly impassable due to a monstrous traffic jam. The roads north of the Schnee Eifel were jammed as well. Sixth Panzer Army units compounded the problem by using roads not assigned to them. According to Oberstleutnant Dietrich Moll, the 18th VGD's operations officer, "two-way traffic [on the Schönberg road toward St. Vith] was almost impossible."[8] Lucht himself bemoaned the area as "difficult pathless forest country."[9]

Quite apart from traffic management, the burgeoning defense at St. Vith also confounded the Germans. Lieutenant Colonel (LTC) Thomas J. Riggs, using BG Clarke's arriving units, spurned hasty attacks on St. Vith. As the 18th VGD's Moll put it, "Without supporting howitzers, even reconnaissance was without value."[10] Having failed to seize the crossroads at St. Vith à outrance, Lucht would have to assemble forces and organize a set piece attack.

South of LXVI Corps, the Fifth Panzer Army had achieved a breakthrough, albeit too late to prevent the 10th AD from putting in roadblocks east of Bastogne, enabling the 101st Airborne Division (ABN) to occupy Bastogne by the morning of December 19. Although the Fifth Panzer Army achieved some success, it had not broken out in the open and lost the race to Bastogne.

The Allied Estimate of the Situation

By the evening of December 18 General Dwight D. Eisenhower believed that the Allies "had sufficient information of the enemy's strength, intentions, and situation, and of our own capabilities, to lay down a specific plan for our counter action."[11] Not only had Eisenhower not panicked, but he was, as Stephen E. Ambrose points out in *The Supreme Commander*, "the first important Allied general to grasp the full import of the attack, the first to be able to readjust his thinking" and to realize that "Hitler had given the AEF [Allied Expeditionary Force] a magnificent opportunity."[12] To describe his vision for first defeating the Germans and then to exploit their defeat, Eisenhower convened a meeting at Verdun, France, on December 19.

There he met with Lieutenant General (LTG) Omar N. Bradley, 12th Army Group commander; LTG Jacob L. Devers of the 6th Army Group; and LTG George S. Patton Jr. of the Third Army. Eisenhower opined that "the present situation is to be regarded as one of opportunity for us and not a disaster." He confirmed his orders to cease offensive operations for the time being. Holding the line of the Meuse River while preparing a counterattack was the essence of his plan. He radioed British field marshal Bernard Law Montgomery to that effect later in the day, "Our weakest spot is in the direction of Namur. The general plan is to plug the holes in the north and launch co-ordinated attack from the south."[13] The very idea was antithetical to many of his subordinates, but Eisenhower explicitly accepted giving up ground east of the Meuse.

Plugging holes in the north was well underway; First Army reserves, supplemented by Ninth Army, were firming up the northern shoulder. What remained undetermined was how soon Third Army could mount a counterattack from the south. When asked, Patton responded, "On December

22, with three divisions; the 4th Armored, the 26th and the 80th." In his diary Patton reported that some present at the meeting "seemed surprised and others pleased."[14] Eisenhower took him seriously, so the broad outline of the response to the German offensive and the Allied riposte was settled. Although not present to sense the feeling of the meeting, Bernard Montgomery at the 21st Army Group nevertheless had strong feelings about the environment in Bradley's 12th Army Group. In a report to Field Marshal Allan Brooke, the chief of the Imperial General Staff, Montgomery claimed the Americans exhibited "great confusion and all the signs of a full scale withdrawal . . . a definite loss of grip and control."[15]

At First Army the situation seemed improved. The entry in the First Army diary for December 18 began starkly: "The situation is rapidly deteriorating." By contrast, the entry for December 19 was upbeat: the diary reported the arrival of Major General (MG) Matthew B. Ridgway to discuss the employment of his XVIII Corps, wearing his "two customary hand grenades strapped to his shoulder." The diarists wrote also that the "the 7th Arm[ore]d which has joined up with one regiment [the 424th Infantry] of the 106th Div not cut off is doing a magnificent job in holding firm at St. Vith against tremendous pressure." The rest of the notes for the day record the arrival of reinforcements, the stiffening of the northern shoulder, and the notice of Third Army's counterattack. In VIII Corps, however, the situation remained "extremely fluid."[16]

MG Troy H. Middleton at VIII Corps would have agreed with this assessment. The Fifth Panzer Army had penetrated the 28th ID in the Corps center. Units of General Erich von Brandenberger's 7th Army had forced the 4th ID back in the south. Although under tremendous pressure, neither division collapsed. Middleton had committed what resources he had, including the arriving 10th AD. He had done what he could but questions remained. First, would the 10th AD prevent the XLVII Panzer Crops, composed of the 2nd PZ, 9th PZ, and the Panzer Lehr Divisions, from taking the road junction at Bastogne before the 101st could get there? Second, how would the defenders at St. Vith fare?[17]

At sunrise on December 19, BG Hasbrouck had control over the units in the horseshoe minus the 424th Infantry (INF) and CCB, 9th AD. As Donald P. Boyer Jr. noted in a report written in 1947, "it was the presence of the enemy to the North, South and *rear*." Hasbrouck knew the enemy had been in contact with his trains as far west as La Roche-en-Ardenne. First Army reported the Germans had taken Stavelot, to his northwest.[18] The units

Hasbrouck sent south to defend his southern flank at Gouvy literally had to fight to establish roadblocks. His situation, like Middleton's, was fluid; he, too, wondered how the defenders would fare.

It is not clear just what transpired between Hasbrouck and Middleton when they met on December 17 other than Middleton intended for Hasbrouck to stiffen the defense at St. Vith and extricate the two regiments from the Schnee Eifel. Middleton's indecision on December 16–17 had the effect of limiting Hasbrouck's options and those of the 422nd and 423rd Infantries. About noon on December 16 Middleton had promised MG Alan W. Jones the 7th AD would arrive at 0700 on December 17. His own after action review and every witness to the conversation contradicted him. The VIII Corps after action report is disingenuous, to say the least, when it claims that Middleton urged Jones to withdraw the two regiments. In any event, Jones declined to do so. According to the VIII Corps report, Jones "felt confident of the security of his position since he had information . . . that 7th Armored Division . . . would close by 1500 the next day." Early on December 17 Middleton had issued "a hold at all costs order." Why, then, would he expect Jones to withdraw?[19]

Middleton further muddied the waters when he ordered Hasbrouck to cooperate with Jones. In *Corps Commanders of the Battle of the Bulge*, Harold R. Winton asserts that by not deciding who was in charge at St. Vith, Middleton "jeopardized the defense." According to Winton, Middleton should have placed the junior but more experienced Hasbrouck in overall command.[20] Despite lack of clear command lines, Hasbrouck knew what he must do. First he had to stem the tide caused when the Germans burst through the Losheim Gap and isolated the Schnee Eifel. Stemming the tide then had to be rationalized with attempting to relieve the two regiments. He would succeed in the first but he lacked the means event to attempt the second.

Establishing Coherent Defense

On December 17–18 Clarke, Hasbrouck, BG William M. Hoge, and Jones flung units hither and yon as threats appeared. Stubborn competence and initiative displayed by soldiers in every grade enabled a defense to accrete around islands of resistance. LTC Thomas J. Riggs and Lieutenant (LT) Joseph V. "Navajo" Whiteman exemplified that kind of effort. The defense began to mature on December 19. This happened in part because the 7th AD leadership and Hoge shared a common conceptual view of how to defend. They appreciated that the road junction at St. Vith was the means to an end for the Germans rather than an objective per se. Clarke articulated this idea clearly: "St. Vith was just a spot on the terrain. It was not important in and of itself."[21] Hasbrouck and his commanders intended to defend St. Vith short of losing their units to retain it.

To organize and fight as their doctrine specified they had to see the battlefield, and to "see" it they had to employ all of their senses. Often they saw with their ears—listening to the radio or even the sounds of battle. They communicated in written form, sending encrypted radio messages or messages carried by courier. Contact patrols between units and reconnaissance patrols provided "visual" acuity, as did debriefing prisoners. Finally, they went forward to see for themselves. Clarke, Hasbrouck, Hoge, COL Dwight A. Rosebaum, and LTC Fred M. Warren communicated frequently and visited both adjacent units and their own when possible. Battalion commanders operated in similar fashion.

LTC Robert C. Erlenbusch, who commanded the 31st TB, believed going forward was essential. He also believed commanders influenced action by their presence because of how their soldiers reacted. According to Erlenbusch, "A lot of these drafted folks were bright, well-educated people. They weren't a bunch of dummies. By the same token, they weren't professional soldiers. When you got up there with them, they were reassured and you enhanced control."[22] By December 1944 the 7th AD had become a veteran unit. The bonds developed in combat flourished when officers and noncommissioned officers worked directly with their soldiers.

Erlenbusch served primarily in Clarke's CCB. Although Clarke was new to the Division, he operated in familiar ways. Erlenbusch recalled that Clarke's orders were "informal, verbal and clear."[23] When it was feasible Clarke brought his team together to "discuss various possibilities and contingency plans to be used as guides when the situation demanded."[24] LTC John P. Wemple, who commanded the 17th TB, described Hasbrouck as "cool, calm and collected" in combat. Furthermore, he believed that both Hasbrouck and Clarke issued "precise and well conceived orders."[25] LTC Roy U. Clay, who commanded the 275th Armored Field Artillery (AFA), compared the 7th AD to the 2nd ID, the first unit he supported. "They inspired confidence, "he said of the two veteran divisions, Regarding Hasbrouck, Clay claimed, "Every member of the 7th Armored respected General Hasbrouck."[26]

Hasbrouck and his commanders fought what they thought of as an "active defense." The idea stemmed from doctrine based on theory, that of Carl von Clausewitz, who used the term in the context of covering a large area by defending it in such a way that the enemy is constrained to attacking along identifiable routes, an action that relied on "mobility, active defense, and even offensive measures." The defender then occupied posts to deny those routes and used mobility to counterattack. US Army armor doctrine reflected this theory.[27] BG Clarke asserted that the key for armor in the defense was to exploit its mobility to counterattack penetrations or "spoil" enemy attacks by hitting the enemy as they prepared to attack or got underway. To them the doctrine of small forces forward backed up by a mobile reserve made perfect sense.[28] Clarke's method included keeping tanks ready to run a counterattack sweep he referred to as a "race track." The method was easy to describe but more difficult in execution. The counterattacking force moved to flank the attackers. Flanking combined with fixing fires and artillery often proved effective.[29]

In a memoir completed in November 1945, Richard L. McBride, a staff sergeant in a mortar platoon of the 23rd Armored Infantry Battalion (AIB), described the US Army's concept for armor in the defense as well as any doctrine writer. McBride believed that "an armored division was essentially and normally a weapon of fast aggressive, assault, rather than defense. With fewer men, greater mobility, and greater firepower than its brother infantry divisions, *defense* decreased its advantages and increased its disadvantages— while the *attack* did just the opposite."[30] McBride reflected the high quality of many draftees. He graduated with honors from Yale University in 1943 and enlisted soon after. He turned down officer candidate school to serve in the ranks and later turned it down a second time to remain in the ranks.[31] McBride arrived in the 7th AD as a replacement in September 1944 and served in A Company, 23rd AIB until April 1945. He understood how his outfit proposed to fight. Like many of his colleagues in the Lucky Seventh, he was a veteran who knew his business.

On Tuesday, December 19, the 7th AD had sufficient forces to organize the defense of the sector. The Division made no effort to break through to the two beleaguered regiments on the Schnee Eifel, however. It is reasonable to wonder whether the 7th AD should have attempted to relieve the 422nd and the 423rd Infantries. Certainly Hugh Cole, the official historian of the battle, believed the Division had a plan to do so, asserting that such an attack planned for December 17 was "postponed," not "canceled." The 7th AD lacked both combat troops and artillery to support such an effort. LTC Roy U. Clay's 275th AFA and the 965th Field Artillery (with towed 155-millimeter howitzers) could have supported, but these two battalions were the only ones available until the division artillery arrived.[32] The artillery arrived and occupied firing positions on December 19, but it was too late to support an attack.

Forging the Horseshoe

At 0930 the Germans settled the question by mounting the first of a series of generally uncoordinated attacks against the "horseshoe." Simultaneously, Lucht's troops fired artillery preparations and followed up with ground attacks against the two regiments in the Schnee Eifel. The FEB made this first attack against CCB, 7th AD. Oberst Otto-Ernst Remer's troops struck toward Hünningen from the village of Nieder-Emmels. Numerous intermingled units formed the defense, all more or less under the command of LTC Erlenbusch. Task Force (TF) Erlenbusch defended the two main roads that ran northwest toward Recht and north toward the Losheim Gap.

The first attack petered out quickly, but a second, stronger attack occurred in the early afternoon. Erlenbusch reported "15 enemy tanks and 300 infantry were coming S[outh] on the road from NDR Emmels [Nieder-Emmels] to Hunningen."[33] During this attack Erlenbusch's troops employed the "active defense." Major (MAJ) William F. Beatty, the battalion executive officer, had positioned an attached platoon of tank destroyers in hull defilade positions astride the road to Nieder-Emmels. These were ideal positions for the long-range, high-velocity ninety-millimeter cannons mounted on the M36 tank destroyers in the platoon because they afforded long-range observation found in few other places near St. Vith. From these well-chosen positions the platoon picked off three enemy tanks at the remarkable range of two thousand yards, while Erlenbusch maneuvered his C Company, 31st TB to flank the Germans. C Company arrived on their flank and drove the surviving Germans off. Supported by artillery and mortars, C Company Sherman tanks "knocked out" two more Panzers and six or seven half-tracks before the enemy withdrew. Erlenbusch called for and received fighter-bombers to support the tank sweep, but visibility was so limited that the fighters could not engage. LT Truman R. Bowman, the officer who led the tank sweep, coordinated by radio directly with Erlenbusch to avoid friendly fire from the tank destroyers.[34] After the successful sweep Bowman retired into defilade, ready to repeat the process. Early in the afternoon the FEB reprised its attack, coming through the valley, and was driven off again. Using tank "sweeps" to defeat the enemy reflected both BG Clarke's intent to fight an "active defense" and armored force doctrine.[35]

Erlenbusch had great faith in tank sweeps and tank destroyers. In his view, tank destroyers "were very effective when they were properly used and sufficiently protected."[36] Because they were thin-skinned and their turrets had no overhead cover, they seldom could stand and fight, but instead had to shoot and move in order to survive. Tank destroyers provided essential firepower that the basic M4 Sherman tank lacked. In fact, Erlenbusch, like many of his colleagues, had found a tactical solution to the problem of the Sherman tank. Erlenbusch described the Army's concept for tanks quite clearly: "Tanks are designed to kill people, not tanks."[37]

The M4 was armed with a low-velocity seventy-five-millimeter cannon that reflected the Army's operational concept for its use: to exploit infantry penetration. The first page of Field Manual 17-12, *Armored Force Field Manual: Tank Gunnery*, explained that the "ultimate objective of the armored division is vital rear installations." In the US Army, tank destroyers had the mission to kill tanks. The seventy-six-millimeter M10 and the even better ninety-millimeter M36 proved effective, even devastating, to enemy armor when used in concert with the infantry and tanks. As soldier-historian David E. Johnson argues convincingly in *Fast Tanks and Heavy Bombers*, the Army concept for armor proved badly mistaken.[38] In 1944 the US Army began fielding Shermans equipped with a high-velocity seventy-six-millimeter cannon. These tanks fared much better against the German Panzers, including the Tiger.

A Troop, 87th CAV, oriented east, occupied ground on the right of Erlenbusch's tank destroyers. While Erlenbusch's tanks and tank destroyers handled the threat from the north, the Cavalry dealt with an abortive supporting attack. A small German combined arms force rolled south from Nieder-Emmels along the railway about a mile or a mile and a half northeast of the crossroads at Hünningen. Tanks attached to LT Lee A. Mestas's A Troop destroyed a tank and an armored car. The enemy withdrew without returning fire.[39]

Despite nearly continuous German pressure, engineers supporting CCB went forward and laid mines at key intersections, including the one at Hünningen, and forward of CCB's defenses. On CCB's left, COL Rosebaum's CCA proved unable to push the Germans far enough out of Rodt to assure control of the road but did keep the Germans from using the road. The situation south of St. Vith remained hazy, but Hasbrouck effectively and perceptibly gained control of the fight on December 19. LT Jack Dillender, a tank destroyer platoon leader, articulated clearly the concept for the defense: "The 7th Armored would fight and withdraw to hold back the drive [Germans] as long as possible to give our side time to build a wall of steel. . . . The Division set up small task forces which would fight to delay."[40]

Combat Command Reserve (CCR) occupied the westernmost tip of the horseshoe in and around Petit-Thier. During the course of the day the

Division stripped CCR of most of its troops. LTC Wemple's 17th TB joined CCB. The 106th ID troops serving in TF Navajo were sent to the rear to reorganize combat capability for the remnants of the 106th ID. What remained was a menagerie, including what amounted to two platoons of the 33rd Armored Engineers and a detachment from B Company, 23rd AIB. Armor support included six tanks from the 31st TB, rounded out by a Forward Observer team mounted on a Sherman tank, two tank destroyers, and two 105-millimeter assault guns.[41]

Hasbrouck ordered this force to "clear and make safe [the] road [to] Vielsalm-Poteau and establish contact with CCA." The order did not relieve CCR of defending Petit-Thier, and the task assigned arguably exceeded CCR's means. Since COL John L. Ryan, Hasbrouck's chief of staff, had visited CCR that day, presumably he and therefore the Division understood the problem but simply could not establish a contiguous well-manned main line of resistance. Securing the road to Vielsalm was essential to inhibiting any German attempt to envelop the horseshoe and reduce it from the rear. Additionally, the road ran from Poteau generally west, all the way to La Roche-en-Ardenne, and it needed to be held. At 1530 hours Hasbrouck reinforced CCR with a provisional cavalry troop composed of three officers and eighty men mounted on eight M8 armored cars.[42] In the vein of the "Division giveth and the Division taketh away," the Division then withdrew the handful of tanks attached to CCR.

The ersatz cavalry troop screened the flank and patrolled the road. The two tank destroyers established a roadblock on the road through Ville-du-Bois. CCR had too few troops to open the road to Poteau fully but claimed lightly armored vehicles could traverse it. The road remained under German observation and occasional fire. Additionally, a CCR patrol reconnoitered a parallel route that unarmored vehicles could use in comparative safety. LTC Fred M. Warren's troops had done well. Late in the afternoon one of his patrols made contact with CCA. The northwestern tip of the horseshoe was as secure as CCR could make it.

Although COL Rosebaum's CCA had managed to gain control of the road through Poteau, it had been unable to secure the town. Similarly, armor and infantry from the 1st SS and 9th SS kept the pressure on Poteau but were unable to retake the town. The resulting tactical stalemate worked to the advantage of the Americans, as it denied a good westbound road to the increasingly frustrated SS troops. Rosebaum's soldiers improved their defenses by establishing a roadblock at Rodt.[43]

The End on the Schnee Eifel

For the infantry on the Schnee Eifel, December 19 began as the day before had—"bitter cold; overcast; snow." The dystopian life of soldiers on both sides showed little improvement. The German GIs, or *Landsers*, enjoyed a modest advantage in comfort over the soldiers in the surrounded regiments. Klaus Ritter certainly felt better having reequipped himself with American underwear and shoepacs made with rubber soles and leather "spats." He rejoiced, claiming, "Like a new-born child I feel in that army outfit 'Made in the U.S.A.!' "[44] Ritter and his buddies in the 1818th Anti-Tank Battalion had fared well. Earlier, on the outskirts of Schönberg, they had enjoyed "hot tea and coffee" provided by German-speaking Belgians. Ritter surprised them by speaking their dialect. He was, after all, a local himself.

But enjoying the hospitality of the citizens of Schönberg did not last long. Early on December 19 Ritter's unit moved to the Skyline Drive between Bleialf and Auw. There it took up positions "to destroy tanks or other vehicles trying to escape the bag." On the way up the road Ritter passed the detritus of the 423rd INF's failed attempt to break out. Along the way he saw "quite a lot of dead Americans."[45] The 422nd and 423rd Infantry Regiments had made some progress but still had not crossed the Ihrenbach River or reached the road that ran north from Schönberg. They had crested the Skyline Drive north of Bleialf and stopped there.

Both regiments were low on ammunition and morale. COL Charles C. Cavender's troops of the 423rd could actually see the way out—Schönberg. If they could take the town, they had a chance to escape via the road to St. Vith. Cavender convened a conference of his commanders shortly before 0900. There he announced, "We will attack at 1000 hours in a column of battalions." The 3rd Battalion would lead, and the 422nd would attack on Cavender's right. Soon after he issued the order, the Germans mounted an attack preceded by an artillery barrage. Rounds from the barrage impacted in and around the command group, wounding several, including the commander of the 1st Battalion. He died of his wounds within minutes.[46]

Despite the barrage, the two regiments attempted to break out under fire and, in the case of the 423rd, while being attacked from the rear. Unable to communicate effectively, the regiments attacked without coordination and indeed fired on each other. Dan Bied, a rifleman in the 422nd, vividly recalled the German artillery preparation: "Flames shot skyward from tree bursts. Limbs fell around us like matchsticks. The ground erupted, spewing smoke and fire." Confusion reigned, and "no one was commanding us per se . . . it was an every-man-for-himself kind of mess."[47] Bied's assessment explains why the breakout failed. By late afternoon both regiments had sput-tered to a halt. Perhaps the final straw occurred when Remer's FEB joined the fray. Fully surrounded and outnumbered, the "doughs" on the Schnee Eifel had run out of options. A few soldiers escaped, but most of the surviv-ing members of the regiments surrendered. LTC Joseph F. Puett, command-er of Cavender's 2nd Battalion, reported that after the surrender they were taken into German "custody."[48]

By 1700 hours the largest surrender of US troops since the Philippines in 1942 had occurred. Just how many surrendered is not known with certainty. In the official history Hugh Cole reports that it was at least seven thousand.[49] About five hundred soldiers of the 422nd hung on until the next morning and then they, too, joined the dreary columns of prisoners heading east.

South of St. Vith

On the morning of December 19, BG Bill Hoge's CCB, 9th AD remained in position southeast of CCB, 7th AD west of the Our River. Shortly after sun-rise, CCB observed movement of infantry, armor, and horse-drawn artillery into Lomersweiler. It took some time for the Germans to assemble, but they eventually mounted two probes. One attack aimed northwest toward Neidin-gen across wooded terrain cut by the ubiquitous *Bachs* (streams). Tanks and infantry from C Company, 27th AIB and B Company, 14 TB maneuvered, destroying three enemy tanks, one of which they believed was a captured US Army Sherman. A second probe moved from Steinebrück northeast up a draw on the German side of the Our River. This second probe appeared aimed at finding a way around the northern flank of CCB.[50]

Enemy probes went on through the course of the day until late afternoon. At 1635, the 14th TB observed German infantry moving toward it in draw. Two tank platoon leaders, LT Stanley J. Dawidczyk and LT Hugh R. Mor-rison, concluded the action when they "charged and overran the enemy in the draw." The two tankers "mowed down" enemy infantry at close range and then called mortars on survivors as they withdrew. The two lieutenants motored around shooting up German Volksgrenadiers for nearly an hour.[51]

Although they were plenty busy with their own action, Hoge's troops took note of what happened elsewhere. They could see "heavy artillery shelling, and several attacks from the north and northeast" on the Prümerberg. Lat-er on December 19, confident his battalion commanders had the situation in hand, Bill Hoge made his way to St. Vith to see Bruce Clarke. There are several accounts that suggest Hoge was truculent, but neither he nor Clarke recalled their meeting that way. Both were straight-talking, confident men. At one point Hoge wanted to know, "Who do I work for?" He pointed out he had been sent south by First Army with orders to work for Jones. To Clarke he wondered aloud, "Maybe I had better go back to Bastogne and find out." In the end Hoge agreed to collaborate with Clarke, who insisted, "You're needed south of St. Vith a lot more than you're needed in Bastogne." Clarke advised Hasbrouck of the arrangement he and Hoge had made by radio.[52]

Afterward, Hoge and Clarke reviewed the tactical situation. It was clear to both men that the only way back or west for Hoge's command ran through St. Vith. Clarke believed he would eventually have to give up St. Vith and was concerned for CCB, 9th AD if it came to that. He suggested that Hoge withdraw his combat command through St. Vith and reposition south of the town and west of the railway running north through it. Hoge concurred. CCB, 9th AD began moving at sunset and completed the move before midnight on December 19–20. The horseshoe took on a less distorted shape.[53]

In two days of hard fighting, COL Alexander D. Reid's 424th INF had nearly been overrun by the 62nd VGD. On the night of December 17 Reid withdrew his regiment west of the Our River. The withdrawal was not as easily coordinated as the laconic sentence devoted to it in the after action report suggests. Some who did get out did so by evading the enemy. Harold D. Allen, a rifleman scout in A Company of the regiment's 1st Battalion, evaded capture on the December 16 when much of A Company was overcome in a night attack. Allen and group of twenty other soldiers from A Company worked their way westward. They finally rejoined their battalion on December 17 and made it out. The next morning Allen and remnants of A Company came to a "cross road, and there was our Regimental commander, Colonel Reid. Boy! Was he a sight for sore eyes."[54]

West of the Our River, Reid stabilized his defense with all three battalions on line. The 1st Battalion defended in the north around the village of Bracht. Hoge's right flank ended about one thousand yards northwest of the 1st Battalion's left. The 3rd Battalion occupied the center between Bracht and Burg-Reuland. The 2nd Battalion extended the line south from Burg-Reuland but not in physical contact with the 112th INF. At the end of the day the 424th occupied defensible positions, and the situation was stabilizing.

Behind or west of the 424th, Hasbrouck positioned TF Lindsey, formed from the remnants of the 14th CAV. Captain Franklin P. Lindsey commanded some 236 troopers equipped with eleven Armored Cars, eleven Stuart light tanks, and six assault guns. Lindsey, who commanded B Troops' 32nd

CAV, had shown skill and resolve during the collapse of the group. Lindsey's task force added some depth to the 424th and provided mobility the 424th lacked. Hasbrouck positioned a smaller cavalry task force of thirty troopers and six vehicles in Bovigny, about two miles north of Gouvy. Both of these measures helped to deepen security on the left flank and the rear of the 7th AD; the CCB, 9th AD; and the 424th INF.[55]

On the morning of December 19, COL Gustin M. Nelson withdrew his 112th INF generally northwest and established a defense south of the village of Huldange. Not long after arriving, the 28th ID ordered Nelson to defend the Lausdorn–Weiswampach–Weiler line.[56] Attempting to comply with an earlier order, the regiment had already moved beyond that line. Nelson's regiment had fought effectively against the 116th PZ and 560th VGD but now could no longer comply with orders that arrived too late for execution. He concluded that the Division "was completely out of touch with the situation."[57] That morning Nelson went north to find Hasbrouck after a patrol from the 7th AD made contact. The two men met at about 1030 hours. Hasbrouck wanted to know, "What are you doing way up here? And where the hell's the rest of your division?" Nelson, a determined and experienced officer, briefed Hasbrouck on his situation, whereupon Hasbrouck called MG Jones at the 106th ID and suggested he take on the 112th. Accordingly, Nelson went on to Jones's command post late in the afternoon and apprised him of his situation. Jones responded with, "From now on you are attached to the 106th Division and I will take full responsibility."[58]

Jones ordered Nelson to tie in his defense with Reid's 424th INF and to maintain contact with them. Jones and Nelson agreed that the 112th would move to high ground between the Luxembourg villages of Beiler and Leithum, oriented south. Jones accepted the idea that Nelson would not have physical contact with the 424th but would run contact patrols between the two regiments. The 112th fended off attacks throughout December 19 as LVIII Panzer Corps pushed west. In fact, the 112th had stymied the 116th PZ and mauled parts of the 560th VGD. But the 112th's infantrymen, who had retreated on foot nearly thirty miles, did not perceive their success. Charles Haug, an infantryman in B Company, 1st Battalion, 112th INF, described German attacks as coming in waves on December 19. He remembered, "Everyone was hungry and tired and cold." Haug had the sense that the 112th was on its own, that "there seemed to be no help coming from anywhere." He and his mates "thought the Germans were winning the war."[59]

However the troops in the 112th felt, they meted out punishment. COL Nelson made a good choice when he chose to exercise his initiative and seek out the 7th AD. MG Jones then solicited and received VIII Corps' approval of the arrangement he had made with Nelson. Together they effectively forged the southern tine of the horseshoe defense. Work remained to be done west of the 112th: the handful of troops around Gouvy still needed help. The day ended with the defense of the St. Vith sector in better shape. The VIII Corps after action review commentary for the day reported that "the St. Vith defenses were solidified and dispositions were improved."[60]

German Reactions

After the war Hasso von Manteuffel described his frustration with the continued failure to take St. Vith. According to Manteuffel, "The result for 19 December in this [LXVI] Corps was on the whole disappointing." The failure to take the town stemmed from the LXVI Corps' difficulty "in assembling sufficient forces for the attack and in securing combined use of all forces as far as timing and placing in the sector were concerned."[61] Around noon Lucht, Manteuffel, and Model met at the LXVI Corps command post at Wallerode Mühle. About five miles from St. Vith, the three were well within the sound of the guns. Model was angry, noting of St. Vith, "It has to be taken fast. It's a stumbling block to my whole offensive." He added, "[Sepp] Dietrich is making complaints all the way back to Wolf's Lair [Hitler's command post]. He says even his 1st SS Panzer Division is being tied up because of the road jam." Lucht, whose units were in the process of reducing the pocket on the Schnee Eifel and attacking toward St. Vith that every moment, vented his own anger: "Dietrich! His people have been using my roads since yesterday. How can I mount an attack with him fouling up my rear?"[62]

Lucht added that he had personally arrested SS officers who refused to vacate roads assigned to his Corps. He further complained, "This morning my horse-drawn artillery couldn't get through because Dietrich's people were stealing my roads. And they still are." Manteuffel exhorted him: "Kick them off [the SS] so they stay off. Without artillery you'll never take St. Vith." Model intervened, saying, "I'll take care of it." With that he went out and literally directed traffic for a time. The intervention helped, but only briefly.[63] The SS showed little regard for following orders from regular army officers.

Model's problems abounded. The Sixth Panzer Army's attacks had produced little beyond the penetration led by Joachim Peiper. American infantrymen from the 30th ID stopped Peiper at La Gleize. The US XVIII Airborne Corps became operational on December 19 at Werbomont, Belgium, with the 82nd ABN, the arriving 30th ID, and the 3rd AD.[64] The Corps effectively shut down the sputtering Sixth Panzer Army and, worse still, turned immediately to the task of reducing Peiper's narrow penetration. Peiper's arrogance and poor march discipline, combined with bad communications, led him to outrun his support. Soon he and his troops would pay for his errors and their arrogance.

Model had already shifted the main effort to Manteuffel and provided the use of the FEB in taking St. Vith. Now he weighted the effort further by ordering Oberstgruppenführer Willi Bittrich's 2nd SS Panzer Corps to the Fifth Panzer Army. Bittrich's 9th SS, already caught up in the congestion behind the 1st SS, was subordinated to the 1st SS Panzer Corps. Model ordered Bittrich to redeploy the 2nd SS, his remaining division, in the Fifth Panzer Army area. Accordingly, the 2nd SS started south toward Prüm, Germany, where it would turn west and be employed on LXVI Corps' left. Success depended on the Fifth Panzer Army.[65]

On the afternoon of December 19 Hasbrouck reported his situation to Middleton. The 7th AD journal noted the message as follows: "7th AD still holds positions shown on overlay. CCB 9th AD, 424th INF and 112th INF on our south and protecting my flanks as far west as Lourth [Ourthe] River as best I can tell with miscellaneous units. Request you establish communications with me. I intend to hold present positions unless you order otherwise."[66] Hasbrouck did not complain about the unclear command lines, but it is interesting to note that he took no notice of the 106th ID headquarters. His frustration with VIII Corps can be seen in his request that the Corps establish communications. Doctrine stipulated that communications responsibility ran higher to lower. Communications with VIII Corps did not improve for the simple fact that the Corps command and control system largely depended on wire, which had been disrupted in far too many places.

Hasbrouck's misshapen horseshoe had dings and gaps in its two tines. Worse still, his lines remained porous. More than once, lightly armed supply columns found they had to fight their way to and from supply points. The command system remained loose, requiring Hasbrouck to tread carefully—with Jones and, to a lesser extent, with Hoge. Although his northern flank had to some extent stabilized, the south remained insecure, as the Fifth Panzer Army flowed west and south through the gap blown through the 28th ID.

At sunset on December 19 the troops in the sector defended an elongated and fragile line that extended more than fifty miles, or more than half the length of the VIII Corps line the day the Germans had first attacked.

NOTES

1. Chester Wilmot, *The Struggle for Europe*, 584. According to John Keegan, *The Second World War*, 598, Wilmot "effectively invented the modern method of writing contemporary military history." Wilmot's narrative has stood the test of time despite his not having access to the Ultra story.

2. Major General Andrew J. Adams (Ret.) to the author, June 14, 1984.

3. 7th Armored Division, G-2 journal, December 1944, entries 2–6 and 10–14.

4. 7th Armored Division, G-3 journal, December 1944, entries 17 and 25.

5. Charles Whiting, *Decision at St. Vith*, 101.

6. On the Hitler Youth Division, see Hubert Meyer, *The 12th SS: The History of the Hitler Youth Panzer Division*, vol. 2, chaps. 8.4 and 8.5. Meyer documented his work using both German and American records. He served as chief of staff of the 12th SS.

7. General der Panzertruppe Hasso von Manteuffel, "An Interview with Gen Pz Hasso von Manteuffel," ETHINT-46, 6.

8. Oberstleutnant Dietrich Moll, "18th Volks Grenadier Division," 47.

9. Walther Lucht, "LXVI Infantry Corps," 2.

10. Lucht, "LXVI Infantry Corps," 46.

11. Dwight D. Eisenhower, *Crusade in Europe*, 350.

12. Stephen E. Ambrose, *The Supreme Commander*, 556.

13. Eisenhower, *Crusade in Europe*, 350. See also Ambrose, *The Supreme Commander*, 556–60. Eisenhower precipitated concern that he might be contemplating a major withdrawal by using the crisis to make the case for solving the infantry replacement problems cited in chapter 1 of the present volume. The meeting included staff officers. Patton, for example, brought his aide, LTC Charles R. Codman, and at least one other staff officer. In his diary Patton noted that in addition to Eisenhower, in attendance were Bradley, Devers, Eisenhower's deputy air marshal Sir Arthur Tedder, "and a large number of staff officers." See Martin Blumenson, *The Patton Papers*, 2:596–97. See also Charles B. MacDonald, *A Time for Trumpets*, 419–24. MacDonald's account of the meeting is important because it is the first important history of the Bulge to account for Ultra in the decisions taken on December 19, 1944.

14. Blumenson, *The Patton Papers*, 599.

15. MacDonald, *A Time for Trumpets*, 416.

16. Major William C. Sylvan and Captain Francis G. Smith Jr., *Normandy to Victory*, 221.

17. Harold R. Winton, *Corps Commanders of the Bulge*, 158.

18. Donald P. Boyer Jr., *St. Vith: The 7th Armored Division in the Battle of the Bulge*, 24, emphasis in the original.

19. Colonel Ernest R. Dupuy, *St. Vith: Lion in the Way*, 23–25, 64. Headquarters VIII Corps, "Report of the VIII Corps After Action against Enemy Forces," 7. The Corps after action review is, plainly and simply, and an ex post facto alteration of the facts.

20. Winton, *Corps Commanders*, 154.

21. General Bruce C. Clarke (Ret.), interview with the author, Falls Church, VA, August 8, 1984, General Bruce C. Clarke Papers.

22. Colonel Robert C. Erlenbusch (Ret.), interview with the author, Point Charlotte, FL, December 8, 1984.

23. Colonel Robert C. Erlenbusch (Ret.) to the author, August 24, 1984.

24. Erlenbusch to the author, August 24, 1984.

25. Colonel John P. Wemple to the author, September 4, 1984.

26. Colonel Roy U. Clay (Ret.) to the author, July 1, 1984. Clay contrasted the 2nd ID and 7th AD with the 106th ID and the 14th CAV. The comment about Hasbrouck is from Colonel Roy U. Clay (Ret.) to the author, July 3, 1984.

27. Carl von Clausewitz, *On War*, 507.

28. Armored force defensive doctrine was thin, but it focused on using tanks to counterattack as the key to success. See US War Department, *Armored Force Field Manual*, FM 17, 39–40; and US War Department, *Armored Force Field Manual: The Armored Battalion, Light and Medium*, FM 17-33, 113. General Bruce C. Clarke (Ret.), interview with the author, McLean, VA, August 20, 1984, General Bruce C. Clarke Papers.

29. Clarke interview, August 20, 1984. The method was described in greater detail in Erlenbusch to the author, August 24, 1984.

30. Richard L. McBride, "Grinding Through with the 7th Armored Division." McBride's memoir is a first-rate account of soldiering in the armored infantry. Although the manuscript itself is undated, McBride dated the foreword November 1945.

31. McBride, "Grinding Through"; "Richard Lee McBride," obituary, *Journal News* (White Plains, NY), December 14, 2009, https://obits.lohud.com/obituaries/lohud/obituary.aspx?n=richard-lee-mcbride&pid=150013341.

32. Hugh M. Cole, *The Ardennes: Battle of the Bulge*, 282; US Department of War, *Armored Force Field Manual: The Armored Battalion, Light and Medium*, FM 17-33, 13. W. Wesley Johnston, in *Combat Interviews of the 38th Armored Infantry Battalion*, believes that Clarke planned to attempt a breakthrough.

33. Johnston, *Combat Interviews of the 31st Tank Battalion*, 14–15. In his postwar debriefing Remer claims he did not mount an attack until noon on December 19. It is possible that the early morning attack came from the 9th SS. Remer clearly wanted to bypass St. Vith rather than support an infantry attack on the town. See Generalmajor Otto E. Remer, "The Führer-Begleit Brigade in the Ardennes Offensive," 4.

34. Johnston, *Combat Interviews of the 31st Tank Battalion*, 15, 51; Erlenbusch interview, December 8, 1984. See also 7th Armored Division, G-3 journal, December 1944, entry 36, reporting the request for air support at 1010 hours. Colonel Erlenbusch remembered these events quite clearly even after forty years. It is remarkable that what he told the author in 1984 matched what he told Robert E. Merriam

in 1944. On the tank destroyers, see Combat Command B, 7th Armored Division, "After Action report, Month of December 1944," 3. See also 814th Tank Destroyer Battalion, "After Action Report December 1944," 3. There may have been only two tank destroyers or a section rather than a platoon. Hitting a target at two thousand yards was an achievement. The tank destroyers, like the tanks, used nonballistic reticles in low-power telescopes. Killing a German tank at that range was generally possible only for the M36 tank destroyer—mounting, as it did, a ninety-millimeter high-velocity cannon.

35. Clarke used the term "active defense" explicitly but did not associate it with the Army "Active Defense" doctrine published in 1976; General Bruce C. Clarke (Ret.) to the author, August 31, 1984, General Bruce C. Clarke Papers. Combat Command R also used the term in its after action review. The usage reflects the thinking that came to be thought of as a mobile defense.

36. Erlenbusch to the author, August 24, 1984.

37. Erlenbusch interview, December 8, 1984.

38. David E. Johnson, *Fast Tanks and Heavy Bombers*, chaps. 5–14, focuses on how the Army adapted but makes clear the concept that drove Armored Force doctrine and development. Johnson's case is compelling. The Army trained, organized, and equipped tanks to exploit breakthrough by infantry and not to fight other tanks.

39. Johnston, *Combat Interviews of the 87th Cavalry Reconnaissance Squadron*, 18.

40. Calvin C. Boykin Jr., *Gare la Bête*, 76.

41. Combat Command R, 7th Armored Division. "After Action Report, Month of December 1944," 9.

42. Combat Command R, "After Action Report, Month of December 1944," 9.

43. Combat Command A, 7th Armored Division, "After Action Report, December 1944," 8; Johnston, *Combat Interviews of the 7th Armored Division Combat Commands*, 12.

44. Klaus Ritter, statements, box 10, Charles B. MacDonald Papers, pt. 1, p. 8.

45. Ritter, statements, pt. 1, p. 9. The Ritter interviews do not include dates. The author's estimate is that Ritter is describing his unit's activity on December 19. Additionally, he reported hearing firing the day before, which is consistent with the 423rd's effort to break out on December 19.

46. Whiting, *Decision at St. Vith*, 113–15.

47. Dan Bied, "Hell on Earth," box 4, Charles B. MacDonald Papers, 19.

48. LTC Joseph F. Puett, "Certificate: Movements and Actions of the 2nd Battalion 423rd Infantry from 16th to 19th December 1944," 5. See also Colonel Charles C. Cavender, "The 423 in the Bulge."

49. Cole, *The Ardennes: Battle of the Bulge*, 170. Cole's estimate, of course, includes the supporting artillery.

50. Combat Command B, 9th Armored Division, "Action South of St. Vith 17–23 Dec 1944," 12; this interview is wide ranging and detailed, but written as a narrative. See also 14th Tank Battalion, "History of the 14th Tank Battalion," 11–12; and 14th Tank Battalion, "After Action Report—1 Dec 44 to 31 Dec 44"; this after action review is accompanied by detailed sketches/overlays at 1:25,000 scale that show

positions of the 14th TB as of the evening of December 18, and final positions after repelling enemy probes on December 19.

51. 14th Tank Battalion, "History of 14th Tank Battalion," 11–12.

52. John S. D. Eisenhower, *The Bitter Woods*, 285. Eisenhower's account seems to have relied on Clarke's recollection, as it varies slightly from the way Hoge recalled the meeting. In any case, the two brigadier generals collaborated effectively. See also General William M. Hoge, *Engineer Memoirs*, 135. Hoge's *Memoirs* is an edited version of the senior officer debriefing program.

53. Eisenhower, *The Bitter Woods*, 285; Hoge, *Engineer Memoirs*, 135. Clarke's version of the decision for CCB, 9th AD to withdraw is given by Eisenhower. Hoge recalled having made the decision himself. Either way it happened, CCB, 9th AD needed to withdraw and did.

54. 424th Infantry Regiment, "After Action Report Ending 31 December 1944," 4. See also Colonel A. D. Reid, interview by Captain K. W. Hechler, 2–3; and Harold D. Allen, "My Experience in the Battle of the Bulge."

55. 7th Armored Division, "After Action Report, Period 1–31 December 1944," 7.

56. Colonel Gustin M. Nelson and Major Justin C. Brainard, interviewer not identified, January 14, 1945.

57. Col. Gustin M. Nelson to his father, May 1945, extract.

58. Nelson to his father, May 1945. Nelson does not mention the conversation with Hasbrouck in his letter. See also John Toland, *Battle: The Story of the Bulge*, 119; and 7th Armored Division, "Battle of St. Vith: 17–23 December," 7.

59. Charles Haug, "Courageous Defenders," 26.

60. Headquarters, VIII Corps, "Report of the VIII Corps After Action Against Enemy Forces," 15.

61. General der Panzertruppe Hasso von Manteuffel, "Fifth Panzer Army Ardennes Offensive."

62. Toland, *Battle: The Story of the Bulge*, 119.

63. Toland, *Battle: The Story of the Bulge*, 119. See also MacDonald, *A Time for Trumpets*, 348. The traffic problem is a theme throughout Oberstleutnant Dietrich Moll, "18th Volks Grenadier Division."

64. Winton, *Corps Commanders*, 172.

65. Michael Reynolds, *Sons of the Reich*, 194–95.

66. 7th Armored Division, G-3 journal, December 1944, entry 13, December 19, 1944.

CHAPTER EIGHT

Crisis at St. Vith

The town was being overwhelmingly attacked in several directions and there appeared to be little prospect of preventing its being cut off.
—Major General James Gavin

The brightest spot along the western front is at St. Vith.
—BBC broadcast, December 1944

If this is a bright spot what the hell is going on everywhere else!
—GI in Combat Command B, 9th Armored Division

In a television documentary after World War II, Brigadier General (BG) Robert W. Hasbrouck commented, "As the morning of twentieth December dawned we of the Seventh Armored Division felt pretty lonely." Major (MAJ) Donald P. Boyer, who fought on the Prümerberg as the operations officer of the 38th Armored Infantry Battalion (AIB), recalled, "The battlefield is an extremely lonely place."[1] Although not quite cut off, the 7th Armored Division (AD) and the other units in the sector had little idea of the situation beyond what they could see. Pressure from continuous enemy probes and frequent attacks kept the defenders on edge, even as a deep sense of isolation, one compounded by the cold, wet, and foggy weather, pervaded.

The troops defending the sector came from four separate divisions, VIII Corps, and First US Army. Disparate or not, they fought effectively and with surprising cohesion. Morale varied, but the troops drew some comfort from the quality of their leaders. Lieutenant Colonel (LTC) Roy U. Clay, who commanded the attached 275th Armored Field Artillery Battalion (AFA), had confidence in the 7th AD leadership, and particularly in Hasbrouck. Clay claimed, "Every member of the Seventh Armored respected General Hasbrouck."[2] BG Bruce C. Clarke believed morale important. He also believed that "spirit and morale comes down from the top in battle, not up from the bottom."[3] Clarke's assertion may be accurate; but initiative at the bottom also stimulated morale, as Lieutenant (LT) Joseph V. "Navajo" Whiteman showed. The remaining soldiers of the 106th Infantry Division (ID) and the 14th Cavalry Group (CAV) redeemed the good name of their units. Together the soldiers weathered the crisis at St. Vith and survived to fight again.

The battle to control the vital crossroads and rail station at St. Vith seemed on the verge of crisis to those manning the so-called horseshoe defense. BG Hasbrouck had intermittent communications with VIII Corps and had little reason to have confidence in the Corps' ability either to restore communications or provide assistance. He therefore decided to contact his next higher headquarters—First US Army. On December 20 Hasbrouck literally "penciled" a note with his assessment of the situation. He addressed the note to his friend, Major General (MG) William B. Kean, who served as First Army Chief of Staff. Hasbrouck sent one of his staff officers, LTC Frederick Schroeder, to find First US Army Headquarters and deliver the note.[4]

The Allied situation, though still grim, had moderated somewhat. The First Army diarists reported "7th and 9th Armd Divs together holding firm at St Vith . . . 101st A/B Div below is very heavily engaged but is still holding at Bastogne. Stavelot is definitely in our hands and we are closing the net around Stoumont where the 1st SS [Schutzstaffel] is."[5] This achievement stemmed from a handful of American combat engineers and scattered units who delayed Obersturmbahnführer Joachim Peiper's thrust westward. On December 19 the veteran 30th ID arrived in time to stop him at Stoumont. The "Hickory Division" also blocked the routes to the north at La Gleize and seized Stavelot in Peiper's rear. By taking Stavelot, the 30th ID cut off Peiper and effectively ended the Sixth Panzer Army's drive on the Meuse River. Southwest of St. Vith the 101st Airborne Division had moved into Bastogne, shielded by the 10th AD. In the far south of the VIII Corps sector, elements of the 4th ID, 9th AD, and 28th ID fought a delaying action against the German Seventh Army.

German Assessments and Orders

In October 1945 General der Panzertruppe Hasso von Manteuffel told his captors that "St Vith was much more important than Bastogne" in the early days of the offensive. The German failure to take St. Vith as planned bought time for First US Army to stiffen the northern shoulder. Major Percy Schramm, the German high command's diarist, described the problem succinctly: "The counter pressure on the right flank still continued and threatened to grow sharper." This pressure from the north or right flank created difficulty for both the Fifth and Sixth Panzer Armies. On December 19 Manteuffel's frustration reached critical mass. Despite having agreed to wait for General der Artillerie Walther Lucht's LXVI Corps to mount a coordinated attack with the entire Corps, he found that he could not wait. Sometime during the night of December 19–20 he reached down into LXVI Corps and ordered Oberst Otto-Ernst Remer to mount an attack with the Führer Escort Brigade (FEB) as soon as he could manage to do so.[6]

Remer, a man of boundless ambition, acted on his own initiative to shift the weight of the FEB from supporting the attack on St. Vith toward the Meuse, where glory could be found. He got off an abortive attack toward Rodt before daylight on December 20, achieving nothing. After the war, perhaps to cover his disregard for orders for the sake of his own ambitions, Remer complained of receiving "contradicting orders" from "Heeresgruppe [Army Group B], the Fifth Army, and the LXVI Corps."[7]

The Germans in the Ardennes did not demonstrate the utility of *Auftragstaktik*, the theory of enlightened obedience or, in contemporary US Army parlance, mission command exercising "disciplined initiative." Early in the attack the main effort in the north came to a bad end as SS commanders clogged scarce road space, each convinced he was enhancing the accomplishment of his assigned mission within acceptable parameters. Remer no doubt believed that exercise of his initiative was justified by the possible outcome, but when his gamble failed to pay off, he ended up further dispersing the German offensive effort against St. Vith. In 1961 Bruce C. Clarke commanded US Army Europe. During his tenure he wrote an article espousing "mission-type" orders. In his view of such orders, subordinates did not decide whether to follow them but were given the freedom to decide how best to execute them.[8] Nevertheless, some orders must be issued—as well as executed—with precision.

As of December 20, the Sixth Panzer Army still floundered in the north because of spirited defense, difficult terrain, and inept tactics by the vaunted SS. Opportunity remained in the Fifth Panzer Army, particularly south of St. Vith and west of Gouvy. Morale based on success remained high in the Fifth Panzer Army. As Oberstleutnant Heinz Günther Guderian, the 116th Panzer Division (PZ) operations officer, recalled, "Our *Landsers* are loaded with cigarettes, chocolates and canned food and are smiling from ear to ear." Better yet, "The combat units were able to fill gaps caused by missing vehicles in their convoys with captured ones."[9]

The 116th PZ reconnaissance element bypassed Houffalize, hoping to find and seize an intact bridge over the Ourthe River. The 116th did not find a bridge just past the town but continued west. Impatient and leery of finding a bridge, General der Panzertruppe Walter Krüger, the commander of LVIII Panzer Corps, ordered the 116th PZ to turn north and attack toward Samrée. He ordered the hard-marching 560th Volksgrenadier Division (VGD) to attack toward Baraque de Fraiture, south and west of St. Vith. Krüger believed that by heading west on the north bank of the Ourthe he was more likely to find open ground and a standing bridge. Krüger may have perceived a second advantage: breaking out to the northwest before the Americans could develop an adequate defense. Meanwhile, the 2nd SS PZ, on the move at Generalfeldmarschall Walther Model's orders since December 19, was coming up behind Krüger's troops heading for an assembly area about nine miles east of Houffalize.[10] Once refueled it could be employed to exploit success. Model's decision to send 2nd SS PZ south and Manteuffel's sense of the battlefield could pay off if the 2nd SS PZ could attack toward Manhay and break through the northern shoulder of the defense.

Allied Assessments and Orders

MG Troy H. Middleton's failure to designate clear lines of command continued to inhibit the defense at St. Vith. Poor communications exacerbated the problem for BG Hasbrouck. Nevertheless, he gradually assumed responsibility for defending the sector despite lacking clear lines of authority over all of the engaged units. Meanwhile, at the theater level, General Dwight D. Eisenhower reorganized his front, dividing it along a line extending from Givet, Belgium, east to Prüm, Germany. That line became the boundary between First US Army and Third US Army, as well as the boundary between British field marshal Bernard Law Montgomery's 21st Army Group north of the boundary, and Lieutenant General (LTG) Omar N. Bradley's 12th Army Group on the south side. Eisenhower also ordered LTG Jacob L. Devers's 6th Army Group to take up part of the 12th Army Group's zone.[11]

Large and fragile egos presided over the war on either side of the new Army Group boundary. Eisenhower's decision provoked controversy and complaint that has endured. He took the right decision for the Allied effort and certainly from the perspective of those fighting at St. Vith. At 1200 hours on December 20, as a result of the change and reinforcement directed by Eisenhower, MG Matthew D. Ridgway and XVIII Airborne Corps assumed control over the St. Vith sector, under First Army. Unlike Middleton, Ridgway eventually made a decision about command relationships at St. Vith.

In his postwar memoir, Montgomery, by then styled Field Marshal the Viscount Montgomery of Alamein, Knight of the Garter, opined that the less he said of the battle the better. That concern did not trouble him in 1944 and 1945. He and his chief, Field Marshal Alan Brooke, were often critical of the Americans generally and Eisenhower specifically. Both believed the British senior staff, and Montgomery in particular, should command Allied ground operations, while the Americans should provide the bulk of the troops and logistics and Eisenhower should limit himself to general oversight. Charles Whiting, a British veteran of the battle who devoted much of his working life to studying and writing about the Battle of the Bulge, summed up Montgomery when he wrote, "In a profession given to drink, whores and profanity, Montgomery was a birdlike, ascetic little saint, popular with his own men, but suspect to many of his fellow officers in the British Army and, even more so, to those hairy-chested, rednecked 'cousins from over the sea.'"[12]

Montgomery carped, complained, and intrigued to advance the argument that a unified ground command separate from Supreme Headquarters Allied Expeditionary Forces was necessary to concentrate forces and speedily end the war. He, of course, was the logical choice for overall ground command. Early in December Eisenhower unequivocally assured Montgomery that he, Eisenhower, would continue to coordinate and command all three Allied army groups. On midmorning that Wednesday, December 20, Eisenhower at last seemed to fulfill much of the Field Marshal's fondest hopes.

Choosing Montgomery to coordinate the fight in the north made sense on several levels. First and foremost, he recognized the danger posed by the German attack far more quickly than did LTG Bradley or LTG Courtney H. Hodges. Like Eisenhower, Montgomery acted decisively. At the outset of the German offensive he dispatched liaison teams code-named Phantom to report on conditions at the front. The Phantom teams moved out rapidly. They crossed army and army group boundaries to get where they needed to go. A Phantom liaison arrived at VIII Corps on the morning of December 18. Montgomery also acted quickly to provide material help. On December 19 he transferred British XXX Corps, composed of four divisions, to the Second British Army with orders to use them to backstop the northern crossings over the Meuse. The XXX Corps units reached positions to defend the crossings on December 20.[13]

Thanks to Phantom, Montgomery did not have to rely on reports coming from the bottom up through multiple filters, but no Phantom liaison had yet reached St. Vith on December 20. In that respect Montgomery was no better informed than LTG Hodges, the First US Army commander. At 1330 on December 20 Montgomery arrived at Hodges's headquarters as part of his approach to taking command of the fight. Montgomery would not command from a telephone handset, and he wanted to set the tone and assess the atmosphere at First Army. One of the British delegation observed that Montgomery had arrived "like Christ come to cleanse the temple."[14] General Francis "Freddie" de Guingand, Montgomery's chief of staff, described him as "looking supremely cheerful and confident."[15] However one perceived his visit, the field marshal definitely made an impression—though not an entirely favorable one.

Montgomery listened but also conveyed his appreciation of the situation and issued orders. He believed the Germans aimed to cross the Meuse south of Liège. Accordingly, he advised Hodges of his orders to XXX Corps to defend the northern Meuse crossings. He directed Hodges to generate a reserve in the area of Marche, Belgium, to use to counterattack after the Germans had been stopped. Furthermore, Montgomery specified that MG J. Lawton Collins would command the counterattacking force.[16] In order to generate forces for Collins's VII Corps, Ninth US Army, already under Montgomery's command, would assume part of the First Army line. Finally, the field marshal wanted Hodges to shorten his line by withdrawing forward units, including those at St. Vith. Hodges, reluctant to a fault to give up ground, demurred. What turn the conversation may have taken thereafter will never be known, because at that juncture LTC Schroeder arrived with Hasbrouck's note to Kean.

Hasbrouck's letter is one of the few events of the fighting at St. Vith that is widely known and widely reproduced. Nevertheless, it bears repeating here.

> Dear Bill:
>
> I am out of touch with VIII Corps and understand XVIII Airborne Corps is coming in.
> My division is defending the line St. Vith–Poteau inclusive. CCB [Combat Command B], 9th AD, the 424th Inf Regt of the 106th Div and the 112th Inf Regt of the 28th Div are on my right and hold from St. Vith (excl[usive]) to Holdingen. Both Infantry regiments are in bad

shape. My right flank is wide open except for some reconnaissance elements, TDs [tank destroyers] and stragglers we have collected and organized into defense teams as far back as Cheram [Cherain] inclusive. Two German Divisions, 116 Pz and 560 VG, are just starting to attack NW with their right on Gouvy. I can delay them the rest of the day but *maybe* cut off by tomorrow.

VIII Corps has ordered me to hold and I will do so but need help. An attack from Bastogne to the NE will relieve the situation and cut the bastards off in the rear. I also need plenty of air support. Am out of contact with VIII Corps so am sending this to you. Understand the 82AB [Airborne] is coming up on my north and the north is not critical.

Bob Hasbrouck

At just over two hundred words, Hasbrouck's note is a model of clarity written by an officer under tremendous stress.[17]

Hasbrouck provided a succinct estimate of his situation and that of neighboring units. He described accurately the envelopment underway at Gouvy. In doing so, he demonstrated his de facto command of the sector. The 116th PZ and 560th VGD appeared to be massing to attack to the northwest. What he did not know was that 2nd SS PZ would soon join that effort. An attack on the road between Baraque de Fraiture and Manhay was particularly dangerous. Hasbrouck communicated the gravity of the situation without resorting to an emotional appeal. Even though the attack from Bastogne could not be undertaken, his recommendation was sound.

Until Schroeder arrived, Hodges appeared to be on the wrong side of a losing argument with his superior. Hearing the contents of the letter, Hodges asserted, "In the light of this new information, Ridgway's XVIII Corps will have to keep driving forward toward St.-Vith to Hasbrouck's relief." Montgomery accepted this view given the new information but made it clear he intended eventually to withdraw the troops in the St. Vith sector from their exposed position.[18]

Protecting the Shanks of the Horseshoe

Hasbrouck's note suggests he was reasonably sanguine about his northern flank, but his actions belie any complacency. In the north, Combat Command R (CCR) and Combat Command A (CCA) remained in contact with elements of the 9th SS and, later in the day, the FEB. CCR with not much other than Task Force (TF) Navajo, sought to control the road from Petit-Thier to Poteau. CCA attempted to deny the Germans use of the road from

Poteau to Recht. Hasbrouck remained sufficiently concerned to issue the kind of order he personally disliked receiving. At 0926 he sent a message to Colonel (COL) Dwight A. Rosebaum: "Imperative that you command road leading into Poteau from Recht."[19] Far to the south, Rosebaum still had a small task force based on a company of light tanks and a company of engineers supporting extemporaneous defense at Gouvy led by the redoubtable LTC Robert O. Stone of the 440th Anti-Aircraft Artillery Battalion (AAA).

Conscious of being bypassed on his southern flank, Hasbrouck was particularly concerned about the southern shank of the horseshoe. He had done what he could to provide back-up to COL Alexander D. Reid's 424th Infantry (INF) by positioning TF Lindsey, formed from the 14th CAV, west of the 424th's line. As noted, CCA had positioned a light tank company and combat engineer company in the area on December 18. They were supporting LTC Stone. But Hasbrouck believed more had to be done. So at 0900 he again "robbed Peter to pay Paul." He thinned out the line in the north once more to generate forces to build TF Jones, commanded by LTC Robert B. Jones, 814th Tank Destroyer Battalion, at the southern tip of the horseshoe.[20]

TF Jones is emblematic both of the flexibility of the armored force and the chaos of the battle. Jones commanded an amalgam. The task force included two of his own tank destroyer companies; LTC John P. Wemple's 17th Tank Battalion (TB), minus one company; three Sherman tanks from the 40th TB; the 40th's light tank company; a combat engineer company; a small cavalry "task force" (less than a platoon) from the 14th CAV; and a second cavalry detachment "composed of 15 scout cars, 5 assault guns (75 millimeter) and 13 light tanks." G Company, 112th INF provided the only infantry. LTC Stone's 440th AAA and some 250 stragglers and Army-level logistics troops rounded out the task force.[21]

Hasbrouck charged Jones with securing the southern flank but withheld the use of the 17th TB without his consent. LTC Wemple's tankers constituted the only reserve available. Hasbrouck further ordered Jones to deny the enemy use of the road junctions at the villages of Deiffelt, Ourth, Gouvy, and Cherain. Holding the crossroads would delay and provide warning of the anticipated enveloping attack. That very morning the Division had captured a 560th VGD order that specified that its axis of advance went through Gouvy.[22]

Parker's Crossroads

When Hasbrouck and his staff examined the intended axis of advance of the 560th VGD they identified another crossroads vital to the 7th AD and ultimately to the troops holding the northern shoulder. A handful of houses stood at the crossroads, called Baraque de Fraiture, where Belgian national highways N15 and N26 intersected. N15 ran generally north and south. From Baraque de Fraiture the road led to Manhay, some five miles or more to the north. Highway N28 ran east and west. Samrée and the 7th AD trains lay five miles west. Going east, N28 ran to Salmchâteau, on the Salm River, slightly more than six miles away. If the Germans took the crossroads, they would cut off the troops in the horseshoe and perhaps penetrate the northern shoulder.

R. Ernest Dupuy's description of the crossroads in *St. Vith: Lion in the Way* is apt: "Baraque de Fraiture was the name of the height where the crossroads hamlet stood, a huddle of typical Belgian peasant homes with its one and only adornment a four-square, concrete road marker."[23] Fortunately, friendly troops had occupied Baraque de Fraiture since December 19. On December 18, the 589th Field Artillery (FA) had attempted to withdraw from exposed positions in the Schnee Eifel. German assault guns and infantry ambushed the battalion as it withdrew. Only three howitzers and about a hundred soldiers led by battalion executive officer MAJ Elliot Goldstein and battalion operations officer MAJ Arthur C. Parker III escaped.[24]

What remained of the 589th arrived in the vicinity of Bovigny on the afternoon of December 18. There they provided close-in defense for the five artillery battalions assigned to COL Herbert Krueger's 174th Field Artillery Group. Subsequently, Krueger "commandeered" the battalion to support his column of artillery as it withdrew. In response to a rumor of German tanks in the area Parker occupied Baraque de Fraiture to hold the road west open. Krueger withdrew through the crossroads and left Parker to his own devices. On December 20, the 106th ID ordered Parker to hold the crossroads "to protect division supply routes against attack from the south or west."[25] MAJ Parker established a sound all-around antitank defense. One howitzer oriented east toward Vielsalm. The second, pointed west, occupied a firing position at the western interior angle where the two highways crossed. The last howitzer went in just across N26 from the second, aiming south.

At 0800 on December 20, BG Hasbrouck met with LT Arthur A. Olson, D Troop, 87th Cavalry Reconnaissance Squadron, at the division command post. Hasbrouck ordered LT Olson to take his troop and "go to Samrée to assist in the defense of that area." Olson and D Troop got underway from Beho. On their way to Samrée, D Troop passed through what soon became known as Parker's Crossroads. At nightfall Olson encountered enemy infantry about a mile and a half east of Samrée. He ordered his scouts into action

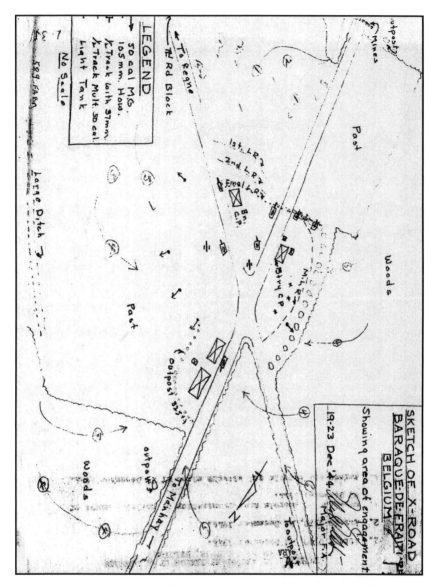

MAP 9. The numbered arrows show various attacks made by the Germans. The first came on the morning of December 20, and the fifth and final came at dusk on December 23, when the 4th Schutzstaffel Panzergrenadier Regiment overran the defenders. The north arrow is on the right-hand side of the sketch. The road to Manhay runs generally north. The road to Règné leads to Vielsalm and the 7th Armored Division rear. The road that exits at the upper left leads to Houffalize. Facsimile of a sketch drawn and signed by Major Elliot Goldstein, executive officer of the 589th Field Artillery, courtesy of John Schaffner. This copy has the edge of Goldstein's legend cut off.

dismounted. The troop's scouts drove the enemy infantry into the forest, whereupon D Troop "plastered the woods with mortar and machine gun fire" until they were satisfied the enemy had retired and then moved on. The troop got within half a mile of Samrée, where they discovered three American 2.5-ton trucks blocking the road. Roughly two companies of Germans manned the extemporaneous roadblock.[26]

Olson withdrew his troop a short distance, intending to develop the situation the next morning. He sent his supply trucks, half-tracks, and assault guns back to the crossroads to report to Parker. D Troop could shelter its logistics and Parker could use the half-tracks and assault guns to help defend the crossroads. Olson also dispatched LT Joseph W. Jones to the division command post to report on the situation and get orders. Jones's report clarified for Hasbrouck the danger in the rear of the Division. LT Jones returned to the troop's night defensive position with the information that the 3rd AD had troops in Dochamps and several nearby villages just north of the highway. He also brought the news that Hasbrouck wanted Olson to make contact with the 3rd AD and coordinate an attack with it.[27]

Action at Samrée

The 7th AD trains had fought direct-fire contacts every day since arriving. COL Andrew J. Adams had positioned his maintenance, ordnance, and fuel at Samrée. In addition to his own units, Adams had two medium truck companies manned by African American troops. His organic transportation units and the two medium truck companies hauled supplies in a loop from supply points forward and then returned for more as required. The main supply route from Samrée went to La Roche-en-Ardenne and beyond to access supply points and back east through Parker's Crossroads to Salmchâteau and ultimately to Vielsalm and then to the units.

Adams could not secure the main supply route in either direction. Because of that, he consolidated his supplies of fuel and rations in Samrée. He also used troops and self-propelled automatic antiaircraft weapons from D Battery, 203rd AAA to run patrols and escort convoys. Tanks and other combat vehicles coming out of repair also provided security when they were available. On December 18–19, Adams had established twelve roadblocks. Small detachments of antiaircraft artillery and combat engineers manned all but two of them. "Clerks, cooks and mechanics," as well as other rear area units, manned these. The roadblocks provided some security and early warning.[28] The ersatz units manning the roadblocks fought off several German patrols.

Until the night of December 19 the meager resources available to COL Adams enabled the trains to support the Division, albeit not without risk. Enemy reconnaissance and advanced guard units shot up more than one convoy. On the night of December 19, two units of LVIII PZ Corps maneuvered in the vicinity of Houffalize. The 116th PZ cleared Houffalize to the west, while the foot-mobile troops of the 560th VGD operated north and east. That night LVIII Corps turned both divisions north. During the night of December 19–20 the 116th PZ backtracked through Houffalize and moved north to attack Samrée.

The Panzer division had to struggle to reverse its march columns to comply with the Corps order. The division commander commented that the countermarch effort "was anything but pleasant." Tanks, half-tracks, trucks, and other gear had to reverse course and sequence in their columns. Sorting out units and their support took all night. Generalmajor Siegfried von Waldenburg, the commander, noted that his troops "didn't understand the necessity of these orders, which resulted in numerous counter questions."[29] It is easy to imagine the kind of questions, rhetorical and otherwise, the *Landsers* may have posed.

By the morning of December 20 the harassed troops of the 116th PZ had reoriented toward the north. While the 116th PZ organized to attack Samrée, MG Maurice Rose, in command of the 3rd AD, now joining the fight, dispatched three identically organized task forces south from Hotton, Soy, and Manhay. They moved toward terrain objectives from where they could screen the rest of the 3rd AD as it arrived. LTC Samuel M. Hogan's task force moved down the right flank boundary of the XVIII Airborne Corps, fielding a reconnaissance troop, a company of Sherman tanks, a platoon of light tanks, and a single battery of self-propelled howitzers. TF Hogan came south along the east bank of the Ourthe River and reached La Roche-en-Ardenne, where he found Adams's troops manning a roadblock. TF Tucker, led by MAJ John Tucker, moved south along the Aisne River to Dochamps and then to Samrée, where it found the 7th AD trains in extremis. On Tucker's left, TF Kane, led by LTC Matthew W. Kane, moved toward Parker's Crossroads to occupy a heavily wooded area overlooking the site. Kane reached his objective without opposition.[30]

Adams and the 7th AD trains suffered a rough day. At 0700 a small reconnaissance formation, probably from the 116th PZ, attacked one of Adams's roadblocks near La Roche-en-Ardenne. The troops on the roadblock drove this first attack off. At noon TF Hogan reached the roadblock and relieved the 7th AD trains troops. Adams then used these troops to reinforce strongpoints elsewhere. At 0945 the 116th PZ mounted an attack in battalion strength on another roadblock near Samrée.[31]

The trains fought for dear life while issuing supplies to five different units. At 1430 the tank company assigned to TF Tucker made its way toward Samrée, where the tankers exchanged fire with the attacking Germans, destroying one Panzer but losing three tanks of their own. The tank company withdrew and, according to Adams, "nothing was heard from it again." Half an hour later the Germans broke into Samrée with three Mark V Panther tanks. In response, Adams mounted a counterattack with two recently repaired Sherman tanks and "a miscellaneous group of service personnel." The Panthers destroyed the two US tanks, forcing Adams to withdraw from Samrée toward the comparative safety of La Roche-en-Ardenne, around which the trains still held several roadblocks.[32]

Meanwhile, in Samrée, the 116th PZ took in a great haul of supplies. More than twenty thousand gallons of fuel and fifteen thousand rations fell into the hands of the 116th's Panzer regiment. To the exultant and fuel-starved Panzer troops and their Panzergrenadier partners this windfall seemed "a present from heaven."[33] Throughout the fight Adams maintained good communications with the Division, so Hasbrouck knew fully the risk developing in the rear. The XVIII Airborne Corps also learned of the developing risks to the northern shoulder.

The King of Battle

Walther Lucht's LXVI Corps finally closed on St. Vith on December 20. His horse-drawn artillery, a rocket artillery brigade, and his infantry still clogged the roads as they made their final approach to enable a coordinated attack to reduce the American defenses. As LXVI Corps closed, the American artillery came into its own. On December 21, COL Orville Martin, the 7th AD artillery commander, gained control of all the artillery in the sector and made good use of it. As of that day the division artillery controlled eight artillery battalions. These included the 7th AD's three organic battalions, the 275th AFA, the 965th FA, and the 592nd FA (the latter two with 155-millimeter guns); the 591st FA (with 105-millimeter guns) from the 106th ID; and the 16th AFA from the 9th AD.

These eight artillery battalions savaged German columns, broke up patrols, hit crossroads, fired counterbattery, and supported limited counterattacks. On December 20 alone, the artillery fired 270 discrete missions expending 6,819 rounds of ammunition. American artillery proved its worth throughout the war but truly shone at St. Vith. Antitank gunner Klaus Ritter found it terrifying. He recalled "a screaming and whizzing . . . and then it impacts, men crying, frightened horses neighing. My body quivers, and fear gets to my throat."[34] Ritter had several harrowing moments thanks to the 7th AD artillery as his antitank unit closed in on Wallerode Mühle, less than a mile from the Prümerberg. The Germans respected American artillery for good reason. According to Oberst Friedrich Kittel, who commanded the 62nd VGD, "American artillery observation was very good, directing the fire of the enemy guns always to the decisive points."[35]

The German LXVI Corps had not been able to use its artillery very effectively as the forward units outran it, but the artillery caught up and emplaced on December 20. The Americans particularly despised the Nebelwerfer multiple rocket launchers known as screaming meemies. General Lucht's corps artillery included the 16th Volkswerfer Brigade fielding eighteen multiple rocket launchers (with six tubes per launcher) of varying size, ranging from 150 millimeters to 300 millimeters. The LXVI Corps fielded a battalion of heavy artillery firing a dozen 150-millimeter howitzers.[36] German artillery doctrine specified that "every attempt must be made to engage the greater part of the enemy's artillery before the start of the infantry attack."[37] The LXVI Corps had successfully supported the attack on December 16 and now, finally, could bring artillery to bear again.

The Apex of the Horseshoe: Clarke and Hoge

The Lucky Seventh's official narrative claimed that on December 20, BG Bruce C. Clarke's CCB, 7th AD enjoyed "a relatively quiet day."[38] That invites the question, Compared to what? During this "quiet" day both the FEB and the 18th VGD patrolled aggressively and exchanged direct fire with CCB. The 18th VGD completed concentrating with the 295th Volksgrenadier Regiment (VGR) in the north in and around Wallerode. The 294th massed astride the road to St. Vith from Schönberg, and the 293rd came up on its left.[39]

BG William M. Hoge's CCB, 9th AD spent much of the day organizing the position it had occupied during the night. That effort included employing engineers to work on the roads to enable movement of reserves and supplies. The 62nd VGD had closed up opposite CCB. Some of Hoge's troops could see horse-drawn artillery pulling into Lomersweiler, within a mile of their own positions. Hoge's combat command had a busy day. LTC Fred S. Cummings Jr.'s 27th AIB, defending on a wide front, repelled several attacks during it. Cummings, a veteran officer who had assumed command the previous day, described the fighting as "furious."[40]

A battalion of Volksgrenadiers from the 62nd VGD attacked the 27th AIB at 1630. In this action, II Battalion of the 190th VGR made a foolhardy move across an open field. Apparently unaware of the proximity of American infantry, the Volksgrenadiers attempted to cross the field in a column. Cummings's infantry called for "time on target" massed artillery. B and C Companies of the 27th opened up with everything they had, supported by several mounted quadruple .50-caliber machine guns, drove off the Volksgrenadiers with high losses.[41]

On December 20, CCB, 9th AD's direct-support artillery, the 16th AFA, fired 3,200 rounds of ammunition primarily in "defensive barrages" like that which helped stop the 190th VGR attack. As a consequence, the battalion ran dangerously low on ammunition. The Germans exacerbated the problem when they ambushed the 16th's supply column as it returned from drawing ammunition at Samrée from the 7th AD's trains. The supply column managed to escape, but five men were missing or killed.[42]

The Infantry Regiments

On Hoge's right, COL Reid's 424th INF fought off one attack on December 20. While CCB, 9th AD battered one of the 190th VGR battalions, what remained of the 190th came against the 424th. Driving off the Germans that afternoon at dusk was a genuine success, but the attack also demonstrated that the 62nd VGD had crossed the Our River. In fact, the 62nd had all three regiments concentrated and their artillery closed up for the first time since December 16.

In the first days of the offensive COL Gustin M. Nelson's 112th INF mauled the 560th VGD and forced the 116th PZ to find another way west. The sheer weight of numbers forced Nelson to delay westward and ultimately north into the St. Vith sector. By midday on December 20, Nelson's infantry had established what he called an island defense in recognition of the porous nature of the main line of resistance. In a letter to his father Nelson described the position more accurately as a "complete circular defense."[43]

Although now attached to the 106th ID, Nelson received an order directly from VIII Corps directing him to send an infantry company to attack enemy forces at Bastogne. The order suggests more than a little ignorance of the situation. Equally remarkable, Nelson, who elsewhere had shown the courage to act without orders when existing instructions made no sense, duly sent G Company, 3rd Battalion, 112th INF toward Houffalize. Surprisingly, G Company survived. Not surprisingly, it did not return for several days.[44]

Day's End

Hasbrouck finally got some good news. At 1230 he heard from LTG Hodges at First Army, who advised, "Ridgway with armor and infantry is moving from west to gain contact with you." On making contact, the 7th AD would be assigned to Ridgway's XVIII Airborne Corps. Then Hodges clarified the chain of command. He assigned Hasbrouck command of the 106th ID, the 112th INF, and CCB, 9th AD.

Despite this welcome news, the 7th AD had little reason to feel less lonely. Probed all along his line and well to the rear, Hasbrouck faced an eminent crisis. He had perceived that the Germans would attack in force on December 20, yet they had not done so. Still, it was clear that the Germans were massing north, east, and southeast of his position at St. Vith. At dusk one more little vignette played out. The quiet day for CCB, 7th AD came to an end.

After two days of pressure and small attacks from Nieder-Emmels, LTC Robert C. Erlenbusch, commanding the 31st TB, and MAJ William F. Beatty, his executive officer, focused on that avenue of approach. Beatty positioned four tank destroyers in hull defilade alongside the road that ran south from Nieder-Emmels to Hünningen. Meanwhile, Erlenbusch ordered the redoubtable Second Lieutenant Truman R. Bowman to "spread out turret down [a reverse slope defense] along the ridge west of Hunningen." Forward observers prepared concentrations in support.

According to Erlenbusch, "The basic plan was to let the lead tanks break over the hill and come abreast of our tanks. Our tanks had all of their guns pointed north. On command the platoon would fire simultaneously to knock out the lead tanks and then move forward to engage subsequent wave, if any. The TDs were to engage whatever came down the road trying to hit them in the belly as they crossed the ridge belly up." At dusk, "Bowman dismounted his bow gunners and equipped them with sound powered phones. They were posted ahead of tank to keep the tank commander informed of the direction the lead tanks were taking relative to his tank. The bow gunner was to withdraw and join his own crew when the enemy tank closed to 50 yards or so from the front." All that remained was to execute.[45]

Not long after dark Beatty's outposts heard movement from Nieder-Emmels. The Germans reached Beatty's tank destroyers an hour or so later, just before 2000. The Germans did not illuminate their advance with flares, as they sometimes did. The tank destroyers destroyed the first four enemy tanks that crossed the ridge at about fifty yards' range. As the enemy tanks in trail maneuvered, Bowman's platoon killed four more at the slightly greater range of one hundred yards. This triggered the planned artillery that "was so perfect . . . we never knew if there was infantry or not behind the tanks."[46] As the Germans withdrew, the tank destroyers destroyed an assault gun and perhaps damaged another.

Units of the 7th AD captured thirty-two German soldiers that day. Most came from the 1st SS, the 18th VGD, and the 560th VGD. Division intelligence was also tracking the 9th SS. Despite this success, Hasbrouck had little reason to celebrate. That day the 7th AD also captured four soldiers from the FEB, all of whom wore the Grossdeutschland Division sleeve flash. This led the intelligence section to assume that the Grossdeutschland had been transferred from the Eastern Front. The 62nd VGD had been identified opposite the 424th INF. Hasbrouck also knew that the 116th PZ had attacked his trains some twenty-five miles to the rear. It seemed reasonable to conclude that he was in contact with seven divisions, of which four were Panzer divisions.

NOTES

1. Army Pictorial Center, *The Battle of St. Vith*, pt. 1.

2. Roy U. Clay, telephone interview with the author, July 3, 1984.

3. General Bruce C. Clarke (Ret.) to the author, November 28, 1984, General Bruce C. Clarke Papers.

4. Hugh M. Cole, *The Ardennes: Battle of the Bulge*, 393–94; Major General Robert W. Hasbrouck (Ret.), interview with the author, Washington, DC, August 20, 1984. Hasbrouck did not think well of First Army's performance. He did not explicitly criticize VIII Corps, but his operations officer did; Colonel Charles E. Leydecker (Ret.) to the author, August 8, 1984.

5. Major William C. Sylvan and Captain Francis G. Smith Jr., *Normandy to Victory*, 223.

6. General der Panzertruppe Hasso von Manteuffel, "An Interview with Gen Pz Hasso von Manteuffel," ETHINT-46, 7. In the years after the war Manteuffel maintained that taking St. Vith had greater importance than taking Bastogne. See also Major Percy Ernst Schramm, "The Course of Events of the German Offensive in the Ardennes," 5. On counterattack orders, see Charles B. MacDonald, *A Time for Trumpets*, 470. Just when Manteuffel issued the order is unclear, but it was certainly on the night of December 19–20.

7. Generalmajor Otto E. Remer, "The Führer-Begleit Brigade in the Ardennes Offensive," 9.

8. Clarke provided the author with a reprint of an article in published in *Military Review*, September 1961, that he used to illustrate what he called "mission type orders"; General Bruce C. Clarke Papers.

9. Heinz Günther Guderian, *From Normandy to the Ruhr*. See also Oberstleutnant Dietrich Moll, "18th Volks Grenadier Division," 49.

10. Cole, *The Ardennes: Battle of the Bulge*, 356–57. See also MacDonald, *A Time for Trumpets*, 535–36.

11. On the reorganization of the front, see Dwight D. Eisenhower, *Crusade in Europe*, 350–53.

12. Charles Whiting, *Decision at St. Vith*, 158. See also Michael Reynolds, *Sons of the Reich*, 199.

13. MacDonald, *A Time for Trumpets*, 416, 424, 479, 596; R. J. T. Hills, *Phantom Was There*, 278; Nigel Hamilton, *Monty: The Battles of Field Marshall Bernard Montgomery*, 484–85.

14. Chester Wilmot, *The Struggle for Europe*, 592.

15. Wilmot, *The Struggle for Europe*, 592.

16. Collins used his initial when signing his name but was known in the Army as Joe.

17. Cole, *The Ardennes: Battle of the Bulge*, 396, emphasis in the original. Cole does not report Schroeder having arrived during the conference with Montgomery. All other major sources do.

18. Whiting, *Decision at St. Vith*, 166. See also John S. D. Eisenhower, *The Bitter Woods*, 288–89.

19. 7th Armored Division, G-3 journal, December 1944, entry 44, December 20, 1944.

20. Division Artillery, 7th Armored Division, "After Action Report, Month of December 1944," 14.

21. 7th Armored Division, "Battle of St. Vith: 17–23 December," 8; Calvin C. Boykin Jr., *Gare la Bête*, 77–78. The division order cited in the G-3 journal has the town names of Cherain and Deiffelt spelled incorrectly, as does the 7th AD narrative cited here. Boykin spelled both correctly.

22. 7th Armored Division, G-3 tactical journal, December 1944, entry 26, December 20, 1944, 0430 hours. CCA captured two soldiers from the 560th, one of whom was a captain. That officer had the planned march order for the 1130th Volksgrenadier Regiment.

23. Colonel R. Ernest Dupuy, *St. Vith: Lion in the Way*, 182.

24. 589th Field Artillery Battalion, "Narrative of Action 589th FA BN," sketch of Parker's Crossroads at Baraque de Fraiture, 5–7.

25. 589th Field Artillery Battalion, "Narrative of Action," 8. For "commandeered," see Dupuy, *St. Vith: Lion in the Way*, 189.

26. W. Wesley Johnston, *Combat Interviews of the 87th Cavalry Reconnaissance Squadron*, 43.

27. Johnston, *Combat Interviews of the 87th Cavalry Reconnaissance Squadron*, 43.

28. Major General Andrew J. Adams (Ret.), interview with the author, August 31, 1984. Andrew J. Adams, MG (Ret.), to the author, June 4, 1984, containing a short paper Adams wrote for the Air Command and Staff School, "Account of the Activities of the Seventh Armored Division Trains from 18th to 22nd December 1944," n.d.

29. Generalmajor Siegfried von Waldenburg, "Commitment of the 116th Panzer Division in the Ardennes 1944/45," pt. 1, p. 15.

30. Cole, *The Ardennes: Battle of the Bulge*, 353–59. Later in the fighting Tucker was reinforced by two armored infantry companies commanded by LTC William R. Orr—thus the task force became Task Force Orr.

31. Adams, "Account of the Activities," 2–3.

32. Adams, "Account of the Activities," 2–3. See also 7th Armored Division, "Action at Samrée, Belgium." Several resupply columns cleared Samrée during the fighting by going to Dochamps and then back and making their way circuitously to Vielsalm and then forward. Adams's short paper recounts the fight at Samrée involving quartermaster troops, a light tank and a half-track from the 87th CAV and others who pitched in. Both the light tank and the half-track expended all of their ammunition in the five hours the fighting lasted. Task Force Tucker's three tanks were damaged, but not destroyed. It is likely the 116th PZ captured them.

33. Guderian, *From Normandy to the Ruhr*, 320.

34. Klaus Ritter, statements, box 10, Charles B. MacDonald Papers, pt. 2, p. 6.

35. Generalmajor Friedrich Kittel, "62nd Volksgrenadier Division," 31.

36. Lieutenant Colonel Joseph R. Reeves, "Artillery in the Ardennes," 176. See also Division Artillery, 7th Armored Division, "After Action Report, Month of December 1944," 14.

37. Bruce Condell and David T. Zabecki, eds., *On the German Art of War: Truppenführung*, 102.

38. 7th Armored Division, "Battle of St. Vith, 17–23 December 1944," 8.

39. Moll, "18th Volks Grenadier Division," 46–47.

40. 27th Armored Infantry Battalion, "After Action Report," 3. See also Headquarters, Combat Command B, 9th Armored Division," After Action Report for the Period 1–31 December 1944," 6.

41. 27th Armored Infantry Battalion, "After Action Report," 3; Headquarters, Combat Command B, 9th Armored Division," After Action Report," 6

42. 16th Armored Field Artillery, "After Action Report (For Period 010001 December to 312400 December, 1944)," 3.

43. Colonel Gustin M. Nelson and Major Justin C. Brainard, interviewer not identified, January 14, 1945. Col. Gustin M. Nelson to his father, May 1945, box 3, Charles B. MacDonald Papers.

44. Col. Gustin M. Nelson, notes from S-2 periodic reports provided by Nelson, January 20, 1045, box 3, Charles B. MacDonald Papers.

45. Robert C. Erlenbusch to the author, August 24, 1984; Erlenbusch also provided to the author a letter he wrote to Hasbrouck, March 23, 1946.

46. Erlenbusch to the author, August 24, 1984.

(*Above*) General Dwight D. Eisenhower, Supreme Commander Allied Expeditionary Force, with Major General Troy H. Middleton, the commanding general of VIII Corps. Signal Corps photo, courtesy of the Dwight D. Eisenhower Library and Museum.

(*Below*) Major General J. Lawton Collins, the commanding general of VII Corps; Field Marshal Bernard Law Montgomery, commander of the 21st Army Group; and Major General Matthew B. Ridgway during the Battle of the Bulge. Signal Corps photo, courtesy of the Dwight D. Eisenhower Library and Museum.

(*Above*) Lieutenant General Courtney H. Hodges, commanding general of First Army, awarding the Silver Star to Brigadier General Robert W. Hasbrouck, commander of the 7th Armored Division, for the defense of St. Vith, Belgium. Signal Corps photo, courtesy of Robert W. Hasbrouck Jr.

(*Left*) Colonel Bruce C. Clarke during his tenure as commander of Combat Command B, 4th Armored Division. Clarke is wearing an Eagle, denoting his rank. Although commissioned as an engineer, Clarke is wearing the World War I tank corps insignia adopted by the Armored Forces. Courtesy of the US Army Armor School Archives.

(*Right*) Brigadier General
William M. Hoge, shortly after
the end of the Battle of the
Bulge. His face bares the cost of
the previous month's fighting.
Signal Corps photo, courtesy
of the US Army Heritage and
Education Center.

(*Left*) Colonel Donald P.
Boyer during his tenure
as commander of the 11th
Armored Cavalry Regiment, an
honor he shared with Colonel
Robert C. Erlenbusch, who
commanded the 31st Tank
Battalion. During the Battle of
the Bulge, Boyer served as the
operations officer of the 38th
Armored Infantry Battalion and
played a key role in the defense
of the Prümerberg. Official
photo, courtesy of Lieutenant
Colonel (Retired) Richard C.
Orth Jr.

(*Right*) General der Panzertruppe Hasso von Manteuffel, commanding general of the Fifth Panzer Army. After the war Manteuffel served in the Bundestag and also met with many of his former adversaries. He and Brigadier General Bruce C. Clarke became friendly. Bundesarchiv, Bild 146-1975-035-19.

(*Left*) General der Artillerie Walther Lucht, the commanding general of LXVI Corps. Bundesarchiv, Bild 101L-1029-30 A.

(*Right*) Oberst Günther Hoffmann-Schönborn, the commanding officer of the 18th Volksgrenadier Division. Bundesarchiv, Bild 183-B7259.

(*Left*) Oberst Friedrich Kittel, commanding officer of the 62nd Volksgrenadier Division. Bundesarchiv, Bild 146-1989-031-34.

(*Above*) Oberstleutnant Heinz Günther Guderian, operations officer with the 116th Panzer Division, wearing the all-black field uniform of the Panzer troops on the occasion of his capture in April 1945 by troops of the 7th Armored Division. Signal Corps photo, courtesy of the 7th Armored Division Association.

(*Below*) A present-day photograph of a 168th Engineer Battalion foxhole on the Prümerberg. Photo courtesy of Carl Wouters.

(*Above*) Infantrymen assigned to the 424th Infantry Regiment, 106th Infantry Division making their way up hill in the German extension of the Ardennes in March 1945. Photo courtesy of the 106th Infantry Division Association.

(*Left*) Volksgrenadiers making their way through the Ardennes during the Battle of the Bulge. Bundesarchiv, Bild 183-J28510.

(*Above*) A 105-millimeter howitzer position of the 106th Infantry Division . Note how deeply the howitzer's wheels have sunk. The 106th Infantry Division had to abandon at least three howitzers frozen so deeply that they could not be moved. Note also the hut in the background, where a stovepipe can be seen smoking at the back end, indicating that it was heated. Photo courtesy of the 106th Infantry Division Association.

(*Right*) Private John Schaffner, an artillery scout with the 589th Field Artillery, 106th Infantry Division, taken shortly after his nineteenth birthday while home on leave in 1943. Schaffner survived the Schnee Eifel to fight on at Parker's Crossroads and through the rest of the war. Note that in this photo, Schaffner is wearing a corporal's stripes. Later he got on the wrong side of his battery commander and lost his stripes, but in the end won them back. Photo courtesy of the 106th Infantry Division Association.

197561-S

(*Above*) This is one of the most famous photos from the Battle of the Bulge, taken by a German combat cameraman on the morning of December 18, 1944, on the road just east of Poteau, Belgium. This soldier was a grenadier assigned to Kampfgruppe Hansen from the 1st Schutzstaffel Panzer Division. He and his colleagues had just routed Task Force Mayes of the 18th Cavalry Squadron, 14th Cavalry Group. He was almost certainly a machine gunner. His *Werkzeugtasche*, or gunner's tool pouch, can be seen just below the belt of machine gun ammunition draped around his neck. His "boot" knife is visible just to the right of his chin, and his entrenching tool can be seen just above his gunner's pouch. The man to his rear may be the assistant gunner, as he is carrying ammunition. Photo courtesy of the National Archives and Records Administration.

(*Above*) Kampfgruppe Hansen grenadiers crossing the Poteau road amid the detritus of Task Force Mayes. This is a frame from a German combat video. Photo courtesy of the National Archives and Records Administration.

(*Below*) Crossroads at the Baraque de Fraiture, known during the war as Parker's Crossroads. It was vital to supplying the 7th Armored Division via the highway from Samrée to Vielsalm. On Christmas Eve 1944 the 2nd Schutzstaffel Panzer Division attacked northward either moving on or parallel to the highway toward Manhay. Photo courtesy of the National Archives and Records Administration.

(*Above*) An M4 Sherman tank equipped with a seventy-five-millimeter cannon dug in near Manhay, Belgium, in late December 1944 or early January 1945 during a brief hiatus from the snow. The soldier in the foreground is wearing the four-buckle rubber overshoes or galoshes, which were more common than the more famous shoepacs. Photo courtesy of the National Archives and Record Administration.

(*Right*) Private Audry Ziegler of C Company, 17th Tank Battalion whitewashing his M4 Sherman tank near Xhoris, Belgium, on January 11, 1945. The snow returned to stay through the end of the Battle of the Bulge. Signal Corps photo, courtesy of Robert W. Hasbrouck Jr.

(*Above*) Tanks and tank destroyers of the 7th Armored Division assembling to attack. The long-barreled vehicles in the background are M36 tank destroyers. Photo courtesy of the National Archives and Records Administration.

(*Below*) Paratroopers assigned to 2nd Battalion, 517th Parachute Infantry Regiment attached to the 7th Armored Division, heading toward St. Vith. As evidenced by antennas, two paratroopers are carrying the backpack Signal Corps Radio 300, which had a range of about three miles. Given the number of radios, this group was probably either a company or the battalion headquarters. Having two radios enabled a commander to speak or listen to both his subordinates and his own commander. During the battle to retake St. Vith, the 509th Parachute Infantry Battalion and the 508th and 517th Parachute Infantry Regiments fought attached to the 7th Armored Division. Photo courtesy of the National Archives and Records Administration.

(*Above*) German photo of US Army bombing near St. Vith. Panicked horses can be seen in the foreground. The horses on the left are drawing a standard German Army supply wagon with a canvas cover. The wagon likely belonged to the 18th or 62nd Volksgrenadier Division. Another team of horses can be seen on the right. Bundesarchiv, Bild 183-J28547.

(*Below*) An M7 howitzer section of the 7th Armored Division supporting the attack to retake St. Vith. Brass casings can be seen in the foreground behind. Waterproofed cardboard canisters in which ammunition was stored and moved can be seen in stacks left and right of center. The canvas tarpaulin covering the self-propelled howitzer provided some protection from the elements. The bows used to support the canvas are visible at the left front of the howitzer. Photo courtesy of the Dwight D. Eisenhower Library and Museum.

(*Above*) Stuart light tanks of the 87th Cavalry Squadron moving down a forest trail. Photo courtesy of the family of William A. Knowlton.

(*Below*) An 18th Volksgrenadier Division Hetzer Jagdpanzer on fire. Infantrymen of the 7th Armored Division can be seen moving behind the stricken antitank gun. Photo courtesy of the National Archives and Records Administration.

(*Above*) The 31st Tank Battalion preparing to seize the village of Wallerode. The battalion then took Hünningen on January 23, 1945. The after action report claimed, "The doom of St Vith was now sealed as Hunnigen commands the heights looking into St Vith." Hünningen is less than a mile north of St. Vith, while Wallerode is just over a mile northeast. Signal Corps photo, courtesy of Robert W. Hasbrouck Jr.

(*Below*) Infantrymen from Company A, 23rd Armored Infantry Battalion fighting as part of the 31st Tank Battalion in its attack toward Hünningen. According to the US Army caption, combat photographer Corporal Hugh F. McHugh took this photograph moments before a German sniper killed him. Photo courtesy of the National Archives and Records Administration.

(*Above*) A battalion surgeon (foreground) and medics treat a wounded American. Photo courtesy of the Dwight D. Eisenhower Library and Museum.

(*Below*) A captured German medic who no doubt had to explain where he obtained the two pairs of US binoculars hooked to his equipment belt. Photo courtesy of the Dwight D. Eisenhower Library and Museum.

(*Above*) Soldiers of the 18th Volksgrenadier Division in the hands of the 7th Armored Division. Photo courtesy of Robert W. Hasbrouck Jr.

(*Below*) Redemption: St. Vith back in the hands of the 7th Armored Division. Scouts from Troop C, 87th Reconnaissance Squadron entering St. Vith. National Archives and Records Administration.

(*Above*) Soldiers of the 48th Armored Infantry Squad in front of their half-track. They have pulled the camouflage cover back far enough so the half-track may be seen. It was young men like these who fought to defend St. Vith and then retook the town. One of the squad, George Myrick (not identified), donated this captivating picture of innocence and optimism. Photo courtesy of 7th Armored Division Association.

(*Right*) Lieutenant William A. Knowlton, who "escaped" from the hospital to rebuild and lead Troop B, 87th Cavalry back to St. Vith. Photo courtesy of the family of William A. Knowlton.

(*Above*) Looking east over the ruins of St. Vith. The densely forested ridge, typical of the Ardennes, is the Prümerberg. Bomb craters and shell holes illustrate just how much effort was spent bombing and shelling St. Vith. Photo courtesy of the National Archives and Records Administration.

CHAPTER NINE

Decision at St. Vith

During the Battle of the Bulge we had real good leadership from our commanding, General Hasbrouck.

—Sergeant Russell J. Weber

They were brave blokes whose resistance could only be broken by concentrated fire.

—Oberst Friedrich Kittel

GENERAL DER ARTILLERIE Walther Lucht finally managed to concentrate his LXVI Corps for an attack on St. Vith late on the afternoon of Thursday, December 21, 1944. In the first hours of the counteroffensive, his 18th and 62nd Volksgrenadier Divisions (VGDs) enveloped the two American regiments on the Schnee Eifel but then failed to take St. Vith as planned. From December 17 until nightfall on December 21, LXVI Corps struggled forward over muddy logging trails and roads clogged by its own horse-drawn artillery, the Führer Escort Brigade (FEB), and various Schutzstaffel (SS) units. On December 20, two of the 18th VGD's three regiments remained tied up, clearing the last Americans from the Schnee Eifel. Consequently, they could not get into position to attack until around 1500 on December 21. That afternoon the 18th VGD assembled near Wallerode, northeast of St. Vith, and along the Schönberg road. With the 18th VGD in place, LXVI Corps, along with elements of the Fifth and Sixth Panzer Armies, had virtually cut off the Americans. More important, they could finally attack in strength.[1]

The troops defending Brigadier General (BG) Robert W. Hasbrouck's horseshoe understood that a big attack was coming. Staff Sergeant (SSG) Richard L. McBride, assigned to A Company, 23rd Armored Infantry Battalion (AIB), sensed trouble as the ammunition supply dwindled. He noticed that "while 'outgoing mail' had diminished, the 'incoming mail' increased by the hour."[2] The LXVI Corps had gotten far enough forward to harass the defenders. The lines that formed the elongated horseshoe ran from Petit-Thier on the northern shank of the horseshoe east and then south along the Prümerberg, where McBride's company fought. From there Combat Command B (CCB), 9th Armored Division (AD) manned the line as it continued south to the 424th Infantry Regiment (INF) and then the 112th INF. Here the line curved west toward Task Force (TF) Jones at Gouvy. Some twenty-five miles long, the horseshoe-shaped perimeter remained porous throughout, but especially on the southern shank.

German Assessments and Orders

From the German point of view there was little more to be done. There were virtually no changes to dispositions on December 21. The situation, however, was not good. In the north, the Sixth Panzer Army remained stymied. The arriving US 30th Infantry Division (ID) first stopped Obersturmbahnführer Joachim Peiper's surge toward the Meuse River and then worked to destroy him. Now, instead of leading the way forward, Peiper required rescue. The Fifth Panzer Army still advanced, led by General der Panzertruppe Heinrich von Lüttwitz's XXXXVII Panzer Corps. His three Panzer divisions and one Volksgrenadier division swirled around Bastogne. In the end, the Panzer divisions bypassed Bastogne. Lüttwitz left the well-led 26th VGD to surround the static 101st Airborne Division (ABN). The most serious problem was that General der Panzertruppe Hasso von Manteuffel's troops could not advance freely with the Americans holding St. Vith.

To Manteuffel's chagrin, his LVIII Panzer Corps missed an opportunity to cross the Ourthe River on December 20. The corps commander, General der Panzertruppe Walter Krüger, diverted the 116th Panzer Division (PZ) from crossing the Ourthe and ordered it to attack Samrée, where the 7th AD trains had located. Krüger's choice cost a significant amount of time the Germans no longer could afford. On the other hand, the 116th PZ captured a trove of US Army gasoline and rations. The Panzer division troops gorged on American chocolate and smoked American cigarettes.[3]

On December 20 the hard-marching 560th VGD reached the vicinity of Parker's Crossroads. The 560th had, however, worn itself down fighting the energetic 112th INF, as well as the 424th INF; CCB, 9th AD; and part of the 7th AD. Oberst Rudolph Langhäuser estimated his effective infantry strength at little more than 1,300 men organized in two Kampfgruppen.

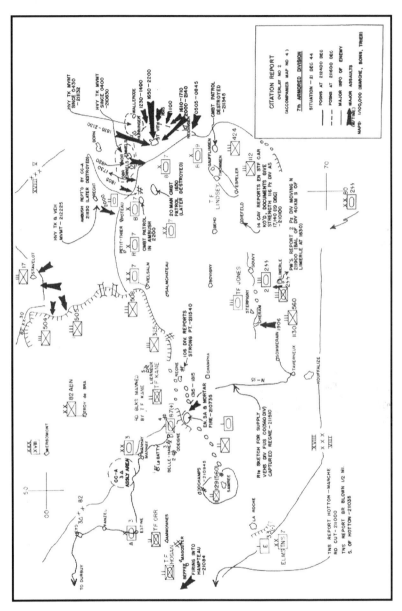

MAP 10. By midnight on December 21, the 82nd Airborne Division had occupied positions to the rear and north of the 7th Armored Division as First Army sought to stabilize the northern shoulder of the Bulge. The situation to the west and south of Vielsalm remained fluid. Nearly continuous German attacks against the Prümerberg positions are evident. Reproduced from Donald P. Boyer, *The 7th Armored Division in the Battle of the Bulge.*

But the "combat strength of the remaining divisional detachments was almost normal."[4] His depleted infantry could count on being well supported by artillery and direct fire assault guns. Most of the Division spent the night near Gouvy. On December 21, Langhäuser planned to attack northwest with one of his Kampfgruppe to cut the road from Salmchâteau to La Roche-en-Ardenne. He intended the other to clear Gouvy and continue generally northwest.[5]

The 2nd SS PZ was en route through Prüm and then west in the wake of the 116th PZ. Though operating in the Fifth Panzer Army zone, the 2nd SS PZ remained subordinated to II SS Panzer Corps of the Sixth Panzer Army. That made sense given that it was to attack northwest to cut off St. Vith and penetrate the northern shoulder. If successful, it would rejoin the 9th SS PZ, its partner in the Corps, and restore movement in the Sixth Panzer Army. The 2nd SS would attack northwest as soon it could refuel in its planned assembly area south of Parker's Crossroads.[6]

Taking St. Vith remained essential to Army Group B. Generalfeldmarschall Walther Model had harangued Manteuffel about taking St. Vith twice on December 18. In turn, Manteuffel flogged General Lucht, whose largely foot-mobile LXIV Corps had been charged with reducing the pocket in the Schnee Eifel as well as taking St. Vith. The crossroads town had become the lone "boulder in the river" that disrupted the flow of the Germans west. If St. Vith fell, the Sixth Panzer Army could move again. Now, three days later, Manteuffel knew that a slim chance for victory remained only if the Fifth Panzer Army could take St. Vith, and soon. In 1950 he wrote a letter describing his view. In it Manteuffel expressed puzzlement at the lack of attention placed on the battle for St. Vith in the early histories of the Battle of the Bulge. To him the stand at St. Vith absolutely disrupted the German counteroffensive, whereas Bastogne was not an immediate hindrance.[7]

American Assessments and Orders

Freshly deployed from England, Major General (MG) Matthew B. Ridgway established his XVIII Airborne Corps command post in a farmhouse at Werbomont, some twelve miles northwest of Parker's Crossroads on Highway N15. Ridgway entered the fray with panache and a theatrical sense second only to that of British field marshal Bernard Law Montgomery, and he had an ego to match. Ridgway wore a grenade and first aid pouch on his combat suspenders. He also carried the World War I–era Springfield rifle rather than the M1. He claimed this was not an affectation, asserting that he carried the Springfield because he was so familiar with it that he reacted with it far more quickly than he could with an M1. This seems farfetched, since he spent little time in troop units prior to World War II. MG Ridgway did operate far enough forward to use his rifle at least once. Whether he genuinely felt he needed to use the Springfield or not he was as effective a showman as Lieutenant General (LTG) George S. Patton Jr.[8]

Ridgway certainly had courage and confidence, and he had good reason to be sure of himself. He had proved himself effective in command of the 82nd ABN in both Sicily and Normandy. Soon after the Normandy landings Ridgway was offered and accepted command of the newly formed XVIII Airborne Corps. Although both the 82nd and 101st jumped into Holland for Operation Market Garden, Ridgway and his corps headquarters had not. He and his staff would fight the corps for the first time in the Ardennes campaign.

Most of Ridgway's corps staff had served with him in the 82nd ABN through the Sicily and Normandy campaigns. Although they had not handled a corps in combat, they, too, had proven able, and they moved into the role of fighting a corps with few missteps. Finally, they were courageous men, steeped in the basic tactical doctrine of airborne and infantry forces. At the outset of its first combat operation, XVIII Corps was assigned three divisions—the 30th ID, the 82nd ABN, and the 3rd AD. Trained for operations employing light infantry units capable of air delivery to the battle area, they would fight a difficult conventional operation instead.

Late on December 18, MG Leland Hobbs's 30th ID stopped Joachim Peiper on the XVIII Airborne Corps' left flank. In the center, MG James M. Gavin's 82nd Airborne fanned out east and southeast toward the Salm River and Parker's Crossroads. One of Gavin's regiments reached Trois-Ponts on December 20. There it made life even more difficult for Peiper and interfered with the advancing 9th SS PZ. The bulk of the 82nd headed south along the west bank of the Amblève River. One regiment, the 325th Glider Infantry, initially occupied a reserve position near Werbomont. Ridgway ordered the 3rd AD into action as it arrived. As noted previously, the 3rd AD task forces moved south on December 20 and made contact with elements of the 7th AD between La Roche-en-Ardenne and Parker's Crossroads. Indecision and confusion did not immediately end when Ridgway arrived, but it would soon.[9]

On December 21, the 82nd ABN made contact with the 7th AD on the Salm River. Hasbrouck described that event succinctly: "We were overjoyed to find that the 82nd ABN had arrived in our general vicinity and had made tenuous contact with us near the Vielsalm Bridge." All along the intermittent positions euphemistically called the line, the troops could see and/or hear the Germans preparing to attack. They also suffered from the cold, but less so than those on the Prümerberg who had no buildings in which they could rest and warm themselves. Shivering in two-man holes separated by several yards, the troops on the Prümerberg suffered through interminable nights punctuated by snow flurries and/or rain. Major (MAJ) Don Boyer recalled that by the night of December 20, "All of us had frostbite." Worse still, "All night long we heard the noise of trucks and the noise of tanks moving into position."[10]

The telephone records and the Division journal reveal a palpable sense of foreboding. For days Hasbrouck had shuttled troops hither and yon, but mostly from the northern shank to stiffen the Prümerberg. By December 20 he had trouble in the south. He now had more problems than solutions. Hasbrouck needed to secure his southern flank and gain more than tenuous contact with the 82nd ABN and the 3rd AD. He also had to consider how to withdraw his command if the situation became untenable. To that end he ordered Lieutenant (LT) Arthur A. Olson and his D Troop, 87th Cavalry Reconnaissance Squadron (CAV) to make contact with the 3rd AD task force that had entered Dochamps the day before.

Olson moved out early on December 21 with two armored cars and two Jeeps planning to link up with friendly forces. The remainder of D Troop remained in defensive positions astride what had been the supply route from Samrée to Salmchâteau. Olson's patrol reached Dochamps and discovered that Germans held the town. As they entered the town, German troops fired on them. Somehow "they managed to turn around, ramming buildings as they went." Despite a lot of shooting, the Germans wounded only one man.

Hasbrouck was no longer directing emergency moves from one part of the sector to another to defend the approaches to St. Vith but instead was managing small unit actions to protect the rear.[11] Over the next forty-eight hours Hasbrouck did little else. His major subordinates, including those who were technically not his subordinates, such as CCB, 9th AD and the 424th INF and 112th INF, all fought a series of small unit actions rather than battle actions orchestrated at higher levels. In the 1965 US Army television documentary *The Battle of St. Vith*, Hasso von Manteuffel described the confusing battle, undertaken mostly in darkness, as one fought by *kleine Leute*—literally, "small people," but more aptly the junior leaders. This included outpost commanders such as MAJ Arthur C. Parker III. Manteuffel, who was describing the initiative of small unit commanders, believed the idea applied to both sides.[12] Poor visibility, multiple ridgelines, and forests made it nearly impossible to employ large forces on any of the avenues of approach into St. Vith and to objectives farther west.

The southward movement of XVIII Airborne Corps units provided Hasbrouck some grounds for optimism, but not enough to relieve the "lonesome" feeling. The troops in the horseshoe remained exposed to a great many Germans. The 7th AD, according to BG Hasbrouck, "had prisoners of war identified in our prisoner of war enclosure who were from five German Divisions." One of these came from the 2nd SS PZ, which seemed to be lurking at the Division's rear.[13] Hasbrouck had more than enough grounds for pessimism.

The LXVI Corps

The Germans also had problems. Friction imposed by muddy forest trails, indiscipline, disoriented units, and a determined enemy prevented LXVI Corps from mounting a well-oiled attack. Instead the two Volksgrenadier divisions and the FEB attacked intermittently and indecisively throughout the day. Generally these attacks included perhaps three hundred or so infantry supported by three to ten tanks. Almost without exception, the Germans attacked along roads or improved trails adequate to support tanks and assault guns.[14] German artillery fired on American positions almost continuously.

The Germans mounted eleven separate attacks against the long perimeter held by the Americans. The American advantage of interior lines no longer mattered. The Germans attacked along the entire front as far west as the Salm River. Small German forces from LXVI Corps, and from both the Fifth and Sixth Panzer Armies, succeeded in penetrating between American positions and attacking command posts, rear area units, and field artillery firing positions throughout the day. There is no neat chronology of the day's events, and none is readily discernible from the record. BG Bruce C. Clarke's personal aphorism, "The job of generals is to keep the confusion from becoming disorganized," became more difficult with each new German attack.[15]

The LXVI Corps had three main avenues into St. Vith and had attacked on all three at various times since December 18. Previous unsuccessful attacks had come from the north via Nieder-Emmels, Ober-Emmels, and Wallerode; from the east on the Schönberg road; and from the southeast on the road from Steinebrück. On December 21 the LXVI attacked on all three avenues yet again. Although Lucht had managed to bring up his artillery, he had trouble positioning it in the rugged terrain of the Schnee Eifel. As Oberstleutnant Dietrich Moll, the 18th VGD operations officer, complained,

"The terrain offered only limited observation and few firing positions for the artillery." According to Moll, "An attack on St. Vith could be supported by artillery only from the narrow Our Valley or from the hill above Wallerode."[16] Despite these difficulties, the Volks-Werfer Brigade, which carried multiple launch rocket systems, was positioned northwest of Wallerode from where it could support attacks along all three axes.

At dawn on December 21, General Lucht visited the commander of the 18th VGD, Oberst Günther Hoffman-Schönborn, and Moll at the 18th's command post in Wallerode. Moll recalled Lucht's instructions clearly: "St. Vith was to be taken during the day regardless of cost."[17] Oberst Friedrich Kittel, commanding the 62nd VGD, received similar dire instructions. Oberst Otto-Ernst Remer, in command of the most powerful unit in the Corps, had the same instruction. Lucht ordered Remer to attack south from Nieder-Emmels and Ober-Emmels. Instead, late in the day, Remer attacked toward Rodt, northwest of St. Vith, so he could bypass the town and get on a good road to head west and cross the Meuse. In a postwar interview he admitted that he had "declined" the order to make an attack south.[18] Remer, the ultimate Nazi and a favorite of the führer, behaved with the arrogance generally confined to the SS. His interpretation of his prerogatives as a commander enabled him to do what he liked rather than commit to what his commander ordered.

The 18th VGD had trouble getting underway. Until the evening of December 20, two of its three regiments and part of the 1818th Anti-Tank Battalion worked to finish off the 422nd and 423rd Infantry regiments. Once the Battalion completed that task, it took until midafternoon on December 21 to assemble for the attack. Accordingly, the first major effort came from the southeast at about 0830, mounted by the 62nd VGD "after the heaviest preliminary bombardment by both divisions [the divisional artillery of the 18th and 62nd VGDs] and the werfer brigade." The 62nd renewed its attack on Neidingen while the southernmost regiment of the 18th VGD supported by attacking toward St. Vith along the Belgian national highway from Steinebrück. The 183rd Volksgrenadier Regiment (VGR) made the main effort against CCB, 9th AD. The attack impressed BG William M. Hoge sufficiently to ask Hasbrouck for help. Hasbrouck released TF Lindsey, formed on the remnants of the 14th CAV, to support Hoge. In the end, the attack petered out, according to the 62nd's commander, because American "tanks were everywhere."[19]

The Calm before the Storm

Despite the anticipation of a major attack, comparatively little happened after the attack on CCB, 9th AD. Still, the noise of movement presaging an attack continued. Combat patrols, desultory firing, and minor attacks punctuated the day. At 1055 that morning BG Bruce Clarke spoke with Lieutenant Colonel (LTC) Charles E. Leydecker, the division operations officer, about the situation and a particular problem with which he wanted help. Aware that Germans might have tapped the phone line, they spoke around the issue Clarke raised. Clarke began by saying, "We seem to be in good humor," to which Leydecker asked, "Everything ok there?" Clarke told him, "The tide is swinging back," meaning Germans were building up to his front. Clarke wanted another artillery battalion in support, or failing that, more artillery ammunition. Clarke point blank asked, "Will you see what you can do?" Leydecker agreed, "I will."[20]

Clarke's concern was legitimate and urgent. On December 20 the division artillery fired 7,819 rounds in 270 missions shifting all across the elongated horseshoe but primarily in support of CCB. The battalions directly supporting CCB, the 434th and 275th, fired 2,439 and 2,057 rounds, respectively. The attack on the 7th AD trains at Samrée and multiple attacks on December 20 had drained ammunition stocks. There was none to be had until the trains could obtain more for resupply and find a safe route forward. The division artillery, free with ammunition on December 20, now fired what they could rather than what they needed to fire.[21] When the inevitable big attack came there would be much less defensive fire.

Elsewhere, Combat Command Reserve (CCR), 7th AD cleared the Poteau road to the point it believed the 14th CAV could recover some of the equipment lost on December 18. CCR also wanted to recover eight eight-inch howitzers and rolling stock abandoned by the 740th Field Artillery Battalion from VIII Corps. At 1100 hours, troops from CCR, the 14th CAV, and the 434th Armored Field Artillery (AFA) set out to retrieve the equipment. The Germans did not take this lying down. They fired both mortars and direct fire at the recovery team. Nevertheless, the Americans recovered their equipment successfully by 1400 hours.[22]

During the day, VIII Corps, overlooking the fact that the troops in the St. Vith sector now belonged to XVIII Airborne Corps, issued several unhelpful orders. In one order, Middleton wanted the 112th INF to attack Houffalize, a forlorn hope if there ever was one, and indicative of how little VIII Corps understood of the battle east of Bastogne. Later, MG Troy H. Middleton ordered CCB, 9th AD to withdraw and rejoin VIII Corps. Neither of these things happened, but they illustrate that without adequate communications VIII Corps headquarters in Neufchâteau, nearly fifty miles away, had lost control of the battle. Direct telephone lines had been cut, and the long route around the penetration proved unreliable. Tactical radios were of little use. The presence of XVIII Airborne Corps at Werbomont, about twenty miles away by reasonably safe routes, supports the wisdom of GEN Dwight D. Eisenhower's quick decision to employ XVIII Airborne Corps and assign it to First Army.

Remer's Initiative

Remer's unauthorized attack toward Rodt also went nowhere against Combat Command A (CCA).[23] At about 1130 Remer did succeed in getting Panzergrenadiers far enough forward to infiltrate the thinly held American lines. Apparently they crossed the Poteau road east of town and headed south.[24] Around nightfall as many as three hundred grenadiers attacked LTC Roy U. Clay's 275th AFA. Clay's battalion was well to the rear, so this attack received immediate attention. Clay began by ordering his two remaining seventy-six-millimeter forward observer tanks into action supported by twenty-five artillerymen from his Battery B. He lost one of the tanks to a Panzerfaust almost immediately. Battery C, the battery directly endangered, turned its tracked howitzers around and went into direct fire mode. The Battery fired 105-millimeter rounds using time fuses set to "zero time," which meant "they would burst at 100 meters." This had devastating effect on the Battery's antagonists.[25]

As the fight got underway, BG Clarke, who could hear firing to his rear, called Clay and asked him to report. Clay did so and asked for help, to which Clarke responded, "Hold on—under no circumstances displace or give up the position. I will send you six light tanks to help out." When the Stuart tanks arrived, Clay organized a tank infantry team with some of his artillerymen and a handful of infantry, and cleared the ground of Remer's troops. All the while the remaining two batteries continued firing in support of Clarke's CCB. When the firing stopped, the artillerymen only one soldier had been killed. Clay's troops captured several Germans, all of whom wore the Grossdeutschland sleeve markings although they came from Remer's brigade. Later that evening several Americans who had been captured by the FEB the day before made their way into the artillery position, having escaped during the fighting.[26]

The Main Attack

Continued movement and periodic German efforts to penetrate the American positions built the expectation of major attack. The 7th AD trains scattered on December 20 and attempted to move to Marche-en-Famenne but fought actions at their remaining roadblocks. In some cases the trains had to fight their way through enemy patrols to reach Marche-en-Famenne and the comparative safety of the arriving 84th ID's newly forming lines.[27]

According to COL Andrew J. Adams, the trains evacuated by getting "together everything that we could find." Once in Marche-en-Famenne and behind friendly lines, Adams and his convoy of some ninety vehicles, including trucks hauling rations, ammunition, and fuel and accompanied by recently repaired combat vehicles, made their way on to Harzé, Belgium. The trip covered some thirty-five miles across two divisions, the 84th ID and the 3rd AD, without having provided advance notice. The trains reached Harzé around midnight on December 21–22 and immediately began to organize to get supplies forward, as none had been delivered for two days.[28]

Hasbrouck had activity all along the southern shank of the horseshoe and growing activity at the apex. At sunset, in bitter cold weather and slushy wet conditions, the Germans made their move. Despite difficulty getting into position, the 18th VGD now had all three infantry regiments able to attack the American positions on the Prümerberg. "Troop morale was excellent, largely because of the division's successes," according to operations officer Moll. All three regiments remained fully fit to attack.[29]

Lucht and Manteuffel were frustrated by their failure to take St. Vith as planned, but the delay did confer one small but important advantage. The FEB and the 18th VGD's lead units had been in contact with the 7th AD long enough to develop a good picture of the defenses on the Prümerberg and as far west as Poteau. The 62nd VGD had not had the time to develop as much combat information, but it, too, found time to develop fire plans and a decent estimate of the enemy's situation.

To a large extent, LXVI Corps could reprise the deliberate attack it had made on December 16. What the Corps could not do was envelop its enemy. Instead, the 18th VGD prepared penetration attacks while the 62nd VGD made a frontal attack. The FEB planned to attack toward Rodt. German military doctrine stressed heavy artillery preparation and support to the infantry in the close assault at the decisive point, or *Schwerpunkt*. Additionally, German doctrine stressed close collaboration between mounted forces—tanks, assault guns, and the infantry. Furthermore, it was imperative that signals

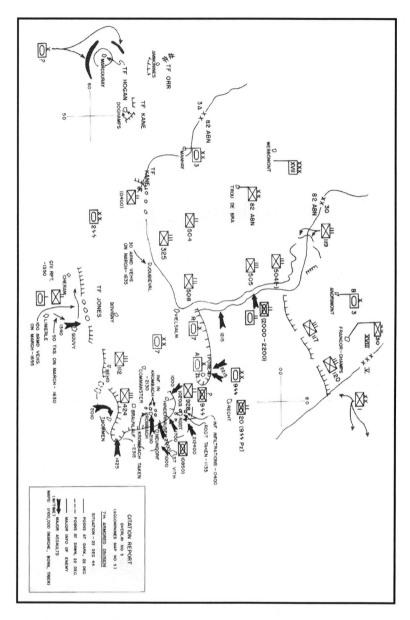

MAP 11. This overlay illustrates the end at St. Vith and the rapidly narrowing corridor to the west. The 30th Infantry Division's 117th and 120th Infantry Regiments are shown firming up the northern shoulder. The dangerous position of the 7th Armored Division is evident. Reproduced from Donald P. Boyer, *The 7th Armored Division in the Battle of the Bulge.*

and communications be "coordinated among participating commanders prior to the attack."[30] For the first time since December 16, the LXVI Corps had the means to execute a combined arms fight.

The LXVI Corps had assembled about one hundred howitzers and thirty Nebelwerfer rocket launchers. The Nebelwerfer ranged from 150 to 300 millimeters in size—they packed a wallop.[31] At 1500 hours LXVI Corps began a punishing artillery preparation on the Prümerberg. Despite otherwise organizing effectively for combat operations on the Prümerberg, BG Clarke expected too much of LTC William H. G. Fuller, commander of the 38th AIB. Clarke assigned him forces well beyond a logical span of control.

On December 21 Fuller controlled a force of around 1,500 men. They were a disparate group, strung out in penny parcels along the ridge. There were four armored infantry companies from two different battalions, a tank company, a platoon of tank destroyers, a cavalry troop, and four hundred combat engineers. The engineers came from two different battalions—LTC Thomas J. Riggs's 81st Engineer Battalion (ENG) from the 106th ID, and LTC W. L. Nungesser's 168th ENG from VIII Corps. Nungesser and Riggs had established the initial defense of the Prümerberg on December 16. German artillery fire increased from 1500 hours until reaching a crescendo at 1600, when LXVI Corps opened up with all it had.[32]

The veteran troops on the Prümerberg had never experienced a barrage like the one they endured that evening. The Germans shifted artillery fires from the Prümerberg to St. Vith and back. Tree bursts among the pines on the ridge killed, wounded, and stunned the defenders. The bombardment sowed particular confusion in A Company, 31st Tank Battalion. The Company suffered the loss of three tank commanders—including the company commander, who was killed during the opening barrage. In the ensuing confusion the five tanks on the ridge withdrew. LT John J. Dunn, who had led the first tanks onto the Prümerberg on December 17, took command. He rounded up the five tanks assigned replacement tank commanders and positioned them on the reverse slope of the ridge. Dunn had several other tanks in positions nearby, probably in support of B Company, 23rd AIB.[33] The confusion in the continuing barrage was such that after the fact neither Dunn nor his tankers knew just where everyone was.

MAJ Donald P. Boyer, Fuller's operation officer, described the sound of the incoming Nebelwerfer rockets as horrendous. To him they sounded like "a huge spring being compressed and then suddenly cut loose. It was a horrible din that came through the air down among the trees."[34] SSG

Richard L. McBride described the method the Germans used to adjust fire: "First their white phosphorous smoke shell burst in the tops of the tall pines along our line, so as to confirm their estimate of the range and mark the target for the following barrage." Once satisfied with the range, "the enemy batteries pounded us into a state of semi-consciousness. We prayed that each incoming shell would somehow avoid our foxholes."[35] Besides traumatizing the troops, the artillery cut telephone communications with the rear as well as along the line.[36]

On the heels of the preparation fires, the Volksgrenadiers attacked in bounds, supported by tanks, antitank guns, and some Hetzer assault guns. Antitank gunner Klaus Ritter, "the old hare," advanced with his mates toward St. Vith. When American artillery and mortars returned fire, Ritter and his men suffered too. His gun crew supported the attack coming out of Wallerode. They could see St. Vith, "but the place is still being held by enemy forces offering violent resistance. . . . Suddenly our road to St Vith is under American mortar fire. It creeps up the road, then moves away into the wood and ceases abruptly," but not before driving the crew into a nearby ditch.[37]

The defenders, despite the shock of the intense barrage, drove off the first effort of the 18th VGD, but soon thereafter Hasbrouck's painfully constructed defense began to unravel. At 1700 hours, Tiger Tanks of the 506th Heavy Panzer Battalion, released from the Army Reserve, joined the attack on the Schönberg road. The tanks LT Dunn positioned occupied reverse slope positions where the Schönberg road crossed the ridge. By now only three remained, as two others had been sent to support infantry elsewhere on the ridge. They were ready to fire when the Tigers crested, but the German tank crews fired high-intensity flares that both blinded the Americans and silhouetted their tanks. In seconds the Tigers destroyed or damaged all three tanks. Once they had dispatched the Shermans, the Tigers and the accompanying Volksgrenadiers turned on the nearby infantry.[38]

LT Harry Balch, a combat engineer assigned to the 168th ENG, thought the German tank infantry attacks "beautiful to observe." Balch described the antagonists' tactics: First an enemy tank "fired a flare and the infantry, grouped forty or fifty in the vicinity of the tank, would get up and fire at everything moving, dark, or near dug-in positions. When the flare died out, the infantry would hit the ground." The Germans also used flare pistols to designate targets.[39] According to LT Balch, the enemy repeated the process with "perfect timing" throughout the night.[40] That night the Germans demonstrated their excellence in combined arms deliberate attack just as they had on December 16.

As the Germans began to penetrate, LTC Fuller asked Riggs to take over, as he was going in to St. Vith for orders. Just what happened when Fuller met with Clarke is the subject of controversy. In *A Time for Trumpets*, Charles B. MacDonald claims that Fuller asked to be relieved. Another version is that Fuller argued with Clarke when the latter concluded that Fuller was exhausted and sent him to the rear. According to Corporal Kenneth M. Neher, who was with Fuller in his forward command post on the ridge, Fuller went back to ask Clarke for permission to withdraw. Regardless of why Clarke evacuated Fuller, command now devolved on LTC Riggs, who had no communications.[41] The junior leaders and individual soldiers—the *kleine Leute*—fought it out.

Coordinating the improvised defense was more than Riggs could manage in extremis. LTC Nungesser argued that the "uncoordinated nature" of the way Clarke placed units complicated defending the "hurried [hastily formed] line" from the outset and may have exhausted Fuller. During the final attack, Nungesser found it "difficult to find the responsible officer for the heterogeneous elements in the line."[42] In the end, Clarke could not prevent the confusion from becoming disorganized. No one, not Clarke nor even those who fought on the ridge, could make sense of what happened that night.

SSG McBride and A Company, 23rd AIB defended just north of the Schönberg road, where the Tigers hit. When the Germans broke through, McBride saw Tiger tanks "with Jerries clinging to their backs . . . with our lines broken, the Nazi infantry and tanks moved down from the wooded hills, out across the open stretch, and felt their way cautiously into the town itself." Passed by the Germans, McBride and a group of about 150 men trudged south of St. Vith, crossing freezing streams and evading the advancing Germans headed toward Crombach. Of this group "perhaps 35 or 50 finally made it." McBride remembered, "There was no such thing as morale or discipline that night—men threw away their equipment to lighten their load, anything to aid the unbelievable strength that kept them plodding to safety."[43]

Elsewhere along the line, units held or even forced the enemy back; but the main penetration widened and had the effect of making otherwise stable positions untenable. At the southern end of CCB's line, Captain Dudley J. Britton and his A Company, 23rd AIB fought effectively, but a regiment of the 62nd VGD moved around them and into the village of Wiesenbach, from where they could fire into the rear of Britton's position. Britton had four tank destroyers supporting him that ran out of high explosive ammunition firing at the enveloping Volksgrenadiers. Worse still, the Germans closed in on the house in which Britton had established his command post. One of the Germans shouted at those in the house, "Come on out," to which Britton responded, "Fuck you, come on in." Britton and some of his company fought their way out, but many others did not escape. At the end of the month, the 23rd AIB reported 218 soldiers missing, many of whom went missing when the Germans overran the Prümerberg.[44]

At 2200 Clarke ordered CCB to withdraw to the ridges west of St. Vith. Before the withdrawal really got underway, the 18th VGD, supported by tanks, entered St. Vith, cutting off as many as six hundred of the defenders. The redoubtable LTC Thomas J. Riggs and MAJ Donald P. Boyer were among those who were unable to escape. The Germans captured both. Riggs later escaped and rejoined the reconstituted 106th ID. Getting the order to withdraw proved nearly as hard as getting out. Messages went by various radio nets and by hand. McBride and many others found their way back in small groups or alone.

The 3rd Platoon, A Company, 814th Tank Destroyer Battalion prevented worse from happening. The M10 tank destroyer platoon manned a strongpoint in the center of town. At approximately 2300 hours one of them knocked out the lead German tank as it reached the center. The destroyed tank prevented those following from getting through. But one of the platoon's M10 tank destroyers had been damaged. A race began between the tank destroyer crews trying to get underway and the Germans trying to clear the road or find a way around the roadblock. The 3rd Platoon crews won the race and headed out of town to the west.[45] With their departure, the defense of St. Vith ended.

At midnight the situation looked grim. The line south of St. Vith held by CCB, 9th AD; the 424th INF; and the 112th INF remained intact, but their positions had become untenable. Hasbrouck was also worried about Parker's Crossroads, where fighting had broken out earlier. He also was concerned about the 2nd SS PZ. He knew it was somewhere to his rear and on his southern flank. He believed it might attack toward Gouvy. To counter an attack toward Gouvy, Hasbrouck ordered LTC Robert B. Jones to swing his task force back to the northwest and "hold like grim death towns of Beho, Bovigny." He also told Jones, "We must have that road [the Beho–Bovigny road north toward Salmchâteau]. Make liberal use of mines and know where they are."[46] If TF Jones failed to hold the towns and the road north, withdrawing the two infantry regiments would be next to impossible.

Just before the end at St. Vith, Clarke called Hoge to tell him he was withdrawing. Hoge prepared to conform to Clarke's movement but could not withdraw until the two infantry regiments to the south could be accounted for. Hoge's CCB, 9th AD had driven off a daylight attack mounted by the 62nd VGD. But the 62nd had the same order the 18th had: get into St. Vith. The 62nd's night attack proved successful.[47] Hoge withdrew under pressure. The two infantry regiments withdrew as well under orders from the 106th ID. Essentially they conformed to the movements of the 7th AD.

As the forward units withdrew, Hasbrouck began to organize a defensive position west of St. Vith. Although CCB had been hit hard, Clarke had the means to reorganize at the edge of St. Vith thanks to LTC Robert C. Erlenbusch's task force, composed of two of his companies, some cavalry, and tank destroyers. TF Erlenbusch formed the core around which the defense west of the city coalesced. Hoge and Clarke established a contact point between them at the village of Bauvenn. CCB, 9th AD would move on south of Bauvenn. The 424th INF and 112th INF would fold themselves in between Hoge's command and TF Jones. At 0200 Ridgway intervened to order all of the units in the St. Vith sector to form a perimeter defense. LTC William F. Train, executive officer of the 112th INF, described the plan in a postwar monograph. Train understood that the intent was for the defenders to remain as "an outpost (enclave) while a new line would be established west of Vielsalm."[48]

Train's assessment reflects LTG Courtney H. Hodges's intention for XVIII Airborne Corps to close up and make firm contact with the troops in the sector. That intention looked less likely to be realized by the hour. In the official history, Hugh Cole noted that Ridgway "regularized" the command situation when he assigned command of all the forces in the sector to MG Allan W. Jones of the 106th ID. In fact he did nothing of the sort, since assigning Jones command had little effect.[49] Hasbrouck was in de facto command. Ridgway would soon realize he had more to do.

Clarke's CCB reeled back but had not given up. The infantry battalions fought dismounted on the Prümerberg. Because they had sent their half-tracks to the rear they had lost very little of their equipment. Neither of the two infantry regiments had suffered serious losses, nor had CCB, 9th AD. The 7th AD's remaining units, CCA and CCR, remained in good shape. How quickly they could reorganize would determine the outcome of the engagement as the night wore on.

Once the Tigers and other armored vehicles moved, the Volksgrenadiers followed as they could. What remained to be seen was whether LXVI Corps could exploit its success and open the crossroads at the center of St. Vith to the Fifth Panzer Army. The Americans—and the Germans, for that matter—had to overcome a condition Carl von Clausewitz described as the *"phase of confusion, the condition of disarray and weakness,"* which marked the crisis of every engagement. Clausewitz called this "the disorganizing effect of victory" and observed that it occurred "even on the victorious side."[50]

The Volksgrenadiers and tankers heading into St. Vith had the potential for hot food. The 164th VGR's colonel spoke for many of them when he noted, "Villages ahead of us are an attractive target providing dry accommodation."[51] SSG Richard L. McBride and a buddy also headed west on foot. They reached Crombach after walking nearly four miles. On the way they passed a 7th AD artillery battery "using up the last of its ammunition in a final gesture of defiance." McBride set about looking for the 23rd AIB. He entered a house and "blurted out, 'Can anyone tell me how to get to the 23d Battalion?'" He and his friend had arrived at Clarke's forward command post, where they saw "several neatly dressed Colonels" studying a map and coordinating what remained of CCB. They invited the two soldiers to rest. McBride fell asleep on a bench from which he slid onto the floor, where he partially blocked the entrance. Staff officers came and went, stepping over him, until he awakened on Friday, December 22.[52]

NOTES

1. Oberstleutnant Dietrich Moll, "18th Volks Grenadier Division," 44–47. In this postwar manuscript Moll complained at length about the difficulty posed by SS units ignoring boundaries, the Führer Escort Brigade's lack of respect for march discipline, and orders from LXVI Corps. Horse-drawn and captured Russian tractors had difficulty moving the Volks-Werfer Brigade into position.

2. Richard L. McBride, "Grinding Through with the 7th Armored Division."

3. Heinz Günther Guderian, *From Normandy to the Ruhr*, 316–17.

4. Generalmajor Rudolph Langhäuser, "560 Volks Grenadier Division" and "12 Volks Grenadier Division," 20.

5. Langhäuser, "560 Volks Grenadier Division," 21.

6. Michael Reynolds, *Sons of the Reich*, 199–200.

7. General der Panzertruppe Hasso von Manteuffel, letter, no addressee, July 30, 1950, box 3, John S. D. Eisenhower, Drafts and Other Materials from *The Bitter Woods*, 1944–68, Dwight D. Eisenhower Presidential Library and Museum, Abilene, KS, 1. Manteuffel likely addressed the letter to Bruce C. Clarke. Manteuffel and Clarke developed a relationship when Clarke commanded 7th Army Europe in the 1950s and renewed it when Clarke returned to command NATO in the 1960s. Manteuffel visited the United States in 1964, and he and Clarke also met at that time. The two "starred" in US Army Pictorial Center, *The Battle of St. Vith*. They collaborated on a NATO study in 1976 and remained correspondents until the 1980s, when both died.

8. Matthew B. Ridgway, *Soldier: The Memoirs of Matthew B. Ridgway*, 112–19. Technically, Ridgway's corps should be rendered XVIII Corps (Airborne), but colloquially it became XVIII Airborne Corps just at the airborne divisions eliminated their parentheses.

9. Charles B. MacDonald, *A Time for Trumpets*, 430–31. James M. Gavin, *On to Berlin*, 218–25, esp. 220, map.

10. Both quotations are from Army Pictorial Center, *The Battle of St. Vith*, pt. 2.

11. *Combat Interviews of the 87th Cavalry Reconnaissance Squadron*, 44–45.

12. Army Pictorial Center, *The Battle of St. Vith*, pt. 2.

13. Army Pictorial Center, *The Battle of St. Vith*, pt. 2. See also 7th Armored Division, "After Action Report, Period 1–31 December 1944," G-2 notes, 9.

14. Division Artillery, 7th Armored Division, "After Action Report, Month of December 1944," 14.

15. On the number of attacks, see 7th Armored Division, "After Action Report, Period 1–31 December 1944," G-2 notes.

16. Moll, "18th Volks Grenadier Division," 47.

17. Moll, "18th Volks Grenadier Division," 49.

18. Generalmajor Otto E. Remer, "The Führer-Begleit Brigade in the Ardennes Offensive," 10–11.

19. Generalmajor Friedrich Kittel, "62nd Volksgrenadier Division," 11. Just when the attack began is unclear. I have chosen 0830 based on 7th Armored Division, G-3 journal, December 1944, entry 40, December 21, 1944. Others have placed the time of the attack as late as 1500. See Samuel W. Mitcham Jr., *Panzers in Winter*, 118. Mitcham believed the attack began at 1100. MacDonald, *A Time for Trumpets*, 472, reports the attack began at 1500. Hugh M. Cole, *The Ardennes: Battle of the Bulge*, also reports the attack began at 1500. In fact, all of these times are correct. The first of eleven attacks the 7th AD reported began about 0830, but the main attack did not occur until 1500. On the reaction to the 62nd's attack, see 7th Armored Division, G-3 journal, December 1944, entries 60–61, December 21.

20. 7th Armored Division, G-3 journal, December 1944, entry 73, December 21, 1944.

21. Division Artillery, 7th Armored Division, "After Action Report, Month of December 1944," 13. See also 434th Armored Field Artillery Battalion, "After Action Report, Month of December 1944," 56. The Division Artillery after action report round count for the 434th on December 20 is off by one thousand rounds. The author checked round counts for each of the subordinate units and used their count where they differed from that of the division artillery.

22. 7th Armored Division, G-3 journal, December 1944, entries 74–84, December 21, 1944. See also Division Artillery, 7th Armored Division, "After Action Report, Month of December 1944," 65. There is some doubt as to whether the number of howitzers still present was seven or eight.

23. Combat Command A, 7th Armored Division, "After Action Report, December 1944," 9.

24. Donald P. Boyer Jr., *St. Vith: The 7th Armored Division in the Battle of the Bulge*, citation report overlay no. 2.

25. Roy U. Clay, "Tinstaafl: Autobiography of Roy U. Clay, Colonel (Ret.)," 90–91. See also Roy U. Clay, *Curbstone: The History of the 275th Field Artillery Battalion in World War II*, 15.

26. Clay, *Curbstone*, 15–16.

27. 7th Armored Division Trains, summary of events, December 1944, 1. See also 7th Armored Division Trains, journal, December 1944, entry for December 21, 1944.

28. MG Andrew J. Adams, (Ret.), interview with the author, Washington, DC, August 31, 1984; 7th Armored Division Trains, summary of events, December 1944, 1. See also 7th Armored Division Trains, journal. Arrival time in the summary for December differs from that in the journal. The journal is more accurate, as it was kept contemporaneously.

29. Moll, "18th Volks Grenadier Division," 49.

30. Bruce Condell and David T. Zabecki, eds., *On the German Art of War: Truppenführung*, 97, 102.

31. George F. Nafziger, *German Army: Battle of the Bulge*, 2–3, 21. Nafziger does not offer a tube count for the FEB. Its 120th Artillery Battalion was probably organized in three batteries of either six 105-millimeter self-propelled howitzers or four 150-millimeter howitzers in direct support. Despite the date on the title page, Nafziger's order of battle includes units that arrived later than December 15, such as the FEB.

32. Cole, *The Ardennes: Battle of the Bulge*, 403.

33. W. Wesley Johnston, *Combat Interviews of the 31st Tank Battalion*, 32–33. Executive officer LT Dunn was west of the ridge in the company rear area. He made his way forward through two separate barrages. The confusion about just what happened confounded even MacDonald, who in *A Time for Trumpets* reports that the A Company commander was wounded while Dunn, who was there, reported him killed in action.

34. Quotation from Army Pictorial Center, *The Battle of St. Vith*, pt. 2.

35. McBride, "Grinding Through," 120–21.

36. W. Wesley Johnston, *Combat Interviews of the 38th Armored Infantry Battalion*, 12.

37. Klaus Ritter, statements, box 10, Charles B. MacDonald Papers, pt. 2, p. 6.

38. MacDonald, *A Time for Trumpets*, 473. MacDonald claims there were five US tanks on the ridge. In his combat interview LT Dunn reports three, but this is likely because tanks moved hither and yon in response to crises. The interview includes a sketch showing the movement of these tanks once Dunn got forward to assume command after the company commander was killed. See Johnston, *Combat Interviews of the 31st Tank Battalion*, 34–35, 38.

39. Lieutenant Colonel W. L. Nungesser, Major Harry W. Brennan, and Lieutenant Harry Balch, interview by Captain K. W. Hechler, 4.

40. Nungesser, Brennan, and Balch interview, 4.

41. MacDonald, *A Time for Trumpets*, 328–29. MacDonald relied on Clarke's version of events. He never interviewed Fuller. The veterans of Fuller's unit did not accept this point of view. MacDonald made a harsh assessment of Fuller, apparently

without confirming the account. Fuller returned to command the 38th until the end of the war. See also Corporal Kenneth M. Neher, "My WWII Story with 38th A.I.B."

42. Nungesser, Brennan, and Balch interview, 5.

43. McBride, "Grinding Through," 123–26.

44. W. Wesley Johnston, *Combat Interviews of the 23rd Armored Infantry Battalion*, 52. See also 23rd Armored Infantry Battalion, "After Action Report, Month of December 1944"; at the end of the report are the lists of those missing in action.

45. 814th Tank Destroyer Battalion, "After Action Report December 1944," 3.

46. 7th Armored Division, "After Action Report, Period 1–31 December 1944," 12.

47. Oberst Arthur Jüttner, "Report by Colonel Jüttner of the 62nd VGD in the Battle of the Bulge," 10–11.

48. Johnston, *Combat Interviews of the 31st Tank Battalion*, 17–20; Lieutenant General William F. Train, "My Memories of the Battle of the Bulge," 14.

49. Cole, *The Ardennes: Battle of the Bulge*, 406–7.

50. Carl von Clausewitz, *On War*, 206, emphasis in the original.

51. Jüttner, "Report by Colonel Jüttner of the 62nd VGD in the Battle of the Bulge," 11.

52. McBride, "Grinding Through," 126–27.

CHAPTER TEN

They Come Back With All Honor

Once again the situation is so fluid that at the end of the period it is impossible to tie down the front occupied by the enemy or ourselves.

—7th Armored Division, G-2 periodic report, December 22, 1944

When the tanks were ordered to retreat, the infantry hung on their sides. They kept firing at the enemy, and laid down particularly heavy fire.

—Captain Walter H. Austey

SUNRISE ON FRIDAY, December 22, 1944, produced very little light and no sunshine. The sky remained overcast, as it had since the German attack began. The conditions remained as they had, bitterly cold. Snow blanketed the earth, but the ground had not frozen so tanks and other vehicles left roads at their peril. Exhaustion, upper respiratory infections, and cold weather injuries including frostbite and trench foot took their toll. On the day the German counteroffensive began the Army issued volume 2, number 48 of *Army Talks*, a cheery little command information product that was part comic book and part newspaper. The December 16 issue featured an article entitled, "What Price Feet?"

Liberally illustrated with cartoon-like sketches, "What Price Feet?" told the story of a GI named Mac who failed to take care of his feet. The article followed the sad tale of Mac's feet and what he should have done. It was good advice, but very little that *Army Talks* advised was feasible. By December 22, Private John Schaffner, who began the battle as an artillery scout on the Schnee Eifel in the 589th Field Artillery (FA), occupied a foxhole at Parker's Crossroads. He had arrived December 10 without ceremony or baggage.

Each day, faithful to the Army's advice, he changed his socks. Once a day, Schaffner removed the dirty socks he kept in his pockets and replaced them with the wet dirty ones from the day before. His method sufficed for him and others. Many others did not do as well as John Schaffner.[1]

Monty at the Helm

Although British field marshal Bernard Law Montgomery did not assume supervision of First US Army until December 20, he had already formed a fairly accurate impression of the battle thanks to his Phantom liaison teams. At his first conference with Lieutenant General (LTG) Courtney H. Hodges at First Army he concluded that the Army commander was exhausted. Hodges was recovering from illness and had ample reason to look a little down given the ferocity of the German attack and the serious losses suffered. On the basis of this first meeting, Montgomery sought to have him relieved, believing that Hodges was no longer up to the task. General Dwight D. Eisenhower assured the field marshal that Hodges was "the quiet reticent type and does not appear as aggressive as he really is." He promised Montgomery that Hodges would do well. Nevertheless, Montgomery closely supervised First Army, and Phantom was one of his means of doing so. Not surprisingly, his liaison teams created some tension, but they "did keep him aware of events at lower echelons in way that the American system had not done for Hodges" and, for that matter, Major General (MG) Matthew B. Ridgway, who resented these officers. Montgomery, tiresome little man that he was, understood the tactical situation around St. Vith better than did Ridgway as late as December 22.[2]

Ridgway had a firm hand everywhere but at St. Vith. The situation there remained dire, and his understanding of it incomplete. But Ridgway—resolute, aggressive, and even stubborn—had the capacity to learn. MG James M. Gavin of the 82nd Airborne Division (ABN) helped develop the picture for Ridgway when Gavin visited MG Allan W. Jones at the latter's command post on December 21. To Gavin, Jones appeared the "picture of dejection."[3] Gavin also visited Brigadier General (BG) Robert W. Hasbrouck later that day and "discussed the situation with General Ridgway." It is likely that he shared his assessment of Jones with Hasbrouck. Ridgway "expressed the view that the St. Vith forces would probably be withdrawn through the 82nd." Furthermore, he instructed Gavin to prepare to withdraw the 82nd north and west.[4]

To Ridgway, ceding ground once it had been gained was anathema, both by inclination and experience. Airborne units expected to fight surrounded or at least behind enemy lines. Moreover, these units lacked mobility, so withdrawing under pressure from mobile troops was to be avoided. Finally, the airborne forces regarded themselves an elite fighting force. They would, they believed, bend but never break. All of this informed Ridgway's point of view, which was distinctly different from Hasbrouck's. The decisions Ridgway made over the next forty-eight hours reflected his best character-istic, the ability to learn (a quality far more rare than might be supposed) and a less desirable impulse to reach firm opinions about others too quickly. Ridgway should be judged in the context in which he found himself: chaos, and a chaos that was at least as profound as that which he had found himself in on December 17.

In contrast with Ridgway, Hasbrouck was urbane and calmly deliberative. Colonel (COL) William S. Triplet, who joined the 7th AD in January, de-scribed Hasbrouck as a "tall, well-built, classically handsome, emotionless officer who gave me the impression that if stabbed would bleed ice water," noting also that Hasbrouck was "coolly courteous." Triplet's observation of Hasbrouck, though intended to be unflattering, is in many ways accurate. Hasbrouck was, in fact, the consummate gentleman and deliberate, neither of which were necessarily admired in the hard-drinking, profane Army in which he served. Equally important, his background in armor, and his be-lief in mobility as fundamental to using armor, placed him at odds with his corps commander.

The Fortified Goose Egg

In 1947, Major (MAJ) Donald P. Boyer, who had been captured on the Prümerberg, wrote the narrative after action report to accompany the rec-ommendation of the 7th Armored Division (AD) for the Distinguished Unit Citation (later known as the Presidential Unit Citation). Boyer wrote that of the troops engaged on the Prümerberg, only two hundred made it back to friendly lines. Of those, "90 had to be evacuated for wounds and exhaus-tion."[5] The cost incurred on the Prümerberg directly affected the 7th AD and its combat capability over the course of the days and weeks to come.

Boyer did the sums for the price paid by the task force formed on the 38th Armored Infantry Battalion (AIB). The task force included the headquarters of the 38th, four armored infantry companies from two different battalions, a troop of cavalry, a tank company, a tank destroyer platoon, and parts of two engineer battalions. The mixed command suffered at least 42 killed, 86 wounded, and 745 missing in action. Although the units that defended the ridge managed to get most of their equipment out, they still lost at least four half-tracks, two tanks, eleven M8 armored cars, and more than a dozen other vehicles. Boyer claimed the task force destroyed fifteen enemy tanks and six assault guns and killed 604 Germans. There is no way to verify the tally, but both sides agreed it was a bitter fight.[6]

MAJ Boyer reckoned the cost also of the effect on the units that fought. He reported that the 38th now had "no Assault Gun, nor Mortar nor Machine Gun Platoons—neither men nor vehicles nor weapons." Of the 38th's A and B Companies, only the antitank platoons, half-tracks, and half-track drivers survived. A Company of the 23rd AIB essentially ceased to exist, and only a platoon remained from the Battalion's B Company. None of the soldiers from the 81st Engineers (ENG) and the 168th ENG came out of the fight—they were killed, wounded, and/or captured. B Troop, 87th Cavalry Reconnaissance Squadron (CAV) was also nearly destroyed. The unexpected reappearance of A Company, 31st Tank Battalion (TB) proved to be the "only bright spot." Thought to have been destroyed, about half of the Company survived by joining forces with Combat Command B (CCB), 9th AD "after fighting their way out [of] ST. VITH." The redoubtable Lieutenant (LT) John J. Dunn escaped south under "considerable" tank fire with seven tanks. He led A Company's survivors to Neubrück, where they joined CCB. Later that morning Dunn and what was left of A Company rejoined the 31st TB.[7]

Hasbrouck had no time to mourn the loss of either the ridge or his soldiers. The few survivors from the Prümerberg and the remaining troops in the St. Vith salient faced serious problems. Some had literally run out of food. The supporting artillery had as few as eight rounds remaining per tube. Although the 82nd ABN had reached the Salm River, it held only a small neck of ground from Salmchâteau to Vielsalm, just over a mile to the north. The only route to sustain the troops east of the Salm led over two bridges, one at Salmchâteau and the other at Vielsalm. With the 2nd Schutzstaffel (SS) Panzer Division at his rear, it looked to Hasbrouck as though the game was up.[8]

Ridgway saw things differently. He believed the troops in the pocket could hold out until relieved. In his memoir *Soldier*, Ridgway described the 7th AD and the others as "surrounded on three sides." This is a generous estimate given how thinly the 82nd ABN held the neck of land between Salmchâteau and Vielsalm. When viewed from the east, the neck looked like that of a sack that could be closed easily by pulling on a string. According to MG Ridgway, "back at Werbomont and Thieux the 82nd and the 3rd Armored gathered," eventually to "move out and make contact with them [the 7th AD et al.] down the narrow corridor that had not yet been cut by the Germans."[9]

Had this sentence been written on December 22 it could be dismissed as hubris from an overconfident corps commander fighting his corps for the first time. Given that Ridgway published this account in 1956, a far less generous assessment is not unreasonable. It reads as though what he imagined feasible in 1944 actually had been the case. But what happened on the battlefield revealed how mistaken he was. To facilitate his plan, XVIII Airborne Corps issued an overlay order dated December 21. Hasbrouck had it before sunup on December 22. The overlay bore the label "Final Defense of St Vith," with no execution date or concept of the operation. The "plan" earned, from the graphics on the overlay, the appellation "Fortified Goose Egg." It is a curious document. The overlay amounted to XVIII Airborne Corps assuming tactical command of both the 7th AD and the 106th Infantry Division (ID) because it assigned individual battle positions to units subordinate to the 7th AD and 106th ID—a serious overreach by the corps commander and/ or his staff.

At daybreak Hasbrouck conferred with Clarke about the overlay plan. Both considered it ill advised. Not given to circumspection, Clarke described it as "Custer's last stand." According to Charles B. MacDonald in *A Time for Trumpets*, Hasbrouck, as well as BG William M. Hoge of CCB and COL Dwight A. Rosebaum of Combat Command A (CCA), 7th AD all opposed the plan.[10] What MG Jones thought is not known, but he ordered the units subordinate to him to withdraw toward positions more or less like those on the overlay.[11]

Before the drama over the order played out, BG Hasbrouck set about the grim tasks of organizing a defense west of St. Vith and determining just where everyone was, including CCB, the 424th Infantry Regiment (INF), and the 112th INF. The first priority was to find troops for BG Bruce C. Clarke to form a line west of St. Vith. If what remained of Combat Command Reserve (CCR) and CCA on the northern shank of the horseshoe held, then Clarke might be able to reconstitute a defense. Doing so would enable the troops to withdraw when necessary.

At 0300 Clarke took the first step to stabilize the defense when he ordered his last reserve into the fight. He ordered Lieutenant Colonel (LTC) John P. Wemple to move his 17th TB "immediately to KROMBACH and report to Brig. Gen. Clarke." It was "snowing like hell" when Wemple led the 17th TB northeast from Bovigny through Maldingen and Braunlauf toward Crombach. According to Wemple, "We couldn't contact CC-B by radio but finally raised the 31st TK BN [Tank Battalion], Lt Col Erlenbusch, who said: 'Come

into town, have REBEL [Wemple's call sign] report to CP [command post]."
On arrival Wemple joined the 31st TB east of Crombach, literally filling in
gaps on the high ground where Clarke was building a new "line." Wemple
still had not seen or spoken with Clarke. He hastily positioned twenty M4
Sherman tanks and three 105-millimeter assault guns. Wemple sent D Company's eleven Stuart light tanks to Hinderhausen, where CCB's artillery was
fighting infantry from the Führer Escort Brigade (FEB).[12]

LTC Robert C. Erlenbusch described the operation as "one of shoving in
just enough stuff to plug the holes as they were made." Before Wemple arrived, Erlenbusch's small contingent of infantry, apparently scraped up by
Clarke and some of the few who made it off the Prümerberg, drove off an attack that came out of St. Vith. Erlenbusch claimed that "our infantry" fought
with "hand grenades or knives or whatever weapons they might have left."
Ruefully he noted that they "were not in organized units" and leadership
depended on "strange officers with strange troops." Although no tanks or assault guns accompanied the first attack, Erlenbusch reported "AT [antitank]
fire from the high ground," south of St. Vith.[13]

Once Wemple came up, he and Erlenbusch built a line nearly five miles
long, oriented toward St. Vith and close enough to engage Germans who
attempted to exit the town.[14] They formed a line on which the remainder of
the 7th AD, CCB, 9th AD, and the two infantry regiments could rally. In essence, the units contracted toward Crombach, forming the Fortified Goose
Egg, not so much in response to the overlay but to the facts on the ground.

When Staff Sergeant Richard L. McBride awakened from sleeping on the
floor of Clarke's command post he went looking for his battalion. He found
it, and the battalion headquarters, nearby. With his company destroyed, he
was sent back to CCB as the 23rd AIB liaison. McBride recalled his duty as
a "marvelous opportunity to watch and listen to what took place at H. Q.
[the CCB command post] that day." McBride watched as Clarke set about
"forging a chain of defense around Crombach. . . . With a large colored
map spread out before him, and a radio-telephone at his side, he directed
his unit commanders to assemble their men at strategic points to fill in our
line."[15] Clarke developed the immediate defense overlooking St. Vith in concert with BG Hoge. Hoge's CCB had made contact with Clarke's right flank
at Bauvenn, as they had agreed.

COL Rosebaum's CCA defended on Clarke's left, centered on the village
of Poteau. LTC Fred M. Warren's CCR extended the line west toward Petit-
Thier. Neither of them had much to work with. Clarke had two of the Division's three tired and diminished tank battalions. The 38th AIB was hors de

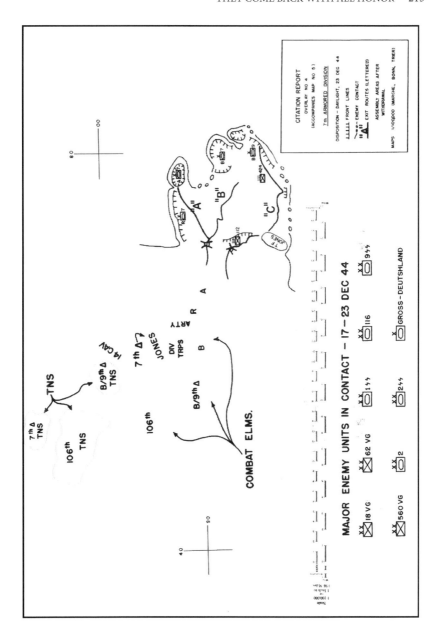

MAP 12. This overlay shows the planned assembly areas intended for the 7th Armored Division; Combat Command B, 9th Armored Division; and the 106th Infantry Division. The salient shown in the east is the last defensible position of the 7th Armored Division. Withdrawal routes A, B, and C can be seen leading out of the salient. Reproduced from Donald P. Boyer, *The 7th Armored Division in the Battle of the Bulge.*

combat, as was half of the 23rd AIB, thanks to the fight on the Prümerberg. Between them CCR had no more than four tank companies from the 40th TB and three infantry companies of the 48th AIB, and none of these were whole. CCR did have a cavalry troop screening the northern flank, but Hasbrouck sent the cavalry on another mission. During the five hours the cavalry was gone, Warren manned the screen with headquarters troops patrolling in jeeps.[16]

CCA held the town of Poteau, where the 14th CAV had suffered at the hands of the 1st SS Panzergrenadier Regiment (PGR). On December 20 Hasbrouck had ordered Rosebaum to retake the town, noting it was "imperative." After a bitter fight with SS Panzergrenadiers, Rosebaum's troops retook Poteau that evening. After the 1st SS and its grenadiers moved on west, relative calm settled from Poteau west to Petit-Thier. The 9th SS, following the 1st SS, made only half-hearted attempts to take Poteau. The relative peace in the north came to an end on the morning of December 22.[17]

German Actions and Orders: Exploitation or Consternation
Sometime during the night of December 21–22 the Fifth Panzer Army issued an order reflecting angst over the delays suffered at St. Vith and elsewhere. It ordered its units to "bypass resistance, only cover the flanks, bulk remains in advance toward the Maas [Meuse River], continue to confuse, split up, surround, reconnoiter in force, deceive."[18] The LXVI Corps realized that while the Volksgrenadier Divisions (VGDs) and FEB had taken St. Vith, they had not fully penetrated the American defenses. To compound their frustration, Oberstleutnant Dietrich Moll, the operations officer for the 18th VGD, observed that "not only had the enemy safely withdrawn he had taken along his weapons and equipment, a remarkable achievement under the circumstances."[19]

Moll's surprise at the Americans' orderly withdrawal turned into consternation. The LXVI Corps ordered artillery and tactical units forward to continue the attack. Accordingly, the 18th VGD required "artillery and heavy infantry weapons to be moved up to just east of St. Vith. All guns were to be clear of the pathless wooded terrain east of St Vith by the evening of 22 December." The Division's march table soon became irrelevant as the road from Wallerode "became congested with the vehicles of neighboring units" including tanks from the Sixth Panzer Army. Some were hoping to use the roads that led out of St. Vith, but many came to see "if the enemy had left anything useable."[20] In the center of town, damaged and destroyed vehicles backed up columns that took hours to untangle. The mess in St. Vith accounts for why no tanks or assault guns supported the infantry attack that Task Force (TF) Erlenbusch drove off before dawn.

The mass of vehicles included many troops of the 18th VGD driving captured Jeeps loaded with the "rich booty of the Schnee-Eifel pocket" and "mobile equipment of the captured American Division (artillery and self-propelled guns) and artillery of the left adjacent unit [the 62nd VGD]." The free-for-all resulted, as it had earlier in the fighting, in a *Stau*, or traffic jam, that Moll claimed took thirty-six hours to clear. Generalfeldmarschall Walther Model found himself in the middle of this immobile collection of rolling stock. In the end he "elected to walk."[21]

Model walked west and found the 18th's Oberst Günther Hoffman-Schönborn and the faithful Moll. On arrival at Hoffman-Schönborn's command post Model unequivocally made known his frustration. Moll, much chastened, complained that the "reprimands given the division by the army group commander were not justified, as higher headquarters was clearly at fault."[22] Not for the first time during the battle had disregard of boundaries, looting, and indiscipline brought a large German formation to a halt. The legendary superiority of German tactical commanders and their troops was not in evidence that day.

Despite the confusion, LXVI Corps crept forward. The Corps planned to envelop the defenders west of St. Vith as it had those on the Schnee Eifel. To do so Oberst Otto-Ernst Remer would attack southwest. The 18th VGD intended to continue the attack west once it got traffic and looters under control. The 62nd VGD attack underway since 0200 continued throughout the day.

Parker's Crossroads at Baraque de Fraiture loomed in importance, as did the bridges over the Salm River. Taking the crossroads could lead to encircling the troops east of the Salm and perhaps a breakthrough on the northern shoulder. The II SS Panzer Corps issued orders to promote this outcome at midday on December 21. The Corps specified that the 2nd SS Panzer Division (PZ) advance detachments were to "position themselves in front of the withdrawing enemy. The Division is to throw back the enemy across the road intersection Baraque de Fraiture and Manhay," which lay five miles north of Baraque.[23] The 2nd SS could not carry out the order until refueled. Meanwhile, the weakened 560th VGD maintained contact and exchanged fire with the handful of Americans at Parker's Crossroads.

Remer and the 62nd VGD Attack from North and South

The FEB assembled near Nieder-Emmels in the predawn hours of December 22. Finally, Otto-Ernst Remer's desire was consistent with that of his corps commander, General der Artillerie Walther Lucht. Remer planned to attack southwest down the extension of the Poteau valley toward Rodt and on to Hinderhausen. He began by sending out "a powerful reconnaissance patrol" operating more or less as an advance guard. Once the patrol made contact, Remer followed with his armored group. At daybreak some of Remer's infantry and tanks entered Rodt, where they encountered part of the 31st TB and a small task force formed on an infantry company from the 48th AIB commanded by Captain (CPT) Harlan C. Stine. Stine had a handful of infantry, nine light tanks, two Shermans, three assault guns (two 105-millimeter guns and one seventy-five-millimeter gun) and five Greyhound armored cars armed with thirty-seven-millimeter cannons. Americans (probably the 31st TB) had also mined the roads coming into Rodt.[24]

According to Remer, the "locality [Rodt] was stubbornly defended by enemy tanks." The FEB suffered losses to both mines and direct fire. Still other vehicles seeking to avoid mines or antitank fire became mired in the soft ground. Finally, about noon, the 828th Grenadier Battalion drove the Americans from Rodt by "lunging from the edge of the woods [north of Rodt] on a broad front." TF Stine covered the 31st TB as it withdrew and then followed with infantry clinging to tanks and armored cars. The task force lost several tanks when they bogged down in soft ground but eventually reached Hinderhausen, southwest of Rodt. Remer's attack came to a halt in the early afternoon, as his brigade had to fight both the Americans and difficult terrain. To add to its difficulties, the FEB also had to fend off the 293rd VGR, which was attacking nearly perpendicular to the FEB's axis. The 293rd attacked in response to an order from LXVI Corps for a regimental attack northwest from Ober-Emmels to prevent any Americans escaping to the north. The order is hard to explain, as it simply created more confusion. Moll "gained the impression that matters were being bungled."[25]

Despite poor coordination and stout resistance, Remer's attack drove a wedge between Rosebaum's CCA and Clarke's CCB. Remer had achieved what neither the 1st SS nor the strangely quiescent 9th SS had. By taking Rodt he effectively turned CCA and CCR, the latter located west of CCA, out of their positions and opened the road from Recht through Poteau and Petit-Thier to Vielsalm. In short, Remer collapsed the northern shank of the old horseshoe defense and threatened Clarke's rear.

Remer's attack demonstrates the military aphorism that an attack along the boundary of enemy units almost always succeeds. Oberst Friedrich Kittel's 62nd VGD also reaped the benefit of such an attack. At 0100 on December 22, CCB, 9th AD withdrew in good order to positions south of Bauvenn, the contact point established with CCB, 7th AD. Kittel's 183rd VGR had reached St. Vith late on December 21, attacking up the small gap between CCB, 7th AD's southernmost unit on the Prümerberg and CCB, 9th AD's northernmost unit. Kittel's other two regiments, the 190th and 164th, did not attack until 0200 but the 190th managed to get a company forward on the forested high ground overlooking the villages of Galhausen and Neubrück.[26] The remainder of the regiment moved forward through the early hours of the morning.

The lead battalion of the 190th VGR moved through Galhausen and then headed southwest along the banks of a creek toward Neubrück, and so got behind the 27th AIB's forward line. Hours earlier Hoge met with LTC Fred S. Cummings Jr., the newly assigned battalion commander of the 27th, as Cummings led his command post troops into Neubrück. BG Hoge had just moved his own command post elsewhere in response to effective artillery fire, and Hoge told Cummings, "Get out of here, don't stop here because it [the town] is under surveillance and they know where we are and for God's sake don't come in here." Cummings ignored Hoge's advice.[27]

At 0930 the grenadiers moved into Neubrück. They struck quickly with "small arms, bazookas, mortars and grenades" and surrounded the very house where Cummings had established his command post despite being told not do so. For nearly two hours the headquarters troops held their own, but at 1130 Cummings capitulated both the command post and the nearby battalion aid station. Oberleutnant Herbert Franke, who commanded the 190th, accepted Cummings's surrender. Franke, who had been wounded during the attack, next attempted to evacuate his prisoners and wounded to Galhausen using captured 27th AIB vehicles. En route, a tank platoon from B Company, 14th TB intervened, and Franke retreated back to Neubrück. In the confusion, one of Franke's prisoners, CPT Glen L. Strange, escaped. Once back in Neubrück, Franke insisted he be returned to his own lines under a flag of truce. The Americans agreed, and Franke and three wounded Germans made their way to Galhausen and safety in a US ambulance flying a white flag.[28]

Meanwhile, CPT Strange, the 27th's intelligence officer, made his way around the Germans in Galhausen and reached A Company, 14th TB. There he organized a relief column composed of a tank platoon and a handful of infantry. Joined by a second tank platoon, Strange and his "task force" retook Neubrück at 1430 and freed most of the Americans captured earlier, including the battalion commander. But the woods east, north, and south of Neubrück were still crawling with Volksgrenadiers.[29]

Oberst Arthur Jüttner's 164th VGR attacked on the 190th's left in three assault columns. Attacking along a forested lane, the 164th took Grüfflingen and Thommen and then continued west. Jüttner reported bypassing some of the enemy and engaging others in house-to-house fighting, while he described others as withdrawing. All three observations are accurate. Both the 424th and the 112th Infantry Regiments had been ordered to withdraw toward St. Vith. Jüttner's Volksgrenadiers would have bypassed some American infantry, fought others, and followed on the heels of still others. By the end of the day Jüttner's troops had reached Aldringen, about four miles southwest of Crombach. Jüttner's success and that of Kittel's other regiments threatened to envelop the Americans from the south, while Remer threatened the same from the north.

Still, taking St. Vith had not produced the outcome that General der Panzertruppe Hasso von Manteuffel had imagined it would. In a postwar interview he told his interrogators that after St. Vith fell, "I thought your troops would immediately withdraw from the entire area, because of the threat Remer [of the FEB] offered when he hit your forces from behind with his tanks."[30] If asked, it is likely Hasbrouck would have agreed with Manteuffel's reasoning. But Hasbrouck could not risk having a withdrawal turned into a rout, and as yet he had no orders to withdraw. More to the point, he had a verbal order from Ridgway requiring him to stay. Even if Ridgway approved a withdrawal, Hasbrouck needed to stabilize the situation first. So he moved units to block Remer in the Poteau valley and tucked in TF Jones at the southwest as the pocket contracted.

On December 21 success for the Fifth Panzer Army and ultimately Army Group B still seemed possible. That day the 116th PZ, leading LVIII Panzer Corps, attacked the village of Hotton on the Ourthe River. But the corps commander, General der Panzertruppe Walter Krüger, ordered the 116th to countermarch a second time and cross at LaRoche-en-Ardenne instead. The 2nd PZ, leading XLVIII Panzer Corps, had already crossed the Ourthe. The LXVI Corps needed to polish off the troops in the Fortified Goose Egg. The 2nd SS PZ had to clear the way through Parker's Crossroads. If LXVI Corps and the 2nd SS succeeded, it might prove possible to save Obersturmbahnführer Joachim Peiper and open the way for the Sixth Panzer Army. On the

morning of December 22, LTG George S. Patton Jr.'s Third US Army began
an attack aimed at relieving Bastogne.[31] For the Fifth Panzer Army, concluding the siege at Bastogne became essential in order to protect the southern
flank if Patton broke through the German Seventh Army in the south.

The Decision to Withdraw

December 21 was Matthew B. Ridgway's third day in command of a corps
in combat. He arrived on the Continent on December 18 and reached XVIII
Airborne Corps' forward command post at Werbomont the next day, at
which point he took over command from MG Gavin. The situation he confronted was dangerous, complex, and riddled with uncertainty. The muddled
chain of command in St. Vith prevented Ridgway from fixing responsibility
for tactical decisions, and he had not formed a favorable impression of what
he had seen so far. To him the "gloom" at VIII Corps, where he spent his first
night, was "thicker than the fog outside."[32]

By the end of the day Ridgway realized he had to decide whether the
troops in what he, too, was calling the horseshoe should stay or go. At 2350,
not long after LXVI Corps penetrated the Prümerberg and took St. Vith,
Ridgway spoke with MG William B. Kean, the First Army chief of staff. The
record of the phone conversation with Kean reveals both the depth of the
tactical dilemma and that Ridgway felt unable to make an informed decision
about withdrawing. He was thinking out loud and using Kean as a sounding
board. Ridgway began by suggesting that Hasbrouck and his "teammates"
could not hold out and that when the 2nd SS attacked Hasbrouck would
have nothing to stop them. But then he wondered if they could be stopped
by bombing or maybe by long-range artillery. What clearly troubled him
most was, "I don't know the ground out there." He also didn't know Robert
Hasbrouck, so he told Kean that he sent his "Deputy Chief"—COL William
B. Quill, a cavalryman—to "find out Bob's attitude." He concluded by asserting he would give Hasbrouck "discretionary authority to pull back there."[33]

Equally certain is that Ridgway was not truly comfortable with ceding
ground if he could avoid doing so. Separately from the phone record Ridgway
dictated a note on Kean's side of the conversation. Kean, he claimed, had
"approved my plan to authorize his [Hasbrouck's] withdrawal." Kean also
felt that Hasbrouck himself "was the only man to make that decision."[34] This
addendum demonstrates that while Ridgway was actively considering withdrawing the troops in the pocket he had not yet reconciled himself to doing so.

The following morning, December 22, one of Montgomery's Phantom officers met briefly with Hasbrouck and asked point blank whether he "wanted to stay there [in the Goose Egg]." BG Hasbrouck replied, "no, not unless higher command thought it was critical terrain."[35] After Montgomery's liaison officer left, Hasbrouck completed an update of his situation to transmit to MG Ridgway. He described his situation in three paragraphs, and made four points in the first paragraph. First, the tons of supplies required daily to sustain the troops in the Goose Egg had to come over two bridges across the Salm River. Second, Hasbrouck pointed out that German artillery could hit the position from nearly 360 degrees. Third, the road net in the shrinking pocket was inadequate to move supplies or troops rapidly. Fourth, if the 2nd SS drove the 82nd ABN back "even as little as 3,000 yards we will be completely severed from any source of supplies."[36]

In the second paragraph, Hasbrouck recommended that the troops be withdrawn west of the 82nd, "where they may be of assistance in halting the possible advance of the 2nd SS Panzer Division." The third paragraph broke no new ground. He suggested that CCB, 7th AD might not hold if attacked in strength. Explicitly, he said, "I don't think we can prevent a complete break-through if another all-out attack comes against CCB tonight." Just as he completed his message, word came of a renewed attack against Clarke. Hasbrouck added a postscript in which he reported that Clarke was retiring under pressure. The remainder of the postscript conveyed how difficult the situation was. "I am throwing in my last chips to halt him [the German attack]. Hoge has just reported an attack [from the 62nd VGD]. In my opinion if we don't get out of here tonight, we will not have a 7th Armored Division left. RWH."[37]

Before sending the message Hasbrouck consulted by telephone with MG Jones at the 106th ID who concurred with the assessment. Hasbrouck transmitted his estimate by radio to XVIII Airborne Corps, where it was received at 1150. Ridgway was not amused. He had not yet reconciled himself to withdrawing and continued to believe, or more likely hope, that the 3rd AD could come to the rescue. To make matters worse, Jones recanted his position without telling Hasbrouck. At 1250 Jones radioed Ridgway, "My intentions are to retain the ground now defended."[38] So from Ridgway's point of view he had contradictory estimates from the two commanders in the pocket.

The 7th AD staff got on with planning the withdrawal in the event that orders came to do so. They had already identified three routes out of the Goose Egg. Much work had to be done, including improving forest trails and roads. On December 21 Clarke had begun to corduroy—to lay tree trunks down as a surface on which to drive—the forest trail leading to Commanster, where he planned an alternate position for his command post. The trail led ultimately to Vielsalm so could be used to withdraw. When Clarke reconnoitered the road on December 22 he got mired. It took twelve soldiers to help get his Jeep "unstuck."[39]

On the day Montgomery assumed operational control of First Army, he was inclined toward withdrawing the troops from the salient he described as shaped like a "sausage." Hodges argued against doing so. When the 7th AD chemical officer made his dramatic appearance and delivered Hasbrouck's letter for MG Kean, Montgomery acquiesced to Hodges's view. The field marshal was with Hodges on December 22 when the news arrived of the penetration of the 7th AD's northern shank of the horseshoe. That evening Montgomery reported the situation and decisions he had taken by radio message to Field Marshal Alan Brooke, the chief of the Imperial General Staff. He advised Brooke that "7 Armd Div and other stray units was heavily attacked this morning . . . and was in grave danger of being done in." He reported to Brooke that he gave orders at once to withdraw the troops. In giving his order he used language that those who fought at St. Vith came to treasure. Montgomery told Hodges, "They can come back with all honor. They can come back to the more secure positions. They put up a wonderful show."[40]

The XVIII Airborne Corps passed on the First Army order, noting that the "request of CG 7 AD" to withdraw was approved. The difference of views between Hasbrouck and Ridgway continued. Ridgway motored down to Vielsalm to visit, as he put it, "the principal bigwigs."[41] There are a number of interesting accounts of what transpired. John Toland's *Battle: The Story of the Bulge* and Charles B. MacDonald's *A Time for Trumpets* are both compelling and differ only in details of the dialogue. The essence is that Ridgway arrived irritated about Hasbrouck's radio message. He, Hasbrouck, and Jones met in the Belgian Army barracks that once housed the Chasseurs Ardennais.

When they met, Ridgway held Hasbrouck's message and asked in a scathing tone, "Did you read this before you signed it?" Hasbrouck responded, "Yes Sir I most assuredly did." Ridgway, a hard man who respected courage, responded favorably. The heat evaporated, and Ridgway asked Hasbrouck to make his case. Hasbrouck did. The two then went forward so Ridgway could see for himself. At Clarke's command post in Commanster they met with Clarke and COL Alexander D. Reid of the 424th INF. Both reported that their commands were at low strength. Ridgway did not ask them whether they favored withdrawing. Lastly, he contacted his old friend Bill Hoge, who had been unable to get to Commanster. He and Hoge arranged a rendezvous. Ridgway trusted Hoge, whom he knew to be a "calm, courageous, imperturbable fellow." Ridgway advised him, "This position is too exposed to try to hold it any longer. . . . I am going to extricate all the forces of the 7th Armored, and attached troops including your own. I plan to start withdrawal tonight. We're going to get you out of here." Hoge responded, "How can you?"[42]

Hoge settled the issue for Ridgway, who returned to Vielsalm and met again with Jones at about 1900 hours. At that session he relieved Jones of command. He also placed Hasbrouck in command of all of the troops in the pocket and ordered him to withdraw. "Bob start pulling your people back as soon as possible. I want them all withdrawn under the cover of darkness tonight." In so doing Ridgway went beyond acquiescing to Hasbrouck's "request." He committed himself fully to that decision. Then he went on record with Hodges's chief of staff, telling Kean "everything is all right" in the pocket and that the commanders "should do exactly as they are doing and [I] ordered them to do so."[43]

The Trains Come Through

Before they could withdraw the troops east of the Salm, the units of the 7th AD needed time and they desperately needed supplies. Ammunition, food, and combat losses had reached a critical stage. COL Andrew J. Adams and his logistics troops had already proven themselves hearty combatants in their fights with various German units, including the 116th PZ. They now demonstrated courage and skill as logisticians. Acting on his own accord, Adams organized what he knew the troops needed and sent supplies forward. He formed the convoy at Marche-en-Famenne, Belgium, on the evening of December 21.[44]

Adams decided to move all the ammunition he had on hand, as well all "gas and rations on hand," and "all replacement vehicles on hand" and deliver all of it to Vielsalm. He organized security from "odds and sods," including lone combat vehicles whose crews had attached themselves to the trains at various times. That gave the convoy two armored cars with thirty-seven-millimeter cannons, a tank destroyer, a Sherman tank, a Stuart light tank, and nine half-tracks. Forty-nine trucks carrying food, fuel, and ammunition formed the bulk of the column. One ambulance and eight wreckers accompanied the convoy to support recovery and evacuate any wounded. MAJ J. D. O'Bryant, a cavalry officer assigned as the trains' intelligence officer, led the menagerie of trucks and combat vehicles from Marche-en-Famenne along the northern shoulder. At 1400 the convoy started crossing the Salm into Vielsalm. There they distributed five thousand rounds of artillery ammunition as well as other required ammunition, gasoline, and rations to every unit in the pocket.[45]

Adams's initiative made a profound difference in morale. No supplies had come through for two days while Adams and his troops fought to survive, but he stayed in touch with the division G-4. Thus he knew what was required and that the 7th AD trains would need to supply all of the forward units, including CCB, 9th AD; the 112th INF; what was left of the 14th CAV; and the 106th ID. As he put it, "We knew they were hurting." Adams was an operator. With the rear in chaos, he sniffed out supplies where he could. He sent trucks north to Holland, where his troops "picked up ammunition, picked up plenty of fuel and plenty of food." In his mind the trains and the division staff functioned so effectively that "it only took a hint before you knew what was needed and what you could do."[46] Adams and his team proved they could do quite a lot.

The division artillery expressed its gratitude for the five thousand rounds brought by O'Bryant and his troops by firing 2,888 of them at the Germans. The artillery fired with great effect on the columns of German troops and equipment stalled in *Staus* of their own making. The artillery "was raising hell with the Germans," which bought time for the combat units to reorganize.[47] After nightfall on December 22, the artillery "raised hell" personally with antitank gunner Klaus Ritter. Ritter, who had survived the Russian front, felt he had helped liberate St. Vith. The "burghers" there spoke the same dialect that he did. That night, west of St. Vith, his good fortune ended. During a bombardment he was sheltering in a ditch with several other soldiers when he got hit with droplets—or, more properly, embers—from a white phosphorous shell. Suffering great pain and great fear he was picked up by medics and evacuated to a makeshift hospital in St. Vith. While he was being carried off he had an idle thought—his wounds would "certainly get me that [wounded] badge in black—perhaps even bronze."[48]

The artillerymen of the 7th AD, and for that matter nearly all of the other Americans in the pocket, exulted in the arrival of ammunition, rations, and food. While sustaining fires, the artillery successfully displaced toward the Salm. As the pocket contracted under pressure, some soldiers were looking over their shoulders but, for the first time in several days, something good had happened.

Parker's Crossroads at Baraque de Fraiture

Charles B. MacDonald and R. Ernest Depuy provide the best descriptions of affairs at Baraque de Fraiture. Even so, their accounts may mislead if read uncritically. Dupuy describes the crossroads as a "height." MacDonald notes Baraque de Fraiture is "high windswept ground" and "at an elevation of 2,200 feet the second highest point in the Ardennes."[49] That said, someone standing at the center of the crossroads can see no perceptible slope, nor will someone driving north on Highway N15 from Houffalize notice any rise. Thick woods grew on all sides of the crossroads. South of the crossroads the forest abutted both N15 and the east–west highway. Any attack had to cross the last four hundred to six hundred yards over open terrain.[50]

Parker's Crossroads was important to both sides. The XVIII Airborne Corps needed to hold it to enable Hasbrouck's command—the equivalent of two divisions—to withdraw, and to protect the 82nd ABN's right flank. The crossroads were important to the Germans, primarily to enable the 2nd SS PZ to break through the northern shoulder. The Americans lacked sufficient resources to defend the place and the implications of not doing so may not have been clear on December 22.

Despite the paucity of resources, the defense had grown far beyond three howitzers and some survivors from the 589th FA. A handful of troops from D Battery, 203rd Anti-Aircraft Artillery (Automatic Weapons) arrived on December 19. The D Battery troops brought three half-tracks. Two mounted quadruple .50-caliber machine guns and one had a thirty-seven-millimeter cannon. The air defense soldiers had been ordered to establish a roadblock by COL Adams as part of his effort to secure his main supply route, which led east through the crossroads to Vielsalm. When their mission to Samrée went sour, D Troop, 87th CAV joined the defense.[51]

The defenders at Parker's Crossroads drove off combat patrols and several attacks by the 560th VGD beginning on the night of December 19–20. On December 21, Parker was wounded. Managing the fight, though not necessarily the command of the various units present, passed to MAJ Eliot Goldstein, the acting battalion commander of the 589th FA. The next day Goldstein and company rebuffed a patrol from the 2nd SS PZ. They captured the patrol leader, so they knew they had the 2nd SS heading their way. Later that day the 2nd SS relieved the 560th VGD so the 560th could continue its march westward.[52]

That evening the 2nd SS received fuel and prepared to move. The Division's Vorausabteilung (Advance Guard) Krag refueled first. Led by SS

Sturmbannführer Ernst Krag, the task group would reconnoiter, fight for combat information, and ultimately find a way north. Krag's guard included his reconnaissance battalion, which was reinforced with assault guns, artillery, combat engineers, and a medical platoon. He had the resources to perform the classic mission of an advance guard—make contact, develop the situation, and provide combat information. Krag did not attack Parker's Crossroads. Instead he sought a way north, farther east toward Salmchâteau.[53]

The 4th SS PGR refueled on December 22 and headed north, but still short of fuel. Many of the regiment's half-tracks and trucks towed other vehicles that still lacked fuel. As the regiment moved north, Otto Weidinger, the regimental commander, turned off N15 and established his command post in Tailles, less than two miles south of Parker's Crossroads. Supported by a few tanks, the regiment moved with one battalion on the left of N15 and a second on the right of it. Weidinger's third battalion moved up on foot in heavy snow. The rest of the 2nd SS would not be able to move until December 23.[54]

After capturing the 2nd SS patrol leader on December 22, Goldstein took his prisoner, "an arrogant SS bastard," with him as an exhibit and headed north looking for help. The XVIII Airborne Corps had chosen to use N15 as a boundary between the 82nd ABN and 3rd AD, a choice that would have earned a failing grade at the Army's Command and General Staff College. But the Staff College graduates in XVIII Airborne Corps knew they could get away with this bad choice by assigning the road to one of the adjoining divisions. They assigned the road to the 3rd AD, which had too few troops to defend it, and had TF Hogan cut off and fighting for its life. Yet when Goldstein asked for help at the crossroads, the 3rd AD provided some tanks, two assault guns, a platoon of armored infantry, and a company from the 509th Parachute Infantry Battalion.[55]

This did not end the confusion. What higher commander owned Parker's Crossroads? Who exercised command on the ground? At the outset of the counteroffensive, various corps and First Army units were scattered throughout the rear areas of the forward divisions, but when the Fifth Panzer Army penetrated the 28th ID and 106th ID in the Losheim Gap, the rear area emptied out as VIII Corps and First Army withdrew artillery, engineers, and logistics troops. Hasbrouck sent D Troop, 87th CAV to Parker's Crossroads to secure his main supply route.

When XVIII Airborne Corps arrived, Ridgway ordered both the 82nd ABN and the 3rd AD south. Gavin's 82nd ABN had advanced south, just as Ridgway ordered, but had only four regiments—not enough to defend the ground he occupied. The 504th held a line that extended in arc from Cheneux to Trois-Ponts. The 505th defended from Trois-Ponts nearly to Salmchâteau, oriented east. Together they held the road-bound 1st SS at bay. The 508th occupied positions from just north of Salmchâteau. At the town their line turned hard right and ran along the road that led through Parker's Crossroads to La Roche-en-Ardenne. The 325th Glider Infantry Regiment defended on the 508th's right, oriented south. The 325th covered the ground as far west as Règné. The infantrymen were spread so thinly that in the 325th's sector individual infantrymen were positioned as far as one to two hundred yards apart. On December 22, Gavin released the 2nd Battalion of the 325th back to the regiment. It had been serving as division reserve. The regimental commander, LTC Max E. Billingsley, positioned the 2nd Battalion on a ridge overlooking the village of Fraiture. The 82nd's disposition did not secure Parker's Crossroads.[56]

Although the 3rd AD had responsibility for Highway N15 and therefore Parker's Crossroads, it had not arrived in sufficient strength to defend it. On December 22 Gavin had explicit responsibility for Parker's Crossroads. He and Billingsley both understood the danger. That same day Billingsley sent CPT Junior R. Woodruff's F Company, 325th Glider Infantry, supported by a towed tank destroyer platoon from the 643rd Tank Destroyer Battalion, to defend the crossroads. That evening at 1812 hours Gavin called Ridgway, "perturbed over the situation on the south in front of Billingsley." Gavin believed there "might be considerable force" south of the crossroads, and he wanted to know when he could expect the 3rd AD to assume defense. Ridgway advised the 82nd would have to hold on at least until December 23.[57]

At nightfall, Goldstein retained unofficial command of troops from the 3rd AD, the 7th AD, the 82nd ABN, and the 106th ID. Just who was there remains unknown. Units came and went as requirements changed. It is clear from postwar interviews that few of the new arrivals concluded that they worked for Goldstein. Because there was no clearly defined chain of command, some who fought there claimed others who also did so were never there. The 643rd most certainly had tank destroyers in the fight, but years later there were some who asserted with absolute belief that no tank destroyers had fought at Parker's Crossroads. The 643rd's role was little known because Woodruff ordered it south of the crossroads, where the Germans promptly captured two of the 643rd's guns. The remaining two guns escaped north and did not stop until they reached Manhay.[58]

Whoever they were, and wherever they came from, everyone located at Parker's Crossroads on December 22 occupied positions astride a road along what soldiers call a high-speed avenue of approach. Since December 19, when Parker first established the roadblock, the defenders had fought off the 116th PZ and the 560th VGD, neither of which were determined to take the crossroads but were focused on moving west. The 4th SS, well supported by tanks, had no mandate to go west—its mandate required it to clear Parker's Crossroads of Americans. Goldstein's menagerie amounted to 110 soldiers from the 589th FA, a cavalry troop, two sections of antiaircraft artillery, two infantry companies, perhaps as many as five tanks and two assault guns, a tank destroyer platoon, and an armored infantry platoon. As night fell on December 22, Goldstein had no real authority other than moral over anyone outside of the 589th. It was snowing heavily, and the 4th SS PGR had closed up on the crossroads.[59]

Otto Weidinger's battalions reported "the presence of strong enemy forces on both sides" of the crossroads. Furthermore, the forward battalions believed it had seen "twelve tanks," and "enemy artillery fire had started." On December 22, the 2nd SS found fuel for a tank company and an assault gun company, and attached them to the 4th SS PGR. On the basis of spirited resistance at the crossroads, Weidinger determined to mount a deliberate attack on December 23 with his infantry supported by tanks (as many as ten 74-millimeter Mark IVs) and assault guns (as many as fourteen seventy-five-millimeter Hetzers) and preceded by an artillery preparation. In other circumstances, Goldstein might have felt flattered.[60]

Escaping the Goose Egg

Having decided to withdraw the forces in the Goose Egg, Ridgway wanted the job done on December 22. That just could not be accomplished. During that afternoon units resupplied, counted noses, shortened their lines where they could, and fought off a series of attacks. Although Field Manual (FM) 17-100, *The Armored Division*, did not list defense as a mission intended for armored divisions, it did list "withdrawal." FM 17-100 described the primary role of the armored division to support the withdrawal of a larger force by making "limited objective attacks" against the enemy to relieve pressure on withdrawing units. When acting alone, or in this case in charge of withdrawing a combined force, the manual required "a covering force of all arms," employing the "cover of darkness" and using "tanks, tank destroyers and, artillery to protect the withdrawal."[61]

Given ambiguity about total numbers of troops and vehicles that had to get out over only two bridges, Hasbrouck and his chief of staff, COL John L. Ryan, led the effort to produce as clear and as simple a plan as possible. Both recalled that the effort took about four hours. Both understood the problem and, Hasbrouck recalled, "I knew what I had to do." Before the staff wrote the plan, Hasbrouck met with BG Herbert T. Perrin, who succeeded Allan W. Jones in command of the 106th ID. Hasbrouck and Ryan also reviewed the plan with the liaison officers of all the subordinate units.[62]

The 7th AD published its written order at 0200 on December 23. Some units did not receive their copy until 0600. The order envisioned withdrawing units from the center while units on the flank withdrew inward and then out, not unlike turning a sock inside out by pulling the toe from the inside. Everyone would cross the Salm at either Salmchâteau or Vielsalm. The order designated three routes. In the north, CCR would use the road from Petit-Thier. CCA would use this route and withdraw through CCR, which would provide cover as CCA crossed the river. CCB, 9th AD would withdraw with Clarke's command on its heels, followed by the 424th INF.

Hasbrouck established three "all arms" covering forces. CCR served as covering force in the north. LTC Vincent L. Boylan of the 87th CAV commanded the main covering force in the center. Boylan had a tank company, an armored infantry company, and a tank destroyer company. Colonel COL Gustin M. Nelson commanded a second covering force south of Salmchâteau that was formed around his 112th INF. Hasbrouck's order specified no covering force could withdraw without explicit authority from him. At two pages, the Division order suggested simplicity, but no one in the pocket assumed it would be easy. After the fact, the division artillery asserted with some hyperbole that this kind of operation was "considered impossible by the best masters of warfare."[63] Because the ground was so soft, Clarke wondered aloud to Hasbrouck, "I don't know how we are going to do it."[64]

BG Hasbrouck wanted to begin withdrawing at 0300, but Hoge could not disengage, as his command was then under heavy attack from the 64th VGD. Hasbrouck agreed to delay start time until 0600, but by then the 2nd SS was attacking Parker's Crossroads. At about 0500 Hasbrouck sent a message to Clarke: "The situation is such on the west of the river south of the 82nd Airborne Division that if we don't join them soon, the opportunity will be gone." A high-pressure area coming from Russia moved in overnight, and when Clarke stepped outside his command post to see what the ground was like, it had frozen. Hasbrouck called Clarke to follow up on his message, asking,

"Bruce, . . . do you think you can get out?" Clarke reported, "A miracle has happened, General! That cold snap that's hit us has frozen the roads. I think we can make it now."[65]

The Division began withdrawing at 0700 hours, pressured heavily by Remer's FEB in the north and the 62nd VGD in the south. Contrary to doctrine, Hasbrouck's command withdrew during a sunny day. That would not have worked at the Command and General Staff College, but he got away with it on that day. If all went well, the Division anticipated that the last unit, less the 112th INF, the final covering force, would cross the Salm not long before dawn on Christmas Eve. The XVIII Airborne Corps originally planned to withdraw the units beaten up at St. Vith to the Corps rear to refit. But First Army intervened by reassigning the 3rd AD to VII Corps. Accordingly, COL Rosebaum's CCA, 7th AD withdrew to defensive positions astride N15 just south of Manhay. The 7th AD half-tracks would do double duty, dropping off their own troops and returning to carry the 112th and 424th Infantry Regiments.[66]

The withdrawal began late but started out as planned, with CCA, 9th AD "withdrawing by echelons from the left side [Bauvenn]." CCA half-tracks and tanks, and one hundred trucks scrounged by the 7th AD, brought out the 424th INF. As many as fourteen infantrymen rode out on a single tank. CCB, 7th AD broke contact and withdrew without incident except for the 17th TB, which got the order late. When he received the order, the 17th's LTC Wemple "immediately issued orders over the radio for the withdrawal of forces." Wemple had to fight his way through Crombach with his tanks firing in all directions. The 17th lost three tanks in the process. The 9th SS attacked CCA, 7th AD as it got underway. Fortunately, the 9th SS also sideswiped the 18th VGD, enabling Rosebaum's tanks to break contact, although Germans managed to get to within one hundred yards of his rear guard. LTC Boylan, commanding the center covering force, passed Wemple through and then he, too, withdrew.[67]

Boylan's operation was textbook perfect compared to the problems TF Jones and the 112th INF experienced. As ordered, LTC Robert B. Jones remained in place at Bovigny until CCB, 9th AD; the 424th INF; and the 112th INF cleared. At 1430 TF Jones began moving north and passed through Cierreaux, where COL Gustin Nelson's 112th held a blocking position to cover Jones as he withdrew. TF Jones continued north, led by its supporting artillery, the 440th Armored Field Artillery (AFA). Remer's tanks and the 62nd VGD reached Salmchâteau as the 440th AFA entered, racing through the southern edge of Salmchâteau and firing on the move. The battalion escaped its "startled enemy" on its self-propelled howitzers and "roared over the bridge."[68]

Effective German antitank fire brought Jones to a halt with Nelson's 112th INF lined up behind him. TF Jones had stumbled into a "perfect" cul-de-sac. Just south of Salmchâteau, Jones had the Salm on his left and high ground on his right. As the light waned on this short winter day the Germans began picking off vehicles in both columns. Nelson made his way forward to Jones, where he discovered the reason for the holdup. He employed his infantry to attempt to clear the town, while Jones withdrew only to have the rear of the column attacked. Although his rear guard of M36 tank destroyers killed six enemy tanks, he lost four of his tank destroyers.[69]

Jones and Nelson searched frantically for a ford while the Germans continued to pick off soldiers and vehicles. Jones's intelligence officer eventually found a ford, and by midnight the survivors finally crossed the Salm, though a few of Nelson's units had to make their way through marshy ground to reach crossing sites. Doing so forced them to abandon some of the trucks carrying them out. The column continued on, with infantrymen clinging to every protuberance on the tanks, tank destroyers, and trucks. One trucker, who refused to abandon his truck, took out more than fifty soldiers. Around 0300 the bedraggled survivors passed through the 82nd ABN and into assembly areas.[70]

Throughout the withdrawal, the division artillery fired continuously. The 7th AD's three organic battalions fired 5,038 rounds in 172 separate missions, and the 275th AFA and a corps battalion supported as well. The 440th AFA fired six hundred rounds in the last phase of the withdrawal and then fought its way out through Salmchâteau. Careful positioning and well-timed movement rearward assured fire support throughout the operation. The artillerymen were justifiably proud of their work and of the Division and crowed about it afterward, but they understood how close it had been. The division artillery after action report noted, "This withdrawal couldn't have been any closer and still been a withdrawal rather than at least a partial destruction."[71]

Despite having little time to prepare to do so, the withdrawing troops passed through the 82nd ABN with few problems. According to Hasbrouck, they were "a very cooperative outfit." Remarkably, the better part of two divisions passed through only two passage points, with no more than twelve hours between the decision to withdraw and the beginning of the operation.

The 82nd experienced one glitch: paratroopers had prepared the bridge at Vielsalm for demolition, but when Hasbrouck cleared them to blow the bridge nothing happened. The 7th AD's engineers finished the job and gratefully withdrew.[72]

The survivors of the St. Vith salient arrived in assembly areas—or, in the case of CCA, 7th AD, new defensive positions—exhausted and well used. During the preceding week they fought against eight different German divisions and the FEB. At no time did they face less than three enemy divisions. The 7th AD's intelligence officer estimated they confronted as many as five hundred enemy tanks and no less than five enemy infantry regiments. Hasbrouck felt somewhat fortunate that the Germans were more intent on making their way west than reducing the small bulge at St. Vith.[73]

The End at Parker's Crossroads

Convinced that he faced a coherent and powerful defensive array, Otto Weidinger massed his 4th SS PGR in an assembly area south of Parker's Crossroads. At 1500 on December 23, Weidinger's supporting artillery fired "a short but very heavy concentration onto the road intersection and the surrounding area." Weidinger's troops attacked as the artillery lifted against an enemy that "resisted bitterly." The Americans fought "tenaciously," but after nightfall the Germans took the crossroads. Weidinger admitted "heavy losses" due to an enemy who "also understood how to fight bravely and to die fearlessly." John Schaffner, the solider who rotated the two pairs of socks he had, was not in his foxhole when the final attack began. He was in a stone building near the center of the crossroads. He and a buddy named Harold Kuizema bolted from the building and made their way in short sprints to a field on the north side of the crossroads where Harold was wounded. Schaffner and two paratroopers carried Kuizema into the woods held by the 82nd ABN. From there he could see the crossroads, and "the whole sky seemed to be lighted by the flames from the burning building."[74]

Although Weidinger took the crossroads he failed to press his advantage. To the east Hasbrouck's troops streamed across the Salm. While Weidinger reorganized, the last act of the withdrawal played out. LT Will Rogers Jr., a former congressman and son of the American humorist, led his reconnaissance platoon of the 814th Tank Destroyer Battalion across the Salm and over the marshy ground toward the 82nd ABN. Rogers's platoon served as the rear guard. As he led his platoon over the Salm, the last unit to cross, a wonderful thing happened: "A full bright moon came up over the hill," and he and his men "came out through the snow [on] this brilliant moonlit night. And then we saw another wonderful sight. About every hundred feet we saw a man in a white parka standing there, and that was the 82nd Airborne."[75]

NOTES

1. "What Price Feet?" *Army Talks* 2, no. 48 (1944): 13–15; John Schaffner, telephone interview with the author, December 3, 2017.

2. David W. Hogan Jr., *A Command Post at War*, 84–85, 220–21. On Montgomery's estimate of Hodge and Eisenhower's response, see Charles B. MacDonald, *A Time for Trumpets*, 426.

3. James M. Gavin, *On to Berlin*, 229.

4. Gavin, *On to Berlin*, 230.

5. Donald P. Boyer Jr., *St. Vith: The 7th Armored Division in the Battle of the Bulge*, 58.

6. Boyer, *St. Vith: The 7th Armored Division in the Battle of the Bulge*, 178–79.

7. W. Wesley Johnston, *Combat Interviews of the 31st Tank Battalion*, 31–40.

8. John S. D. Eisenhower, *The Bitter Woods*, 298. There is no mention of this order in the 7th AD journals, but all of the senior commanders except COL Reid of the 424th INF mentioned it. Hoge is not on record personally, but his after action review refers to the order as establishing an "enclave." Col. Gustin M. Nelson to his father, May 1945, box 3, Charles B. MacDonald Papers, called it an "island defense."

9. Matthew B. Ridgway, *Soldier: The Memoirs of Matthew B. Ridgway*, 119.

10. MacDonald, *A Time for Trumpets*, 478; Colonel R. Ernest Dupuy, *St. Vith: Lion in the Way*, 172–73. Dupuy's account suggests that MG Allan W. Jones, 106th ID, received a similar order and in compliance had the 112th and 424th Infantry Regiments withdrawing toward their positions in the Goose Egg. Jones also ordered CCB, 9th AD to withdraw while retaining contact with CCB, 7th AD on his left.

11. Harold R. Winton, *Corps Commanders of the Bulge*, 253, 257.

12. Winton, *Corps Commanders*, 186; Wemple's narrative is in W. Wesley Johnston, *17th Tank Battalion, 7th Armored Division*.

13. Johnston, *Combat Interviews of the 31st Tank Battalion*, 19–20.

14. Johnston, *17th Tank Battalion, 7th Armored Division*, 25.

15. Richard L. McBride, "Grinding Through with the 7th Armored Division," 132.

16. Combat Command R, 7th Armored Division, "After Action Report, Month of December 1944," 11. Armored formations referred to Jeeps as peeps. That affectation is ignored in this narrative. Some sources claim the name Jeep originally applied to the three-quarter-ton truck rather than the quarter-ton truck that became universally known as a Jeep.

17. Michael Reynolds, *Sons of the Reich*, 197. Reynolds believes the apparent indolence of the 9th SS reflected "confusion and incompetence within the overall command organization."

18. Heinz Günther Guderian, *From Normandy to the Ruhr*, 324.

19. Oberstleutnant Dietrich Moll, "18th Volks Grenadier Division," 49.

20. Moll, "18th Volks Grenadier Division," 51.

21. Moll, "18th Volks Grenadier Division," 51.

22. Moll, "18th Volks Grenadier Division," 51.

23. Otto Weidinger, *Das Reich*, vol. 5, *1943–1945*, 269. Weidinger commanded the Panzergrenadiers Regiment of the Division. An unabashed and unreformed Nazi, Weidinger's history is an apologia for one of the most reprehensible of the many reprehensible SS units. The Division massacred by shooting or burning to death nearly two hundred French civilians at Oradour-sur-Glane on June 10, 1944. On June 14 Weidinger took command of the battalion that committed the outrage. It is possible he was there for the massacre. The author visited Oradour-sur-Glane in 1955 when he was not quite six years old. It was an unforgettable experience and one that makes it hard to even use the acronym for the various SS units.

24. W. Wesley Johnston, *Combat Interviews of the 87th Cavalry Reconnaissance Squadron*, 52–53. See also W. Wesley Johnston, *Combat Interviews of the 48th Armored Infantry Battalion*, 22–23, 36–37. It is difficult to determine just who was where and who did what in Rodt that morning.

25. Generalmajor Otto E. Remer, "The Führer-Begleit Brigade in the Ardennes Offensive," 14; Johnston, *Combat Interviews of the 87th Cavalry Reconnaissance Squadron*, 52–53; Moll, "18th Volks Grenadier Division," 50. Remer noted that the 828th, composed of older men, was intended for security duties.

26. Generalmajor Friedrich Kittel, "62nd Volksgrenadier Division"; Hugh M. Cole, *The Ardennes: Battle of the Bulge*, 410. See also Oberst Arthur Jüttner, "Report by Colonel Jüttner of the 62nd VGD in the Battle of the Bulge," 13.

27. Combat Command B, 9th Armored Division, "Action South of St. Vith 17–23 Dec 1944," 15–20. On Hoge's warning to Cummings, see General William M. Hoge, *Engineer Memoirs*, 133. Cummings replaced LTC George W. Seeley, who died of a heart attack on December 17. Cummings assumed command two days later. According to Hoge, Cummings "was the biggest damned fool I'd ever run into." In March 1945 Hoge relieved him of his command.

28. Combat Command B, 9th Armored Division, "Action South of St. Vith," 17–18. See also Jüttner, "Report by Colonel Jüttner of the 62nd VGD in the Battle of the Bulge," 12. According to Jüttner, Franke commanded the regiment and was wounded.

29. Combat Command B, 9th Armored Division, "Action South of St. Vith," 19–20. The tactical improvisation by CPT Strange; A Company, 14th TB; and a tank platoon from B Company, 14th TB make fascinating reading. The 27th AIB withdrew from Neubrück at 2330. See also 14th Tank Battalion, "After Action Report—1 Dec 44 to 31 Dec 44," 10–11.

30. General der Panzertruppe Hasso von Manteuffel, "An Interview with Gen Pz Hasso von Manteuffel," ETHINT-46, 6.

31. MacDonald, *A Time for Trumpets*, 514–15, 540–41. Most of this paragraph reflects the author's understanding of the situation based on Manteuffel's responses to questions found in ETHINT-45 and ETHINT-46, as well as his postwar comments

in several interviews. It is clear that Model and Manteuffel were growing more concerned each day.

32. Ridgway, *Soldier: The Memoirs of Matthew B. Ridgway*, 114.

33. Record of General Matthew B. Ridgway's side of a conversation with Major General William B. Kean, 212350 December 1944, Matthew B. Ridgway Papers, 1–2.

34. Record of Ridgway conversation with Kean, 2.

35. W. Wesley Johnston, *Combat Interviews of the 7th Armored Division Headquarters*, 19.

36. Johnston, *Combat Interviews of the 7th Armored Division Headquarters*, 21.

37. Johnston, *Combat Interviews of the 7th Armored Division Headquarters*, 21. This message is quoted in its entirety in Cole, *The Ardennes: Battle of the Bulge*, 412.

38. Cole, *The Ardennes: Battle of the Bulge*, 412.

39. General Bruce C. Clarke (Ret.), interview with the author, Falls Church, VA, August 8, 1984, General Bruce C. Clarke Papers.

40. Nigel Hamilton, *Monty: The Battles of Field Marshall Bernard Montgomery*, 507–8.

41. Matthew B. Ridgway, war diary, entry for December 22, 1944, 2210 hours, Matthew B. Ridgway Papers.

42. MacDonald, *A Time for Trumpets*, 479–80; Ridgway, *Soldier: The Memoirs of Matthew B. Ridgway*, 119–20.

43. Ridgway, war diary, entry for December 22, 1944, 2210 hours.

44. 7th Armored Division Trains, summary of events, December 1944, 2; 7th Armored Division Trains, journal, December 22, 1944.

45. 7th Armored Division Trains journal, December 22, 1944. Just how many trucks O'Bryant used is lost in the mists of time. He signed a report in December stating that only thirty-one had gone forward. John Toland, *Battle: The Story of the Bulge*, 186, quotes an aide to Clarke claiming there were ninety. Other sources have used this number as well. The author uses the number reported in the trains journal, as it is contemporary to the convoy.

46. Major General Andrew J. Adams (Ret.), interview with the author, Washington, DC, August 31, 1984.

47. Division Artillery, 7th Armored Division, "After Action Report, Month of December 1944," 17.

48. Klaus Ritter, statements, box 10, Charles B. MacDonald Papers, pt. 2, pp. 8–9. Ritter believed an American mortar wounded him. It's possible, but not likely, given the range of 81-millimeter mortars in use at St. Vith.

49. Dupuy, *St. Vith: Lion in the Way*, 18; MacDonald, *A Time for Trumpets*, 541.

50. MacDonald, *A Time for Trumpets*, map 7.

51. 7th Armored Division, "Battle of St Vith: 17–23 December," 11. See also MacDonald, *A Time for Trumpets*, 542.

52. MacDonald, *A Time for Trumpets*, 543.

53. Otto Weidinger, *Das Reich*, vol. 5, *1943–1945*, 270; MacDonald, *A Time for Trumpets*, 543.

54. Weidinger, *Das Reich*, 5:272–73.

55. MacDonald, A *Time for Trumpets*, 544. For "arrogant SS bastard," see Frank Evans to Charles B. McDonald, n.d., box 1B, Charles B. MacDonald Papers, 2. Evans, who was assigned to D Troop, 87th CAV wrote a pithy account of the fighting at Parker's Crossroads in his letter to MacDonald.

56. Gavin, *On to Berlin*, 233, and 234, fig. 18.

57. MacDonald, A *Time for Trumpets*, 541–45. See also Ridgway, war diary, December 1944, 221812.

58. MacDonald, A *Time for Trumpets*, 543; Elliot Goldstein, *On the Job Training*, 52–65.

59. There are contradictory accounts about what units were there, and when. This narrative relies heavily on Goldstein, *On the Job Training*; the recollections of those from the 589th who survived and of LT Arthur Olson, in Johnston, *Combat Interviews of the 87th Cavalry Reconnaissance Squadron*, 43–47; and 7th Armored Division, "The Battle of St. Vith."

60. Weidinger, *Das Reich*, 5:272; Michael Reynolds, *Sons of the Reich*, 202.

61. US War Department, *Armored Command Field Manual: The Armored Division*, FM 17-100, 22, 78–79.

62. Major General Robert W. Hasbrouck (Ret.), interview with the author, Washington, DC, August 20, 1984; Johnston, *Combat Interviews of the 7th Armored Division Headquarters*, 19, 30.

63. Division Artillery, 7th Armored Division, "After Action Report, Month of December 1944," 18.

64. MacDonald, A *Time for Trumpets*, 481.

65. John S. D. Eisenhower, *The Bitter Woods*, 302.

66. 7th Armored Division, "Order for Withdrawal of 7th Armored Division West of Salm River."

67. Hoge, *Engineer Memoirs*, 137; Headquarters, Combat Command B, 9th Armored Division, "After Action Report for the Period 1–31 December 1944," 10; Cole, *The Ardennes: Battle of the Bulge*, 407–22. See also Moll, "18th Volks Grenadier Division," 53.

68. Cole, *The Ardennes: Battle of the Bulge*, 421; Calvin C. Boykin Jr., *Gare la Bête*, 82–91, covers the withdrawal. See also 814th Tank Destroyer Battalion, periodic reports, December 1944, 4–5.

69. 814th Tank Destroyer Battalion, periodic reports, December 1944, 4–5. The 814th's periodic reports account accurately only for its own losses. Losses incurred by Task Force Lindsey traveling with the 814th are not clear. On the cul-de-sac, see Lieutenant Jack T. Shea, "Fourteenth Cavalry Group," 56.

70. 814th Tank Destroyer Battalion, "After Action Report December 1944," 2–3. See also 440th Anti-Aircraft Artillery Battalion, "After Action Report, December 1944," 12. See also Headquarters, 112th Infantry Regiment, "Unit Report No. 6, from 1 December 1944–31 December 1944," 3–4.

71. Division Artillery, 7th Armored Division, "After Action Report, Month of December 1944," 20.

72. Major General Robert W. Hasbrouck (Ret.), interview with the author, Washington, DC, August 20, 1984.

73. Hasbrouck interview, August 20, 1984.

74. Weidinger, *Das Reich*, 5:272–73; Goldstein, *On the Job Training*, 67.

75. Army Pictorial Center, *The Battle of St. Vith*; Rogers's quotation comes near the end of pt. 2.

CHAPTER ELEVEN

Reversal and Reconstitution

A major German attack was certain to come up the main highway through Manhay.

—James M. Gavin

Instead of passing wrecked vehicles, intentionally destroyed supplies and equipment, abandoned artillery guns and positions by contrast we began to meet convoys of troops headed towards the front.

—Staff Sergeant Richard L. McBride

Field Marshal Model and General von Manteuffel expressed appreciation: they stressed we had been fighting with the same efficiency as the far better equipped Panzer Divisions!

—Arthur Jüttner

As PRIME MINISTER Winston Churchill observed about Dunkirk, wars are not won by evacuations. Nor are battles won by withdrawal. As the bedraggled survivors of the defense of St. Vith passed through the 82nd Airborne Division (ABN) they hoped for a chance to rest in relatively secure assembly areas north of the 82nd's lines. The beating they had taken on the Prümerberg would not soon be forgotten. That and the act of withdrawal affected morale. Nonetheless, they felt grateful to the 82nd and thankful to be momentarily out of danger. Eugene Morrell, an artilleryman in the 106th Infantry Division (ID), recalled stopping briefly just to the rear of the 82nd ABN, where he saw the corpses of paratroopers laying together side by side. When his battery moved on, Morrell found that he could not shake the sight of these men "who lost their lives while helping to clear this road for our escape, remained with us."[1]

The team that fought to hold St. Vith moved to assembly areas north of Werbomont in reserve to XVIII Airborne Corps. Combat Command B (CCB), 9th Armored Division (AD), along with the 424th Infantry Regiment (INF), closed on assembly areas in the early evening. The three combat commands of the 7th AD closed on their assembly areas by midnight on December 23. The covering force, including Task Force (TF) Jones and the 112th INF, fought their way across the Salm River after midnight. The 112th suffered most during the withdrawal, simply because it never received the radio message clearing it to withdraw. Colonel (COL) Gustin M. Nelson vowed never again to accept an order that required him to "remain in position" until ordered out. Sergeant Charles Haug, one of Nelson's riflemen, finally made it back to American lines on Christmas Day, more than two days after the withdrawal began. The thing he remembered best about what happened once he made it behind the lines was his first meal, the "biggest meal you would ever want to lay your eyes on."[2]

Although determining losses during the defense is not an exact science, the bill was steep for all of the units that fought alongside the 7th AD. Hugh Cole's reckoning for the 7th AD, in *The Ardennes: Battle of the Bulge*, is "59 medium tanks, 29 light tanks and 25 armored cars." The attached 814th Tank Destroyer Battalion (TD) lost thirteen ninety-millimeter M36 tank destroyers, and one seventy-six-millimeter M10 of the thirty-five tank destroyers it had on hand on December 17. The Division suffered nearly 20 percent casualties, included those killed, wounded, missing, and lost to nonbattle injury or disease. By any measure, the Lucky Seventh had taken a beating.[3]

Allied Assessments and Orders

Major (MAJ) William C. Sylvan's First Army war diary entry for December 24 expressed continued concern, though with a measure of optimism. There was some good news: the Allied air forces flew and attacked the Germans with success. Better still, the 30th ID polished off Obersturmbahnführer Joachim Peiper's overextended Kampfgruppe. Peiper's troops abandoned their equipment and attempted to escape on foot. A handful made it out, but they left "38 tanks, 78 half-tracks, 8 armored cars and 6 self-propelled guns." Even so, of the daily afternoon conference with British field marshal Bernard Law Montgomery, Sylvan wrote, "The outlook this afternoon is not good."[4] In the 3rd AD, TF Hogan remained surrounded. One of General der Panzertruppe Hasso von Manteuffel's Panzer divisions, the 2nd, was closing on the Meuse River, and the 2nd Schutzstaffel (SS) Panzer (PZ) stood poised to attack north along Highway N15. The Allied command feared that the Germans aimed at taking Liège.

Despite concern expressed by his diarist, Lieutenant General (LTG) Courtney H. Hodges sensed that the worst was over and leaned toward counterattacking. Field Marshal Montgomery, however, did not share Hodges's optimism. On Christmas Eve he ordered Hodges to shorten his lines. By the time the order made its way through First Army and down to the corps, it was late in the day, putting the operation at risk, because it would have to be done in haste.

Montgomery remained rightly concerned over the growing weakness of the American infantry divisions. At the end of the month First Army reported receiving 15,295 infantry replacements for some 41,116 losses. On Christmas Day, Montgomery made his concern explicit in a conference with LTG Omar N. Bradley, 12th Army Group. "The American divisions are all very weak," he said, "and any major offensive action from the north against the right flank of the enemy penetration is definitely not possible at present."[5]

Major General (MG) J. Lawton Collins, commanding the still arriving VII Corps, saw an opportunity to strike the overextended 2nd Panzer Division (PZ) near Celles, Belgium. Hodges's operations officer, mindful both of the order to shorten the lines and Hodges's own desire to strike back, issued an order that allowed Collins the latitude to do what he wished. Collins ordered his 2nd AD to attack. The next day the 2nd AD attacked the 2nd PZ and gutted the advanced element. Although it was not immediately apparent, the 2nd AD's attack essentially put paid to the German counteroffensive.[6]

To facilitate setting the conditions for returning to the offensive, Hodges and his staff reassigned the 3rd AD to Collins and left Highway N15 as the boundary between VII and XVIII Airborne Corps. Despite not anticipating the counteroffensive, nor recognizing when it began that indeed it was a counteroffensive, Hodges and his team wanted very much to counterattack. In their eagerness to enable Collins to do so they aggravated a serious vulnerability that grew more serious by the hour. The 2nd SS PZ posed a very real threat along N15 toward Manhay and ultimately Liège. When the hodgepodge defense at Parker's Crossroads gave way, it left XVIII Airborne Corps' right flank at risk—and, for that matter, the left flank of the offensive-minded Collins. MG Matthew B. Ridgway had no option but to use CCB, 9th AD and the 7th AD to protect the XVIII Airborne Corps flank by securing the approaches to Manhay at the town of Malempré and at Manhay itself.

First, Ridgway attached Brigadier General (BG) William M. Hoge's CCB, 9th AD to the 82nd ABN. MG James M. Gavin planned to deploy Hoge at Malempré, where his tanks overlooked N15. Second, Ridgway ordered the 7th AD to send a combat command to defend Manhay. Soon after sunup on a bright clear day, both exhausted combat commands returned to the battle. Hoge's CCB arrived in Malempré at 1315 hours. COL Dwight A. Rosebaum's Combat Command A (CCA), 7th AD made its way back south and relieved CCB, 9th AD that same afternoon. Rosebaum had the 40th Tank Battalion (TB) and the 48th Armored Infantry Battalion (AIB), the two least beat-up units of the Lucky Seventh's six maneuver battalions.[7]

German Assessments and Orders

Although the 2nd SS PZ seized Parker's Crossroads, it chose not to exploit its success. Dedicated SS man Otto Weidinger, commander of the 4th SS Panzergrenadier Regiment, considered the loses taken at the crossroads "heavy." He lost four tanks and described the losses in the two grenadier battalions as "especially high." In part because of high losses at the crossroads, SS Brigade Führer Heinz Lammerding, commanding the 2nd SS, determined not to attack straight up N15 but rather to move cross-country along both sides of the highway.[8] Lammerding also wanted to wait for the arrival of Oberst Otto-Ernst Remer's Führer Escort Brigade (FEB). Field Generalfeldmarschall Walther Model had assigned the FEB to support the 2nd SS.

Model still had some reason to hope. Driving the Americans west of the Salm, and unhinging the 82nd ABN's western flank, opened the way to employ the 9th SS in the attack. Combined, the 9th SS, 2nd SS, and FEB might yet force the way open for the Sixth Panzer Army. Manteuffel ordered LXVI Corps to close on the Salm, but his confidence in success had ebbed. On Christmas Eve he (almost certainly with Model's concurrence) spoke with Generalfeldmarschall Alfred Jodl, Adolf Hitler's chief of staff. Manteuffel asked for the authority to "change to the 'smaller solution' which called for a sharp swing north, with our left flank on the Meuse River." Jodl passed on Hitler's affirmative reply the day after Christmas. Hitler also released other units to join the offensive, but they lacked sufficient fuel to move.[9]

On Christmas Eve, Manteuffel, like Model, "believed in success of a battle east of the Meuse." But "from that date on, we discarded the plans calling for the crossing of the Meuse."[10] Nevertheless, seizing Manhay might open the way for the FEB, 2nd SS, and 9th SS to support the Fifth Panzer Army's efforts east of the Meuse and maybe even unstick the Sixth Panzer Army. The 7th AD would bear the brunt of the German attack designed to enable success east of the Meuse.

Defeated and Routed: Christmas Eve 1944

When Ridgway ordered the 7th AD to provide a combat command to relieve CCB, 9th AD to defend the approaches to Manhay, BG Robert W. Hasbrouck had little to choose from, as all of his units were worn down. The 17th TB, for example, had only twenty-nine tanks remaining. Rosebaum's CCA included Lieutenant Colonel (LTC) John C. Brown's 40th TB, comparatively robust with thirty medium tanks, nine light tanks, and five assault guns. LTC Richard D. Chappuis, 48th (AIB), added three shopworn armored infantry companies to the mix. C Company, 48th AIB was, in particular, short-handed, so a platoon of paratroops from the newly arrived 517th Parachute Infantry Regiment (PIR) filled it out. The 814th TD provided CCA a platoon of ninety-millimeter M36 tank destroyers. LTC Robert L. Rhea brought down his 23rd AIB—or, rather, what was left of it. Rhea had "regrouped" the Battalion after eight hours' rest. The 23rd was at best at half strength and included dismounted tankers who had lost their tanks. These unfortunates filled out some of the missing files in the 23rd.[11]

Around noon COL Rosebaum sought out BG Doyle Hickey, commanding CCA, 3rd AD in Manhay to discuss "arranging occupation of the area." According to John Toland in *Battle: The Story of the Bulge*, Hickey and LTC Walter B. Richardson, 32nd Armor, "were unfavorably impressed." In the passage, Hickey asserted that Rosebaum must extend his defense to cover Hickey's TF Brewster, located near Belle Haie, just north of Parker's Crossroads. Rosebaum agreed to do so. Hugh M. Cole writes simply that Hickey and Rosebaum "worked out a plan to co-ordinate the efforts of their two commands." A middle path between these two interpretations seems most likely. Whatever else he might have been, Rosebaum was neither bored nor complacent, as Toland reported Hickey saying. The 40th TB did patrol farther south along N15 until it drew fire not far north of Parker's Crossroads. CCA's sector ran from east of Malempré west, then northwest to Grandménil, or about three miles, with N15 splitting the sector.[12]

Montgomery's sensible order to shorten the lines added to the confusion created by First Army. Tenuous relations between Rosebaum and Hickey may have aggravated what followed. The new XVIII Airborne Corps defensive plan called for the 7th AD to defend a line along the high ground north

of Vaux-Chavanne, Manhay, and Grandménil, parallel to the east–west highway that intersected N15 at Manhay. On CCA's left, or east, the 82nd ABN
would defend east to Trois-Ponts. The 30th ID defended east of the 82nd.
The 3rd AD and VII Corps would extend the line west from Grandménil.[13]

To establish the revised line required several complex evolutions, which in
the event were interrupted by a German night attack. First, the 82nd had to
withdraw west and then wheel north, pivoting on Trois-Ponts. CCB, 9th AD
would withdraw through Manhay. TF Brewster would withdraw and, finally,
CCA would retire to the line north of Manhay. Ridgway's Corps order arrived at 1800, with orders for CCA to begin withdrawing at 2200. The order
did not direct TF Brewster to retire, as it was subordinate to the 3rd AD,
assigned to VII Corps. C Company, 40th TB dug in its tanks to hull defilade
in a meadow just south of a tree line overlooking N15.[14]

South of CCA the 2nd SS prepared to attack, with tanks coming north on
N15 supported by Panzergrenadiers both east and west of the road. West of
N15 the Panzergrenadiers attacked from Odeigne through Oster to Grandménil. In the east they moved from Parker's Crossroads through Malempré
to Vaux-Chavanne. That it happened to be a clear night facilitated the German attack.

Believing that TF Brewster had withdrawn via some other route, the 40th
TB began to move. But TF Brewster—with seven tanks of H Company, 2nd
Battalion, 32nd Armor; an airborne infantry company from the 509th Parachute Infantry Battalion; and C Company, 1st Battalion, 290th INF, 75th
ID—had not yet received orders to withdraw. The Germans began their attack on time and bypassed TF Brewster heading north. A captured Sherman
preceded the German column. C Company, 40th TB could see the Germans
approaching, but the backfiring Sherman in the lead coupled with uncertainty about the whereabouts of TF Brewster led to confusion. The Americans
concluded mistakenly that the unidentified tanks belonged to TF Brewster.[15]

As A Company, 40th TB began pulling out to head toward Manhay, SS
Panzergrenadiers knocked out four Shermans with Panzerfaust rocket
launchers. Next, German tanks obliterated C Company, first firing flares that
blinded the tankers, then knocking out five of the Company's eight tanks in
the first few seconds. Lieutenant (LT) Gerald Reeves, a platoon leader in C
Company, believed the Company got off only a few shots. Only three tanks
of the seventeen assigned to A and C Companies managed to get out un-
scathed. The remaining survivors walked out. Reeves reached friendly lines
at 0430.[16]

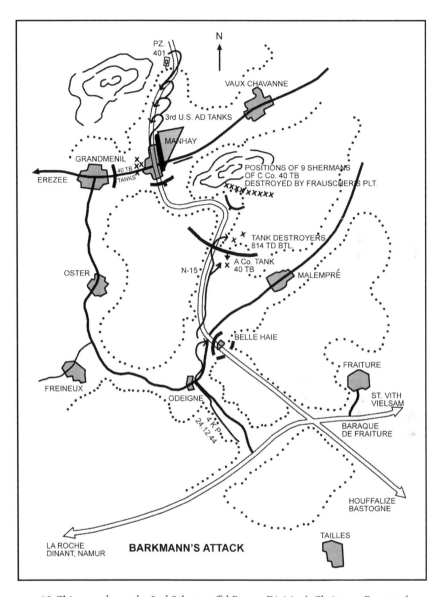

MAP 13. This map shows the 2nd Schutzstaffel Panzer Division's Christmas Eve attack toward Manhay that routed Combat Command A, 7th Armored Division. Tanker Ernst Barkman and the crew of Panther 401 got north of Manhay in their unintentional "hussar's ride." Rapid response by the 7th Armored Division prevented the 2nd SS from breaking through. Much of the supporting data shown here is from George Winter, *Manhay, the Ardennes, Christmas 1944,* and Otto Weidinger, *Das Reich,* vol. 5, both courtesy of J. J. Fedorowicz Publishing.

The withdrawal turned into a rout as intermingled Germans and Americans roared up the road to Manhay. In Manhay itself, LTC Brown, operating in his command tank, attempted to stem the tide supported by the two A Company tanks. Several SS tanks reached the crossroads at the center of town, where they destroyed three of D Company's light tanks. Brown and the two A Company tanks destroyed perhaps three German tanks before he was "blown out of his tank," knocked out and badly concussed. In the midst of this chaos CCB, 9th AD drove into town.[17]

The retreat into Manhay created problems for LTC Robert L. Rhea's 23rd AIB. Rhea withdrew north of Vaux-Chavanne, "astride the paved highway north and south above Vaux Chavinnes [sic]." According to Staff Sergeant (SSG) Richard L. McBride, "We were more than weary and morale was low after the recent setbacks . . . that night as at no other time LTC Rhea had to lead his Battalion personally, exerting his influence *directly*, to inspire the men to take courage and dig in one more time." Rhea made it clear to the troops: "There will be no chance for relief until we hold a defensive line *long enough* to be relieved." McBride believed that Rhea's personal example, as well as that of MAJ Sid Frasier and the ubiquitous Lieutenant (LT) Joseph V. "Navajo" Whiteman, made the difference that night.[18]

The crowning touch came when SS tanker Ernst Barkman, in command of Panther number 401, conducted his "hussar's ride" through Manhay. Barkman unintentionally found himself on N15 just behind an American tank, probably from A Company, 40th TB. He wanted nothing more than to return to the bosom of his platoon. He passed the dug-in tanks of C Company, 40th TB, whose turrets tracked him as he went by, but none fired, perhaps because they could not see him clearly, as trees shielded the road and Barkman was following American tanks. As he headed toward Manhay, still believing he had fallen behind his Company mates, he encountered American infantry on the road. The infantry, mistaking him for an American, made way for him with a few salty curses. When he reached Manhay he headed north to avoid three Sherman tanks. Once north of Manhay he began passing American tanks pulled over on the side of the road.[19]

Finally, some of the Americans recognized number 401 for what it was. In series of events reminiscent of the Keystone Kops, Barkman ran over a Jeep and got his track locked up with those of a Sherman tank. After breaking free, and shooting the other tank and setting it afire, he headed farther north, screened by a smoke grenade. Eventually Barkman found a sheltered clearing from which he could overlook N15 and the crossroads. There he witnessed the unsuccessful last stand of the 40th TB. Once the shooting stopped, Barkman exhibited commendable gall. He drove back through the crossroads past burning Sherman tanks and headed south as fast as number 401 would go. One wonders what Carl von Clausewitz, the famous Prussian military theorist, would have made of this.[20]

Fortuitously, the Germans were as disorganized by success as were the Americans by defeat. The Germans took the town but did little else that night, in part because of fuel shortages. What Hugh Cole has called a sauve qui peut retreat ended at a roadblock Rhea established north of Manhay on N15. Land mines laid by the 3rd AD complicated matters. CPT Walter Hughes, D Company, 40th TB ran over a "friendly" antitank mine and lost his tank and his life. At Rhea's roadblock, Hasbrouck and Rosebaum rallied CCA around CCB, 7th AD, which rushed LTC Robert C. Erlenbusch's 31st TB into the fight from the assembly area they had withdrawn to the night before. Erlenbusch established his command post near the roadblock. At about 0100 hours LTC Brown stumbled in, "completely dazed, dirty and disheveled."[21] The same could be said of his battalion, which lost eighteen tanks that night.[22]

Humiliated

MG Ridgway, who considered the conduct of the 7th AD on December 23 "exemplary," described the event at Manhay as a "fiasco." Because Manhay was critical to the Corps defense, Ridgway ordered Hasbrouck to retake the town and restore the planned main line of resistance. Hasbrouck assigned the mission to BG Bruce C. Clarke's tired troops, who had been thrown back into the line on Christmas Eve.[23] The attack got underway at 1450 but was stillborn.

Clarke launched the attack down two logging trails that led through dense woods, intending to debouch close to Manhay. However, the 3rd AD had mined one of the trails and placed an abatis across the other one. Four M4 Sherman tanks succumbed to 3rd AD mines in the first four hundred yards. The abatis stymied Clarke's second column. Only the infantry attached from the 424th reached Manhay, where the Germans drove them off. Clarke's attack failed because of poor coordination with CCB, 3rd AD, which had laid the mines, and inadequate reconnaissance. Clarke, circling the debacle in a Piper Cub, later said, "I never had a Christmas as depressing as this one."[24]

To add to the humiliation, Ridgway had CCA's defeat investigated. Although his inspector general, COL C. F. Barnett, concluded that the 3rd AD deserved the "primary blame for this debacle" due to inaccurate reporting and poor coordination, he savaged CCA. First and foremost, Barnett asserted, "There was a failure to establish local security." Failure in this basic task he found "difficult to understand" given the high probability of attack made known to the command. Furthermore, he contended in his report that CCA had "numerical and fire superiority over the enemy." COL Barnett harangued at length but also observed, "Troops were nearing exhaustion" and "were seriously depleted." He found no evidence of cowardice, though it was plain he looked for some. His recommendations were straightforward. Chief among these was that he wanted CCA and its constituents "officially castigated for their lack of aggressive spirit" but held out hope they might "redeem themselves in future operations."[25]

Over the next few days, a tired and chagrined 7th AD prevented the Germans from breaking out but achieved little else. The Lucky Seventh held on for three reasons. First, the Allied air forces had good flying weather and freely attacked the Germans. Second, the division artillery stopped strong German attacks on December 25–26 with effective time-on-target missions. Massed fire consumed 6,319 rounds on December 26 and "literally picked to pieces" the towns of Manhay and Vaux-Chavanne. Finally, the German attacks north of Manhay were not pushed very hard, as the German effort shifted west.[26]

Ridgway wanted Manhay back but realized that the 7th AD, even with the 112th INF and 424th INF attached, was too weak to retake it. On December 26 the Corps attached the 3rd Battalion, 517th PIR to the 7th AD with orders for the Battalion to take Manhay that night. The 3rd Battalion, led by LTC Forest Paxton, motored to an assembly area near Manhay. At Hasbrouck's command post, LTC Paxton, his regimental commander LTC Rupert Graves, Hasbrouck, and Hasbrouck's staff planned the operation to retake Manhay. The attack went in after "a very heavy artillery preparation of 20 minutes duration." The paratroopers, supported by 7th AD tanks, cleared the village and crossroads of Germans by 0345.[27]

Reorganization and Reconstitution

The newly arrived 75th ID relieved the Lucky Seventh on the night of December 29, concluding the relief by 0410. SSG McBride's platoon had bottomed out that last week of December. With only eighteen soldiers, the platoon had fewer than half its authorized complement. Two of these were tankers learning on the job how to be infantry. McBride and what remained of A Company, 23rd AIB were pleased to see the new troops arrive. They passed on what information they could and walked out following "the tall lanky, unmilitary-looking Navaho [*sic*]." On their way to where their half-tracks awaited, A Company encountered a "snappy little Major" in a "clean new jeep." The major stopped and exchanged salutes with 'Navaho' [*sic*] who announced, "Sir, the situation is strictly *non-tactical* today."[28]

The Company troops boarded their half-tracks and headed north. As McBride later recalled, "Past one artillery battery after another, we rolled along good paved roads through the Ardennes hills and occasional small villages, until we descended once again into the Ourthe River Valley and arrived back at Hamoir," where they had been briefly on December 23. By 1230 on December 30, the 7th AD was out of the line for the first time in weeks. As Hasbrouck's December after action report concluded with pride, "December 1944 was an epoch-making month for the 7th Armored Division. The Division's stand at ST VITH brought commendations from General EISENHOWER and Field Marshal SIR BERNARD L. MONTGOMERY."[29]

The 7th AD desperately needed time to refit, receive new equipment, repair what it could, and receive and integrate individual replacements. Two weeks of hard fighting outnumbered had taken an incredible toll. The Division lost seventy-three Sherman tanks (almost half of its authorization), five Sherman assault guns, thirty-two Stuart light tanks, thirteen tank destroyers, and other combat and support vehicles amounting to 406 pieces of equipment. The human toll had been just as bad. The Division suffered 1,165 killed, wounded, and missing—more than 10 percent of its authorized strength. Given the confusion of administrative reporting lines, it is possible this number is understated. Nondivisional units such as the 814th TD were sometimes omitted in accounting for losses.[30]

With respect to strength, the Division and various attachments reached their nadir on Christmas Day. That day the personnel officer accounted for 7th AD units, the 814th TD, the 203rd Anti-Aircraft Artillery, an VIII Corps artillery battalion that had withdrawn with them, and the 14th Cavalry Group (CAV). He reported that of 8,921 assigned, 478 were killed, wounded, or missing on Christmas Eve. The 40th TB had 240 missing, and the 48th AIB some 178. Some of these soldiers eventually made their way back, but no one could know that on Christmas Day. The accounting for the 14th CAV could not be made until the following day; on December 26 the Cavalry reported 1,014 soldiers assigned versus an authorized strength of 1,567.[31]

Obviously, casualties did not occur evenly. In the 7th AD the infantry and cavalry suffered disproportionately. Three troops of the 87th CAV virtually ceased to exist. B Troop, the first 7th AD unit to go in the line at St. Vith, was in the worst shape. First Sergeant (1st SGT) Leonard Hoyle Ladd, senior surviving man in the troop, crossed the Salm River with thirty-five soldiers of the 135 authorized. On Christmas Eve the 87th CAV combined the remnants of the 14th CAV to produce from three squadrons (the 18th, 32nd, and 87th) one at full strength. The armored infantry battalions had already reorganized using dismounted tankers to fill out their ranks. The 23rd AIB had 285 killed, wounded, or missing. An armored infantry rifle company had an authorized aggregate strength of 251. Of these, 163 were trigger pullers. The remainder drove vehicles, maintained equipment, fed the company, supplied the company, or provided administrative support. The 23rd AIB had a major rebuilding job to do, exacerbated by the fact that infantrymen replaced any driver killed, wounded, or missing.[32]

The problem of rebuilding a unit or, what postwar Army doctrine calls reconstitution, is different from reorganizing or combining understrength units to form one fully capable unit. Reconstitution rebuilds a unit. The 7th AD units reorganized on the fly to meet tactical requirements, but it would be a mistake to assume that a reorganized unit was as capable as the original. Reconstitution of a unit presumes some time out of the line, as well as support to accept new equipment, incorporate replacements, and train. During a mandated stand-down to reconstitute, a division can plan tasks sequentially and allot time efficiently. During the Battle of the Bulge that luxury was not possible. There were simply too few divisions. MG Ridgway could not afford to assure Hasbrouck a long stand-down, and Hasbrouck understood. In a matter of days the worn-out battalions of the 7th AD had to be ready to conduct decentralized combined arms operations in compartmented terrain against defensive positions protected by obstacles and mines.

The original concept of sustaining units in combat assumed two hundred divisions. That concept afforded time to rotate units out of combat to enable them to refit and retrain. By 1943 the number of planned divisions had declined to 141, then 114, down ultimately to ninety. The manpower crunch resulted in eighty-nine Army divisions and six Marine divisions. In the European theater that reality assured there were few opportunities to rotate units out of the line.[33]

On January 1, 1945, Hasbrouck would issue his guidance for retraining the Division to join the rest of XVIII Airborne Corps when it took the offensive.

Hasbrouck's guidance reflected his estimate of the forthcoming mission and what he had learned in two weeks of fighting in the Ardennes. Hasbrouck "ordered training in the use of small teams of infantry, tanks, and engineers. Where mass employment of tanks would be impossible [almost anywhere in the Ardennes], these small teams could operate over roads or trails to gain the rear of enemy forces to make surprise seizures of important road centers or defiles."[34] Hasbrouck further stipulated that "the tank component of these teams was to be small, rarely, if ever, over a platoon. The infantry component was to be comparatively large to provide reconnaissance and security for the tanks, while the engineers were for mine detection, removal of roadblocks, and pioneer work."[35]

Field Manual (FM) 100-10, *Field Service Regulations Administration*, addressed the basics of replacing men and materiel. The corps might serve as an advocate but the field army and the communications zone led the effort. After the 7th AD crossed the Salm and had good communications, First Army set out to rebuild it. On December 17, First Army began to identify replacement requirements and queried the Division on how many full crews it could provide to man replacement tanks. On December 29, 204 enlisted soldier replacements arrived and twenty-nine soldiers returned to duty. That same day, First Army agreed to find three infantry majors and two armored force majors. The following day 140 tank crew replacements arrived. The XVIII Airborne Corps reported seventeen officers and 283 enlisted soldiers en route. On New Year's Eve, a doctor and 268 soldiers arrived. First Army advised it was sending two majors to interview for assignment. The system worked much as FM 100-10 claimed it would.[36]

Better still, it worked quickly. By New Year's Day 1945, First Army had passed on 992 replacements, bringing the Division up to 9,915 assigned. By January 8 the Division had reached 10,097. In another week the 7th AD reached 10,568, and its regularly attached units had prospered as well. Training the arrivals proceeded apace, as did small unit training. In A Company, 23rd AIB the formidable Navajo Whiteman "introduced himself to the new men of A Co. at a formal meeting, giving them an idea of what was expected of them, and also passing on to them the history of our Division in which we took so much pride."[37]

Hasbrouck specified training goals but let his subordinates determine how to achieve them while he continued to plan the deployment of the Division in the days to come. As he put it, each unit commander "did it in his own way. I couldn't prescribe any particular way to assimilate equipment and train troops. . . . But when we went back on the line again we were in pretty good shape." Yet Hasbrouck did believe it necessary to initiate replacements, many of whom arrived right from the Army Specialized Training Program, which set aside bright young men to go to college instead of war. One cavalry troop commander described these soldiers as "bright but scared kids—upset at being rocketed from the Ivy League to the Battlefield."[38] To initiate replacements Hasbrouck established "little reception centers" where new arrivals were indoctrinated on why they were needed and what was expected of them. From there they joined their units.

James E. Thompson joined the 38th AIB on January 11, 1945. By then the Division had moved to assembly areas near Verviers. Thompson had been inducted on June 15, 1944, and trained at Camp Wheeler near Macon, Georgia. In October, at the end of training, he was hospitalized for an infection. He returned to duty in November and completed his basic training. After a short furlough, he began the trip to the front in December 1944. On Christmas Eve, Thompson boarded a Dutch vessel named *Volendam* and was packed with 239 other soldiers, sardine-like, in the hold of what he described as "an ancient Dutch freighter." The *Volendam* sailed on December 26. One of the few who had not been seasick, Thompson had survived sixteen days of bad food and the nauseating smell of infrequently emptied fifty-five-gallon drums used by those who had been. The venerable *Volendam* landed in Le Havre on January 8.[39]

On arriving in the Division, Thompson lived with a Belgian family who took quite good care of him. He recalled with fondness the waffles and fried potatoes. He liked his new outfit, and especially the food, including "chops, steak, stew, apples, pineapple pie, chocolate cake and other good things." On January 19 he experienced his first day in combat. Like his colleagues, he faced freezing temperatures, bland food (some of which arrived frozen), and fear. Within days he was a veteran who had learned he could urinate on his frozen .30-caliber machine gun in order to fire it, and he had frostbite.[40]

The same day that Thompson joined the Division the debacle at Manhay claimed one more victim. On January 11, Hasbrouck relieved Dwight A. Rosebaum of the command of CCA, "more for his failure to make any effort to get his troops assembled than anything else. He simply sank into a morose state and did nothing." COL William S. Triplet, who took over from Rosebaum, believed that Rosebaum had no inkling of his relief and on hearing that Triplet was to take command called Hasbrouck and "had a heated conversation." There is no evidence to doubt Triplet's account, but it is inconsistent with the way Robert W. Hasbrouck comported himself. The tension over the Fortified Goose Egg defense, coupled with that over the defeat at Manhay, remained between Ridgway and the 7th AD, particularly with Hasbrouck and Clarke, both of whom remained ill disposed toward Ridgway the remainder of their lives. Triplet, who had not witnessed the contretemps over the Goose Egg, did not share their view of Ridgway, of whom Triplet wrote, "I rate him number one." However he felt, Triplet took over rebuilding CCA and proved himself both acerbic and effective.[41]

Receiving new equipment proved less difficult than receiving and assimilating replacements. First Army proved ambitious in reequipping the 7th AD. On the 27th of December, First Army advised the 7th AD that January 3, 1945, was the target date to have the Division reequipped. On December 28, 1944, the 7th AD received twenty-three tanks, some of which required extensive repair. The next day, First Army ordnance promised the Division would be rebuilt to 168 Sherman tanks, or just over 100 percent authorization. As it turned out, forty-one of these rebuilt Shermans, originally built for the British, came with diesel engines, and this created fuel compatibility and maintenance issues. But these problems could be resolved internally, as there were some diesel engine mechanics already assigned and diesel fuel was available.[42]

All of the tanks in the 7th AD, both old and new, came with olive drab paint. With more than a foot of snow on the ground, "OD Green" was not the best color. First Army provided whitewash, and tanks and anything else likely to be in close contact with the enemy got a coat. The Sherman tanks also needed some modification so that they could move better on snow and ice. The Shermans, whether shod with rubber track pads or steel track, behaved like "40 ton toboggans" on icy, snow-covered roads and ground. LTC Reginald H. Hodgson, the division logistics officer, and LTC George E. Hughes, the division ordnance officer, "devised a cleat to be installed on the 'duck feet' track extensions." This solution was applied to all variants of the Sherman chassis, including the self-propelled howitzers.[43]

Not surprisingly, there were not enough welding sets to weld cleats on nearly three hundred tanks, howitzers, and tank destroyers. Undaunted, some enterprising soldier devised a way to wire two tank auxiliary generators ("Little Joes") together to produce an effective if bizarre and dangerous electric welder. The Stuart light tanks could not take the cleats, but ingenuity triumphed again. LTC Erlenbusch recalled that the 31st TB discovered that when the Stuarts ran over barbed wire fence or a barbed wire entanglement, "the wire wove itself around the track and track connectors and provided a reasonable amount of . . . traction. You could get about 20 miles with this arrangement and then you had to find another fence to run over."[44]

In addition to reequipping, the Division needed to resupply and refit. In the last two weeks of December, the 7th AD consumed supplies voraciously. The division artillery fired more than fifty-three thousand rounds. Tanks and tank destroyers pumped out thirteen thousand rounds of seventy-five- and seventy-six-millimeter ammunition. The troops burned through 596,074 .30-caliber rounds and nearly three thousand grenades. Engineers, tankers, and infantrymen laid nearly four thousand mines. Besides issuing supplies to replace those used or lost in combat, the service units needed to rebuild authorized stocks of ammunition, fuel, and rations. The 7th AD's logistics troops found 1,500 mattress covers, 125 snow capes, and 1,500 two-piece camouflage suits to provide to the infantry and cavalry.[45]

Coming out of the line for a few days enabled the troops to thaw out and sleep with both eyes shut. Even better, the troops got trips to shower points, though such occurrences were sufficiently rare to warrant comment in after action reports. Most of the troops lived in Belgian homes. In many cases, quartering with a Belgian family had a rejuvenating effect. SSG Mc-Bride's platoon found solace and good company in the home of Georges and Madame Jadot, where troops slept on the floor for several days before having to move. They enjoyed the Jadots so much, however, that they often returned. Madame Jadot always provided "a heaping bowl of fried potatoes and a pot of hot coffee for us. . . . In turn, we brought extra rations from the mess truck."[46]

The Division did what it could for its soldiers. On January 3 the finance officer paid the troops—always a morale booster. The division personnel officer established post exchange facilities and brought in American Red Cross club mobiles. These vehicles were staffed by female volunteers and had on-board kitchens that dispensed doughnuts, coffee, and other treats. The first club mobiles made it to the 7th AD on January 6. Young American women handing out doughnuts and coffee to lonely young men also improved morale. Ten truckloads of mail arrived on January 7. The division special services officer acquired back issues of the *Stars and Stripes* newspaper, so the troops could catch up on the news. On January 17 the Division issued quotas for three-day passes to Paris. Hasbrouck considered all of this vital to restoring the morale. He visited his units to instill enthusiasm for the inevitable return to combat.[47]

Hasbrouck's subordinates shared his views on morale. On January 9, BG Bruce C. Clarke visited the 434th Armored Field Artillery Battalion (AFA). At an evening officers' call he commended the Battalion for its work in December. He then "started on the projected operation and exactly what he wanted done to insure success." According to the Battalion's after action report, "The General clearly stated that aggressiveness and offensive action must be instituted in the minds of all. Our object is not gaining of ground but the extermination of the German Army, which must and will be destroyed."

LTC James G. Dubuisson anticipated Clarke's ideas. At a battery commanders' call on January 5, Dubuisson told his commander to "pass on to the troops the spirit of the offensive."[48] Hasbrouck and his officers understood that moral preparation of the Division was as important as reequipping and retraining.

Retraining began soon after coming off the line. Although Hasbrouck issued guidance, he did not specify the means. Battalions trained according to their needs and on the preliminary plan of operation issued on January 12 (based on XVIII Airborne Corps' order, published the day before) that aimed ultimately to retake St. Vith. The artillery battalions tended to concentrate on individual skills they hoped they would not need. They were concerned about infiltrating infantry or armor. The 440th AFA, for example, trained all hands on the bazooka and clearing mines. The infantry focused on small unit training with "emphasis on aggressiveness and control." The 23rd AIB practiced reduction of obstacles and roadblocks. The 48th AIB tried its hand at demolitions. The 48th after action review claimed that "the spirit and enthusiasm was good and good training resulted."[49]

In addition to individual training, the tank battalions had to process, test fire, and zero replacement tanks. This was no mean feat given that the tank battalions had lost nearly half of their tanks. The 40th TB—the worst hit—drew, processed, and fired thirty-five tanks in ten days. According to BG Clarke, most tank engagements in western Europe occurred at about four hundred yards. Speed in acquiring and engaging targets became an obsession in the tank battalions. The Ardennes, as the veterans knew, posed a special challenge. Thick woods and rolling hills precluded massing tanks and made target acquisition difficult. As a consequence, the 31st TB drilled its crews in "hitting of unexpected targets by a single tank."[50]

The combat commands managed unit training. The small task forces envisioned by Hasbrouck rolled through field exercises designed to train them to operate effectively as combined arms teams. Conceptually the idea was to "infiltrate this fairly powerful striking force through lightly defended areas, over secondary roads to strike the enemy from the rear."[51] Repetition and criticism played vital roles in improving performance. Clarke considered critiques essential and conducted many of them himself. CCA experimented with movement techniques designed to minimize detection of attacking units, and found that thanks to deep snow muffling the sound of their approach, "tanks could get within two hundred yards of infantry before the ground troops heard them."[52]

Leader training and retraining of individual soldiers occurred at several levels. The division artillery operated a forward observer school for officers and noncommissioned officers, including tank commanders and infantry squad leaders. Maneuver battalions also worked on training junior leaders. LTC John P. Wemple of the 17th TB developed platoon exercises to train his five new platoon leaders. He also conducted a battalion officers' school where "current problems and past battle experiences were discussed . . . as well as plans for movement." Wemple kept his battalion staff active developing plans that kept pace with the changing tactical picture as the rest of XVIII Airborne Corps returned to the offensive. He believed that "detailed planning is one effective way of keeping all elements of the Task Force oriented at all times."[53]

LT William A. Knowlton rebuilt B Troop, 87th CAV. B Troop's story is indicative of what it took for the 7th AD to recover its verve. When 1st SGT Ladd brought out the survivors of the fighting on the Prümerberg he could not bring out the troop's equipment. B Troop was the hardest hit company-size unit in the 7th AD. The troop's service and administrative section survived as a base, but very few of the "trigger pullers" made it out. Knowlton missed the fighting as he was recovering from a head-on collision of his Jeep with a 2.5-ton truck. He and his injured driver went absent without leave from the hospital and made their way back to their unit via Holland and a firefight in Belgium.

On New Year's Eve 1944, LTC Vincent L. Boylan gave command of B Troop to Knowlton. Knowlton began with identifying platoon sergeants. He got one from A Troop, and he appointed two B Troop men just back from the hospital to the other platoons. The junior man, Corporal Harry Gill, had just made it back after recovering from wounds suffered in France nearly two months earlier. Because B Troop had suffered most, it was the last priority. It made more sense to fill units on the basis of which of them could get back into action most quickly. Until January 12 Knowlton had only the survivors, the service and administrative troopers, and hospital returnees. On that day B Troop received its first tranche of replacements, all of whom had trained as cavalrymen. On January 18, three officers arrived. One had experience. The other two were brand new. Cooks and antiaircraft artillerymen rounded out B Troop.[54]

Knowlton's first priority was to make a "conscious effort to make them [replacements] feel at home; so they would not say 'Oh my god, everyone in this outfit is dead.'" By January 19 Knowlton could begin small unit training, although B Troop did not receive all of its equipment until near the end of the month. B Troop went back to war with just four days of training, and most of that dismounted. As Knowlton put it, the whole thing "sounds pretty helter-skelter, and it was—but it worked."[55]

The rebuilt 7th AD returned to battle on January 20, 1945, attacking across ground it knew in hip-deep snow. Now was the Division's chance for redemption. It had clearly been imperative to withdraw across the Salm in December, but it had still stung.

NOTES

1. Veterans of the Battle of the Bulge, Inc., *The Battle of the Bulge: True Stories of the Men and Women Who Survived*, 305.

2. Col. Gustin M. Nelson to his father, May 1945, box 3, Charles B. MacDonald Papers; Charles Haug, "Courageous Defenders," 35.

3. Hugh M. Cole, *The Ardennes: Battle of the Bulge*, 422. Casualty numbers are drawn from Headquarters, 7th Armored Division, "Battle of St Vith: 17–23 December 1944," 83. Tank destroyer losses are from 814th Tank Destroyer Battalion, "After Action Report December 1944."

4. Major William C. Sylvan and Captain Francis G. Smith Jr., *Normandy to Victory*, 232–33.

5. Nigel Hamilton, *Monty: The Battles of Field Marshall Bernard Montgomery*, 520. See also David W. Hogan Jr., *A Command Post at War*, 223–25.

6. General J. Lawton Collins, *Lightning Joe: An Autobiography*, 289–90.

7. James M. Gavin, *On to Berlin*, 238. The combat interviews of the 40th TB and the 48th AIB edited by W. Wesley Johnston are the best source for CCA 7th AD movements.

8. Otto Weidinger, *Das Reich*, vol. 5, *1943–1945*, 273; Charles B. MacDonald, *A Time for Trumpets*, 547.

9. General der Panzertruppe Hasso von Manteuffel, "An Interview with Gen Pz Hasso von Manteuffel," ETHINT-46, 7. See also Major Percy Ernst Schramm, "The Course of Events of the German Offensive in the Ardennes." Employing the

Oberkommando der Wehrmacht reserves made little practical difference given the lack of fuel.

10. General der Panzertruppe Hasso von Manteuffel, "An Interview with Gen Pz Hasso von Manteuffel," ETHINT-45, 13.

11. 17th Tank Battalion, "After Action Report, Month of December 1944," 15–16; 40th Tank Battalion, "After Action Report, Month of December 1944," 2, 10; Combat Command A, 7th Armored Division, "After Action Report, December 1944," 2; Robert L. Rhea to Robert W. Hasbrouck, 25 March 1946, Major General Robert W. Hasbrouck Collection. On the 517th PIR, see W. Wesley Johnston, *Manhay and Grandmenil Belgium*, 24.

12. One platoon of D Company, 40th TB moved south at 1405 hours to attempt linking up with the 2nd Battalion, 325th Glider Infantry Regiment at Baraque de Fraiture, just east of Parker's Crossroads; Johnston, *Manhay and Grandmenil Belgium*, 23. See also John Toland, *Battle: The Story of the Bulge*, 221, 229–30; and Cole, *The Ardennes: Battle of the Bulge*, 585–86. The 2nd AD and 3rd AD were the only two armored divisions organized with two tank regiments and an armored infantry regiment.

13. Cole, *The Ardennes: Battle of the Bulge*, 587.

14. Cole, *The Ardennes: Battle of the Bulge*, 588.

15. Both MacDonald, *A Time for Trumpets*, 550, and Cole, *The Ardennes: Battle of the Bulge*, 589, agree that a Sherman led the German column. Curiously, none of the 40th TB survivors made that claim explicitly.

16. W. Wesley Johnston, *Combat Interviews of the 40th Tank Battalion*.

17. 40th Tank Battalion, "After Action Report, Month of December 1944," 14.

18. Richard L. McBride, "Grinding Through with the 7th Armored Division," 145, emphasis in the original. See also 23rd Armored Infantry Battalion, "After Action Report, Month of December 1944," 4.

19. There are a number of sources for Barkman's ride; they include George J. Winter, *Manhay The Ardennes Christmas 1944*, 17–21; MacDonald, *A Time for Trumpets*, 550–53; and Weidinger, *Das Reich*, 5:278–82.

20. Winter, *Manhay*, 17–21; MacDonald, *A Time for Trumpets*, 550–53; Weidinger, *Das Reich*, 5:278–82. Ernst Barkman assisted George Winter with *Manhay*. Barkman returned to the area in the mid-1980s, and took a photograph of a monument to the 7th AD. On the back of it he wrote, "My special foe in the Ardennes, for whom I have great respect." See Winter, *Manhay*, 23.

21. LTC Robert C. Erlenbusch, interviewer not identified [probably John Toland], n.p., n.d., John Toland Papers.

22. Johnston, *Manhay and Grandmenil Belgium*, 27. The postcombat interview reports that seventeen tanks were lost—fifteen belonging to the 40th TB, plus two forward observer tanks, two tank destroyers, three half-tracks, and two Jeeps. The count includes three light tanks. CPT Walter Hughes, who commanded the light tank company, died that night when his M5 light tank ran over a land mine. Thus the 40th TB lost eighteen tanks that night.

23. Matthew B. Ridgway to James M. Gavin, October 6, 1978, Matthew B. Ridgway Papers. See also Major General Matthew B. Ridgway to General William B. Kean, December 25, 1944, Matthew B. Ridgway Papers.

24. Brigadier General Bruce C. Clarke, interviewer not identified [probably John Toland], n.p., n.d., John Toland Papers.

25. Headquarters XVIII Corps (Airborne), Office of the Inspector General, "Report of Investigation, CCA 7 AD, Manhay, 24–25 December 1944," 2–5.

26. Division Artillery, 7th Armored Division, "After Action Report, Month of December 1944," 21–23. See also Cole, *The Ardennes: Battle of the Bulge*, 599. Starting December 27, the 2nd SS focused west.

27. XVIII Corps (Airborne), G-3 operations journal, 260001 to 262400, entry at 261550; Division Artillery, 7th Armored Division, "After Action Report, Month of December 1944," 23; Gerald Astor, *Battling Buzzards*, 243–48. Astor claims the 460th Parachute Field Artillery Battalion supported the operation, but that may be an error, as the XVIII Airborne Corps journal and 7th AD Division Artillery after action report say otherwise. I am no stranger to error of this kind. In a master's thesis completed in 1985, I identified LTC Richard J. Seitz as the 3rd Battalion commander whereas he commanded the 2nd Battalion. What is devastating about this mistake is that I knew Dick Seitz well. He reached the rank of lieutenant general, and when he retired he returned to his hometown of Junction City, Kansas. He became a mentor to many of us who served in the 1st Infantry Division at nearby Fort Riley.

28. McBride, "Grinding Through," 158, emphasis in the original.

29. McBride, "Grinding Through," 159; 7th Armored Division, "After Action Report, Period 1–31 December 1944," 93.

30. 7th Armored Division, "After Action Report, Period 1–31 December 1944," 95. Casualty reporting can be found in 7th Armored Division, G-1 journal, December 1944. This is not the daily log of messages, but rather the daily strength report. The online 7th Armored Division Documents Repository (https://www.7tharmddiv.org /docrep/) is the easiest way to access these reports.

31. 7th Armored Division, G-1 journal, December 1944, 141–42.

32. 87th Cavalry Reconnaissance Squadron, "After Action Report, Month of December 1944," 11–12; 23rd Armored Infantry Battalion, "After Action Report, Month of December 1944," 20–22, which gives casualties for the month of December. The author found two different lists of casualties. The one cited here listed 268. The author found the same after action report at the Dwight D. Eisenhower Presidential Library and Museum, but that report has a list of casualties appended rather than a separate casualty report. That list has one more missing and seventeen more wounded. Either way, the 23rd AIB had a great many killed, wounded, or missing. On aggregate authorized strength, see US War Department, *Cavalry Reconnaissance Squadron, Mechanized*, Table of Organization 2-25; and US War Department, *Rifle Company, Armored Infantry Battalion*, Table of Organization 7-27. On Ladd and B Troop, see William Donohue Ellis and Colonel Thomas J. Cunningham Jr., *Clarke of St. Vith*, 121.

33. Kent Roberts Greenfield, Robert R. Palmer, and Bell I. Wiley, *The Organization of Ground Combat Troops*, 212–27.

34. 7th Armored Division, "After Action Report, Period 1–31 January 1944," 22.

35. 7th Armored Division, "After Action Report, Period 1–31 January 1944," 22.

36. G-1 daily reports, 143–49. For personnel replacements, see US War Department, *Field Service Regulations: Administration*, FM 100-10, chap. 8.

37. 7th Armored Division, G-1 journal, January 1945, 151, 159, 169; McBride, "Grinding Through," 167.

38. General William A. Knowlton, (Ret.) to the author, November 15, 1984; Major General Robert W. Hasbrouck (Ret.), interview with the author, Washington, DC, August 20, 1984.

39. James. E. Thompson, "A Journal of Papa T's Army Days in World War II Europe," 3–5.

40. Thompson, "A Journal of Papa T's Army Days in World War II Europe," 7–11.

41. Clay Blair, *Ridgway's Paratroopers*, 397. See also William S. Triplet, *A Colonel in the Armored Divisions*, 164–65.

42. 7th Armored Division, G-4 journal, December 1944, 36–43.

43. The army issued track extensions that could be hammered on to the track links to provide wider ground contact. The 7th AD homemade cleats enabled better traction on ice and in soft ground but wore down quickly. 7th Armored Division, "After Action Report, Period 1–31 January 1944," 23–24.

44. Robert C. Erlenbusch to the author, August 20–24, 1984.

45. 7th Armored Division, "After Action Report, Period 1–31 December 1944," 96. See also 7th Armored Division, "After Action Report, Period 1–31 January 1945," 25. Army-produced snow camouflage arrived on January 20, just in time.

46. McBride, "Grinding Through," 164.

47. 7th Armored Division, G-1 journal, January 1945, 153–77. By mid-January the strength returns show the Division nearly at full strength.

48. 434th Armored Field Artillery Battalion, "After Action Report, Month of January 1945," 2, 4.

49. 440th Armored Field Artillery Battalion, "After Action Report, Month of January 1945," 1; 48th Armored Infantry Battalion, "After Action Report, Month of January 1945," 8; 23rd Armored Infantry Battalion, "After Action Report, Month of January 1945," 1.

50. General Bruce C. Clarke (Ret.) to the author, April 1, 1984, General Bruce C. Clarke Papers; 40th Tank Battalion, After Action Report, January 1945, 1; 31st Tank Battalion, "After Action Report, January 1945," 1.

51. 31st Tank Battalion, "After Action Report, January 1945," 1.

52. Clarke to the author, April 1, 1984; 40th Tank Battalion, "After Action Report, Month of January 1945," 1; 31st Tank Battalion, "After Action Report, January 1945," 1.

53. 17th Tank Battalion, "After Action Report, Month of January 1945," 1–2, 5.

54. General William A. Knowlton (Ret.) to the author, November 15, 1984, with attachment entitled "Statement of General William Allen Knowlton." The statement was one he provided in response to a request from a military museum in Bastogne, Belgium.

55. Knowlton to the author, November 15, 1984, 3.

CHAPTER TWELVE

Redemption at St. Vith

It had been a beautiful town prior to the German attack. War is a poor method, costly in lives and property, of solving or resolving political problems.

— Lieutenant Colonel Roy U. Clay

I found the esprit of the Seventh to be high. This was surprising since they had been forced to retreat from St. Vith and then were defeated at Manhai [*sic*]. They were proud of the fact that it had taken six German divisions to whip them.

— Colonel William S. Triplet

NEITHER XVIII AIRBORNE Corps nor First Army could afford to leave the 7th Armored Division (AD) idle. The 7th AD refitted while in reserve to the Corps. During refitting, the Division prepared continuously for how it might be committed when the Corps returned to the offensive. As the Corps reserve, the 7th AD repositioned as required in order to remain responsive. For example, on the afternoon of January 6, 1945, XVIII Airborne Corps alerted the Division for possible commitment in the 82nd Airborne Division's zone. The 7th AD reconnoitered routes, but the Corps did not commit them. The division artillery continued to support the forward units. It fired missions on January 3–4 but still found time to carry out "extensive maintenance and . . . required training."[1] On January 11, 1945, the Lucky Seventh moved to assembly areas near Verviers and Spa, Belgium, in preparation for attacking on January 13.[2]

Allied Assessments and Orders

While the 7th AD restored itself and trained as it could, XVIII Airborne Corps went back on the offensive. On January 3, 1945, First and Third Armies launched converging attacks from north and south, aimed to cut through the Bulge and link up at Houffalize. The attacks reflected a compromise between competing strategic views. The American commanders wanted to attack at the base of the German penetration to cut off German mobile forces, while British field marshal Bernard Law Montgomery preferred a deliberate, methodical advance that would "see off" the Germans. Montgomery believed that anything else amounted to wasting troops in the Bulge when the real prize lay to the northeast across the Rhine River in the Ruhr River industrial zone. The offensive that resulted was closer to Montgomery's view than that of the Americans.

At the same time this debate over strategy occurred, there was a climax to a command crisis that had been festering within the Grand Alliance since General Dwight D. Eisenhower had assumed direct command of all Allied ground forces in September 1944. Montgomery had precipitated continued irritation over his insistence that Eisenhower name a single ground commander—one named Montgomery, to be precise. Eisenhower eventually became frustrated, and in a series of meetings in September brought Montgomery to heel. But in late December Montgomery again raised the issue. Eisenhower had had enough. Not only did the Supreme Allied Commander believe he had already put the matter to bed, but he did not appreciate Montgomery's personal criticism, and this at a time when US commanders were sensitive about being caught by surprise. General Eisenhower made it clear that if Montgomery persisted, he would force the combined chiefs to choose between them.[3]

The situation eventually required Prime Minister Winston Churchill's personal intervention with the British press in January 1945 to smooth over the resulting friction within the Alliance. Although Montgomery and Churchill did their best to make amends, the incident generated national bitterness that, in some quarters, never dissipated. Still, as commander over the northern half of the Bulge, Montgomery's view largely prevailed in the design of a counteroffensive operation that concluded the battle in a manner less aggressive and decisive than that envisioned by senior American commanders on the other side of the Bulge. The First Army counterattack plan reflected Montgomery's caution. It envisaged no dashing thrusts, but instead established phase lines. Major General (MG) James M. Gavin compared the plan of attack to "a huge stable door . . . being closed."[4]

Gavin's metaphor seems especially appropriate in retrospect since the horse, however swaybacked and tired, did bolt the stable before the door was closed. First Army advanced southeast with MG Clarence R. Heubner's V Corps on the left, MG Matthew B. Ridgway's XVIII Airborne Corps in the center, and MG J. Lawton Collins's VII Corps on the right. The 7th AD remained in XVIII Corps reserve. Besides the 7th, Ridgway's Corps included the 30th Infantry Division (ID), the 75th ID, the 82nd Airborne, and what remained of the 106th ID. South of the German Bulge, Third Army attacked northeast with three corps as well. From left to right these included MG Troy H. Middleton's VIII Corps, MG John Millikin's III Corps, and MG Manton S. Eddy's XII Corps. As a consequence of not attacking at the base of the salient, the German mobile forces were never in great danger of being cut off. But with twenty-nine American divisions attacking, the outcome was never in doubt.[5]

German Assessments and Orders

In a postwar report made for his captors, Generalmajor Carl Wagener, chief of staff of the Fifth Panzer Army, wrote that as of Christmas Day 1944 "it was evident that the Ardennes offensive had failed."[6] Generalfeldmarschall Walther Model's Army Group B order of battle still looked formidable and its spearheads remained close to the Meuse River, but the Germans reached their high-water mark on Christmas Eve. The 2nd AD's attack on the 2nd Panzer Division (PZ) marked the turn of the tide. For the Germans, things grew worse from then on. By the end of December the 116th PZ had only twelve operable tanks and five assault guns. Some replacements arrived, including assault guns, but too little and too late to change things. As Siegfried von Waldenburg, who commanded the 116th PZ, wrote on his calendar on New Year's Eve, "The last attack gave us a lift. Even if the major objectives have not been reached, we keep on hoping. We have to persevere or we will be ruined!"[7]

On Christmas Day Generalfeldmarschall Alfred Jodl told Adolf Hitler point blank, "We must face the facts squarely and openly, we cannot force the Meuse River." Nevertheless, Hitler claimed, "All is not lost," and he now insisted that Bastogne be taken. Afterward, he believed, Model could reorganize and then cross the Meuse and seize Antwerp. Later, on New Year's Eve, Hitler announced Nordwind, a comparatively small counteroffensive against the American 6th Army Group that was thinned out to assume part of Third Army's frontage in response to the December offensive. Nordwind, Hitler believed, would draw off US forces from the Ardennes, enabling Model to resume the effort to cross the Meuse and seize Antwerp.[8]

Nordwind began on New Year's Day when three German corps attacked in the Vosges Mountains toward Saarburg, Germany. This second German offensive aimed at Lieutenant General Alexander Patch's Seventh US Army defending 126 miles of front. Patch had only six American divisions to defend a salient bulging eastward into the German lines. Not surprisingly, the German attack enjoyed initial success, but after a gain of some ten miles, it was stopped by Patch's troops. In the end, Nordwind did not change the outcome in the Ardennes.[9]

After driving the 7th AD from St. Vith, LXVI Corps cleared the ground to the Salm River and then turned northward. The 18th Volksgrenadier Division (VGD) and the 62nd VGD did find some time to rest and warm up, having wrested St. Vith and other nearby villages from the Americans. Warm or not, the buildings in St. Vith attracted Allied bombers. On Christmas Day medium bombers from the Ninth Air Force dropped 137 tons of bombs. The next day, British Lancaster bombers savaged St. Vith, leaving very few undamaged buildings. From then on, when the weather permitted, the Allies bombed likely targets, including many small towns and villages.[10]

The LXVI Corps closed up north with the 18th VGD on the right and the 62nd VGD on the left. On Christmas Day, the 18th received orders to relieve the 1st PZ in the area of Baugnez and Trois-Ponts, a frontage of about seven miles. On December 27 the 18th VGD began displacing and took over the sector the next day, with its left boundary on the Salm River. The frontage exceeded what the 18th could defend effectively, but it made do. In the early days of the defense, the 18th VGD suffered little except from Allied air and artillery bombardments, with the result that "daylight movement of troops and vehicles" became ill advised. The 18th prepared as well as it could in accordance with German doctrine by building "in depth of the main defense area a series of strong points." Oberstleutnant Dietrich Moll, the operations officer of the 18th VGD, believed that "morale was generally good, although the Luftwaffe and naval personnel assigned to the division were not always able to endure the constant hardships." Bitterly cold weather and air and artillery bombardment became chief among these.[11]

The misery of air bombardment began for the Germans in St. Vith on December 25–26. At Ridgway's request, Allied bombers reduced most of the town to rubble. Antitank gunner Klaus Ritter, the "old hare" who had survived the Russian front, endured the bombardment in a German field hospital in town, having been wounded by American white phosphorus. He could hear the aircraft approach, then the antiaircraft artillery, and finally the bombs exploding. Sheltering against a wall of the building, Ritter recalled that several wounded Americans with whom he shared the ward "leapt to their feet, trying to find better shelter." Ritter yelled at them sarcastically, "Don't be afraid, these are your fighters [bombers]." In the end, every one ran out into the street. Hours later, a German doctor advised the German walking wounded that they should make their way to facilities in the Schnee Eifel. Ritter began trudging east, but then, "One sign catches my eye. It reads Prüm 33 Km." Instead of heading east, Ritter headed home to Weinsheim, five kilometers closer. Months later, on March 3, when the Americans swept through his hometown, they missed him. For Ritter the war was over.[12] He escaped, but his comrades in the 18th VGD would once again confront the 7th AD.

On January 8, Hitler finally began to see that his notion of returning to the offensive was unrealistic. On that day he authorized the tip of Fifth Panzer Army to withdraw and ordered the Sixth Panzer Army out of the line. On January 12, the Russians began an offensive in the east. That led Hitler to order the Sixth Panzer Army and his two escort brigades redeployed to fight the Russians.[13]

Planning to Retake St. Vith

On January 11, the XVIII Airborne Corps published Field Order Number 2, ordering a Corps attack in two phases. First, the Corps would attack to "secure a line La Neuville–Houvegnez–Waimes." The second phase required the 7th AD "to pass rapidly through the 1st Infantry Division in zone of action; attack and destroy enemy wherever found in ST. VITH area; destroy his road traffic; seize ST. VITH; and on further Corps order, organize and defend this road center; reconnoiter to south and east of ST. VITH; protect the Corps left (east) flank." To assure adequate infantry, XVIII Corps attached the 509th Parachute Infantry Battalion (PIB), commanded by Lieutenant Colonel (LTC) Edmond J. Tomasik, and the 2nd Battalion, 517th Parachute Infantry Regiment (PIR), commanded by LTC Richard Joe Seitz.[14] MG Ridgway intended to commit the 7th AD through the 1st ID and down "a defile south of Waimes."[15]

Brigadier General (BG) Robert W. Hasbrouck's baseline plan conformed nicely with both the ground and Field Manual (FM) 17-100, *The Armored Division*. He intended to attack with Combat Command A (CCA) and Combat Command B (CCB) each having three task forces. Each had tanks, engineers, infantry, and tank destroyers. Colonel (COL) William S. Triplet's

CCA included Task Force (TF) Wemple, formed on the 17th Tank Battalion (TB); TF Rhea, formed on the 23rd Armored Infantry Battalion (AIB); and TF Seitz, formed on the 2nd Battalion, 517th PIR. BG Bruce C. Clarke's CCB included TF Chappuis, formed on the 48th AIB; TF Tomasik, formed on the 509th PIB; and TF Erlenbusch, formed on the 31st TB. Combat Command Reserve (CCR), now led by COL Francis P. Tompkins, retained task forces formed on LTC Marcus S. Griffin's 38th AIB and LTC John C. Brown's 40th TB.[16]

Hasbrouck's scheme, and Ridgway's, for that matter, reflected their familiarity with the ground. Hasbrouck understood that a narrow axis of advance, limited by the terrain, meant his forces would fight for crossroads and were likely to be surprised by antitank fires. Hasbrouck's concept of operations articulated in his training scheme enabled what FM 17-100 called attack in a mobile situation. The manual noted, "Such attacks are usually made in successive objectives each attack being a separate operation." To succeed required establishing a base of fire with artillery, tanks, and/or tank destroyers to support the advance. Maintaining a reserve was crucial, as was displacing the base of fire by echelon—thus assuring continued fire support. FM 17-100 stipulated that the "*maneuvering force* consists of the bulk of the tanks, some artillery, infantry and engineers." Hasbrouck's task force organization reflected this doctrine and his own experience fighting his combat command and as a division commander.[17]

Both the 509th PIB and the 2nd Battalion, 517th PIR jumped off with XVIII Airborne Corps on January 3. The 509th had worked with the 7th AD, but Seitz and his paratroopers had not. Still, exploiting the synergy of combined arms was not foreign to the infantry, so melding the parachute infantry and mounting the troops on tanks proved to be no challenge. The paratroopers routinely operated with attachments, or as attachments, and both had considerable experience—the 509th since North Africa in 1942, and the 517th having operated in Italy, southern France, and in the Bulge. Neither unit missed a beat when the two were pulled out of the fight and attached to CCB and CCA, respectively.

The Road Back

MG Ridgway briefed his division commanders on the First Army attack plan on New Year's Eve. The plan disappointed Ridgway. He believed the attack should aim directly toward St. Vith. He respected the Germans in the defense, and he told his subordinate they faced "a bitter savage fight like the

Falaise Gap all over again." Ridgway wanted to cut off the German mobile forces, and that meant attacking toward St. Vith. Despite his belief that it would be a difficult fight, Ridgway remained confident, telling his generals, "there isn't anything to stop this attack; it's just overwhelming."[18]

First Army's three corps forced their way southeast in truly awful conditions. Cold overcast weather and deep snows rendered the roads icy and dangerous. The Germans, too, exacted a toll, demonstrating their competence in defense even in a lost cause. First Army measured gains in yards per day. Ridgway issued his final instructions for the second phase on January 13. Historian Robert E. Merriam has described the result as "poetic justice." The 7th AD would have a chance to not only destroy part of General der Panzertruppe Hasso von Manteuffel's Fifth Panzer Army but also to avenge the Division's honor and recapture St. Vith. On January 19 Ridgway ordered Hasbrouck to pass forward, and to attack the next day. That same day, Seitz and Tomasik moved their battalions to assembly areas to form the planned task forces. Later Ridgway attached the 508th PIR to secure the ground taken.[19]

The 7th AD moved into attack positions near Waimes on the night of January 19–20, and the two parachute battalions joined them. LTC Seitz's first encounter with COL Triplet took the form of each taking the measure of the other. Seitz's battalion had two Jeeps as its entire rolling stock. Both Jeeps were hauling ammunition when the battalion commander was called to a commanders' conference with the CCA commander. With no other choice, Seitz walked the two miles to CCA's command post. When he arrived there late, just as the meeting was breaking up, Triplet came "unglued" and raised hell about it. Seitz retorted that he was late because of "the fact that I walked to this so and so meeting." At this, Triplet calmed down, and even equipped Seitz with a half-track and two 2.5-trucks to improve the mobility in Seitz's battalion. Each man regarded the other as a great commander.[20] There were no reported bumps between LTC Tomasik of the 509th PIB and BG Clarke at CCB. The next morning the 7th AD started down the road back to St. Vith.

The road back was, however, not without obstacles. At the outset the Division had to negotiate the Ondenval defile, a narrow passage between two densely wooded hills. A railway and highway came together at the narrowest point. From there all the way south to St. Vith, the Lucky Seventh's task forces had to negotiate the wooded hills surrounding Deidenberg, Born, and Hünningen, and then, finally, the same ridge they had defended in December. Hasbrouck and most of his soldiers knew from personal experience that the ground favored the defenders. Waist-deep snow in the firebreaks of the forests would now slow the Division down, regardless of cleats on tracks. Infantry deployed on the flanks would have to be relieved frequently, as they would have to wade through the deep snow.

It was less than five miles from Deidenberg to St. Vith, but there were only two roads—roughly parallel—between them, both of which went through Born. South of Born the 7th would have to negotiate the Emmels valley, where they had bloodied Oberst Otto-Ernst Remer's Führer Escort Brigade (FEB). The Wallerode Bois, the forest just east of the town of Wallerode, posed an additional threat to mobility.

Terrain was one of many hindrances to the 7th AD's progress back toward St. Vith. The weather that had helped keep the Germans at bay and saved the Division when the ground froze on December 23 now favored the enemy. Snow followed in the wake of the high-pressure area coming from Russia that had produced the miracle freeze and the clear flying weather the last week of December. Now the weather grew even colder and the snow deeper, with the result that the roads were treacherous. Weather and terrain robbed the 7th AD of the inherent advantage of armor—speed.

The Lucky Seventh's chief antagonists were once again the 18th VGD and its colleagues in the newly formed XIII Corps. General der Infanterie Hans Gustav Felber's XIII Corps began its life on New Year's Day as Korpsgruppe Felber but received the dignity of corps status on January 13. On that day Felber commanded the 18th VGD, a regiment of the 246th VGD, the 326th Volksgrenadier Regiment, and Obersturmbahnführer Joachim Peiper and the survivors of Kampfgruppe Peiper. Felber had some corps artillery, perhaps as many as thirty-one tubes, and he had twenty-three antitank guns. His infantry divisions were at roughly half strength but still able to conduct a delaying action.[21]

Oberst Günther Hoffman-Schönborn's 18th VGD straddled the Lucky Seventh's zone of action. The 18th fared well through the capture of St. Vith, suffering comparatively few casualties. The grenadiers rested from Christmas Day through December 28. On New Year's Day, the 18th VGD's three regiments still had about one thousand *Landsers* each. Felber described the 18th's morale as good, and he believed his grenadiers still capable of mounting limited objective attacks. Since the American counterattack had begun, the 18th had fought a determined delay against the far more powerful XVIII Airborne Corps. By January 15, the 18th VGD had received five hundred replacements but had lost one regiment detached to support another unit. By January 20, when the 7th AD attacked, the 18th VGD had no more than two

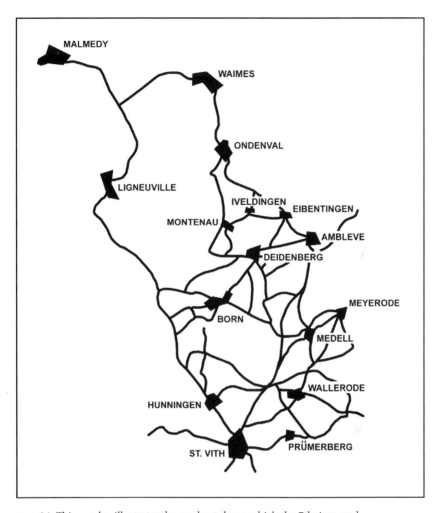

MAP 14. This overlay illustrates the road net down which the 7th Armored Division attacked in the effort to retake St. Vith against the antagonists of the 18th Volksgrenadier Division. It is just under six air miles from Waimes to St. Vith. Reproduced from 7th Armored Division, "After Action Report, Period 1–31 December 1944."

thousand riflemen. The 18th disposed itself in a web defense of strongpoints and roadblocks that the operations officer believed incapable of defeating a "systematic enemy attack." To stiffen the defense, the 18th had mined the obvious armor approaches and built strongpoints "in the depth of the main defense area."[22] The grenadiers had accomplished these tasks as far back as St. Vith by January 19, albeit with very few mines to that depth. Supported by a few tanks and their own antitank battalion they were as ready as they could be.

The 7th AD closed on its assembly areas by 0330 on January 20 and started forward at 0730. Staff Sergeant Richard L. McBride described passing forward. First he and his mortar squad saw artillery, then Jeeps "carrying officers clutching maps," then supply vehicles and ambulances heading in both directions. As they moved toward the front, they saw 1st ID and 30th ID shoulder patches. Finally they began to pass destroyed equipment from both sides until they reached their dismount point. From there they made their way forward, pushing through snow packed hard to a depth of three feet on the level (when a level stretch was found), and up to six or seven feet in drifts. They reached their first objective, only to find light tanks had already taken it.[23]

The Lucky Seventh advanced south with CCA and CCB abreast, the two advancing by alternate bounds so they could support each other. Hasbrouck did not expect a stiff defense, but with his units essentially roadbound, he did not propose to leave them vulnerable to ambush. The Division planned to advance along a four-kilometer front from Ondenval south, slightly more than seven road miles to St. Vith. Along the way the Division's units had to cross the Amblève River and several smaller streams. The highway that ran through the defile just south of Ondenval to St. Vith via Born formed the main avenue of approach. A secondary avenue extended south out of Born toward St. Vith along the Born–St. Vith highway. The Division would have to clear the villages of Deidenberg, Born, and Hünningen, as well as the dense woods north and to the east of Born.

Hasbrouck's scheme of maneuver required close coordination between the two attacking combat commands but also enabled them to support each other and to strike towns from more than one direction. Attacking on more or less parallel routes permitted shifting the main effort rapidly. Finally, Hasbrouck could commit CCR on either axis. Execution would demonstrate whether the concept would work as envisaged.

Triplet's CCA began the attack, with TF Wemple attacking in two columns from the tiny village of Am Kreuz, about two thousand yards southeast of Ondenval and east of the defile. On the left Captain (CPT) Dudley Britton's company-size combined arms task force led with dismounted infantry leading his tanks. Britton's B Company, 23rd AIB had been one of the first units on the Prümerberg. A Lieutenant (LT) Wilson led the right-hand or western column of TF Wemple and started south about one hour after Britton.

Britton reached Deidenberg by 1130, opposed only by small arms and anti-tank fire from the east. By noon Britton had cleared the town and captured four Germans. Wilson had a more difficult time reaching the flyspeck village of Am Stein, some two thousand yards west. Nevertheless, by noon he was in position to assault the village. Wilson went into Am Stein on the heels of an artillery preparation to suppress small arms fire. He secured the village by 1600. By 1730 hours TF Wemple had taken CCA's first objective and Wilson's troops had captured fifty-four *Landsers*.[24]

TF Rhea followed Wemple and passed through Deidenberg just after noon, while Britton was clearing the town and before Wilson reached Am Stein. LTC Robert L. Rhea moved east of Deidenberg and then, against light resistance, up onto the high ground just south of town. From this ridge, just over a thousand yards southeast of Deidenberg, Rhea's task force could dominate the approaches to and interdict movement north from St. Vith.[25]

At nightfall on January 20, TF Seitz came up behind Wemple at Deidenberg. Despite small arms fire from Born, LTC Seitz sent patrols forward to reconnoiter routes that would enable him to seize a forested ridge named Auf der Hart. After Seitz reached that ridge he planned to bring up his tanks. With Triplet's approval, Seitz decided to attack that night under cover of darkness because he had to cross a thousand yards of open terrain. The paratroopers moved out at 0400, and Seitz remembered, "It was bitterly cold and snowing." The dismounted paratroopers clambered up the ridge, where they surprised the "outpost screen with six Germans killed, 30 wounded, and 15 taken prisoner. At first light, I had my tank company close—and pass through—over running the main German defense. After sharp close-in fighting we secured the objective."[26]

Hasbrouck's scheme required complicated maneuvers such as those Triplet's CCA undertook that day. In his first operation Triplet had managed all the moving parts quite well. BG Clarke could not say as much. CCB had numerous problems taking its objective, Born. Clarke's command advanced on two separate axes. TF Tomasik and TF Chappuis passed through the 75th ID zone of attack and approached Born from the west. TF Erlenbusch followed CCA through the Ondenval defile. The V Corps' 1st ID attacked on the 7th AD's left. At Montenau, a small settlement just south of the defile, LTC Robert C. Erlenbusch left the highway and climbed the densely wooded ridge west of the highway using a logging trail. From the crest of the ridge Erlenbusch intended to move along it southwest to a point where it appeared, he noted from studying maps, that he could position tanks to overlook Born. At that time Tomasik's task force and his supporting tanks would attack Born from the west while Erlenbusch's infantry would attack the town from the north. TF Chappuis, in reserve, would follow TF Tomasik.

From the outset, TF Erlenbusch had trouble. South of the defile the task force moved at the pace set by a tank with a dozer blade that cleared the highway of snow. Despite the makeshift snowplow, one of the tanks slid off the road, causing further delay. When the task force left Montenau, the pace slowed due to the terrain and caution posed by Germans firing on LT Wilson's troops in Am Stein. C Company of the 509th PIB provided an advance guard for the tanks as they labored along firebreaks and trails leading south. Erlenbusch himself moved with the lead rifle platoon or the lead tank platoon. The remainder of the task force trailed.[27]

Erlenbusch finally reached his intended position at about 1600 hours. There he found he could only get two tanks in position, both of which were picked off by well-sited German antitank guns. At this point, the best he could do was to get his infantry down off the ridge. The infantry duly trudged downhill, crossed the Ondenval highway, forded a stream east of the highway, and reached a position five hundred yards north of Born. Here they waited for Tomasik to close in from the west.[28]

Tomasik fared even worse than had Erlenbusch. TF Tomasik passed through the 75th ID's 120th Infantry Regiment (INF). Due to coordination issues with the 120th, Tomasik missed his start time. Then he sent reconnaissance forward to make contact with the Germans and assess the defense. This perfectly reasonable step took far longer than planned, so the attack began at 1130 instead of 0730. As Tomasik's tanks debouched from the woods 1,100 yards west of Born, two of them struck mines. Finally, when TF Tomasik reached Born at 1630, it encountered antitank and small arms fire. Tomasik's attack petered out by 1800.[29]

When CCB struggled to get forward, Hasbrouck intervened. In a session at Hasbrouck's forward command post with Clarke and Triplet present and Ridgway as an interested observer, Hasbrouck directed Triplet to mount a coordinated attack on Born with Clarke. Triplet considered Clarke a rival. It is likely the reverse is true as well. Triplet took some advantage of the situation, claiming he could take the town without Clarke. Triplet spelled out his scheme and left believing he would take Born with "the approval of everybody except Clarke."[30] In the end, Hasbrouck called him off and left the mission to Clarke.

Clarke, presumably stung by his failure, "directed that Task Forces reorganize prepared to continue the attack on order that night." Clarke made preparations with Hasbrouck to attack at 2345 following a forty-five-minute artillery preparation delivered by thirteen battalions of division and corps artillery. The 18th VGD remained game, putting up "very heavy resistance which included tanks, SP guns [self-propelled guns from the 1818th Anti-Tank Battalion] and infantry." Tomasik's paratroopers broke into Born at 0132 on January 21. The attack cost B Company, 31st TB thirteen tanks but only five troops were wounded and one killed. The paratroopers suffered far more.[31]

The carnage going into Born had not ended the fight. As many as two hundred grenadiers hung on. The German defenders employed their remaining antitank guns and infantry effectively, preventing TF Chappuis and TF Erlenbusch from closing. LTC Richard D. Chappuis committed his B Company at 0200 and followed with A Company. Finally, at daybreak, Erlenbusch's tanks clawed their way into town against intense accurate fire. LT Henry G. Taliaferro, a tank platoon leader in C Company, 31st TB, described the scene as he came up on the hill overlooking the town; he could see "six friendly tanks burning on the slope." Taliaferro, as any prudent soul might, hesitated to descend the slope with his own platoon. Clarke was there to give instructions. In his "charming voice" he ordered Taliaferro "to secure the rest of this town in twenty minutes." Taliaferro preferred to face the Germans rather than Clarke and followed his general's precise and succinct instructions to the best of his ability. Even so, it took until 1800 on December 21 to secure Born.[32]

Even when it was finally forced out, the 18th VGD "closed by demolition" the trails and woods leading south through the Emmels forest north of St. Vith. Two avenues of approach led more or less south toward St. Vith. One on the west went through Nieder-Emmels, and the other from the Auf der Hart woods, which TF Seitz controlled, went south along the highway and railway through Wallerode. The 18th VGD withdrew slowly along routes it had reconnoitered previously. The 18th's strongpoints and outposts, bolstered by antitank guns and artillery, prevented the 7th AD from breaking through rapidly. The German defensive positions were mutually supporting, arrayed in depth, and protected by both natural and artificial obstacles. By the time the Lucky Seventh cleared Born, its antagonists had completed obstacles and laid minefields part way back to St. Vith.[33]

Despite Clarke's difficulty, the first day on the road to St. Vith illustrated the wisdom of Hasbrouck's training directive and his plan of attack. The 7th AD retained the initiative because its organization and training enabled the Division and the combat commands to reorient rapidly. When Clarke's set piece attack failed, he organized a night attack that required his three task forces to synchronize their efforts. Tomasik and Erlenbusch maintained contact with the enemy, enabling Chappuis to enter the town at low risk of friendly fire and with some idea of the enemy situation. CCB could mount a night attack without reconnaissance or a moonlit night, as specified in FM 17-100.[34] CCB retained the tactical initiative because of individual initiative and unit agility stemming from training and combined arms organization.

The XVIII Airborne Corps envisaged a change during the next stage of the operation. The Corps planned for the 7th AD to continue the attack south along the highway from Born toward St. Vith, as far as the line at Hünningen and Wallerode. From here, Hasbrouck's troops would support the 30th ID. The 30th was to attack from the northwest and advance across the 7th AD's right front to seize St. Vith. With CCB caught up most of the day on December 21 clearing Born, using the 30th ID for the final attack made sense, as it was comparatively fresh. Like the fight for St. Vith in December, the fight in January involved intermingled forces and no clear front lines. The Germans still held the town of Medell in CCA's left rear and Wallerode to its left front. In fact, the 18th VGD command post remained in Wallerode until the evening of January 21.[35]

For most of that same day, in accord with Corps orders, the 7th AD reorganized and resupplied. Two battalions of the 508th PIR arrived midafternoon to relieve CCA so it could organize for the next thrust. First Army adjusted the boundary between V Corps and XVIII Airborne Corps as the advance continued. The consequence of shifting units and stubborn defenders was that XVIII Airborne Corps permitted the German XIII Corps a breather.

Felber and his units made good use of the breather. The 18th VGD occupied a minor salient extending northward because the 30th ID and the 75th ID had pushed back the 326th VGD on the 18th's left flank. To buy time for the 18th to shorten its lines, Felber used a battalion attached from the 246th VGD to mount a limited counterattack from near Nieder-Emmels northwest. The grenadier battalion's attack passed through the 18th VGD. Though the attack petered out, it did manage to stop the 30th ID. That night the 18th VGD withdrew back toward St. Vith unhindered. Both Felber and the leadership of the 18th believed they had avoided disaster thanks to the few hours they had on January 21. Dietrich Moll, the 18th VGD's operations officer, believed the US Army was obsessed with security. Of the Americans, he observed, "entire companies sometimes being stopped by the fire of a few automatic rifles."[36]

That afternoon, Clarke, Hasbrouck, Ridgway, and Triplet conferred. When Triplet arrived in "an amazingly clean cellar" in Born he found the three generals, who "didn't like each other," discussing the next day's operation. Ridgway wanted Hünningen taken on January 22. To do that from Born required looping west or east and then south on one of the two avenues of approach. According to Triplet, Clarke believed that, given the terrain, it would take as much as three days to take the town. Clarke had defended that ground and believed he knew it. Ridgway intervened to say, "If you can't take Hunnange [Hünningen] tomorrow Hasbrouck, I'll have the Thirtieth Infantry Division do it." Clarke still demurred, so Hasbrouck turned to Triplet and told him to take it. Because this account is based on Triplet's memoir, it reflects his tone. Triplet did not care for Clarke, and his assessment of the atmosphere in the cellar is almost certainly exaggerated. For one thing, in his diary Ridgway nearly always referred to his division commanders by their first names. Even when he confronted Hasbrouck about the Goose Egg defense, he called him Bob. Nevertheless, Triplet's account is plausible, as Triplet did get the mission. It is also true that Clarke and Ridgway mixed like oil and water.[37]

During the breather the Americans permitted on January 21, the 18th VGD had withdrawn as best it could east of Schönberg. With the infantry regiments shorthanded, the Division reinforced the "security line" with the division staff, who defended Wallerode.[38] The 18th still had a few tanks and antitank guns forward, as well as a battery of seventy-five-millimeter howitzers deployed in direct-fire mode; it was a poor man's antitank weapon, but very handy against troops.[39]

Hasbrouck issued his order at 0200 on January 22 with 0800 as the start time for CCB and 1000 for CCA. The attack, if successful, would set the stage for the assault on St. Vith. At 0800 hours CCB attacked to clear the woods south of Born and protect CCA's right flank. Triplet attacked at 1000 in column, with TF Seitz in the lead, followed by TF Wemple. TF Rhea brought up the rear. TF Beatty, a small combined arms force from the 31st TB, would attack south from CCB's zone on order. Triplet's three task forces motored straight south from Deidenberg on the eastern avenue of approach. TF Triplet planned to deploy on line with TF Seitz, with TF Wemple attacking from the northeast and east and TF Beatty from the north. Rhea's orders required him to clear a wooded ridge about a thousand yards north of Hünningen.[40]

Still another foot of snow had fallen, delaying CCA. The Sherman tanks simply could not push their way through the snow. Tank dozers had to lead the way, reducing the attack to the width of the blade. CCA found that "the plowing was extremely slow work and we barely made it [up the slope north of Hünningen]. By the time we reached the crest, three dozers were immobilized with burned out or frozen clutches." The remaining dozer tank got everyone down the slope on the south side and into marshy ground with a stream that now confounded Triplet. The tanks struggled through the morass but the half-tracks finally could not move at all. To the rear the combat command bunched up, inviting and receiving artillery. At 1500 hours CCA was well and truly stuck.[41]

Meanwhile, Hasbrouck had become frustrated enough to launch TF Beatty, and the task force encountered and destroyed a German strongpoint just north of Nieder-Emmels. The strongpoint consisted of six dugouts by at least twenty-two grenadiers, of whom two were killed, four wounded, and sixteen captured. MAJ William F. Beatty's infantry from B Company, 48th AIB got hit by both "screaming meemies" and US artillery supporting CCA. Even so, LT Roland Lavrenz, a platoon leader, ran off a German tank with his M1 rifle. Serendipity played a role: one of Lavrenz's rifle rounds set fire to a gasoline can stored on the tank. Beatty sent a tank platoon across the 30th ID boundary to seize Nieder-Emmels because he was taking fire from the village. LT Rex E. Waldrop "disabled two German tanks, killed a number of German infantrymen and disorganized resistance in the town." Beatty lost two tanks but reached and took his share of Hünningen, destroying four German tanks in the process.[42]

MAJ Beatty made effective use of three 105-millimeter assault guns that he had. The 18th VGD had turned nearly every house in Nieder-Emmels into a fortified position, and the task force took fire from nearly all of them. Each time that occurred, Beatty or someone else vectored one of the assault guns to the offending house and fired a canister round into it with satisfying results. The canister round was a new tool, and the tankers loved it. When fired at the comparatively fragile timber frame walls of a Belgian home they literally brought the house down. TF Beatty got into Hünningen at 1700 and had nearly cleared it when TF Wemple and TF Seitz arrived. When the firing stopped, MAJ Beatty made his way to the tavern where he had left his rubber overshoes when he had been evacuated with pneumonia on December 21. The innkeeper had them still and reunited the galoshes with their owner.[43]

German artillery played hell with TF Wemple while it was mired in the marshy ground in the Emmels valley. Finally, Wemple got underway again with TF Seitz on his left and slightly behind him. As CPT Jack Howison,

Wemple's operations officer, described it, "At 1730 we got the order to move out. The tanks drew anti-tank fire. The tanks provided overhead fire while the infantry cleaned out houses. There was little opposition except for small arms fire and some anti-tank fire. The tanks practically destroyed the houses in the eastern part of Hunningen. The infantry had little trouble. At Hunningen the paratroops with Task Force Seitz took prisoners who tried to escape to the north as Task Force Wemple came in." Taking Hünningen spelled the end for the Germans in St. Vith, as the ridge that ran from Hünningen east to Wallerode dominated the northern approach to the town as surely as did the Prümerberg to the east. At the end of the month the 31st TB crowed in its after action report that on January 22 the "doom of ST VITH was now sealed."[44]

At dusk COL Triplet saw "an example of the remarkably good shooting that was characteristic of the gunners of the Seventh Armored." A German antitank gun hit one of LTC Wemple's tanks and it exploded. It was, Triplet recalled, "A hellish sight. But the red line of the German tracer had barely faded from the retina when one of our tanks and a tank destroyer in the second wave [of TF Wemple] lanced converging pair of shots that exploded the German vehicle." The fight for the ridge had ended. Triplet reported as much, though perhaps a little early, at 1737.[45]

CCA, like CCB before it, needed some time to reorganize. CCB would get the nod to take St. Vith, as planned days earlier. John Toland recorded Hasbrouck's order to Bruce C. Clarke in *Battle: The Story of the Bulge*. On the evening of January 22 Hasbrouck called Clarke and said, "Bruce . . . you got kicked out of St Vith. Would you like to take it back?" Clarke wanted very much to take the town back. Hasbrouck gave him some help from CCA, including TF Chappuis and most of TF Rhea. Clarke also had TF Beatty. Clarke's plan was straightforward: TF Chappuis would move cross-country west of and parallel with the Hünningen–St. Vith highway. Beatty would attack south on the highway, just as the FEB had done in December. Rhea would come up on the ridge overlooking St. Vith and use his tanks to provide a base of fire for his infantry.

That same night Clarke sent B Company, 38th AIB on a reconnaissance in force into St. Vith. That mission required the company commander to continue until resistance proved too strong. In plain English, B Company was to learn whether the Germans had left. If they had, Clarke would move into St. Vith immediately. The infantry reached the edge of town, where it encountered a roadblock. It appeared the Germans would fight.[46]

Clarke's troops attacked St. Vith at 1415 on January 23. The attack proved to be anticlimactic. Snow and cold were the chief resistance. The 18th VGD had evacuated St. Vith the night before, leaving only a few combat patrols and roadblocks to delay the attackers. Still, Hasbrouck, circling overhead in a Piper Cub, took satisfaction in the attack. It was, he thought, "pretty to watch." CCB overwhelmed the few remaining German troops. The message to XVIII Airborne Corps read, "ST VITH fell at 1745 to CCB, 7 AD. Little resistance."[47]

Anticlimactic or not, the capture of St. Vith did not mean the 7th AD was finished. That same night Hasbrouck ordered CCA to take Wallerode and CCB to expand both east toward the Schnee Eifel and south. Allied air force bombing had rendered the roads in St. Vith impassable, so division engineers set to work to build a bypass so the roads beyond the town leading to the Siegfried Line and Germany could be used. Linking up with Third Army units would constitute the final act of reducing the Bulge. As First and Third Armies closed on each other they made first contact near Houffalize at 0930 on January 16. Fittingly, two privates made that contact.[48]

The rest of the "first contacts" each occurred farther east. The task of effecting linkup outside of St. Vith fell to LTC Erlenbusch. His task force occupied an arc of ground that extended south and west of St. Vith along the very road his tankers used to withdraw from St. Vith in December. On January 27 Erlenbusch set out from St. Vith in a light tank borrowed from D Company to make contact with an approaching Third Army unit. As he later recalled,

I proceeded west on the Neundorf road to try to contact the unit [the 346th INF, 87th ID] that was to the west. The light tank was a good vehicle for this job. At idle speed, the two Cadillac engines made practically no noise. The foot and a half of snow pretty well deadened the noise of the tracks. It was a cold, crisp, clear night and the starlight reflecting from off the snow gave us enough light to see where we were going. About halfway down the road to Neundorf we idled up to a still standing farmhouse. This would be a likely place for an outpost, so we stopped our movement even though we could see no one or any sign of occupancy. As we stood there frozen into the scene we heard the distinctive click of a rifle bolt being pulled into position and simultaneously a challenge in English. We had made contact with a battalion outpost. In due course, the battalion commander arrived and I explained to him where our units were and that we expected friendly units to be coming from the south, probably on the Grüfflingen–St. Vith road. He explained to me what he knew of his unit's positions, and I was off in my tank, hopefully to get by C Company on my way home without being shot. After a number of attempts I finally got them on the radio and explained where I was and where I was going. Finally arrived at my CP [command post] about 2100 and was treated to a hot toasted cheese sandwich someone made for me on the top of an old wood-burning range salvaged from the rubble and brought to our basement CP.

For the 7th AD, the Battle of the Bulge was well and truly over. The Lucky Seventh then fought its way across Germany and eventually reached the Baltic Sea. The cost for the recapture of St. Vith had been high. The 7th AD suffered 1,466 casualties in January, and these losses did not include the casualties incurred by the parachute battalions. The fighting rendered the 509th PIB combat ineffective. That proud battalion had been reduced to fifty-four soldiers; the rest had been wounded or killed. LTC Seitz's 2nd Battalion, 517th PIR also suffered serious casualties, with nearly two-thirds of the Battalion killed or wounded. How many Germans the 7th AD and its paratroopers killed cannot be known with certainty, but they captured 1,013. More important, they helped destroy the last significant German reserve in the west.[49]

NOTES

1. Division Artillery, 7th Armored Division, "After Action Report, Month of January 1945," 2.

2. 7th Armored Division, "After Action Report, Period 1–31 January 1944," 5.

3. Stephen E. Ambrose, *The Supreme Commander*, 574–76.

4. Forrest C. Pogue, *George C. Marshall*, 421–37, addresses the crisis that occurred between Eisenhower and Montgomery that rose to the level of George C. Marshall and Winston Churchill. See also Ambrose, *The Supreme Commander*, 527–35, on the September crisis in command and 571–79 in an aptly named chapter "Showdown, with De Gaulle and Brooke" on the post-Bulge dispute. On the British point of view, see Nigel Hamilton, *Monty: The Battles of Field Marshal Bernard Montgomery*, 334–35, 368–71, 388–410, 530–34. Hamilton is a partisan supporter of Montgomery, as Ambrose is for Eisenhower, but even Hamilton acknowledges that "Montgomery dug his own professional grave." The idea that "Monty knew best" brought him down, and it is by no means clear what he proposed was best.

5. Most histories of the Battle of the Bulge treat the reduction of the bulge almost as an afterthought. Charles B. MacDonald's chapter "Erasing the Bulge" in his *A Time for Trumpets*, is concise. Peter Caddick-Adams's chapters "End of the Bulge," "Performance of a Lifetime," and "Beyond the Bulge" in his *Snow and Steel* are

brilliant. Clarence R. Huebner assumed command of V Corps on January 15, 1945. He had been in command of the 1st ID. See Harold R. Winton, *Corps Commanders of the Bulge*, 311.

6. Generalmajor Carl Gustav Wagener, "Results of the Ardennes Offensive," 1.

7. For tanks and assault guns, see Heinz Günther Guderian, *From Normandy to the Ruhr*, 343; the Waldenburg quotation is on 344.

8. MacDonald, *A Time for Trumpets*, 588; see chap. 26, "Crises in Command," on planning to reduce the Bulge, the specifics on Montgomery's contretemps with Eisenhower, and *Nordwind*.

9. Caddick-Adams, *Snow and Steel*, 636–40.

10. Brigadier General George C. McDonald, "Allied Air Power and the Ardennes Offensive," 53–54. See also Winton, *Corps Commanders*, 210–15, on the return of the air forces of both sides to the battle during the Russian high-pressure event.

11. Oberstleutnant Dietrich Moll, "18th Volks Grenadier Division," 60–61.

12. Klaus Ritter, statements, box 10, Charles B. MacDonald Papers, pt. 2, pp. 10–12.

13. Robert E. Merriam, *Dark December*, 206–7.

14. 7th Armored Division, "After Action Report, Period 1–31 January 1944,", 5–6.

15. Division Artillery, 7th Armored Division, "After Action Report, Month of January 1945," 3.

16. 7th Armored Division, "After Action Report, Period 1–31 January 1945," 6. Tompkins took command from LTC Warren, who assumed command when COL Ryan became chief of staff of the 7th AD. See also Combat Command R, 7th Armored Division, "After Action Report, Month of January 1945."

17. US War Department, *Armored Command Field Manual: The Armored Division*, FM 17-100, 51–53, emphasis in the original. In Major General Robert W. Hasbrouck (Ret.), interview with the author, Washington, DC, August 20, 1984, the author specifically asked General Hasbrouck on the utility of the staff college course that he attended. Hasbrouck's answer was simple: "I knew what to do."

18. Major General Matthew B. Ridgway, war diary, entry for commanders' conference, 1345, December 31, 1944, Matthew B. Ridgway Papers.

19. Merriam, *Dark December*, 207; XVIII Corps (Airborne), G-3 operations journal, January 1945, entry for 191445, January 1945.

20. Richard Joe Seitz, "Chronology of Important Events in the Life of Richard Joe Seitz," 70; William S. Triplet, *A Colonel in the Armored Divisions*, 166. Triplet, who comes across in his memoir as a bully, respected those who pushed back. He wrote that Seitz "was one of the best soldiers I have known."

21. General der Infanterie Hans Felber, "Defensive Fighting in the Ardennes."

22. Felber, 3. Moll, "18th Volks Grenadier Division," 62, 64.

23. Richard L. McBride, "Grinding Through with the 7th Armored Division," 178.

24. 17th Tank Battalion, "After Action Report, Month of January 1945," 6–8; W. Wesley Johnston, *The 7th Armored Division Goes Back*, 22–23; this book has good sketches.

25. 23rd Armored Infantry Battalion, "After Action Report, Month of January 1945," 1.

26. Seitz, "Chronology," 71; Combat Command A, 7th Armored Division, "After Action Report, January 1945."

27. Combat Command B, 7th Armored Division, "After Action Report, Month of January 1945," 2; Colonel Robert C. Erlenbusch (Ret.), interview with the author, Point Charlotte, FL, December 8, 1984. See also 31st Tank Battalion, "After Action Report, January 1945," 3.

28. Combat Command B, 7th Armored Division, "After Action Report, Month of January 1945," 2; 31st Tank Battalion, "After Action Report, January 1945," 3.

29. Combat Command B, 7th Armored Division, "After Action Report, Month of January 1945," 2. See also 31st Tank Battalion, "After Action Report," 3; and Johnston, *The Seventh Armored Division Goes Back*, 25–26.

30. Triplet, *Colonel in the Armored Divisions*, 173.

31. Triplet, *Colonel in the Armored Divisions*, 173; Combat Command B, 7th Armored Division, "After Action Report, Month of January 1945," 2. The 509th attacked with élan but took great casualties. Tomasik had only seventy paratroopers still in action at St. Vith. After St. Vith, the Army deactivated the 509th rather than rebuild it. See Clay Blair, *Ridgway's Paratroopers*, 424–25. See also Johnston, *The Seventh Armored Division Goes Back*, 28–30.

32. US 7th Armored Division Association, *The Lucky Seventh*, 307.

33. Moll, "18th Volks Grenadier Division," 79. In his manuscript Moll reports the Americans taking Born on January 19, but he was mistaken. It is one of the few errors in his account, which he recorded without the benefit of his unit journal.

34. US War Department, *Armored Command Field Manual: The Armored Division*, FM 17-100, 89.

35. This surmise is based on Moll, "18th Volks Grenadier Division," 79.

36. Moll, "18th Volks Grenadier Division," 81; Felber, "Defensive Fighting in the Ardennes." 17. See also Robert L. Hewitt, *Work Horse of the Western Front*, 206, which notes that the counterattack was "beautifully planned." The 102th Regiment did not detect the Germans until they were "practically in the positions of the 1st and 3rd Battalions."

37. Triplet, *Colonel in the Armored Divisions*, 174–75.

38. Moll, "18th Volks Grenadier Division," 80.

39. Moll was not clear on just what remained in Hünningen. The data on enemy equipment comes from Combat Command A, "After Action Report, January 1945"; 17th Tank Battalion, "After Action Report, Month of January 1945"; and 31st Tank Battalion, "After Action Report, January 1945."

40. Johnston, *The Seventh Armored Division Goes Back*, 32; Combat Command A, "After Action Report, January 1945," 9.

41. Triplet, *Colonel in the Armored Divisions*, 179; for Triplet's account of the action that day, including struggling through the marshy ground and across a small stream, see 178–87.

42. Johnston, *The Seventh Armored Division Goes Back*, 35. See also 31st Tank Battalion, "After Action Report, January 1945," 4.

43. Erlenbusch interview, December 8, 1984.

44. Johnston, *The Seventh Armored Division Goes Back*, 18–21; 31st Tank Battalion "After Action Report, January 1945," 4.

45. Triplet, *Colonel in the Armored Divisions*, 186–87.

46. Combat Command B, 7th Armored Division, "After Action Report, Month of January 1945," 3.

47. Combat Command B, 7th Armored Division, "After Action Report, Month of January 1945," 3; Hasbrouck interview, August 20, 1984.

48. MacDonald, *A Time for Trumpets*, 615.

49. Erlenbusch interview, December 8, 1984; 7th Armored Division, "After Action Report, Period 1–31 January 1945," appendix 1; Blair, *Ridgway's Paratroopers*, 425.

After the Battle

I heard a story . . . that some wounded German said, hell this is no green Division, this is the 7th Armored.

—Brigadier General Robert W. Hasbrouck

THE AIM OF this narrative has been to tell the story of a draftee armored division that is not among the "fabled" of World War II such as the 1st Infantry Division (ID), the 82nd Airborne Division (ABN), or the 4th Armored Division (AD). All of these units earned their fame. The 1st ID made three assault landings including, most famously, on Omaha Beach. The 82nd ABN won its fame in Sicily, Normandy, and Operation Market Garden. The 4th AD earned its reputation during the breakout and pursuit after Operation Overlord, and again in relieving Bastogne. But these famous divisions did not win the war by themselves. Some divisions had poor reputations they did not deserve. Arguably, the 90th ID is among these. But in the US share of the fighting on the Western Front, plain old vanilla draftee divisions carried the load; the Lucky Seventh was among these.

Why, one may ask, does that matter? It matters because Army concepts, both sound and unsound, led to choices at the strategic level in structure and equipment that Americans, literally from all walks of life, had to implement in a short amount of time against first-rate opponents. In contemporary terms, the United States fought against its near peers. By the end of the war, American industrial capacity exceeded that of any of its rivals or allies. That capacity did not, however, translate into capability without the officers and noncommissioned officers who led units and the soldiers who served in them. In the end, the soldiers of the 7th AD and those who fought alongside them made the difference in stopping the last major German offensive of the war.

The 7th AD's story matters also as a corrective—both to the sometimes exaggerated achievement of other units and, more important, to the largely underappreciated excellence of the US Army's average units as compared to the 1944 edition of the German Army. Apologists for the 1944 Wehrmacht, who contend that it was but a shadow of its 1940 edition, forget or overlook the fact that the US Army was insignificant in size and capability in 1940 but within four years was at least as good as the German Army it faced and arguably as good as the German Army ever was.

The qualitative advantage of German equipment is often mentioned in histories of World War II battles. That has not been a theme herein, but it requires at least passing reference. In March 1945, at the direction of III Corps, Lieutenant Colonel (LTC) Robert C. Erlenbusch of the 31st Tank Battalion (TB) wrote a paper comparing the "merits of the American tank vs. the German tank." He admitted the qualitative superiority of German tanks in cross-country mobility and tank guns. The German high-velocity seventy-five- and eighty-eight-millimeter guns penetrated "the Sherman and Stuart tanks anywhere without fail even at ranges over 1500 yards." American tanks, according to Erlenbusch, had to close to between eight hundred and a thousand yards to have any chance of penetrating a German Panther or Tiger tank. American tankers fought successfully only if they were "tactically clever" and then fired rapidly or hit "lucky shots." Erlenbusch concluded by arguing that "superiority in numbers, industrial ability to replace casualties, the boldness, the fearlessness and just plain 'guts' of the American tanker" were the deciding factors. Erlenbusch's tank crews proved their ability in the summer of 1944 during the pursuit, in the fall in Holland, and certainly at St. Vith.[1]

Deservedly, the Lucky Seventh received high accolades for its performance during the Battle of the Bulge, including a Distinguished Unit Citation for Combat Command B (CCB) and its attached units. For six days, the 7th AD denied the Germans the use of the road and rail network that went through St. Vith. The stand there ruined the German timetable and enabled First Army to reinforce the northern shoulder. The 7th AD's soldiers held off the Germans as long as they did against tremendous odds for three reasons. First, they held good defensive positions in what General der Artillerie Walther Lucht, the commander of LXVI Corps, described as a "difficult, pathless forest country."[2] Second, by December 1944 the 7th AD and its leadership were experienced, aggressive soldiers who took the battle to the Germans at every opportunity. And third, leaders—including those General der Panzer-truppe Hasso von Manteuffel characterized as *kleine Leute* (small people)—fought the doctrine they had learned and capitalized on the initiative of their subordinates.

Edwin B. Coddington's observation in his magnificent *The Gettysburg Campaign* about the importance of "enterprising officers" applied in 1944 as surely as it did 1863, and is as likely to matter in the future.[3] Soldiers such as MAJ Elliot Goldstein, LT William A. Knowlton, 1st Sergeant Leonard Hoyle Ladd, Staff Sergeant (SSG) Richard L. McBride, LT Arthur A. Olson, Major (MAJ) Arthur C. Parker III, Lieutenant (LT) Joseph W. "Navajo" Whiteman, and many others proved themselves enterprising whether or not they were commissioned officers.

Brigadier General (BG) Robert W. Hasbrouck deserved Chester Wilmot's honorific as "one of the great men of the Ardennes." Hasbrouck proved himself enterprising, and he capitalized on the initiative of Olson, Parker, and Whiteman, to name a few. He showed the ability to read the battlefield with his eyes and his ears. Equally important, Hasbrouck functioned well in an ambiguous command situation in which he had to assume leadership over a number of orphan commands without formal authority. He showed the kind of moral courage that Prussian military theorist Carl von Clausewitz wrote about in *On War*. Even more important, Hasbrouck had "sensitive and discriminating judgment." Hasbrouck had the kind of mind that, "*even in the darkest hour, retains some glimmerings of the inner light which leads to truth; and second, the courage to follow this faint light wherever it may lead*."[4] When the time came, he stood by his assessment that the 7th AD should be withdrawn, confronting Major General (MG) Matthew B. Ridgway, who was perhaps second only to Lieutenant General (LTG) George S. Patton Jr. in the practice of intimidating subordinates.

BG Bruce C. Clarke, BG William M. Hoge, Colonel (COL) Gustin M. Nelson, COL Dwight A. Rosebaum, and COL William S. Triplet at the combat command and regimental levels demonstrated that they, too, shared at least some of the traits Clausewitz attributed to military genius. At the battalion level, LTC Roy U. Clay, LTC Robert C. Erlenbusch, MAJ Donald P. Boyer, LTC Thomas J. Riggs Jr., and LTC Robert O. Stone were among those who showed similar capacity. The 7th AD and its attached units manifested the capacity to execute what Clarke called "mission-type orders," not unlike the celebrated *Auftragstaktik* of the German Army.[5]

MG Ridgway was not an easy man to work for. For that matter, neither were his key subordinates. LTC Frank W. Moorman, who served in the 82nd ABN with Ridgway, General (GEN) Maxwell Taylor, and MG James M. Gavin had this to say of them: "Ridgway would cut your throat and then burst into tears. Taylor would cut your throat and think nothing about it. Gavin would cut your throat and then laugh."[6] Ridgway may have been a hard man, but unlike MG Troy H. Middleton at VIII Corps, he was crystal clear about what he intended and expected. Clay believed Ridgway remained upset with the 7th AD's leadership over withdrawing from the shrinking pocket west of St Vith. When interviewed forty years later, both Clarke and Hasbrouck believed that Ridgway would not have withdrawn the Division—they believed that British field marshal Bernard Law Montgomery's intervention saved the 7th AD to fight another day. Perhaps they were right. It is even likely they were right, but what Ridgway might have done is irrelevant.

What is relevant is that Ridgway did not know Hasbrouck. He needed to hear from Hoge before he was comfortable with the decision to withdraw. Once he made up his mind, Ridgway embraced completely the necessity of withdrawing from the dangerous pocket east of the Salm River. What is most important about Ridgway is that he learned in execution. That he drove the 7th AD in January 1945 is true, and it was within his purview. That neither Clarke nor Hasbrouck liked it is also true—and understandable.[7]

Personal interactions and relationships in combat are important and can be decisive. MG Middleton and MG Alan W. Jones failed to communicate clearly, partly because Jones lacked confidence. Middleton did not make his intentions clear, and Jones failed to assert himself about the risks to the 422nd and 423rd Infantry Regiments on the Schnee Eifel. Confusion led to indecision and ultimately to chaos, the unnecessary loss of two infantry regiments and most of their supporting artillery. When Ridgway confronted Hasbrouck about withdrawing, Hasbrouck stood his ground and made his case. Ridgway respected that: whatever ill will remained between the two did not materially affect operations.

The US Army developed a robust body of doctrine during World War II. Army field manuals (FMs) enabled bright but inexperienced officers and soldiers to employ sophisticated tactics that made use of mobility both to defend St. Vith and then retake it. FM 17-12, *Tank Gunnery*, published in April 1943, is a good example. The manual is clear, concise, and useful in the training of inexperienced troops in how to bore sight their weapons, lay and fire the tanks as artillery, measure angles by hand, and solve complicated problems using formulas that require simple arithmetic. What it does not do is provide techniques to solve the problem of firing rapidly at an enemy tank that has a better gun than your own. The troops in the field solved that problem. Hasbrouck published a letter for his soldiers on January 30, 1945, that claimed they had destroyed 126 tanks and self-propelled guns. Their gunnery, as COL Triplet observed, was excellent and they took pride in that excellence. Training to the standard in the manuals worked for draftees who ranged from men who did not finish high school to those like SSG McBride, who graduated with honors from Yale University.

The smaller armored division that resulted from the reorganization required to accommodate the general shortage of manpower produced highly mobile units with arguably too few infantry. The concept of employing armored divisions to exploit penetration by infantry divisions proved mistaken. The infantry divisions needed tanks and tank destroyers, and the armored divisions needed more infantry. The combined arms structure of the 7th AD proved flexible both in defense and offense. Fighting in the hilly wooded terrain of the Ardennes, the Division needed infantry, particularly in the fight to retake St. Vith. The armored infantry battalions assigned to the 7th AD used their half-tracks for tactical mobility but fought on foot. The leg infantry and paratroopers they fought alongside lacked tactical mobility. The 7th AD did what it could to provide vehicles to the supporting infantry units to afford them basic mobility. Without trucks, half-tracks, or tanks on which to ride, the infantry arrived too late or risked being destroyed. Surprisingly, much of the US Army's infantry remains foot mobile in the twenty-first century.

On Christmas Eve 1944, the 2nd Schutzstaffel (SS) Panzer Division (PZ) humiliated Combat Command A (CCA). This disaster happened in part because First Army used a road as a corps boundary; this would be a definite failure on an Army Command and General Staff College examination, and for good reason. Roads, especially in the Ardennes, are avenues of approach. Using one as a boundary complicated coordination and fire control between adjacent units and thus created a seam the Germans could and did exploit. To compound matters, the 3rd AD and 7th AD did not coordinate effectively. At least part of the 3rd AD withdrew without notice, which caused confusion. Deception, fatigue, and the loss of control all played a role in the routing of the 40th TB, which had fought well in the preceding week. The 7th AD managed to stop the 2nd SS PZ, but the Division grew increasingly feeble until it needed help to retake Manhay. The endurance of the 7th AD, or the obduracy that Manteuffel believed essential, had declined by the end of December.

Even before Ridgway took the 7th AD out of the line, First Army, with XVIII Airborne Corps as an advocate, was working to restore and reequip it. Meanwhile, the manpower problems addressed by reduction in end strength of both armored and infantry divisions grew worse rather than better. A postwar study of combat casualties in seventeen divisions employed in the European theater of operations showed their losses averaged 3,933 infantry privates from April to September 1944. This amounted to losing nearly two-thirds of the authorized establishment of 6,195 privates in these divisions in five months. Put another way, the divisions required nearly seventy thousand replacements in that period, roughly the end strength of six divisions.[8] The problems of replacing manpower and retraining stemmed also from the inability of the United States to build ninety Army divisions, let alone two hundred, as had originally been deemed necessary.

First Army staff and the theater communications zone depots did a remarkable job finding replacements. First Army managed to restore the 7th AD nearly to full strength in less than two weeks. That meant, however, that many of the replacements had just over a week to train with their unit and find their place within it. Replacing equipment was no less difficult. LTG Courtney H. Hodges appealed directly to Field Marshal Montgomery for help in getting 250 tanks earmarked for British forces sent to First Army instead. That is the chief way the 7th AD obtained replacement tanks. Again, that left little time for tank crews to train. Thankfully, although the Division lost a lot of tanks, it lost relatively few crews. Yet despite incredible effort, the 7th AD did not return to battle at 100 percent.

On January 24, 1945, LT Knowlton's B Troop had no armored cars, and his soldiers each had a single clip or magazine of ammunition. B Troop, 87th Cavalry Reconnaissance Squadron was the incarnation of shortages of all kinds and proof that the 7th AD set priorities. Knowlton knew when he took B Troop it would be last to get anything in order to fill infantry and armor units. On January 24, Combat Command R (CCR) ordered Knowlton's "troop" into action. He complained that the troop had "no machine guns and little ammunition; each man had five rounds for his personal weapon." Knowlton recalled the response, "80 bodies are 80 bodies" and, further, CCR did not care if B Troop had to use "rocks instead of snowballs."[9]

Although B Troop suffered, Hasbrouck's training scheme fit the conditions in the field and the raft of replacements his units had to assimilate. When the

7th AD went back on the offensive on January 19, they had spent just over two weeks out of the line and even then had not been without commitments. As corps reserve, they could not afford to stand down; indeed, they executed local missions and trained within the sound of the guns. In the offense, the Division necessarily ceded the advantage of terrain to its protagonists. Snow, bitter cold, and the 18th Volksgrenadier Division (VGD) made the 7th AD pay for every gain. At times, the Lucky Seventh moved slowly both because of the conditions and, by the last week in December, perhaps because its troops had lost some of their confidence. In 1945 Charles McMoran Wilson, Lord Moran, personal physician to Prime Minister Winston Churchill, published a study of courage. A battalion medical officer in World War I, Moran made notes of what he saw in that conflict and added to it as he watched World War II from afar. Moran observed that courage can be used up—it is finite—but that rest helps restore courage or at least extend the reserves.[10]

Attacking against even weakened German forces in January 1945 after having survived the defense of St. Vith required enormous reservoirs of courage. In January the Division seemed tentative on occasion. Years after the fact, LT Knowlton, by then a retired general, explained how that might have been so. During the pursuit of the Germans in the summer of 1944, morale was so high that Knowlton recalled that when someone would say, "There is a company [of Germans] over in that woods, a few soldiers would yell 'let's go get them.' " In the Bulge, such exchanges played out differently: "When someone would say, 'There is a sniper in the woods,' everyone would hunker down in nervousness." Knowlton concluded, "It makes a great deal of difference if the troops think they are winning in a breeze."[11] In the late fall, the Germans seemed beaten, but in December they shocked the US Army in Europe—including the 7th AD.

Oberstleutnant Dietrich Moll, the 18th VGD operations officer, believed the Americans reluctant to fight at night. Certainly that was true of the 106th ID and, at least on the offense, the 7th AD. At night, tank telescopes were of little use and armor unsupported by infantry did not do well. More to the point, armored force doctrine and Army ground force doctrine did not extoll the virtues of fighting at night. FM 100-5, *Operations*, lists dire warnings of what could go wrong. FM 100-17, *The Armored Division*, argues for attacking only on moonlit nights and only to support daylight operations. The fact that the manual does not contain a single word about the advantages of attacking at night compels the conclusion that the authors could think of none. Not surprisingly, when Ridgway urged Hasbrouck to mount his first attack on the road back to St. Vith at night, Hasbrouck demurred, noting that "it is difficult to operate tanks at night"—this from an officer who during the defense of St. Vith did not blanche in the face of attacks from several divisions.[12]

The Germans took a decidedly different view. Manteuffel's chief of staff argued that night fighting took less skill than fighting in daylight. Moll said much the same thing. This view was alien to Americans and diametrically opposed to US Army doctrine. The Army avoided night operations except as means of inserting paratroops. FM 100-5, *Operations*, notes that the night attack "has assumed importance as employed by troops especially trained to overcome the difficulties of the operation and exploit its advantages."[13]

The US Army in World War II used firepower delivered from the air or by artillery to great advantage. Russell Weigley, in *The American Way of War*, has argued convincingly that resorting to firepower first and maneuver second is an American tradition dating to the Civil War. Contemporary soldiers channel that idea, saying, "Send a projo [projectile] so Joe don't go." Weigley's argument may go too far, but not by much. The US Army had an abundance of artillery in World War II and used it effectively. US and Allied air forces made it difficult for the German Army to move at all in the daylight. Artillery, and lots of it, fired time on targets and supported maneuver, sometimes even making maneuver unnecessary.

CCA maneuvered to take Deidenberg and several small villages. COL Triplet, in command of CCA, orchestrated complex maneuver on multiple approaches. In December, LTC Erlenbusch's task force shattered several attacks by combining maneuver by tanks with a base of fire provided by tank destroyers. Fire and maneuver combined to assure that the 7th AD retained or gained the initiative in both offense and defense. Officers in the 7th AD considered they were fighting an active defense by using the inherent mobility of their units to advantage. By using tanks in local counterattacks and maneuvering from one danger spot to another, the 7th AD led the Germans to perceive that the Division was stronger than it actually was.[14]

The speed of the American reaction surprised the Germans as well. Within hours of the German counteroffensive, General (GEN) Dwight D. Eisenhower had the 7th and the 10th Armored Divisions on the move, with the 82nd and 101st Airborne Divisions moving soon after. First Army responded quickly, as did Field Marshal Montgomery. The Allies not only acted rapidly but operated with far better march discipline than did their German antagonists. Third Army attacked on December 22 with three divisions. This was beyond what the Germans imagined possible.

The performance of the US Army in what combat historian Robert E. Merriam has called a "Dark December" was impressive. Initially, hubris led the Allied command to misread German intentions despite having accurately tracked German reinforcements moving forward. Nevertheless, the Allies—or, rather, mostly the Americans—responded with alacrity, courage, and competence, from Eisenhower all the way down to Private John Schaffner, a 106th ID artillery scout who escaped both the Schnee Eifel and Parker's Crossroads. BG Hasbrouck kept the chaos from becoming confused, to use BG Clarke's term. What is most impressive, however, is that the Lucky Seventh not only survived the beating it took in December but in two weeks the troops revived themselves sufficiently to operate with competence and even bursts of brilliance in January. Theirs is a great American story.

The Germans

Generalfeldmarschall Walther Model, one of the few Germans officers who stood up to Adolf Hitler, fought an increasingly desperate and losing battle. Beset by the Allies and forbidden to withdraw, his Army Group B withered away. On April 18, 1945, 325,000 of his troops surrendered.[15] On April 21, 1945, rather than be captured, Model committed suicide. Hasso von Manteuffel survived the war and a few months as a prisoner of war. Later he served in the Bundestag. He traveled to France, the United Kingdom, and the United States, where he met with some of his old adversaries, including LTG Omar N. Bradley, BG Clarke, GEN Eisenhower, BG Hasbrouck, and Field Marshal Montgomery. When he met with Manteuffel, Bradley wondered aloud, "How could a man so small cause us so much trouble in the Battle of the Bulge?"[16]

Oberst Otto-Ernst Remer survived the war but remained the quintessential unreconstructed Nazi. There are several videos of him on the internet denying the Holocaust and generally asserting the old ideology. The most chilling of these is from a meeting of ultranationalist and German expatriates hosted by a publishing house owned by a Holocaust denier.[17]

Obersturmbahnführer Joachim Peiper survived the war. He was tried with others for the Malmedy Massacre and other outrages. Although sentenced to death, Peiper's sentence was commuted to life in prison. Even so, he was released in 1956 after having served a bit more than ten years. He worked in civilian industry for a time and then retired in 1972 to a country house in Traves, France. On July 13, 1976, a group of assailants stormed Peiper's home and set it ablaze with him in it. His charred remains were removed from the ruins the next day.[18]

Antitank gunner Klaus Ritter, the "old hare," survived the war. According to a 1983 account by Heino Brandt, who assisted Charles B. MacDonald with *A Time for Trumpets*, Ritter was a teacher who had written several articles. He also coauthored a book called *Menschen zwischen Trummern and Weideraufbau: Die Stadt Prüm von 1944 bis 1950* (People between drudgery and reconstruction: The city of Prüm from 1944 to 1950).[19]

Heinz Günther Guderian, son of Generaloberst Heinz Guderian and operations officer of the 116th PZ, survived the war. On April 16, 1945, 7th AD troops captured him near Menden, Germany, during the mass surrender of the Germans trapped in the Ruhr Pocket. In addition to writing *From Normandy to the Ruhr*, he served in the West German Bundeswehr, ultimately reaching the rank of Generalmajor and serving as inspector of Panzer troops, just as his father had. Guderian retired from the Bundeswehr in 1974 and died in 2004.[20]

The Americans and Monty

The stories of those at the highest levels of command are well known and so are mentioned here only in passing. After the war Bernard Law Montgomery served as chief of Britain's Imperial General Staff. Elevated to the peerage as Viscount Alamein, he proved as ungracious after the war as he had been during it, managing to alienate practically everyone with whom he had been close. He died in 1976.[21]

Obviously, Dwight D. Eisenhower continued to serve in the early postwar era as Supreme Allied Commander in Europe, and then as chief of staff of the US Army, for a time as president of Columbia University, and finally two terms as president of the United States. He died in 1969.[22]

Two months and a week after V-E Day, Omar N. Bradley reluctantly accepted President Harry S. Truman's request to take over as the administrator of veterans affairs from 1945 to 1948. Thereafter he succeeded Eisenhower as chief of staff (in 1948) and then served as the first chairman of the Joint Chiefs of Staff from 1949 to 1953. He died in 1981.[23]

At the end of the war in Europe, Courtney H. Hodges prepared to move his headquarters to the Pacific to participate in the invasion of Japan. When that proved unnecessary, Hodges took First Army to Fort Jay on Governor's Island in New York City. He commanded First Army there until he retired in 1949. He died in San Antonio, Texas, in 1961.[24]

Matthew B. Ridgway was promoted to lieutenant general in June 1945 and served in a number of important staff positions. In 1949 he became deputy chief of staff for operations, reporting to his West Point classmate J. Lawton Collins, who had commanded VII Corps alongside Ridgway's XVIII Airborne Corps in the Battle of the Bulge. In December 1950 Ridgway became commander of Eighth Army in Korea after LTG Walton H. Walker was killed in an accident. Ridgway then succeeded Douglas MacArthur in 1951 as the US Forces Far East commander and was promoted to full general. He then served as Supreme Allied Commander Europe and, finally, as chief of staff of the Army. He retired in 1955 and died in Fox Chapel, Pennsylvania, in 1993.[25]

General Hodges promoted Robert W. Hasbrouck to major general on January 4, 1945. Hasbrouck commanded the 7th AD until August 1945, when he returned to the United States, where he served as chief of staff for Army ground forces until he retired in 1947. After the war Hasbrouck served on the Hoover Commission, which was chartered to make recommendations on the organization of the executive branch of the government. He also served as a director on two corporate boards. He died in 1985.[26]

Bruce C. Clarke and William M. Hoge had long and successful careers. Both commanded during the Korean War. In late 1945 Clarke commanded the 4th AD in Germany. Later he commanded the 1st AD at Fort Hood, Texas, from 1951 to 1953. Then he commanded I Corps in Korea. Clarke served as commander in chief for US Army Europe in his final assignment, retiring as a full general in 1962. He died in 1988.

William M. Hoge, who, like Clarke, was commissioned in the Army Corps of Engineers, led CCB through March 1945, capping off his tenure by seizing the Ludendorff Bridge at Remagen on the Rhine. He then took command of the 4th AD until July 1945, when he returned to the United States. Hoge served on various staffs and then commanded IX Corps in Korea. He served as commander in chief for US Army Europe from 1953 to 1955, retiring as a full general. After serving on various corporate boards, he retired to Missouri but eventually moved to his son's home in Easton, Kansas. He died in 1979.[27]

Thomas J. Riggs, who led the initial defense on the Prümerberg, remained in the Army and retired as a colonel. He died in 1998.[28]

Robert C. Erlenbusch of the 31st TB stayed in the Army. He later commanded the 11th Cavalry Regiment on the inner-German border during the Cold War. He died in 1985.[29]

John P. Wemple, who commanded the 17th TB, left the Army to return to Louisiana, where he worked in the oil business. He died in 1988.[30]

Donald P. Boyer, the operations officer of the 38th Armored Infantry, re-turned home from a German prisoner of war camp. He, too, commanded the 11th Cavalry Regiment on the inner-German Border and retired as a colonel. He died in 2001.

Roy U. Clay, 275th Armored Field Artillery Battalion, retired as a colonel, ran physical plants for two different colleges, and then prepared tax returns in Boiling Springs, Pennsylvania. He died in 1993.[31]

Fred M. Warren, who commanded Combat Command Reserve during the Bulge, returned to his law practice but remained in the Army Reserve. Eventually he commanded the Army Reserve as a major general. He died in 1986.[32]

Owen E. Woodruff Jr., who served as Clarke's operations officer in CCB, made a career in the Army. He served in the postwar constabulary in Berlin, and later applied for specialized training and went to law school at the University of San Francisco. After law school Woodruff transferred to the Judge Advocate General Corps. He retired as a colonel in 1963. Eventually he became a magistrate in the Federal District Court for San Francisco, where he served until 1997. He died in 2008.[33]

Will Rogers Jr., who gave up a seat in the House of Representatives to serve with the 814th Tank Destroyer Battalion, left the Army in 1946. He ran unsuccessfully for a Senate seat in California that same year. He remained active in the Democratic Party and in American Indian Affairs. In 1993 he committed suicide.[34]

John Schaffner, the 106th Infantry Division soldier who fought on the Schnee Eifel and at Parkers' Crossroads, as of this writing remains hale and hearty and helpful to anyone who would like to know the story of those who fought in the Bulge. He left the Army in November 1945 at Camp San Luis Obispo, California. The Army issued him a new uniform and sent him on his way. Schaffner believed his postwar career was "not unusual for his generation." He worked in what would later become known as information technology, retiring as senior computer systems analyst. He married his "love," Lil, and was married for over seventy years. Sadly, Lil passed in April 2019. John Schaffner and his "love" raised three children, and he has six grandchildren and nine great-grandchildren.[35]

Charles Haug's memoir "Courageous Defenders" is a compelling narrative of the fighting withdrawal of the 112th Infantry Regiment. Haug made it home to Minnesota, where he returned to banking, ultimately running a bank in the city of Sleepy Eye. He died in 2017.[36]

Richard L. McBride, who led a mortar section in A Company, 23rd Armored Infantry Battalion, continued on with his outfit, led by Navajo Whiteman. McBride described the battle to reduce the Ruhr Pocket as particularly harrowing. In some villages the Germans festooned their windows with bedsheets, and in others determined Nazis and/or German patriots confronted the Division. On April 4, 1945, McBride's luck ran out when a German mortar peppered his back with shrapnel near the village of Küstelberg, Germany, some thirty miles north of the university town of Marburg on the eastern side of the Ruhr Pocket. McBride made his way through the evacuation system to the United Kingdom following his first ride in an airplane—a C-47. He recalled there were twenty-four wounded on the evacuation flight, including two Nazi "supermen" cared for by a "pretty young nurse" whose "presence helped a lot." McBride missed the rest of the war. On May 3, 1945, he embarked on the troop ship USS *General Meigs* and arrived in the "zone of interior" on May 15, 1945.[37]

McBride concluded his memoir by writing that he hoped "the friends we have all made during the fighting overseas will never be forgotten, and that our pride in our outfit will remain a strong bond, helping to unite us and make still firmer our time of friendship." His division drove on, literally to the beaches of the Baltic Sea, on May 3, 1945, where Robert W. Hasbrouck indulged himself by wetting the tracks of his tank in the sea. He and his soldiers had done what they were asked.[38]

NOTES

1. LTC Robert C. Erlenbusch to Commanding General, III Corps, March 22, 1945, Major General Robert W. Hasbrouck Collection.

2. General der Artillerie Walther Lucht, "LXVI Infantry Corps," 2.

3. Edwin B. Coddington, *The Gettysburg Campaign*, 186.

4. Chester Wilmot, *The Struggle for Europe*, 584, emphasis in the original.

5. Clarke provided the author with a reprint of an article in published in *Military Review*, September 1961, that he used to illustrate what he called "mission type orders"; General Bruce C. Clarke Papers.

6. Clay Blair, *Ridgway's Paratroopers*, 53.

7. Roy U. Clay, "Tinstaafl: Autobiography of Roy U. Clay, Colonel (Ret.)," 94; General Bruce C. Clarke (Ret.), interview with the author, McLean, VA, August 20, 1984, General Bruce C. Clarke Papers; Major General Robert W. Hasbrouck (Ret.), interview with the author, Washington, DC, August 20, 1984. Clarke, in particular, resented Ridgway.

8. Major William R. Keast, *Provision of Enlisted Replacements*, Army Ground Forces Study No. 7 (Washington, DC: Historical Section, US Army Ground Forces, 1946), 22.

9. "Statement of General William Allen Knowlton," 6. The statement accompanied General William A. Knowlton (Ret.) to the author, November 15, 1984, and was one he provided in response to a request from a military museum in Bastogne, Belgium.

10. Lord Moran, *The Anatomy of Courage*. Lord Moran's work remains a classic in the effort to understand human limits.

11. General William A. Knowlton (Ret.) to the author, December 13, 1984.

12. US War Department, *Armored Command Field Manual: The Armored Division*, FM 17-100, 88–91. See also Major General Matthew B. Ridgway, war diary, entry for commanders' conference, at XVIII Airborne Corps, 1605, January 14, 1945, Matthew B. Ridgway Papers.

13. US War Department, *Field Service Regulations: Operations*, FM 100-5, 241.

14. Generalmajor Friedrich Kittel, "62nd Volksgrenadier Division," 10. Manteuffel expressed surprise at the speed of the reaction as well.

15. Matthew Cooper, *The German Army 1933–1945*, 527.

16. Donald Grey Brownlow, *Panzer Baron*, 158, 159–64.

17. The publishing house was Samisdat; see "Samisdat Publishers," Revolvy, https://www.revolvy.com/page/Samisdat-Publishers. There are at least three different YouTube videos of postwar interviews or presentations; all of them reveal that Remer had not abandoned fascism.

18. Danny S. Parker, *Hitler's Warrior*, 270–85. Parker devoted the chapter "Ghosts of the Past" to recount the theories about who killed Peiper and the outrages perpetrated by Nazi sympathizers after Peiper's death.

19. In March 1999, Klaus Ritter answered a questionnaire about his war experience that was in 2008 posted to a website; see "Klaus Ritter Letter, dated 4 June 1999," Stenger Historica, http://www.stengerhistorica.com/History/WarArchive/Veteran Voices/RitterQuestionairre.htm. See also Klaus Ritter, statements, box 10, Charles B. MacDonald Papers, pt. 1.

20. Heinz Günther Guderian, *From Normandy to the Ruhr*, 608. See also "Guderian, Heinz Günther Jr.," World War II Graves, https://ww2gravestone.com/people/guderian-heinz-gunther.

21. See Bernard Law Montgomery, *The Memoirs of Field-Marshal the Viscount Montgomery of Alamein*; and Nigel Hamilton, *Monty: The Battles of Field Marshal Bernard Montgomery*.

22. The chief source on Eisenhower used in this narrative is Stephen E. Ambrose, *The Supreme Commander*.

23. Omar N. Bradley and Clay Blair, *A General's Life: An Autobiography*, 446, 448. On Bradley's service as chief of staff and chairman of the Joint Chiefs, see 449–663.

24. David W. Hogan Jr., *A Command Post at War*, 294. Hodges's personal papers are at the Dwight D. Eisenhower Presidential Library and Museum.

25. Harold R. Winton, *Corps Commanders of the Bulge*, 352–53. See also Matthew B. Ridgway, *Soldier: The Memoirs of Matthew B. Ridgway*.

26. Robert Wilson Hasbrouck, military biography, box 7, Charles B. MacDonald Papers; see also "Gen. Robert Hasbrouck, 89, Dies," *Washington Post*, August 21, 1985, https://www.washingtonpost.com/archive/local/1985/08/21/gen-robert-hasbrouck -89-dies/999276b4-2e0e-4c6c-bc16-11846474fe87/?noredirect=on&ut m_term=.246ce37c5bb6.

27. General William M. Hoge, *Engineer Memoirs*; see also "Retired Gen. William Hoge, 85," *Washington Post*, October 29, 1979, https://www.washingtonpost.com /archive/local/1979/11/04/retired-gen-william-hoge-85/e6ce0c4c-06d9-4724-869b-90cec0239b0b/?utm_term=.e7c5c6c0ef3e.

28. "Thomas J. Riggs, Colonel, United States Army," Arlington National Cemetery, www.arlingtoncemetery.net/tjriggs.htm.

29. Information on Robert C. Erlenbusch comes from Erlenbusch's papers, in the possession of the author.

30. For more on Wemple, see "John Patton Wemple," Home of the Wemple Family History, https://www.wemple.org/getperson.php?personID=I3679&tree=Wemple; and William S. Triplet, *A Colonel in the Armored Divisions*, 166.

31. "Roy Udell Clay," Justin Museum, http://www.justinmuseum.com/oralbio /clayrubio.html. The Justin Museum commemorates the Civilian Conservation Corps.

32. For more on Frederick M. Warren, see David E. Hilkert, *Chiefs of the Army Reserve*, 192–203.

33. Woodruff remained in touch with Clarke throughout Clarke's life. The data on Woodruff's postwar career is taken from his obituary in the *San Francisco Chronicle*, which ran September 9–14, 2008; see "Judge Owen E. Woodruff Jr.," SF-Gate, https://www.legacy.com/obituaries/sfgate/obituary.aspx?n=owen-e-woodruff &pid=117163078.

34. Sonia Nazario, "Ailing Will Rogers Jr., 81, Commits Suicide," *Los Angeles Times*, July 11, 1993, https://www.latimes.com/archives/la-xpm-1993-07-11-me-12271-story.html.

35. John Schaffner, email to the author, October 16, 2018. John Schaffner, telephone interview with the author, December 3, 2017.

36. "Charles Alden Haug, 1922–2017," Sturm Funeral Home, https://sturmfh. com/tribute/details/6007/Charles-Haug/obituary.html. See also Haug, "Courageous Defenders."

37. Richard L. McBride, "Grinding Through with the 7th Armored Division," 311–15.

38. McBride, "Grinding Through," 316; Seventh Armored Division, *From the Beaches to the Baltic*, 57; Major General Robert W. Hasbrouck (Ret.), interview with the author, August 20, 1984. McBride returned home to Westchester County, New York, to work in the family business, and died there in 2009. The author regrets never knowing him.

Table of Ranks through Lieutenant Colonel

US Army	German Army	Schutzstaffel
General of the Army	Generalfeldmarschall	Reichsfürhrer
General	Oberstgeneral	Oberstgruppenführer
Lieutenant General	General (der Infanterie, etc.)	Obergruppenführer
Major General	Generalleutnant	Gruppenführer
Brigadier General	Generalmajor	Brigadeführer
No equivalent	No equivalent	Oberführer
Colonel	Oberst	Standartenführer
Lieutenant Colonel	Oberstleutnant	Obersturmbannführer

Troop List—7th Armored Division

Organic Units

Headquarters and Headquarters Company, 7th Armored Division

Headquarters and Headquarters Company, Combat Command A

Headquarters and Headquarters Company, Combat Command B

Headquarters and Headquarters Company, Combat Command Reserve 87th Cavalry Reconnaissance Squadron (Mechanized)

23rd Armored Infantry Battalion

38th Armored Infantry Battalion

48th Armored Infantry Battalion

17th Tank Battalion

31st Tank Battalion

40th Tank Battalion

Headquarters and Headquarters Battery Division Artillery

    434th Armored Field Artillery Battalion

    440th Armored Field Artillery Battalion

    489th Armored Field Artillery Battalion

Headquarters and Headquarters Company Division Trains

33rd Armored Engineer Battalion

77th Armored Medical Battalion

129th Armored Ordnance Maintenance Battalion

147th Armored Signal Company

Military Police Platoon

Habitually Attached Units

203rd Anti-Aircraft Artillery Battalion (Automatic Weapons)

814th Tank Destroyer Battalion

446th Quartermaster Troop Transport Company
3967th Quartermaster Truck Company

Attached or Supporting Units in December 1944

From VIII Corps
14th Cavalry Group
18th Cavalry Reconnaissance Squadron (Mechanized)
32nd Cavalry Reconnaissance Squadron (Mechanized)
275th Armored Field Artillery Battalion
965th Field Artillery Battalion (155-millimeter howitzer)
168th Engineer Combat Battalion
440th Anti-Aircraft Artillery Battalion (Automatic Weapons)

From the 106th Infantry Division
Headquarters and Headquarters Company
820th Tank Destroyer Battalion (Towed)
424th Infantry Regiment
3rd Platoon, Company F, 423rd Infantry Regiment
Headquarters and Headquarters Battery Division Artillery 589th Field Artillery Battalion
    591st Field Artillery Battalion
    592nd Field Artillery Battalion (155-millimeter howitzer)
81st Engineer Combat Battalion
Note: The 106th ID service support units are not included.

From the 9th Armored Division
Headquarters and Headquarters Company, Combat Command B
Troop D, 89th Cavalry Reconnaissance Squadron (Mechanized)
with platoons from Troop E (assault guns) and Troop F (light tanks)
27th Armored Infantry Battalion
Company C, 131st Ordnance Maintenance Battalion
14th Tank Battalion
16th Armored Field Artillery Battalion
Company B, 9th Armored Engineer Battalion
Company A, 811th Tank Destroyer Battalion
Battery B, 489th Anti-Aircraft Artillery Battalion (Automatic Weapons)
Company B, 2nd Armored Medical Battalion

From the 28th Infantry Division
112th Infantry Regiment

229th Field Artillery Battalion
Company C, 103rd Engineer Combat Battalion

From the 517th Parachute Infantry Regiment

3rd Battalion, 517th Parachute Infantry Regiment

Attached or Supporting in January 1945

From XVIII Airborne Corps

275th Armored Field Artillery Battalion
987th Field Artillery Battalion (155-millimeter howitzer)
Company B 738th Tank Battalion (Special) (mine exploders)
Detachment, 994th Treadway Bridge Company (floating bridge with two tracks)
299th Engineer Combat Battalion
2nd Battalion, 517th Parachute Infantry Regiment
509th Parachute Infantry Battalion

From the 82nd Airborne Division

508th Parachute Infantry Regiment

German Units in Contact with 7th Armored Division

The primary sources for this list of German combatants include 7th Armored Division after action reports and G-2 (intelligence) notes; Charles B. MacDonald, *A Time for Trumpets*; Dietrich Moll, "18th Volksgrenadier Division, 1 Sep 1944–25 Jan 1945"; and Hubert Meyer, *The 12th SS: The History of the Hitler Youth Division*, vol. 2.

December 1944

Sixth Panzer Army
  506th Heavy Panzer Battalion (Tiger II or King Tiger)
  I Schutzstaffel (SS) Panzer Corps
    1st SS Panzer Division
      Kampfgruppe Peiper (formed on 1st SS Panzer Regiment)
      Kampfgruppe Hansen (formed on 1st SS Panzergrenadiers Regiment)
  II SS Panzer Corps
    2nd SS Panzer Division
      Kampfgruppe Krag (formed on 2nd SS Reconnaissance Battalion)
      2nd SS Panzer Regiment
      3rd SS Panzergrenadier Regiment
      4th SS Panzergrenadier Regiment
    9th SS Panzer Division
      9th SS Panzer Regiment
      19th SS Panzergrenadier Regiment
      20th SS Panzergrenadier Regiment
Fifth Panzer Army
  Führer Escort Brigade
  LVIII Panzer Corps

116th Panzer Division
  16th Panzer Regiment
  60th Panzergrenadier Regiment
  156th Panzergrenadier Regiment
  226th Anti-Tank Battalion (probable)
560th Volksgrenadier Division
  1128th Volksgrenadier Regiment
  1129th Volksgrenadier Regiment
  1130th Volksgrenadier Regiment
  1560th Anti-Tank Battalion
LXVI Corps
  244th Assault Gun Brigade
  16th Volks-Werfer Brigade
    86th Werfer Regiment
    87th Werfer Regiment
  460th Heavy Artillery Battalion (155-millimeter howitzer)
  18th Volksgrenadier Division
    293rd Volksgrenadier Regiment
    294th Volksgrenadier Regiment
    295th Volksgrenadier Regiment
    1818th Anti-Tank Battalion
    1818th Artillery Regiment (four battalions: two 75-millimeter, one
    105-millimeter, and one 150-millimeter)
  62nd Volksgrenadier Division
    164th Volksgrenadier Regiment
    190th Volksgrenadier Regiment
    193rd Volksgrenadier Regiment
    162nd Anti-Tank Battalion
    162nd Artillery Regiment (four battalions: two 75-millimeter, one
    105-millimeter, and one 150-millimeter)

Note: Artillery used in direct support of LXVI Corps is included. Supporting units are not included unless there are verifiable reports of direct contact.

January 1945

When the 7th Armored Division (AD) went on the offensive on January 20, 1945, it went against the newly formed XIII Corps and the 18th Volksgrenadier Division (VGD). The 18th VGD received some support from several units originally assigned to the Sixth Panzer Army. On January 21, 1945, the 18th VGD supported by tanks from the 1st SS Panzer

Division and infantry from the 246th VGD. After the fall of St. Vith, the 12th SS Panzer Division, 246th VGD, and 326th VGD all defended against the 7th AD.

The 12th SS, like the 2nd SS, had been redeployed from the Sixth Panzer Army to the Fifth Panzer Army. By mid-January, however, the Division chief of staff accurately considered the Division to be understrength in men and equipment. On January 12, for example, the 12th SS employed three tanks and "several" Panzerjäger IVs. Several tanks were being repaired, but by the end of January, when the 12th SS withdrew to be redeployed east, it had to be rebuilt.

Bibliography

Documents take varying forms, and are inconsistent in how authors are credited and how the documents are titled and dated. In general, all such elements are cited as they appear in the original documents, with only minor changes made where deemed necessary for clarity.

Books

Ambrose, Stephen E. *The Supreme Commander: The War Years of General Dwight D. Eisenhower.* Garden City, NY: Doubleday, 1969.

Astor, Gerald. *Battling Buzzards: The Odyssey of the 517th Parachute Regimental Combat Team, 1943–1945.* New York: Fine, 1993.

———. *A Blood-Dimmed Tide: The Battle of the Bulge by the Men Who Fought It.* New York: Fine, 1992.

Atkinson, Rick. *The Guns at Last Light: The War in Western Europe, 1944–1945.* New York: Holt, 2013.

Bastrup, Boyd L. *King of Battle: A Branch History of the US Army's Field Artillery.* Fort Monroe, VA: Office of the Command Historian, US Army Training and Doctrine Command, 1992.

Beevor, Anthony. *The Ardennes 1944: The Battle of the Bulge.* New York: Viking, 2015.

Bergstrom, Christer. *The Ardennes 1944–1945: Hitler's Winter Offensive.* Havertown, PA: Casemate, 2014.

Blair, Clay. *Ridgway's Paratroopers: The American Airborne in World War II.* Garden City, NY: Dial, 1985.

Blumenson, Martin. *Breakout and Pursuit.* Washington, DC: Office of the Chief of Military History, 1961.

———. *The Patton Papers.* Vol. 2, *1940–1945.* Boston: Houghton Mifflin, 1974.

Boykin, Calvin C., Jr. *Gare la Bête (Beware the Beast): A History of the 814th Tank Destroyer Battalion, 1942–1945.* College Station, TX: C and R, 1995.

Bradley, Omar N. *A Soldier's Story.* New York: Popular Library, 1964.

Bradley, Omar N., and Clay Blair. *A General's Life: An Autobiography.* New York: Simon and Schuster, 1983.

Brown, John Sloan. *Draftee Division: The 88th Infantry Division in World War II.* Lexington: University Press of Kentucky, 1986.

Brownlow, Donald Grey. *Panzer Baron: The Military Exploits of General Hasso von Manteuffel.* North Quincy, MA: Christopher, 1977.

Burning, John R. *The Battle of the Bulge: The Photographic History of an American Triumph.* Minneapolis: Zenith, 2009.

Butcher, Harry C. *My Three Years with Eisenhower: The Personal Diary of Captain Harry C. Butcher, USNR.* New York: Simon and Schuster, 1946.

Caddick-Adams, Peter. *Snow and Steel: The Battle of the Bulge, 1944–45.* New York: Oxford University Press, 2015.

Cameron, Robert S. *Mobility, Shock, and Firepower: The Emergence of the U.S. Army's Armor Branch, 1917–1945.* Washington, DC: Center of Military History, 2008.

Cavanagh, William C. C. *The Battle East of Elsenborn and the Twin Villages.* South Yorkshire, England: Pen and Sword, 2004.

Cavanagh, William C. C., and Karl Cavanagh. *A Tour of the Bulge Battlefields.* South Yorkshire, England: Pen and Sword, 2004.

Cirillo, Roger. *Ardennes-Alsace, 1944–1945.* Washington, DC: Center of Military History, 1995.

Citino, Robert M. *Blitzkrieg to Desert Storm: The Evolution of Operational Warfare.* Lawrence: University Press of Kansas, 2004.

Clausewitz, Carl von. *On War.* Edited and translated by Michael Howard and Peter Paret. Princeton, NJ: Princeton University Press, 1984.

Clay, Roy U. *Curbstone: The History of the 275th Field Artillery Battalion in World War II.* Jackson, TN: Richerson, 1978.

Coddington, Edwin B. *The Gettysburg Campaign: A Study in Command.* New York: Scribner's, 1979.

Coffman, Edward M. *The Regulars: The American Army, 1898–1941.* Cambridge, MA: Belnap, 2004.

Cole, Hugh M. *The Ardennes: Battle of the Bulge.* Washington, DC: Center of Military History, 1965.

———. *The Lorraine Campaign.* Washington, DC: Office of the Chief of Military History, 1950.

Collins, General J. Lawton. *Lightning Joe: An Autobiography.* Baton Rouge: Louisiana State University Press, 1979.

Condell, Bruce, and David T. Zabecki, eds. *On the German Art of War: Truppenführung.* Boulder, CO: Rienner, 2001.

Cooper, Matthew. *The German Army 1933–1945: Its Political and Military Failure.* New York: Stein and Day, 1978.

Corum, James S. *The Roots of Blitzkrieg: Hans von Seeckt and German Military Reform.* Lawrence: University Press of Kansas, 1992.

Crosswell, D. K. R. *Beetle: The Life of General Walter Bedell Smith.* Lexington: University Press of Kentucky, 2010.

Davis, John, with Anne Riffenburg. *Up Close: A Scout's Story, from the Battle of the Bulge to the Siegfried Line.* Bennington, VT: Merriam, 2012.

Dupuy, Colonel R. Ernest. *St. Vith: Lion in the Way; The 106th Infantry Division in World War II.* Washington, DC: Infantry Journal Press, 1949.

Dupuy, Trevor N. *A Genius for War: The German Army and the General Staff, 1801–1945.* Garden City, NY: Military Book Club, 1977.

Eisenhower, Dwight D. *Crusade in Europe.* Garden City, NY: Doubleday, 1948.

Eisenhower, John S. D. *The Bitter Woods: The Battle of the Bulge.* New York: Putnam's, 1969.

Ellis, William Donohue, and Colonel Thomas J. Cunningham Jr. *Clarke of St. Vith: The Sergeants' General.* Cleveland: Dillon/Leiderbach, 1974.

Elstob, Peter. *Hitler's Last Offensive.* Barnsley, England: Pen and Sword, 2003.

Fey, Will. *Armor Battles of the Waffen-SS 1943–1945.* Winnipeg, MB: Fedorowicz, 1990.

Forty, George. *U.S. Army Handbook, 1939–1945.* New York: Barnes and Noble, 1998.

Forty, Simon. *American Armor: 1939–1945 Portfolio.* Harrisburg, PA: Stackpole, 1981.

Freeman, Douglas Southall. *Lee's Lieutenants: A Study in Command.* New York: Simon and Schuster, 2001.

Frieser, Karl Heinz, with John T. Greenwood. *The Blitzkrieg Legend: The 1940 Campaign in the West.* Annapolis, MD: Naval Institute Press, 2005.

Fritz, Stephen G. *Front Soldaten: The German Soldier in World War II.* Lexington: University Press of Kentucky, 1995.

Gavin, James M. *On to Berlin: Battles of an Airborne Commander, 1943–1946.* New York: Viking, 1978.

Giles, Janice Holt. *The Damned Engineers.* Washington, DC: Office of the Chief of Engineers, 1985.

Goldstein, Elliot, 589th Group. *On the Job Training: An Oral History of the Battle of Parker's Crossroads and of the Fate of Those Who Survived.* Self-published, 1999.

Greenfield, Kent Roberts, ed. *Command Decisions.* Washington, DC: Center of Military History, 1987.

Greenfield, Kent Roberts, Robert R. Palmer, and Bell I. Wiley. *The Organization of Ground Combat Troops.* Washington, DC: Center of Military History, 1947.

Gross, Gerhard P. *The Myth and Reality of German Warfare: Operational Thinking from Moltke the Elder to Heusinger.* Edited by Major General David T. Zabecki, USA (Ret.). Lexington: University Press of Kentucky, 2016.

Guderian, Heinz Günther. *From Normandy to the Ruhr: With the 116th Panzer Division in World War II.* Bedford, PA: Aberjona, 2001.

Guillemot, Philippe. *The Battle of the Bulge: The Failure of the Final Blitzkrieg.* Translated by Marie-France Renwick. Paris: Histoire and Collections, 2015.

Hamilton, Nigel. *Monty: The Battles of Field Marshal Bernard Montgomery.* New York: Random House, 1994.

Hanson, Victor Davis. *The Second World Wars: How the First Global Conflict Was Fought and Won*. New York: Basic Books, 2017.

Hewitt, Robert L. *Work Horse of the Western Front: The Story of the 30th Infantry Division*. Washington, DC: Infantry Journal Press, 1946.

Hilkert, David E. *Chiefs of the Army Reserve: Biographical Sketches of the United States Army Reserve's Senior Officers*. Fort McPherson, GA: Office of Army Reserve History, 2004.

Hills, R. J. T. *Phantom Was There*. London: Arnold, 1951.

Hogan, David W., Jr. *A Command Post at War: First Army Headquarters in Europe, 1943–1945*. Washington, DC: Center of Military History, 2000.

Hoge, General William M. *Engineer Memoirs: General William M. Hoge, US Army*. Washington, DC: US Army Corps of Engineers, 1993.

Ingersoll, Ralph. *Top Secret*. New York: Harcourt, Brace, 1946.

Johnson, David E. *Fast Tanks and Heavy Bombers: Innovation in the U.S. Army, 1917–1945*. Ithaca, NY: Cornell University Press, 1998.

Keegan, John. *The Second World War*. New York: Penguin, 2005.

Kelly, C. J. *Red Legs of the Bulge: Artillerymen in the Battle of the Bulge*. Bennington, VT: Merriam, 2014.

Kershaw, Alex. *The Longest Winter: The Battle of the Bulge and the Epic Story of World War II's Most Decorated Platoon*. Cambridge, MA: Da Capo, 2004.

Kirkpatrick, Charles E. *An Unknown Future and Doubtful Present: Writing the Victory Plan of 1941*. Washington, DC: Center of Military History, 1990.

Koch, Brigadier General Oscar W., with Robert G. Hays. *G-2: Intelligence for Patton*. Atglen, PA: Schiffer Military History, 1999.

Liddell Hart, B. H. *History of the Second World War*. New York: Putnam's, 1970.

Ludewig, Joachim. *Rückzug: The German Retreat from France, 1944*. Edited by David T. Zabecki, AUS (Ret). Lexington: University Press of Kentucky, 2012.

MacDonald, Charles B. *Company Commander*. New York: Bantam, 1978.

——. *The Mighty Endeavor: American Armed Forces in the European Theater in World War II*. New York: Oxford University Press, 1969.

——. *The Siegfried Line Campaign*. Washington, DC: Office of the Chief of Military History, Department of the Army, 1963.

——. *A Time for Trumpets: The Untold Story of the Battle of the Bulge*. New York: Morrow, 1985.

Mansoor, Peter R. *The GI Offensive in Europe: The Triumph of the American Infantry Divisions, 1941–1945*. Lawrence: University Press of Kansas, 1999.

Martin, Harry F., Jr. *I Was No Hero in the Battle of the Bulge*. Self-published, CreateSpace, 2016.

Matloff, Maurice. *Strategic Planning for Coalition Warfare: 1943–1944*. Washington, DC: Center of Military History, 1959.

McManus, John C. *Alamo in the Ardennes: The Untold Story of the American Soldiers Who Made the Defense of Bastogne Possible*. New York: NAL Caliber, 2008.

Merriam, Robert E. *Dark December: The Full Account of the Battle of the Bulge*. Yardley, PA: Westholme, 2011.

Meyer, George C. *Mud, Dust and Five Stars: The Story of Your Battalion from Activation to the Close of the War.* Dusseldorf: Bagel, 1945.

Meyer, Hubert. *The 12th SS: The History of the Hitler Youth Panzer Division.* 2 vols.
Translated by H. Harri Henschler. Mechanicsburg, PA: Stackpole, 2005.

Miller, Edward G. *Nothing Less Than Full Victory: Americans at War in Europe,
1944–1945.* Annapolis, MD: Naval Institute Press, 2007.

Mitcham, Samuel W., Jr. *Panzers in Winter: Hitler's Army and the Battle of the Bulge.*
Mechanicsburg, PA: Stackpole, 2006.

Montgomery, Bernard Law. *The Memoirs of Field-Marshal the Viscount Montgomery of Alamein.* Cleveland: World, 1958.

Moran, Lord [Charles McMoran Wilson, 1st Baron Moran]. *The Anatomy of Courage.* Garden City Park, NY: Avery, 1987.

Morelock, Jerry D. *Generals of the Bulge: Leadership in the U.S. Army's Greatest
Battle.* Mechanicsburg, PA: Stackpole, 2015.

Morse, John W. *The Sitting Duck Division: Attacked from the Rear.* Lincoln, NE:
Writers Club Press, 2001.

Nafziger, George F. *German Army: Battle of the Bulge, 15 December 1944.* Nafziger
Orders of Battle Collection, Ike Skelton Combined Arms Research Library, Fort Leavenworth, KS. https://usacac.army.mil/cac2/CGSC/CARL/
nafziger/944GLAA.pdf.

Nance, William Stuart. *Sabers through the Reich: World War II Corps Cavalry from
Normandy to the Elbe.* Lexington: University Press of Kentucky, 2017.

Pallud, Jean-Paul. *Battle of the Bulge: Then and Now.* London: After the Battle, 1984.

Parker, Danny S., ed. *The Battle of the Bulge: The German View.* Mechanicsburg, PA:
Stackpole, 1999.

———. *Hitler's Warrior: The Life and Wars of SS Colonel Jochen Peiper.* Boston: Da
Capo, 2014.

Perret, Geoffrey. *There's a War to Be Won: The United States Army in World War II.*
New York: Random House, 1991.

Phillips, Robert F. *To Save Bastogne.* New York: Stein and Day, 1983.

Pogue, Forrest C. *George C. Marshall: Organizer of Victory, 1943–1945.* New York:
Viking, 1973.

Price, Frank James. *Troy H. Middleton: A Biography.* Baton Rouge: Louisiana State
University Press, 1974.

Reynolds, Michael. *The Devil's Adjutant: Jochen Peiper, Panzer Leader.* Barnsley,
England: Pen and Sword, 2009.

———. *Sons of the Reich: II SS Panzer Corps; Normandy, Arnhem, Ardennes, Eastern Front.* Havertown, PA: Casemate, 2002.

Rickard, John Nelson. *Advance and Destroy: Patton as Commander in the Bulge.*
Lexington: University Press of Kentucky, 2011.

Ridgway, Matthew B., with Martin H. Martin. *Soldier: The Memoirs of Matthew B.
Ridgway.* New York: Harper, 1956.

Ruppenthal, Roland G. *Logistical Support of the Armies: Volume II: September
1944–May 1945.* Washington, DC: Office of the Chief of Military History,
Department of the Army, 1959.

Schrijvers, Peter. *Those Who Hold Bastogne: The True Story of the Soldiers and Civilians Who Fought in the Biggest Battle of the Bulge.* New Haven, CT: Yale University Press, 2014.

———. *The Unknown Dead: Civilians in the Battle of the Bulge.* Lexington: University Press of Kentucky, 2005.

Seventh Annual Convention Committee of the 106th Infantry Division Association. *The Lion's Tale: Short Stories of the 106th Infantry Division.* N.p: Seventh Annual Convention Committee of the 106th Infantry Division Association, 1953.

7th Armored Division, *From the Beaches to the Baltic: The Story of the 7th Armored Division.* Heidelberg: Heidelberger Gutenberger-Druckerei, n.d. https://www.7tharmddiv.org/docrep/images/7AD/Wartime%20Publications/From-the-Beaches-to-the-Baltic.pdf.

Smith, Walter Bedell. *Eisenhower's Six Great Decisions: Europe 1944–1945.* New York: Longmans, Green, 1956.

Sparks, Richard D. *A Walk through the Woods.* Self-published, 1991.

Stars and Stripes. *The 106th: The Story of the 106th Infantry Division.* Paris: Stars and Stripes, n.d.

Sylvan, Major William C., and Captain Francis G. Smith Jr. *Normandy to Victory: The War Diary of General Courtney H. Hodges and the First U.S. Army.* Edited by John T. Greenwood. Lexington: University Press of Kentucky, 2008.

Tapper, Jake. *The Outpost: An Untold Story of American Valor.* New York: Little, Brown, 2012.

Toland, John. *Battle: The Story of the Bulge.* New York: Random House, 1959.

Triplet, William S. *A Colonel in the Armored Divisions: A Memoir, 1941–1945.* Edited by Robert H. Ferrell. Columbia: University of Missouri Press, 2001.

US 7th Armored Division Association. *The Lucky Seventh.* Dallas: Taylor, 1982.

Van Creveld, Martin. *Fighting Power: German and U.S. Army Performance, 1939–1945.* Westport, CT: Greenwood, 1982.

Veterans of the Battle of the Bulge, Inc., ed. and comp. *The Battle of the Bulge: True Stories of the Men and Women Who Survived.* Reading, PA: Aperture Press, 2014.

Weidinger, Otto. *Das Reich.* Vol. 5, *1943–1945: 2 SS Panzer Division.* Translated by Klaus Scharley and Fred Steinhardt. Winnipeg, MB: Fedorowicz, 2012.

Weigley, Russell F. *Eisenhower's Lieutenants: The Campaign of France and Germany, 1944–1945.* Bloomington: Indiana University Press, 1981.

Wheeler, James Scott. *Jacob L. Devers: A General's Life.* Lexington: University Press of Kentucky, 2015.

Whiting, Charles. *Death of a Division.* New York: Stein and Day, 1981.

———. *Decision at St. Vith.* Havertown, PA: Casemate, 2014.

———. *Ghost Front: The Ardennes before the Battle of the Bulge; The Story of America's Worst Intelligence Blunder of World War II.* Cambridge, MA: Da Capo Press, 2002.

———. *The Last Assault: The Battle of the Bulge Reassessed.* Aylesford, England: Bookzat, 2018.

Wilmot, Chester. *The Struggle for Europe.* Old Saybrook, CT: Konecky and Konecky, 1952.

Wilson, John B. *Maneuver and Firepower: The Evolution of Divisions and Separate Brigades.* Washington, DC: Center of Military History, 1998.

Winter, George J. *Manhay, the Ardennes, Christmas 1944.* Winnipeg, MB: Fedorowicz, 1990.

Winton, Harold R. *Corps Commanders of the Bulge: Six American Generals and Victory in the Ardennes.* Lawrence: University Press of Kansas, 2007.

Yale, Wesley W., Isaac D. White, and Hasso von Manteuffel. *Alternative to Armageddon: The Peace Potential of Lightning War.* New Brunswick, NJ: Rutgers University Press, 1970.

Articles

Barrows, Frederick M. "The Einheit Theory." *Military Review* 21, no. 83 (1942): 41–43.

Benitez, Lieutenant Colonel E. M. "Field Organization of the Services of Supply in the German Army." *Military Review* 19, no. 74 (1939): 49–53.

Blumenson, Lieutenant Colonel Martin. "Relieved of Command." *Army,* August 1971, 30–37.

Hargreaves, Patrick. "With the Company Commander." *After the Battle* 73 (1991): 4–10.

Judge, Colonel D. J. "Cavalry in the Defense Dec. 16–18 1944." *Armor,* October–December 2014, 70–79.

Kelley, Lieutenant Colonel Kevin. "All He Ever Wanted to Be Was a Soldier." *Armor* 102, no. 6 (1993): 46–49.

Lary, 1st Lt. Virgil P., Jr. "The Massacre at Malmedy." *Field Artillery Journal* 36, no. 2 (1946): 80–82.

MacDonald, Charles B. "The Neglected Ardennes." *Military Review* 43, no. 4 (1963): 74–89.

Raymond, Captain Allen D., III. "The Battle of St. Vith." *Armor* 73 (1964): 5–11.

Reeves, Lieutenant Colonel Joseph R. "Artillery in the Ardennes." *Field Artillery Journal* 36, no. 3 (1946): 138–42, 173–84.

"What Price Feet?" *Army Talks* 2, no. 48 (1944): 13–15.

Whipple, Colonel William. "Logistical Problems during the German Ardennes Offensive." *Military Review* 28, no. 2 (1948): 18–26.

Unpublished Manuscripts

Clay, Roy U. "Tinstaafl: Autobiography of Roy U. Clay, Colonel USA Retired." N.d. Courtesy of the family of Colonel Roy U. Clay.

Compana, Victor W. "The Operations of the 2nd Battalion, 504th Parachute Infantry (82nd A/B DIV) in the German Counter Offensive, 18 December 1944–10 January 1945 (Ardennes Campaign)." Written for advanced infantry officers' course, class of 1946–1947, US Army Infantry School, Fort Benning, GA.

DiNardo, Richard Louis. "Germany's Panzer Arm: Anatomy and Performance." PhD diss., City University of New York, 1988.

Haug, Charles. "Courageous Defenders: As I Remember It." 1947. US Army Heritage and Education Center, Carlisle, PA.

Hollinger, Major John C. "The Operations of the 422nd Infantry Regiment (106th Infantry Division) in the Vicinity of Schlausenbach, Germany, 16–20 December 1944 (Ardennes-Alsace Campaign) (Personal Experience of an Assistant Regimental S-3)." Written for advanced infantry officers' course, US Army Infantry School, Fort Benning, GA, 1949–50.

Jones, Captain Allan W., Jr. "The Operations of the 423rd Infantry (106th Infantry Division) in the Vicinity of Schönberg during the Battle of the Ardennes, 16–19 December 1944, (Ardennes-Alsace Campaign) (Personal Experience of a Battalion Operations Officer)." N.d. Written for advanced infantry officers' course, US Army Infantry School, Fort Benning, GA, 1949–50.

Moon, Major William P., Jr. "The Operations of the 1st Battalion, 422nd Infantry Regiment, (106th Infantry Division) in the Vicinity of Schlausenbach, Germany, 10–19 December 1944 (Ardennes-Alsace Campaign) (Personal Experience of a Battalion Executive Officer)." N.d. Written for advanced infantry officers' course, US Army Infantry School, Fort Benning, GA, 1949–50.

9th Armored Division. Combat Command 'B' Battle of the Bulge, 16 December 1944–25 December 1944: Combat Narrative." US Army Heritage and Education Center, Carlisle, PA, n.d.

Pietranton, 1st Lt. Inf. Frank A., ed. "History of Company 'B' 820th Tank Destroyer Battalion." January 1946. https://www.tankdestroyer.net/images/stories/ArticlePDFs2/820th_TD_Bn_History_of_Co.__B_-_Edit.pdf.

Seitz, Richard Joe. "Chronology of Important Events in the Life of Richard Joe Seitz." 2000. Courtesy of the family of Richard Joe Seitz.

Allied Forces Official Documents

Supreme Headquarters Allied Expeditionary Force
Air Staff, Office of the Assistant Chief of Staff, A-3. "Report of Allied Air Force Operations from 17th–27th December 1944." N.d. US Air Force Historical Research Center, Maxwell Air Force Base, AL.

Office of the Assistant Chief of Staff, G-2. "Weekly Intelligence Summary: No. 37 week ending December 3, 1944." N.d. N-12426, Ike Skelton Combined Arms Research Library, Fort Leavenworth, KS.

———. "Weekly Intelligence Summary 40, week ending December 24, 1944." N.d. N-12426, Ike Skelton Combined Arms Research Library, Fort Leavenworth, KS.

US Armed Forces Official Documents

Official Publications

Army Talks, Dwight D. Eisenhower
Presidential Library and Museum, Abilene, KS

Army Talks was a command information periodical published for the European Theater of Operations. Many examples can be found online at the University of

Richmond Boatwright Memorial Library's "America at War" web database, http://dlxs.richmond.edu/w/wtp/titlebrowse.html.

Studies

European Command, Intelligence Division. "Tactical Study of Weather and Terrain." August 24, 1951.

Kays, Marvin D. *Weather Effects during the Battle of the Bulge and the Normandy Invasion.* White Sands Missile Range, New Mexico: US Army Electronics Research and Development Command, Atmospheric Sciences Laboratory, August 1982.

Keast, Major William R. *Provision of Enlisted Replacements.* Army Ground Forces Study No. 7. Washington, DC: Historical Section, US Army Ground Forces, 1946.

Thompson, Royce L. *American Intelligence on the German Counteroffensive 1 November–15 December 1944.* 2 vols. Washington, DC: Center of Military History, 1949.

US Army Armor School. *The Battle at St. Vith Belgium, 17–23 December 1944: An Historical Example of Armor in the Defense.* Fort Knox, KY: US Army Armor School, n.d. [1947?].

University of Oklahoma Research Institute. "Disaster in Battle: Two Pre-atomic Military Disasters." Operations Research Office, Johns Hopkins University, August 25, 1952.

Von Luttichau, Charles V. P. *The Ardennes Offensive, Germany's Situation in the Fall of 1944; Part II: The Economic Situation.* Washington, DC: Office of the Chief of Military History, March 1953.

US Army Air Force

Headquarters, 9th Air Force. "Report of Larger Ninth Air Force Organizations." December 12, 1944. US Air Force Historical Research Center, Maxwell Air Force Base, AL.

McDonald, Brigadier General George C. "Allied Air Power and the Ardennes Offensive: 15 December 1944–16 January 1945." March 16, 1945. US Air Force Historical Research Center, Maxwell Air Force Base, AL.

US War Department

US War Department. *Armored Command Field Manual: The Armored Division.* FM 17-100. Washington, DC: Government Printing Office, January 15, 1944.

——. *Armored Force Field Manual.* FM 17. Washington, DC: Government Printing Office, n.d.

——. *Armored Force Field Manual: Tank Gunnery.* FM 17-12. Washington, DC: Government Printing Office, April 22, 1943.

——. *Armored Force Field Manual: The Armored Battalion, Light and Medium.* FM 17-33. Washington, DC: Government Printing Office, September 18, 1942.

——. *Armored Force Field Manual: The Tank Company, Light and Medium.* FM 17-32. Washington, DC: Government Printing Office, August 2, 1942.

——— . *Armored Infantry Battalion*. FM 17-42. Washington, DC: Government Printing Office, November 1944.

——— . *Cavalry Reconnaissance Squadron, Mechanized*. Table of Organization 2-25. Washington, DC: US Department of War, September 15, 1943. http://www. warestablishments.net/U.S.A/Reconnaissance/Cavalry%20Reconnaissance %20Squadron%20Mechanized%20September%201943.pdf.

——— . *Dictionary of United States Army Terms*. TM 20-205. January 18, 1944.

——— .*Field Artillery Field Manual: Tactics and Technique*. FM 6-20. Washington, DC: Government Printing Office, July 10, 1941.

——— . *Field Service Regulations: Administration*. FM 100-10. Washington, DC: Government Printing Office, November 15, 1943.

——— . *Field Service Regulations: Operations*. FM 100-5. Washington, DC: Government Printing Office, May 22, 1941.

——— . *Infantry Field Manual: Rifle Regiment*. FM 7-40. Washington, DC: Government Printing Office, 1942.

——— . *M4 Sherman Medium Tank Crew Manual*. FM 17-76. Washington, DC: Government Printing Office, September 15, 1944.

——— . *M4 Sherman Medium Tank Technical Manual*. TM 9-759. Washington, DC: Government Printing Office, August 4, 1942.

——— . *Rifle Company, Armored Infantry Battalion*. Table of Organization 7–27. Washington, DC: US Department of War, September 15, 1943. http://www .militaryresearch.org/7-27%2015Sep43.pdf.

——— . *Technical Manual: Basic Half-Track Vehicles, M2, M3*. TM 9-710. Washington, DC: Government Printing Office, February 23, 1944.

——— . *Water Transportation: Ocean Going Vessels*. FM 55-105. Washington, DC: US Government Printing Office, September 25, 1944.

Manuscript Collections

General Bruce C. Clarke Papers and Correspondence

Bruce C. Clarke commanded Combat Command B, 7th Armored Division during the Battle of the Bulge. The author interviewed General Clarke in August 1984 and corresponded with him over the course of four years (1984–87). Clarke provided the author with copies of correspondence, interviews, published articles, and short papers that he wrote, annotating many of these. Often he returned a letter with his notes written on the back of the original and in the margins. There are more then one hundred pages of these notes, articles, and presentations in the author's possession.

J. Lawton Collins Papers, 1896–1975. Dwight D. Eisenhower
Presidential Library and Museum, Abilene, KS.
History of VII Corps While Operating in Belgium during the Period January 1–31
    1945. Box 5.
Hugh M. Cole: The Ardennes Offensive and Correspondence. Box 68.

William E. DePuy Papers, US Army Heritage and Education Center, Carlisle, PA

Correspondence 1975–1976. Box 7, Letters to and from General Bruce C. Clarke,
1976.

John S. D. Eisenhower, Drafts and Other Materials from The Bitter Woods,
1944–68. Dwight D. Eisenhower Presidential Library and Museum, Abilene, KS.

There are nineteen boxes of materials, including notes, interviews, sources, and
drafts. The letters in this collection provide insight into the point of view that general Dwight D. Eisenhower took, as well as observations from key participants in
the battle, ranging from young soldiers to senior officers.

Hasbrouck, Robert W., to John S. D. Eisenhower, April 14, 1966. Box 2.
Manteuffel, General der Panzertruppe Hasso von. Letter, no addressee, July 30,
    1950.
Montgomery, Field Marshal the Viscount Bernard L., to John S. D. Eisenhower,
    March 6, 1966. Box X.
Riggs, Thomas J., Jr., to John S. D. Eisenhower, March 10, 1966. Box 3.
Umstattd, PFC Walter. "Diary of PFC William Umstattd, Machine Gunner 423rd
    Infantry Regiment, 106th Division." Box 3.
Wilson, Lt. Col. James T., to John S. D. Eisenhower, March 24, 1966. Box 3.

Major General Robert W. Hasbrouck Collection, US Army
Heritage and Education Center, Carlisle, PA

Box 1 contains correspondence related to the support of the nomination of the 7th
Armored Division for the Presidential Unit Citation.

Boylan, Lieutenant Colonel Vincent L., to Major General Robert W. Hasbrouck,
    5 April 1946. Includes his unit after action report and an endorsement dated
    January 25, 1945, by Brigadier General Bruce C. Clarke recommending a unit
    citation for Troop B, 8th Cavalry Reconnaissance Squadron.
Brown, John C., to Major General Robert W. Hasbrouck, April 5, 1946.
Dailey, Tom, to Major General Robert W. Hasbrouck, March 19. No year given, but
    likely written in 1946 based on dates for similar correspondence associated
    with the nomination of the 7th AD for a Distinguished Unit Citation.

Erlenbusch, Lieutenant Colonel Robert C., to Commanding General, III Corps, March 22, 1945.

Erlenbusch, Lieutenant Colonel Robert C., to Major General Robert W. Hasbrouck, March 23, 1946.

Martin, Colonel O. W., to Major General Robert W. Hasbrouck, March 18, 1946. Includes an extract from the 7th Armored Division Artillery after action report, December 1944.

Rhea, Lieutenant Colonel Robert L., to Major General Robert W. Hasbrouck, March 25, 1946.

Warren, Fred M., to Major General Robert W. Hasbrouck, March 28, 1946.

John W. Leonard Collection, US Army
Heritage and Education Center, Carlisle, PA
Undated manuscript Leonard wrote on the employment of his division in the Ardennes.

Charles B. MacDonald Papers, US Army
Heritage and Education Center, Carlisle, PA

Charles B. MacDonald served in the 2nd Infantry Division during World War II and fought as a company commander during the Battle of the Bulge. After World War II he served as an Army historian with the Center of Military History. The collection of research materials used in his book *A Time for Trumpets* is contained in twelve boxes.

Bechtel, Ernest W. "Untold Story of Battery B." N.d. Box 7.

Bied, Dan. "Hell on Earth." N.d. Box 4.

Cavender, Colonel Charles C. "The 423 in the Bulge." In Seventh Annual Convention Committee of the 106th Infantry Division Association, *The Lion's Tale: Short Stories of the 106th Infantry Division.* N.p.: Seventh Annual Convention Committee of the 106th Infantry Division Association, 1953. Box 5.

Clarke, General Bruce Cooper. Military biography. Box 7.

Dickson, Colonel B. A., former G-2 of First Army. Interview by Forrest C. Pogue, Washington, DC, February 6, 1952, based on Dickson's reading of a Pogue manuscript. Pogue Interviews folder, box 1.

Eisenhower, John S. D. Notes from interview with General der Panzertruppe Hasso von Manteuffel, October 12, 1966. Box 6.

Evans, Frank, to Charles B. MacDonald, n.d. Box 1B.

Extracts from G-2 journals and files, December 10–15, 1944, from 2nd Infantry Division, 99th Infantry Division, 106th Infantry Division, and VIII Corps. Pogue Interviews folder, box 1.

Ford, Private First Class Homer D. "Statement of PFC Homer D. Ford, Company C, 518th Military Police Battalion, 18 December 1944 with Supporting Documents." Box 7.

"The German Attack." Chap. 1 in "Intelligence History," unpublished manuscript of an after action review, declassified in 2010. Box 6.

Hansen, Chester B. Diary. Box 7.

Hasbrouck, Robert Wilson. Military biography. N.d. Box 7.

Merriken, William H. "Answers to Questions Concerning: The Bulge Ardennes 1944 (Baugnez)." December 14, 1981. Box 7.

Middleton, Lieutenant General Troy H., to the Theater Historian, "Questions Answered by Lieutenant General Troy H. Middleton," July 30, 1945. Box 7.

Nelson, Col. Gustin M., to his father, May 1945. Extract. Box 3.

———. Notes from S-2 periodic reports provided by Nelson. January 20, 1945. Box 3.

Parker, Danny S. "The Tigers of Winter." N.d. Box 11.

Puett, Lieutenant Colonel Joseph F. "Certificate: Movements and Actions of the 2nd Battalion 423rd Infantry From 16th to 19th December 1944." N.d. Box 5.

Ringer, Robert C., 591st FA. "The Boy at the Bank Barn Berg Reuland Dec. 10–11 1944." Box 5.

Rosengarten, Adolph C. Interview by Forrest C. Pogue, Philadelphia, December 22, 1947. Pogue Interviews folder, box 1.

Sibert, Brigadier General Edwin L., director of staff, Inter-American Defense Board. Interview by Forrest C. Pogue, Washington, DC, May 11, 1951. (Col. William H. Jackson, deputy director of the Central Intelligence Agency, was also present.) Pogue Interviews folder, box 1.

Sibert, Major General Edwin L., and Colonel Alexander Standish. "Military Intelligence Aspects of the Period Prior to the Ardennes Counter Offensive." N.d. Box 6.

Strong, Major General Sir Kenneth W. D. Interview by Forrest C. Pogue, n.p., December 12, 1946. Extract. Pogue Interviews folder, box 1.

Train, Lieutenant General William F. "My Memories of the Battle of the Bulge (16 Dec 1944–15 Jan 1945)." N.d. Box 3.

Weber, Lt. Col. Richard E., 592nd Field Artillery. Undated and untitled manuscript describing combat actions, December 9–30, 1944. Box 4.

Wilkey, Malcolm Richard. "Personal Narrative of Malcolm Richard Wilkey (then Major, Later Lt. Col.) 174 FA Gp. and VIII Corps Hq." N.d. Box 1.

Williams, Brigadier E. T. Interview by Forrest C. Pogue, n.p., May 30–31, 1947. Extract. Pogue Interviews folder, box 1.

106th Division Association Collection, US Army
Heritage and Education Center, Carlisle, PA

Helms, Major Sanda B., to Colonel C. C. Cavender, August 4, 1945. Box 4.

Huyett, Captain J. B., Jr., to Colonel C. C. Cavender, July 30, 1945. Box 4.

Hynes, Captain William J., to Colonel Charles C. Cavender, n.d. Box 4.

Wessels, First Lieutenant Robert R., to Colonel S. L. A. Marshall, August 24, 1945. Box 4.

Matthew B. Ridgway Papers, US Army
Heritage and Education Center, Carlisle, PA
Ridgway, Major General Matthew B. War diary.
———. Record of Major General Matthew B. Ridgway's side of a conversation with Major General William B. Kean, 212350 December 1944.
Ridgway, Major General Matthew B., to General William B. Kean, December 25, 1944.
Ridgway, Matthew B., to James M. Gavin, October 6, 1978.

James E. Thompson Papers, US Army
Heritage and Education Center, Carlisle, PA
Thompson, James E. "A Journal of Papa T's Army Days in World War II Europe as Viewed Forty Years Later." N.d. Box 1.

John Toland Papers, National Archives and records
Administration, Washington, DC

Toland donated the notes and files associated with his research for *Battle: The Story of the Bulge.*

US 7th Armored Division Association, US Army
Heritage and Education Center, Carlisle, PA
Grant, Colonel Joseph H., Jr. "My Recollection of Events for the Period 16–22 Dec. 1944." Transcriptions of documents written by Colonel Joseph H. Grant.
Griffin, Lieutenant Colonel Marcus S., to Mrs. Mildred Johnson, January 5, 1945.
McBride, Richard L. "Grinding Through with the 7th Armored Division (September 1944 to April 1945)." N.d.
Moore, Howard. Company B, 17th Tank Battalion. "Memoir of a World War II Experience." November 2005.
17th Tank Battalion, Activation Order, September 20, 1943.
Winter, George. Assault on Baraque de Fraiture Crossroads, situation sketch of the final German assault. N.d.
Yates, Ross. "Battle of the Bulge: Emerson Wolfe's Story." *Hillside Highlights*, November 2000. Transcribed by Walter C. Johnston.

George J. Winter Collection, George C Marshall Research Library, Lexington, VA
Winter, George J. "Barkman in the Ardennes." N.d.
———. "The Capture of Poteau." N.d.

Combat and Senior Officer Interviews and Debriefings

7th Armored Division
Clarke, Bruce C. "Oral History Interview with Bruce C. Clarke." Interview by Jerry N. Hess, Arlington, VA, January 14, 1970. Harry S. Truman Library and Museum, Independence, MO.

Knowlton, General William A. (Ret). by Lieutenant Colonel David W. Hazen, Carlisle, PA, 1982. William A. Knowlton Papers, Box 1, US Army Heritage and
Education Center, Carlisle, PA.

Combat Command B, 9th Armored Division
Combat Command B, 9th Armored Division. "Action South of St. Vith 17–23 Dec
1944," based on interviews of Brig Gen Benjamin [*sic*: William] Hoge and
twenty-nine others from across the combat command at several sites, January
15–23, 1945. Interviews by 2d Lt George E. Moise. Box 1B, Charles B. Mac-
Donald Papers, US Army Heritage and Education Center, Carlisle, PA.

14th Cavalry Group
Lindsey, Captain Franklin F., Commander, B Troop, 32nd Cavalry Reconnaissance
Squadron, and others. Interview by Lieutenant Jack Shea, January 7, 1945.
Norman D. Cota Collection, Dwight D. Eisenhower Presidential Library and
Museum, Abilene, KS.
Williamson, Captain Henry H., Assistant S-2, 14th Cavalry Group. Interview by
Lieutenant Robert E. Merriam, St. Roch, Belgium, January 1, 1945. Record
Group 331, National Archives and Records Administration, Suitland, MD.

106th Infantry Division

Soldier historians assigned to the 2nd Information and Historical Service attached
to VIII Corps conducted these interviews. All can be found in Record Group 331,
National Archives and Records Administration, Suitland, MD.

Belzer, Lieutenant Colonel Carl, Division Surgeon, 106th Division. Interview by
Captain K. W. Hechler, Anthisnes, Belgium, January 6, 1945.
Berwick, Captain Lee, S-3, 3rd Battalion, 424th Regiment, 106th Division. Inter-
view by Captain K. W. Hechler, vicinity of Aisomont, Belgium, January 11,
1945.
Forty-one American prisoners of war from the 106th Infantry Division, attached
units, the 28th Infantry Division, and a single soldier from the 99th Infantry
Division. Group interview by Lieutenant Jack Shea, casern at Erfurt, Germany,
May 10, 1945.
Freeland, Captain Joseph, Commander, Cannon Company, 424th Regiment, 106th
Division, and fifteen Cannon Company soldiers. Interview by Captain K. W.
Hechler, vicinity of La Reid, Belgium, January 8, 1945.
Glatterer, Lieutenant Colonel Wilton S., G-4, 106th Division, and Major Raymond
Priniski, Assistant G-4, 106th Division. Interview by Captain K. W. Hechler,
vicinity of Spa, Belgium, January 11, 1945.
Logan, Lieutenant Robert, S-3, 2nd Battalion, and Lieutenant Colonel Orville
Hewitt, Commander, 2nd Battalion, 424th Regiment, 106th Division. Inter-
view by Captain K. W. Hechler, vicinity of Bronhomme, Belgium, January 8,
1945.

Long, 1st Lieutenant Ivan H., Platoon Leader, Intelligence and Reconnaissance Platoon, 423rd Infantry. Interview by Captain K. W. Hechler, vicinity of Desnié, Belgium, January 6, 1945.

Marshall, Major Walter Alden, Battalion Commander, 81st Engineer Battalion; Major Harry D. Evans, Battalion Executive Officer; Captain Hal Mosley, S-3; Captain Nathan Ward, Headquarters and Service Company; Captain Harold M. Harman, Company A; and Don Carmichael, Supply Officer. Interview by Captain K. W. Hechler, vicinity of Spa, Belgium, January 11, 1945.

Matthews, Lt. Col. Joseph C., Executive Officer, 422nd Infantry. Interview by Capt. William J. Dunkerley, Moosburg, Germany, May 3, 1945.

McKinley, 2nd Lieutenant Harold W., Ammunition and Pioneer Platoon, 1st Battalion, 423rd Infantry. Interview by Captain K. W. Hechler, vicinity of Trois-Ponts, Belgium, January 13, 1945.

Oseth, Major Frederick W., Executive Officer, 3rd Battalion, 422nd Infantry Regiment, 106th Infantry Division. Interview by Maj. J. F. O'Sullivan, Camp Lucky Strike, St. Balery en Caux [sic: Saint-Valery-en-Caux], France, May 11, 1945.

———. "German Breakthrough in the Ardennes." Interview by Capt. William J. Dunkerly, Moosburg, Germany, May 3, 1945.

Post, Major Douglas E., 422nd Infantry Regiment. Interview by Captain K. W. Hechler, vicinity of Bronhomme, Belgium, January 7, 1945, with further information from Lieutenant Scott Proffitt, S-2, 2nd Battalion, 422nd Infantry Regiment.

Puett, Lieutenant Colonel Joseph F., and Captain Joshua P. Sotherland. Interview by John G. Westover, Camp Lucky Strike, St. Valery en Caen [sic: Saint-Valery-en-Caux], France, April 17, 1945.

Reid, Colonel A. D., Commander, 424th Infantry Regiment. Interview by Captain K. W. Hechler, vicinity of Trois-Ponts, Belgium, January 10, 1945.

Roadruck, Lieutenant Colonel Max, G-1, 106th Division. Interview by Captain K. W. Hechler, vicinity of Spa, Belgium, January 12, 1945.

Surmont, Chief Warrant Officer Albert, Assistant Regimental Communications Officer, and Technical Sergeant Robert Sherbondy, Radio Operator. Interview by Captain K. W. Hechler, vicinity of Bronhomme, Belgium, January 9, 1945.

Underwood, Captain R. D., Information and Education Officer, 424th Infantry Regiment. Interview by Captain K. W. Hechler, vicinity of Spa, Belgium, January 12, 1945.

Weber, Lieutenant Colonel Richard E., Jr., Commanding Officer, 592nd Field Artillery Battalion. Interview by Major J. F. O'Sullivan, n.p., n.d.

Williams, Lieutenant Colonel Earle, Signal Officer, 106th Division. Interview by Captain K. W. Hechler, vicinity of Anthisnes, Belgium, January 11, 1945.

112th Infantry, 28th Infantry Division

Allen, Lieutenant Colonel William H., CO, 1st Bn, 112th Inf; and 1st Lieutenant Joseph W. Morgan S-3, 1st Bn, 112th Inf. Interviewer not identified, Montfaucon, France, January 16, 1945.

Cannon Company, 112th Infantry Regiment, 28th Infantry Division; 1st Lt. Robert
    W. Black, Commanding Officer; 1st Kt. Richard V. Purcell, Executive Officer
    (Reconnaissance Officer); and First Sergeant George E. Mortimer. Interview
    by Tech 3rd Grd William Henderson, 2d info & Hist. Sv, VII [VIII] Corps
    Team, First U. S. Army, Hachinette, France, January 23 [1945].
Macsalka, Lt Col Joseph L., C. O., 2d Bn, 112 Inf; Captain William G. McLaughlin,
    Arty Liaison Officer, 229 FA Bn; 1st Lt Walton Fitch, S-2, 2nd Bn, 112 Inf; 2d
    Lt Edwin B. Cline, 4th Plat, C. O. F, 112 Inf; and S/SGT Owen A. Paul, Opera-
    tions Sgt, 2d Bn, 112 Inf. Interviewer not identified, in the mountains south of
    Kaysersberg, France, January 22, 1945.
Nelson, Colonel Gustin M., and Major Justin C. Brainard. Interviewer not identi-
    fied, Montfaucon, France, January 14, 1945.
Woodward, Major Walden F., C. O. 3rd Bnd., 112th Infantry Regiment, 28 Infan-
    try Division; Captain Guy T. Piercey, C. O., Company M; Captain William B.
    Cowan Jr., S-1, 3rd Bn, and C. O. Hq. Co. Interview by Tec 3rd Grd William
    Henderson, 2nd Info and Hist Team, 1st U. S. Army, Lapoutroie, France,
    January 20, 1945.

168th Engineer Battalion
Nungesser, Lieutenant Colonel W. L., Major Harry W. Brennan, and Lieutenant
    Harry Balch. Interview by Captain K. W. Hechler, Nadrin, Belgium, February
    4, 1945.

Johnston Collection of US Army Combat Interviews

W. Wesley Johnston, son of a 7th Armored Division combat veteran, collected
Center of Military History combat interviews, which he then self-published. I
have used these for convenience despite being in possession of copies of many of
the original interviews. Johnston also interviewed veterans to provide context to
the original combat interviews, and annotated and/or provided commentary on
each of the resulting sets of interviews. Johnston collected the following, compiled
them, and self-published them through CreateSpace in 2014.

*Combat Interviews of the 7th Armored Division, Division Artillery: St. Vith and
    Poteau, Belgium, December 1944.*
*Combat Interviews of the 7th Armored Division Combat Commands: St. Vith and
    Manhay, Belgium, December 16–23, 1944.*
*Combat Interviews of the 7th Armored Division Headquarters: St. Vith and Manhay,
    Belgium, including the 14th Cavalry Group, December 17–23, 1944.*
*Combat Interviews of the 23rd Armored Infantry Battalion, 7th Armored Division:
    The St. Vith Salient, including Task Force Navajo, December 17–23, 1944.*
*Combat Interviews of the 31st Tank Battalion, 7th Armored Division: The St. Vith
    Salient, Belgium, December 17–23, 1944.*
*Combat Interviews of the 33rd Armored Engineer Battalion, 7th Armored Division:
    The St. Vith Salient, Belgium, December 17–23, 1944.*

Combat Interviews of the 38th Armored Infantry Battalion, 7th Armored Division: The St. Vith Salient and Manhay, December 17–23, 1944.

Combat Interviews of the 40th Tank Battalion, 7th Armored Division, December 1944.

Combat Interviews of the 48th Armored Infantry Battalion, 7th Armored Division: Poteau, Rodt, Malempre and Manhay Belgium, December 18–25, 1944.

Combat Interviews of the 87th Cavalry Reconnaissance Squadron, 7th Armored Division: The St. Vith Salient, December 17–23, 1944.

Manhay and Grandmenil Belgium, December 24–30, 1944. Combat Interviews of the 7th Armored Division and Some Attached Units.

17th Tank Battalion, 7th Armored Division: Combat Interviews, Morning Reports, After Action Reports, Germany and Belgium.

The 7th Armored Division Goes Back: The Retaking of St. Vith, Belgium, January 20–23, 1945.

Author's Interviews and Correspondence

INTERVIEWS

Adams, Major General Andrew J. (Ret.). Washington, DC, August 31, 1984,

Cirillo, Roger. Telephone conversation with the author, April 5, 2019.

Clay, Colonel Roy U. (Ret). Carlisle, PA, August 28, 1984, and numerous telephone interviews, 1984.

Erlenbusch, Colonel Robert C. (Ret). Point Charlotte, Florida, December 8, 1984.

Hasbrouck, Major General Robert W. (Ret.). Washington, DC, August 20, 1984.

Schaffner, John. Telephone interview, December 3, 2017.

CORRESPONDENCE

Adams, MG Andrew J., to the author, June 14, 1984, including the manuscript of a short paper Adams wrote for the Air Command and Staff School, "Account of the Activities of the Seventh Armored Division Trains from 18th to 22nd December 1944," n.d.

Clay, Colonel Roy U. (Ret.), to with the author, eleven letters between April 1984 and November 1984. Colonel Clay also provided an undated memorandum on the 275th AFA actions during the fighting. The memorandum is supported by a World War II–era sketch of the unit's area.

Erlenbusch, Colonel Robert C. (Ret.), with the author, September 25–30, 1983, and April 21, May 10, and August 20–24, 1984.

Griffin, Colonel Marcus S. (Ret.), to the author, December 2, 1984.

Knowlton, General William A. (Ret.), with the author, November 8, 1984, November 15, 1984, and December 13, 1984, The November 15 letter included an undated transcript of "Statement of General William Allen Knowlton," which was made for a military museum in Bastogne, Belgium.

Leydecker, Colonel Charles E. (Ret.), to the author, August 8, 1984.

John Schaffner, email to the author, October 16, 2018.
Wemple, Colonel John P. (Ret.), to the author, September 4, 1984, with a sketch
    showing 17th Tank Battalion defense of Crombach, Belgium.

Unit Journals, Orders, and Reports

Documents listed here come from the Charles B. MacDonald Papers at the US
Army Heritage and Education Center, Carlisle, PA; the Dwight D. Eisenhower
Library and Museum in Abilene, KS; the Ike Skelton Combined Arms Research
Library at Fort Leavenworth, KS; and the National Archives and Records Admin-
istration in Suitland, MD. Entries in this section are listed in an order that reflects
the hierarchy of Army units.

US Army Unit Records

12TH ARMY GROUP

Assistant Chief of Staff G-2. "Weekly Intelligence Summary No. 19 for week ending
    16 December 1944." December 19, 1944.
AAA [Anti-Aircraft Artillery], Armd, Arty, Sig, CWS. "Report of Operations (Final
    After Action Report), Volume XI: Antiaircraft Artillery, Armored, Artillery,
    Chemical Warfare and Signal Sections." July 31, 1945.

FIRST US ARMY

The author consulted all of the First US Army estimates and reports for December
1944 and January 1945 but has listed here only those used or cited.

Headquarters, First US Army. *G-2 Estimate No. 36.* November 20, 1944.
——. *G-2 Estimate No. 37.* December 10, 1944.
——. "Annex No. 3 to G-2 Periodic Report No. 56, Translation of German Docu-
    ments." December 15, 1944.
——. Summary of G-2 estimates regarding the Battle of the Bulge, November 15,
    1944–March 9, 1944.
——. "After Action Report, 1–31 December 1944," April 7, 1945.

VIII CORPS

These documents are not the entire records but rather the records essential to the
7th Armored Division Story.

Headquarters, VIII Corps. "Report of the VIII Corps After Action Against Enemy
    Forces in France, Belgium, Luxembourg and Germany, for the Period 1–31
    December 1944." April 6, 1945.

———. "Intelligence Annex: To Accompany Operation Memorandum No. 3." December 15, 1944.

Headquarters, VIII Corps Artillery. "Action Against Enemy, Reports After / After Action Reports." January 10, 1945.

174th Field Artillery Group. "Report After / After Action Reports for the Month of December 1944." N.d.

XVIII CORPS (AIRBORNE)

Headquarters, XVIII Corps (Airborne), G-3 operations journals, December 22, 1944–January 23, 1945, including selected situation reports.

———. "Summary of Operations. December 18, 1944–February 13, 1945." March 1, 1945.

Headquarters, XVIII Corps (Airborne), Office of the Inspector General. "Report of Investigation, CCA 7 AD, Manhay, 24–25 December 1944." January 6, 1945.

3RD ARMORED DIVISION

"3rd Armored Division Artillery After Action Report." January 25, 1945.

7TH ARMORED DIVISION

Boyer, Donald P., Jr. *St. Vith: The 7th Armored Division in the Battle of the Bulge 17–23 December 1944. A Narrative After Action Report.* N.p: n.p., July 22, 1947.

Reports and Orders

7TH ARMORED DIVISION

7th Armored Division. "Action at Samrée, Belgium." December 22, 1944.

———. "After Action Report, Period 1–31 December 1944." N.d.

———. "After Action Report, Period 1–31 January 1945." N.d.

———. "Battle of St. Vith: 17–23 December." N.d.

———. G-1 journal, January 1945.

———. G-2 journal, December 1944.

———. G-2 journal, January 1945.

———. G-3 journal, December 1944.

———. G-2 periodic reports, December 1944.

———. G-2 periodic reports, January 1945.

———. G-3 journal, January 1945.

———. G-3 periodic reports, December 1944.

———. G-3 periodic reports, January 1945.

———. G-3 tactical journal, December 1944.

———. G-4 journal, December 1944.

———. "Order for Withdrawal of 7th Armored Division West of Salm River." December 23, 1944.

———. Tactical headquarters journal, December 1944.

Combat Command A, 7th Armored Division. "After Action Report, December 1944." January 1, 1945.

———. "After Action Report, January 1945." N.d.

Combat Command B, 7th Armored Division. "After Action Report, Month of December 1944." January 1, 1945.

———. "After Action Report, Month of January 1945." February 1, 1945.

Combat Command R, 7th Armored Division. "After Action Report, Month of December 1944." December 31, 1944.

———. "After Action Report, Month of January 1945." January 31, 1945.

7th Armored Division Trains. Journal, December 1944.

———. Summary of events, December 1944.

Division Artillery, 7th Armored Division. "After Action Report, Month of December 1944." January 1, 1945.

———. "After Action Report, Month of January 1945." February 1, 1945.

33rd Armored Engineer Battalion, "After Action Report December 1944." January 4, 1945.

203rd Anti-Aircraft Artillery Battalion. "After Action Report." January 3, 1945.

———. *203 AAA.* N.p.: n.p., n.d. Postwar unit history published locally and signed by the Battalion Commander.

434th Armored Field Artillery Battalion. "After Action Report, Month of December 1944." December 31, 1944.

———. "After Action Report, Month of January 1945." January 31, 1945.

440th Anti-Aircraft Artillery Battalion. "After Action Report, December 1944." January 6, 1945.

440th Armored Field Artillery Battalion. "After Action Report, Month of December 1944." January 1, 1945.

———. "After Action Report, Month of January 1945." February 2, 1945.

489th Armored Field Artillery Battalion. "After Action Report, Month of January 1945." February 1, 1945.

23rd Armored Infantry Battalion. "After Action Report, Month of December 1944." January 2, 1945.

———. "After Action Report, Month of January 1945." February 1, 1945.

38th Armored Infantry Battalion. "After Action Report, Month of December 1944." January 3, 1945.

———. "After Action Report, Month of January 1945." February 2, 1945.

48th Armored Infantry Battalion. "After Action Report." January 2, 1945.

———. "After Action Report, Month of January 1945." February 1, 1945.

87th Cavalry Reconnaissance Squadron. "After Action Report, Month of December 1944." January 8, 1945.

———. "After Action Report, Month of January 1945." N.d.

17th Tank Battalion. "After Action Report, Month of December 1944." December 31, 1944.

———. "After Action Report, Month of January 1945." January 31, 1945.

31st Tank Battalion. "Operational History—December 1944." N.d.
———. "After Action Report, January 1945." N.d.
40th Tank Battalion. "After Action Report, Month of December 1944." December 31, 1944.
———. "After Action Report, Month of January 1945." January 31, 1945.
814th Tank Destroyer Battalion, "After Action Report December 1944." January 7, 1945.
———. Periodic reports, December 1944.
———. Periodic reports, January 1945.
446th Quartermaster Troop Transport Company. "1944 Historical Record of the 446th Quartermaster Troop Transport Company (attached to 7th Armored Division)." N.d.

9TH ARMORED DIVISION, COMBAT COMMAND B

Combat Command B. "Battle of the Bulge 16 December 1944–25 December 1944, Combat Narrative." N.d.
Headquarters, Combat Command B, 9th Armored Division. "After Action Report for the Period 1–31 December 1944." January 9, 1945.
16th Armored Field Artillery. "After Action Report (for Period 010001 December to 312400 December, 1944)." January 1, 1945.
27th Armored Infantry Battalion. "After Action Report." January 3, 1945.
14th Tank Battalion. "After Action Report—1 Dec 44 to 31 Dec 44." N.d.
———. "History of the 14th Tank Battalion." N.d.
811th Tank Destroyer Battalion. "History of the 811th Tank Destroyer Battalion." N.d.
811th Tank Destroyer Battalion, Company A. "After Action." N.d.

14TH CAVALRY GROUP

Headquarters, 14th Cavalry Group Mechanized. "Action against the Enemy, Reports After / After Action Report." January 10, 1945.
Shea, Lieutenant Jack T., "Fourteenth Cavalry Group (Mecz.) and Its Work in the Counter-Offensive: 16–31 Dec. 1944." January 25, 1945.
———. "After Action Report of the 14th Cavalry Group Mechanized, Ardennes 16 December–24 December 1944." February 1, 1945. Historical narrative by a field historian.
18th Cavalry Reconnaissance Squadron. "Action against the Enemy, After / After Action Reports." January 8, 1945.

28TH INFANTRY DIVISION

Headquarters, 112th Infantry Regiment. Periodic reports, December 1944.
———. S-2 journal, December 1944.
———. "Unit Report No. 6, from 1 December 1944–31 December 1944." January 16, 1945.

82ND AIRBORNE DIVISION

Headquarters, 82nd Airborne Division. *Belgium: The Story of the Bulge, Dec 1944–Feb 1945.* N.p.: n.p., n.d.
———. "Historical Data on the 82nd Airborne Division." July 3, 1945.

106TH INFANTRY DIVISION

Headquarters, 106th Infantry Division. "Report of Enemy Action against the 106th Infantry Division, 11 December to 31 December 1944." N.d.
———. Unit citation, 81st Engineer Combat Battalion. May 25, 1945.
Hechler, K. W., Captain. "German Breakthrough 16–30 December 1944, 106th Infantry Division (General Summary)." N.d.
424th Infantry Regiment. "After Action Report Ending 31 December 1944." N.d.
Division Artillery. "After Action Report." December 31, 1944.
———. "Report of 106th Div Arty's Air OP[erations]." Compiled by field historian Lieutenant Jack Shea. February 19, 1945.
589th Field Artillery. "After Action Report." N.d.
———. "Narrative of Action 589th FA BN." N. d. Compiled from interviews by US Army field historian Major J. F. O'Sullivan.
591st Field Artillery Battalion. "After Action Report." December 31, 1944.
592nd Field Artillery Battalion. "History—592nd FA Battalion, 10th–31st December 1944." N.d.
820th Tank Destroyer Battalion. "After Action Report." February 9, 1945.
Company A, 820th Tank Destroyer Battalion. "After Battle Report, December 1944." N.d.

German Manuscripts and Official Interviews

Many of the German manuscripts cited herein are from the US foreign military studies conducted from 1945 to 1960. European Theater Historical Interrogations (ETHINT) documents are interviews of German officers that were conducted at the end of the war. A-series manuscripts are interviews done of German officers held as prisoners of war, and B-series manuscripts are narrative histories of units on the Western Front written by German officers, and can be found in the Ike Skelton Combined Arms Research Library, US Army Command and General Staff College, Fort Leavenworth, KS.

Blumentritt, General der Infanterie Günther. "The Ardennes Offensive: A Critique." N.d. MS B-740.
Büchs, Generalleutnant Herbert. "Defense of the West Wall." September 28, 1945. ETHINT-37.
———. "An Interview with MAJ Buechs, The Ardennes Offensive: Sep–Dec 44." August 31, 1945. ETHINT-34.

Dietrich, Oberstgruppenführer Sepp. Untitled manuscript prepared for Colonel Burton F. Ellis, trial judge advocate for the Malmedy war crimes trial. N.d. N 17480, Ike Skelton Combined Arms Research Library, Fort Leavenworth, KS.

Felber, General der Infanterie Hans. "Defensive Fighting in the Ardennes." January 1–15, 1945. MS B-039.

Jodl, Generaloberst Alfred. "An Interview with Genobst Alfred Jodl: Ardennes Offensive." July 31, 1945. ETHINT-51.

———. "An Interview with Genobst Alfred Jodl: "Planning the Ardennes Offensive." July 26, 1945. ETHINT-50.

Jüttner, Oberst Arthur. "Report by Colonel Jüttner of the 62nd VGD in the Battle of the Bulge." Translated by Heino Brandt, 1982. Box 10, Charles B. MacDonald Papers, US Army Heritage and Education Center, Carlisle, PA. May have originally appeared in *Alte Kameraden*.

———. "With the Same Efficiency as the Panzers! The 62nd Volksgrenadier Division in the Battle of the Bulge." *Alte Kameraden*, 1977. Translated by Heino Brandt, 1982. Box 10, Charles B. MacDonald Papers, US Army Heritage and Education Center, Carlisle, PA.

———. Personal impression during the offensive in the "Ardennen." Translated by Heino Brandt, but neither attributed nor dated. Box 10, Charles B. MacDonald Papers, US Army Heritage and Education Center, Carlisle, PA.

———. Interview. Interviewer not identified. October 16, 1982. 62nd VGD folder, box 10, Charles B. MacDonald Papers, US Army Heritage and Education Center, Carlisle, PA.

Kittel, Generalmajor Friedrich. "A New 62nd Inf. Div.—the 62nd VGD." *Alte Kameraden*, November 1958. Translated by Heino Brandt, 1982. Box 10, Charles B. MacDonald Papers, US Army Heritage and Education Center, Carlisle, PA.

———. "62nd Volksgrenadier Division (16 Dec 1944–27 Jan 1945)." January 1946. MS B-028.

Kraemer, Generalmajor Fritz. "An Interview with Genmaj (W-SS) Fritz Kraemer SIXTH PZ ARMY (16 Nov 44–4 Jan 45)." August 14–15, 1945. ETHINT-21.

———. "An Interview with Genmaj (W-SS) Fritz Kraemer SIXTH PZ ARMY (24–27 Dec 44)." October 11, 1945. ETHINT-22.

———. "An Interview with Genmaj (W-SS) Fritz Kraemer SIXTH PZ ARMY (16–19 Dec 44)." October 11, 1945. ETHINT-23.

———. "Operations of Sixth Panzer Army, 1944–45." N.d. MS A-924.

Langhäuser, Generalmajor Rudolph. "560 Volks Grenadier Division, 15–29 Dec 1944" and "12th Volks Grenadier Division, 1–28 Jan 1945." MS B-027.

Lucht, General der Artillerie Walther. "LXVI Infantry Corps, 23 Dec 44–2 Jan 45." N.d. MS B-477.

Manteuffel, General der Panzertruppe Hasso von. "Fifth Panzer Army (Ardennes Offensive Preparations) 16 Dec 44–25 Feb 45." N.d. MS B-151.

———. "Fifth Panzer Army Ardennes Offensive." Sequel to MS B-151. N.d. MS B-151B.

———. "An Interview with Gen Pz Hasso von Manteuffel, FIFTH PZ ARMY (11 Sep 44–Jan 45)." June 21, 1945. ETHINT-45.

———. "An Interview with Gen Pz Hasso von Manteuffel, FIFTH PZ ARMY (Nov 44–Jan 45)." October 29 and 31, 1945. ETHINT-46.

———. Untitled remarks made on July 26, 1950, at a meeting of veterans of the Battle of the Bulge. Box 8, Charles B. MacDonald Papers, US Army Heritage and Education Center, Carlisle, PA.

Manteuffel, General der Panzertruppe Hasso von, to General Bruce C. Clarke, July 5, 1976. Box 8, Charles B. MacDonald Papers, US Army Heritage and Education Center, Carlisle, PA.

Moll, Oberstleutnant Dietrich. "18th Volks Grenadier Division, 1 Sep 1944–25 Jan 1945." MS B-688.

Oberkommando der Wehrmacht. "Führer Directive 51." November 3, 1943. World War II Database. https://ww2db.com/doc.php?q=331.

Peiper, Obersturmbahnführer Joachim. "Brief Review and Reflections about the Battle in the Russian Theater of Operations." April 7, 1946. Manuscript prepared for Colonel Burton F. Ellis, trial judge advocate for the Malmedy war crimes trial. N.d. N 17480, Ike Skelton Combined Arms Research Library, Fort Leavenworth, KS.

———. "An Interview with Obst. Joachim Peiper, 1 SS PZ REGT (11–24 Dec 44)." September 7, 1945. ETHINT-10.

———. "Kampfgruppe Peiper: 15–26 December 1944." N.d. MS C-004.

Peiper, Obersturmbahnführer Jochen [Joachim], to Col. [John S. D.] Eisenhower, April 4, 1967. Box 1, Charles B. MacDonald Papers, US Army Heritage and Education Center, Carlisle, PA.

Praun, Albert. "German Radio Intelligence." March 1950. MS P-038.

Remer, Generalmajor Otto E. "The Führer-Begleit Brigade in the Ardennes Offensive, December 16 1944 to January 26, 1945." N.d. MS B-592.

Ritter, Klaus. Statements. N.d. Translated by Heino Brandt, 1983. Box 10, Charles B. MacDonald Papers, US Army Heritage and Education Center, Carlisle, PA. There are two separate undated documents—the author labeled them parts 1 and 2, based on chronology.

Rundstedt, Generalfeldmarschall Gerd von. "An Interview with Genfldm Gerd von Rundstedt, The Ardennes Offensive." Interview by Major Kenneth W. Hechler. July 12, 1949. ETHINT-47.

Schmager, Gert. "Regiment 'DF' [Der Führer] 22nd until 27th December 1944." Der Freiwillige, 1964, 13. Box 10, Charles B. MacDonald Papers, US Army Heritage and Education Center, Carlisle, PA.

Schramm, Major Percy Ernst. "The Course of Events of the German Offensive in the Ardennes: 16 Dec 44 to 14 Jan 45." MS A-858.

———. "The Preparations for the German Offensive in the Ardennes: Sep to 16 Dec 1944." 1946. MS A-862.

Skorzeny, Oberstleutnant Otto. "Ardennes Offensive: An Interview with Obstlt Otto Skorzeny." August 12, 1945. ETHINT-12.

Staudinger, Generalleutnant Walter. "Sixth Pz Army Artillery in the Ardennes Offensive: An Interview with Genlt SS Walter Staudinger." August 11, 1945. ETHINT-62.

Stumpf, General der Panzertruppe Horst. "Tank Maintenance in the Ardennes Offensive: An Interview with Gen Pz Horst Stumpf." August 11, 1948. ETHINT-61.

Wagener, Generalmajor Carl Gustav. "Fifth Panzer Army (2 Nov 44–16 Jan 45)." MS B-235.

———. "Fifth Panzer Army—Ardennes (Special Questions)." Interview by Master Sergeant Leonard Beck, Hersfeld, Germany, October 18, 1945. MS A-961. This interview was based on written questions provided to Wagener.

———. "Results of the Ardennes Offensive." N.d. MS A-964.

Waldenburg, Generalmajor Siegfried von. "Commitment of the 116th Panzer Division in the Ardennes 1944/45." N.d. MS A-873.

Warilmont, General der Artillerie Walter. "Reciprocal Influence of East and West Fronts." August 2, 1945. ETHINT-3.

Weidinger, Otto, and Gert Schmager. Extract from *Kameraden bis Zum Ende* [Comrades to the end]. N.d. Translated by Hans Holtkmap, 1983. Box 9, Charles B. MacDonald Papers, US Army Heritage and Education Center, Carlisle, PA.

Wortmann, Karl. "Memories of the Last Days of December 1944." Box 10, Macdonald Collection, US Army Heritage and Education Center, Carlisle, PA.

Soldiers' Stories from Veterans Organizations, Associations, Museum Archives, and Soldier Monographs

Allen, Harold D. "My Experience in the Battle of the Bulge." February 10, 2015. Battle of the Bulge Memories. http://www.battleofthebulgememories.be/stories26/us-army25/855-my-experience-in-the-battle-of-the-bulge.html.

Awalt, Arlos L. "Curley." Interview by William G. Cox, May 29, 2007. National Museum of the Pacific War, Fredericksburg, TX. http://www.indianamilitary.org/106ID/Diaries/None-POW/Await-Arlos-424/07-13-2007/Awalt%20Arlos%20L.%20%207-13-2007.pdf.

Chamness, Earl T. "'HQ' Company, 112th Infantry Regiment, 28th I.D." September 17, 2012. Battle of the Bulge Memories. http://www.battleofthebulgememories.be/stories26/32-battle-of-the-bulge-us-army/725-hq-company-112th-infantry-regiment-28th-id.html.

Eaton, Captain Henry A. "Interview with Captain Henry A. Eaton, 203rd AAA." Battle of the Bulge Memories. http://www.battleofthebulgememories.be/en/stories/us-army/626-interview-with-captain-henry-a-eaton-203rd-aaa.

Haas, Technician Fifth Grade Bernard J. "Roadblock Overrun 12 Hours Baraque de Fraiture (Parker's Crossroad) December 22–23, 1944." October 23, 2012. Battle of the Bulge Memories. http://www.battleofthebulgememories.be/stories26/32-battle-of-the-bulge-us-army/738-roadblock-overrun-12-hours-baraque-de-fraiture-parkers-crossroaddecember-22-23-1944.html. Originally appeared in the *Bulge Bugle*, August 2010.

Hokanson, Lieutenant Colonel William (Ret.). "The Forgotten Epic Defense of St. Vith, Belgium in the Battle of the Bulge." N.d. US 7th Armored Division Association. https://www.7tharmddiv.org/docrep/X-168-Hokanson.doc.

Kline, Sergeant John P. "The Service Diary of German War Prisoner #315136." Box 4, 106th Division Association Collection, US Army Heritage and Education Center, Carlisle, PA.

Kunselman, Sergeant Maurice H. "424th Infantry Regiment, 106th Infantry Division." September 17, 2011. Battle of the Bulge Memories. http://www.battleofthebulgememories.be/stories26/32–battle–of–the–bulge–us–army/649–424th–infantry–regiment–106th–infantry–division.html. Originally appeared in the *Bulge Bugle*, August 2002.

McIlroy, Sergeant James R. "A Soldier's Story . . . Krinkelt, 1944," May 23, 2014. Battle of the Bulge Memories. http://www.battleofthebulgememories.be/stories26/32-battle-of-the-bulge-us-army/836-a-soldier-s-story-krinkelt-1944.html. Originally appeared in *The Checkerboard*, October 1985, the newsletter of the 99th Division Association.

Morrison, Ian A. "Three Days in December." Temporary box 7, Veterans of the Battle of the Bulge Collection, US Army Heritage and Education Center, Carlisle, PA.

Neher, Corporal Kenneth M. "My WWII Story with 38th A.I.B." December 4, 2005. Battle of the Bulge Memories. http://www.battleofthebulgememories.be/stories26/us-army25/193-my-wwii-story-with-38th-aib.html.

Oxford, Sergeant Paul G. "Excerpts from a Letter." January 26, 2016. Battle of the Bulge Memories. http://www.battleofthebulgememories.be/stories26/us-army25/867–excerpts–from–a–letter.html. Originally appeared in *The Cub of the Golden Lion* 69, no. 4 (1993): n.p.

Pope, Robert W. "How I Survived World War II." Stories of the 106th, 106th Infantry Division Association. http://106thinfdivassn.org/stories/robert_pope.html.

Prell, Second Lieutenant Donald B. "My Story." US 7th Armored Division Association. https://www.7tharmddiv.org/docrep/X-106-422-Prell.pdf.

Rangsdale, Corporal Floyd D. "A Gargantuan Battle." December 28, 2012. Battle of the Bulge Memories. http://www.battleofthebulgememories.be/stories26/us–army25/759–a–gargantuan–battle.html. Originally appeared in the *Bulge Bugle*, February 2003.

Schober, Milton J. "Manhay, Christmas Day—Memoir." Milt's WWII Letters (blog). https://dadswwiiletters.wordpress.com/2001/09/14/manhay-christmas-day-memoir/.

Video

Army Pictorial Center. *The Battle of St. Vith*, parts 1 and 2. Aired on *The Big Picture*, January 31, 1965. https://www.c-span.org/video/?323173-1/reel-america-the-battle-st-vith-1965.

Index

1st Infantry Division, 23, 86, 267, 272–273, 285

1st Schutzstaffel (SS) Panzer (PZ), 42–43, 66–67*map*, 75, 98, 103, 118, 147

2nd Infantry Division, 24–25, 49–50, 56, 60, 76

2nd Schutzstaffel (SS) Panzer Division (PZ), 42–43, 190, 241–242, 245*map*, 289

4th Infantry Division, 24–25, 56, 149

Sixth Panzer Army, 62, 64–65*map*, 96–99, 105, 120–121, 160–161, 169

9th Fallschirmjäger Regiment (FJR), 77–78, 98, 104

9th Schutzstaffel (SS) Panzer (PZ), 43, 118, 147, 155, 161, 183, 191, 216, 231

10th Armored Division, 86, 122, 148–149, 168

12th Army Group, 14, 20*map*, 23–24, 122

14th Cavalry Group (CAV), 24–25, 56, 59, 66–67*map*, 69, 76–82, 106, 118–119, 126–127

XVIII Airborne Corps, 149, 161, 171–173, 178–179, 182, 190–196, 213, 223, 226–228, 241–244, 263–265

18th Cavalry Squadron Mechanized, 25, 59–60, 76–77, 79–80

18th Volksgrenadier Division (VGD)
  beginning of battle and, 75
  encirclement by, 133
  on eve of battle, 69
  looting and, 126

main attack and, 197
  movement of, 216–217, 266
  operational planning and, 37
  organization of, 39–43, 42*fig*
  performance of, 120–121
  retaking of St. Vith and, 270–271, 271*map*, 275–276
  at St. Vith, 147–148, 180, 194
  troop movements and, 98–101, 105, 187

21st Army Group, 7, 15, 20*map*, 23–24, 170

28th Infantry Division, 24–25, 66–67*map*, 85

32nd CAV, 60, 76, 79–80, 82, 84, 103, 105, 127

62nd Volksgrenadier Division (VGD), 40–42, 76, 83–84, 100, 105, 180–181, 187, 194, 197, 218–221, 231–232

LXVI Corps, 42, 66–67*map*, 75, 88, 99–101, 121, 147–148, 160–161, 179–180, 187–188, 193, 197, 199, 217, 220, 242, 266

82nd Airborne Division, 189*map*, 191–192, 227–228, 232–234, 239

84th Infantry Division (ID), 55, 94, 197

99th Infantry Division ID), 59–60, 66–67*map*, 75, 80

106th Infantry Division "Golden Lions"
  arrival of, 24–25, 37
  collapse of, 106–107
  conditions for, 50–51
  on December 16, 82–85

dispositions of, 59–62
on eve of battle, 55–56
joining with, 8
Jones with, 159
Lucht and, 38
LXVI Corps attack on, 66–67*map*
manpower shortages and, 12
missed opportunities of, 119
orders to, 58–59
organization of, 13*fig*
prior to battle, 68–69
remnants of, 137, 155
Ritter and, 43, 45
troop movements and, 80, 101–102, 126
XVIII Airborne Corps and, 213
112th Infantry Regiment, 24, 59–62, 76, 85,
    100, 103, 132–133, 158–160, 181, 195,
    203, 231–232, 240
116th Panzer Division (PZ), 42, 43*fig*,
    63, 66–67*map*, 68, 70, 85, 100, 170,
    178–179, 188, 265
293rd Volksgrenadier Division (VGD),
    75–76, 100
325th Glider Infantry Regiment, 228
422nd Infantry Regiment (INF), 61, 101,
    102*map*, 156–157
423rd Infantry Regiment (INF), 83, 88, 101,
    102*map*, 156–157
424th Infantry Regiment (INF), 83, 100, 103,
    158–159, 174, 181, 188, 240
440th AAA (Automatic Weapons), 136–137
589th Field Artillery (FA), 101–102

Aachen, 23
active defense, 151–153
Adams, Andrew J., 146, 177–179, 197,
    224–226
Albrick, Edgar J., 130
Allen, Harold D., 158
"Allied Air Power and the Ardennes
    Offensive" (McDonald), 34
Alpeter, Milan K., 135–136
Ambrose, Stephen E., 85, 148
American Red Cross, 254
American Way of War, The (Weigley), 292
Archimede, Dante, 79

Ardennes
    description of, 18–19, 56, 58
    Hitler's strategy and, 32
    importance of, 5
    map of, 20*map*
Ardennes, The (Cole), 34, 46, 108, 240
armored divisions, organization of, 10–14
army field manuals, 4, 9, 288–289
Army Ground Forces Reduction Board, 10
Army Group B, 19, 21
Army Specialized Training Program, 11
Atkinson, Rick, 82

Balch, Harry, 200
Baraque de Fraiture, 226–229
Barkman, Ernst, 245*map*, 246–247
Barnett, C. F., 247–248
Battle of St. Vith, The, 5, 192
Battle of the Bulge, size of, 7–8
Battle: The Story of the Bulge (Toland), 87,
    223, 243, 279
Beatty, William F., 153, 182, 277–279
Berwick, Lee, 84
Bied, Dan, 156–157
Billingsley, Max E., 228
Bitter Woods, The (Eisenhower), 45–46
Bittrich, Willi, 161
Blair, Horace N., 80
Blitzkrieg Legend, The (Frieser), 120
Boos, Frank, 25
Born, 270, 272–275, 277
Born-Wallerode line, 127
Bouck, Lyle, 60, 78
Bowman, Truman R., 153, 182–183
Boyer, Donald P., Jr., 108–109, 137, 149, 167,
    192, 199, 202, 211–212, 287, 296
Boylan, Vincent L., 97–98, 230–231, 256
Bradley, Omar N.
    Ardennes and, 20*map*, 32–33
    assessment by, 85–86
    command of, 14, 24
    Eisenhower and, 148
    Kasserine Pass and, 122
    later life of, 294
    Manteuffel and, 293
    Middleton and, 46–47

refusal to withdraw, 56, 133
reorganization and, 170
on Runstedt, 21
Silvester and, 17
strategy and, 49
withdrawal and, 241
Brandenberger, Erich von, 35, 149
Brandt, Heino, 294
breakout, 14–16
Britton, Dudley J., 109, 272–273
Brooke, Alan, 149, 171, 223
Brown, John C., 135, 243, 246, 268
Buckman, Clarence L., 68
Butcher, Harry C., 70, 122

Caddick-Adams, Peter, 33, 78
casualties, 8, 17, 23–24, 211, 240, 249–250,
    281, 290
Cavender, Charles C., 25, 59, 61, 69, 83, 88,
    133–134, 156
Chamness, Earl T., 85
Chappuis, Richard D., 135–136, 243, 268,
    273–276, 279
Christmas Eve attack, 243–247, 245map
Churchill, Winston, 239, 264
civilian casualties, 8
Clarke, Bruce C.
    active defense and, 153
    assessment of, 287
    at Bastogne, 94
    Clay and, 196
    on December 20, 180
    establishing defense and, 150–152
    expected attack on, 146
    Fuller and, 201
    Hoge and, 157–158
    later life of, 295
    Leydecker and, 195
    main attack and, 199, 202–203
    Manhay and, 247
    Manteuffel and, 293
    on "mission-type" orders, 5, 169
    on morale, 168
    on organization, 193
    overlay plan and, 213–214
    Remer's attack and, 218

retaking of St. Vith and, 268, 273–277,
    279–280
retraining and, 255–256
Ridgway and, 253, 288
Riggs and, 104, 130–131
at St. Vith, 106–108, 123–126, 136
troop movements and, 109, 111
withdrawal and, 222–223, 230–231
Clausewitz, Carl von, 4, 15, 32–33, 51, 58,
    74, 94–95, 104, 151, 204, 287
Clay, Roy U., 60, 77, 107–108, 151–152,
    167–168, 196, 287, 296
Coddington, Edwin B., 287
Cole, Hugh M., 32, 34, 38, 46–47, 60, 108,
    152, 157, 203, 240, 243, 247
Collins, J. Lawton, 172, 241, 265, 295
Combat Command A (CCA), 95, 124,
    134–136, 154–155, 173–174, 196,
    203, 218, 230–231, 241–242, 244, 248,
    276–280
Combat Command B (CCB), 83–88, 98,
    104, 124–125, 131–132, 131map,
    146, 154–158, 180–181, 188, 203,
    218–219, 231, 240–242, 247–248,
    276–280, 286
Combat Command R (CCR), 95, 109–113,
    118–119, 125–126, 154–155, 173, 195,
    203, 230
communications, poor, 82–83, 87, 288
Communications Zone (COMZ), 24
Company Commander (MacDonald), 49
confirmation bias, 35, 47
convoy, supply, 224–225
Corps Commanders of the Bulge (Winton),
    123, 150
Cota, Norman D. (Dutch), 132–133
Craig, Malin, 87
Crawford, Max, 79
Creel, SGT, 103
Creveld, Martin van, 119
Crusade in Europe (Eisenhower), 85
Cummings, Fred S., Jr., 180–181, 219

Damon, William F., 60, 77, 79, 126, 128
Dark December (Merriam), 34
Dawidczyk, Stanley J., 157

Descheneaux, George L., Jr., 59, 61, 69, 84, 133–134
Devers, Jacob L., 16, 20map, 76, 148
Devine, Mark A., 59–60, 79–80, 100–101, 106–107, 117–118, 126, 170
Dickson, Benjamin A. "Monk," 48
Dietrich, Sepp, 35, 38, 42, 146, 160
Dillender, Jack, 154
doctrinal rates of march, 97
Drueke, Wilhelm, 76
Dubuisson, James G., 129, 255
Dugan, Augustine D., 126–127
Dunkirk, 239
Dunn, John J., 109, 199–200, 212
Dupuy, R. Ernest, 51, 175, 226
Dupuy, Trevor N., 119

East, Wilbur S., 126
Eaton, Henry A., 130
Eddy, Manton S., 265
Eisenhower, Dwight D.
    command crisis and, 264
    concerns of, 70
    German deception of, 35
    on Hodges, 210
    later life of, 294
    Manteuffel and, 293
    reorganization and, 170–171
    situational assessment by, 148–149
    speed of response from, 292
    on status of Germans, 15, 21
    strategy and, 18, 85–86, 122
    XVIII Airborne Corps and, 196
Eisenhower, John S. D., 45–46, 56
Enigma code, 31
enterprising officers, 287
Erlenbusch, Robert C., 131, 151, 153–154, 182, 203, 213–214, 247, 253–254, 268, 273–276, 280–281, 286–287, 295
Ersatzheer (replacement army), 4

Falter, Alfred, 108–109
Farrens, Kenneth C., 78–79
Farris, James W., 128
Fast Tanks and Heavy Bombers (Johnson), 154

Felber, Hans Gustav, 270, 276
Fifth Panzer Army, 62–63
Fighting Power (Creveld), 119
Fortified Goose Egg, 213–214, 220, 222, 229–233, 253
Foster, Robert, 109
Franke, Herbert, 219
Frasier, Sid, 246
Frieser, Karl Heinz, 120
From Normandy to the Ruhr (Guderian), 63, 294
Führer Escort Brigade (FEB), 43, 121, 147, 153, 157, 161, 169, 173, 187, 197, 218, 242
Fuller, William H. G., 131, 199, 201

Gavin, James M., 122, 191, 210, 221, 227–228, 242, 264, 288
Generals of the Bulge (Morelock), 123
Genius for War, A (Dupuy), 119
German equipment, 286
German forces, preparations of, 33–35
Germans
    assessment, intentions, and orders of, 62–63, 68, 119–122, 168–170, 188–190, 216, 242–243, 265–267
    operational planning of, 35–39
    organization, training, and planning of, 39–42
    situational assessment of, 146–148
    troop movements of, 98–100
Gerow, Leonard, 15, 21, 47, 86
Gettysburg Campaign, The (Coddington), 287
Ghost Front (Whiting), 44
Gill, Harry, 256
Goldstein, Elliot, 175, 226–229, 287
Goodman, Irving, 118
Graves, Rupert, 248
Griffin, Marcus S., 268
Gross, Gerhard P., 120
Guderian, Heinz, 33
Guderian, Heinz Günther, 63, 70, 169–170, 294
Guingand, Francis "Freddie" de, 172
Guns at Last Light (Atkinson), 82

Hansen, Chester, 122
Hansen, Max, 118–119, 127–128
Hardin, Richard A., 108
Hasbrouck, Robert W.
  14th Cavalry Group and, 128
  82nd Airborne Division and, 191–192
  anticipation of attack on, 187
  assessment of, 145, 212, 287
  at Bastogne, 108, 111
  Boylan and, 98
  calmness of, 211
  Clarke and, 106
  Clay and, 168
  command of, 124, 182
  on December 16, 93–94
  enemy positions and, 149–150
  equipment and, 243
  establishing defense and, 150–151
  on eve of battle, 55
  Gavin and, 210
  Hoge and, 158, 194
  Kean and, 172–173
  later life of, 295
  main attack and, 197, 202–203
  Manhay and, 247
  Manteuffel and, 293
  Middleton and, 150
  morale and, 254–255
  night attacks and, 291–292
  Olson and, 175
  orders from, 174
  overlay plan and, 213, 216
  pessimism of, 193
  prisoners and, 183
  recollections of, 167
  as replacement for Silvester, 17
  report from, 161
  retaking of St. Vith and, 267–270, 272,
    274–275, 277–280
  Ridgway and, 288
  role of, 5
  Rosebaum and, 134, 136, 252–253
  at St. Vith, 112, 137, 145–146, 154–155
  strategy and, 124–127
  Task Force Navajo and, 129
  training and, 250–252, 255, 290–291

troop movements and, 158–159
  withdrawal and, 221–223, 230–233
Haug, Charles, 159, 240, 296
Herbstnebel (Autumn Mist), 34
Heubner, Clarence R., 265
Heydte, Friedrich August Freiherr von der,
    36, 99
Hickey, Doyle, 243
Hitler, Adolf
  Clausewitz and, 32
  operational planning and, 38–39
  planning and, 31
  prior to battle, 44
  Skorzeny and, 35
  SS divisions and, 42
  strategy and, 7, 18, 265
  troop movements and, 267
  Western Front and, 21–22
  withdrawal and, 242
Hobbs, Leland, 191
Hodges, Courtney H.
  assessment of, 122–123
  command of, 14, 24
  equipment and, 290
  Estimate 37 and, 48
  Hasbrouck and, 173, 182
  later life of, 294
  main attack and, 203
  Middleton and, 83
  Montgomery and, 172, 210
  prior to battle, 70
  refusal to withdraw, 56
  Ruhr River dams and, 23
  Siegfried Line and, 133
  on status of Germans, 86
  withdrawal and, 223, 241
Hodgson, Reginald H., 253
Hoffman-Schönborn, Günther, 39, 44–45,
    75–76, 100, 103, 105, 194, 217, 270
Hogan, Samuel M., 178, 227, 240
Hoge, William M.
  assessment of, 287
  Cummings and, 219
  establishing defense and, 150–151
  Hasbrouck and, 161
  horseshoe defense and, 124–125, 180

later life of, 295
main attack and, 202–203
overlay plan and, 213–214
Peiper and, 110
Ridgway and, 224
at St. Vith, 157–158, 194
strategy and, 101
troop movements and, 86–88, 98, 131
at Winterspelt, 104, 111
withdrawal and, 223–224, 230, 242
Hollinger, John C., 83
Hondorp, Donald, 97
horseshoe defense, 124–127, 153–155, 161–
162, 168, 173–174, 180–181, 187–188
Howison, Jack, 278–279
Hughes, George E., 253
Hughes, Walter J., 137, 247
Hürtgen Forest, 23–24

infantry divisions, organization of, 10–14
intelligence, 45–50
island defense, 181

Jadot, Georges and Madame, 254
Jamiel, Morphis A., 97
Jodl, Alfred, 22, 35, 120–121, 242, 265
Johnson, David E., 154
Jones, Alan W.
Clarke and, 94
command of, 203
communication and, 288
establishing defense and, 150
evaluation of battle and, 82–83
on eve of battle, 55–56
Gavin and, 210
Hasbrouck and, 161
Middleton and, 150
Nelson and, 159–160
Robertson and, 49, 133
at St. Vith, 106–107, 123–124
strategy and, 61, 80, 84
troop movements and, 59, 100, 102,
102map
withdrawal and, 86–88, 213, 222, 224,
230
Jones, Alan W., Jr., 83

Jones, Joseph W., 177
Jones, Robert B., 97–98, 174, 202, 231–232
Jüttner, Arthur, 40, 76, 82, 103–105, 220

Kampfgruppe Peiper, 75, 98, 110, 118
Kane, Matthew W., 178
Kasserine Pass, 122
Kean, William B., 168, 172–173, 221,
223–224
Kittel, Friedrich, 39, 100, 180, 194, 219
Kline, John K., 25
Knowlton, William A., 98, 256–257, 287,
290–291
Koch, Oscar, W., 46
Kracke, John L., 80
Krag, Ernst, 226–227
Kriz, Robert, 60, 68
Krueger, Herbert, 175
Krüger, Walter, 38, 42, 68, 88, 100, 122, 170,
188, 220
Kuizema, Harold, 233

Ladd, Leonard Hoyle, 250, 256, 287
Lammerding, Heinz, 242
Langhäuser, Rudolph, 100, 188, 190
Lavrenz, Roland, 278
Lee, John C. H., 24
Leydecker, Charles E., 126, 195
Lindsey, Franklin P., 101, 103, 105, 158–159,
174, 194
Losheim Gap, 25, 76–82
Lucht, Walther
main attack and, 197
Manteuffel and, 190
mission objective for, 37–38
role of, 42
Schramm and, 169
at St. Vith, 121–122, 147–148, 153, 160,
179–180, 187, 193–194
strategy and, 44–45
on terrain, 286
troop movements and, 76, 88, 99–100
Lüttwitz, Heinrich von, 88, 188

M4 Sherman tanks, 153–154
MacArthur, Douglas, 295

MacDonald, Charles B., 3, 18–19, 23, 48–49, 86, 127, 201, 213, 223, 226, 294
Malmedy Massacre, 110
Manhay, 243–248
manpower, shortage of, 3, 10, 18, 22, 250
Manteuffel, Hasso von
  assessment of, 121
  attack by, 42, 63
  beginning of battle and, 74, 88–89
  Clausewitz and, 33
  description of, 45
  failure to take St. Vith and, 160–161
  fuel and, 68
  later life of, 293
  main attack and, 197
  Model and, 147, 190
  night attacks and, 292
  recollections of, 5, 192, 220
  at St. Vith, 10
  on St. Vith, 168
  stalling of, 188
  strategy and, 35–36, 38–39
  troop movements and, 112–113
  withdrawal and, 240–242
Marche-en-Famenne, 197
Marshall, George C., 10, 45
Martin, Harry F., Jr., 25–26, 68
Martin, Orville, 179
Matthews, Church, 112, 117
Mayes, James, 80
Mayes, Walter J., 127–129
McBride, Richard L., 152, 187–188, 200–201, 204, 214, 246, 248–249, 254, 272, 287, 289, 297
McDonald, George C., 34–35
McIlroy, James R., 74
McMahon, Leo T., 50–51, 101, 107
McNair, Lesley J., 10
Menschen zwischen Trümmern and Weideraufbau (Ritter), 294
Merriam, Robert E., 34, 269, 293
Mestas, Lee A., 154
Metz, 17
Meuse River, 122, 148, 242–243, 265
Meyers, John C., 127–128
Meyers, Samuel L., 123

Middleton, Troy H.
  Ardennes and, 45–46
  arrival of, 24
  beginning of battle and, 83, 86–88
  career of, 45
  Clarke and, 94
  command failure and, 47
  communication and, 288
  Hasbrouck and, 108, 150, 161
  Hodges and, 133
  intelligence and, 49
  January 1945 attacks and, 265
  Jones and, 106–107
  lack of direction from, 170
  orders from, 195–196
  Robertson and, 56
  situational assessment and, 149
  strategy and, 123
  troop formations and, 25, 36
  troop movements and, 101–102
Millikin, John, 265
Mills, Aubrey L., 78
Mills, Roger B., 110
mission-type orders, 5
Model, Walther, 19, 35–36, 38–39, 42, 112–113, 120, 146–147, 160–161, 170, 190, 217, 242, 293
Moll, Dietrich, 37, 39–40, 88, 100, 147–148, 193–194, 197, 216–218, 266, 276, 291–292
Montgomery, Bernard Law
  "airborne carpet" of, 16
  on Americans, 56
  Ardennes and, 20*map*
  Bradley and, 148–149
  command of, 14, 24
  Eisenhower and, 264
  Hitler's strategy and, 32–33
  Hodges and, 210
  January 1945 attacks and, 264
  later life of, 294
  Manteuffel and, 293
  reorganization and, 170–173
  speed of response from, 292
  on status of Germans, 48
  withdrawal and, 222–223, 240–241

Moorman, Frank W., 288
Morell, Eugene, 74
Morelock, Jerry D., 123
Morrell, Eugene, 239
Morrison, Hugh R., 157
Morse, John W., 68–69
Murray, Everett W., 93
Myth and Reality of German Warfare, The
    (Gross), 120

Nebelwerfer rockets, 199–200
Neese, Alonzo A., 104
"Neglected Ardennes, The" (MacDonald), 18
Neher, Kenneth M., 201
Nelson, Gerald, 135
Nelson, Gustin M., 24, 62, 76, 85, 100, 103,
    122, 132–133, 159–160, 181, 230–232,
    240, 287
Nelson, Roy "Big Moose," 135–136
night attacks, 36–37, 291–292
Nordwind, 265–266
Nungesser, W. L., 104, 111–112, 199, 201

O'Bryant, J. D., 224–225
Olson, Arthur A., 175, 177, 192, 287
Omaha Beach, 16
On War (Clausewitz), 4, 15, 287
Ondenval defile, 269
Operation Greif, 35–36
Operation Market Garden, 16
Oseth, Frederic W., 83
Our River, 25, 56, 58, 158
Oxford, Paul G., 84–85

Parker, Arthur C., III, 175, 192, 226, 287
Parker's Crossroads, 174–177, 188, 202, 217,
    226–229, 233–234, 243–244
Patch, Alexander, 266
Patton, George S., Jr., 14, 17, 45–46,
    148–149, 221, 287
Paxton, Forest, 248
Peiper, Joachim
    attack by, 104–105, 160–161
    clearing way for, 220
    end of drive of, 168
    later life of, 293

    at Malmedy, 130
    Mills and, 110
    rescue of, 188
    stopping of, 191
    troop movements and, 75, 86, 98–99, 118,
        147
    withdrawal of, 240
Pergin, David E., 110
Perrin, Herbert T., 84, 230
Phantom teams, 171–172, 210
photoreconnaissance, 49
Porché, Stanley E., 79
Poteau, 134–136
Puett, Joseph F., 82, 84, 157

Quill, William B., 221

Recht, 118–119
reconstitution, 248–257
Reeves, Andrew R., 48–49
Reeves, Gerald E., 135–136, 244
Reichsbahn, 34–35
Reid, Alexander D., 59, 61–62, 83–84, 100,
    103–104, 111, 124, 131, 158, 174, 181,
    223
Remer, Otto-Ernst, 43, 121, 153, 157, 169,
    194, 196, 217–221, 231–232, 242, 293
replacements, 4
Reppa, Robert P., 103
retraining, 250–252, 255–257
Rhea, Robert L., 131, 243, 246–247, 268,
    273, 277, 279
Richardson, Walter B., 243
Ridge, Paul A., 60, 79–80, 126
Ridgway, Matthew B.
    arrival of, 149
    assessment of, 288
    bombing campaign and, 266
    CCB and, 241–243
    command of, 171, 210–211
    description of, 190–191
    Fortified Goose Egg and, 229
    Hasbrouck and, 287
    January 1945 attacks and, 265
    later life of, 294–295
    on Manhay, 247

night attacks and, 291–292
refusal to withdraw, 212–213, 220
retaking of St. Vith and, 268–269, 274,
    277–278
at St. Vith, 203
tension with, 253
troop movements and, 173, 182, 227–228
withdrawal and, 221–224
Riggs, Thomas J., Jr., 104, 107, 109, 125,
    130–131, 147–148, 150, 199, 201–202,
    287, 295
Ritter, Klaus, 43–45, 63, 69–70, 73, 88,
    105, 112, 126, 156, 179–180, 200, 225,
    266–267, 294
Robertson, Walter M., 49, 56, 82, 133
Rogers, Will, Jr., 233–234, 296
Rose, Maurice, 178
Rosebaum, Dwight A., 111–112, 134–135,
    151, 154–155, 174, 213–214, 216, 218,
    231, 242–243, 247, 252–253, 287
Ruhr, attempt to protect, 7
Ruhr River dams, 23
Rundstedt, Gerd von, 21, 35, 38, 121–122,
    146–147
Ryan, John L., Jr., 97–98, 111, 155, 230

Samrée, 177–179
Scarborough, Leon T., 110
Schaffner, John, 209–210, 233, 293, 296
Scheldt Estuary, 16
Schramm, Percy E., 32, 120, 169
Schrijvers, Peter, 8
Schroeder, Frederick, 168, 172–173
Seitz, Richard Joe, 267–269, 273, 277–278,
    281
Shakespeare, William V., 84
Shea, Jack, 79
Sibert, Edwin L., 47–48
Siegfried Line, 15–16, 23–24, 56
Silesia, defense of, 31–51
Silvester, Lindsay McDonald, 10, 16–17, 125
Simpson, William H., 123
Skorzeny, Otto, 35–36, 84, 99, 127
Skyline Drive, 58, 82, 101, 104, 156
Slayden, William M., 51, 88
Small Slam, 35, 38

Snow and Steel (Caddick-Adams), 33
Soldier (Ridgway), 212
Soldier's Story, A (Bradley), 21
Spencer, Gayle H., 135–136
St. Lo, Battle of, 14
St. Vith
    beginning of battle and, 73–89
    crisis at, 167–183
    decision at, 187–204
    disposition of troops for, 57map
    eve of battle at, 55–70
    main attack at, 197–204, 198map
    maps of, 57map, 66–67map
    plan to retake, 267–268, 271map
    redemption at, 263–281
    stand at, 145–162
St. Vith: Lion in the Way (Dupuy), 51, 175
Stafford, George, 104
Stine, Harlan C., 218
stomach battalions, 22
Stone, Robert O., 136–137, 174, 287
Strange, Glen L., 219–220
Strong, Kenneth, 48
Struggle for Europe, The (Wilmot), 17
Supreme Commander, The (Ambrose), 85,
    148
surprise, element of, 33
Swantack, Frank A., 108
Sweat, Fred C., 111
Sylvan, William C., 48, 70, 122–123, 240

Taliaferro, Henry G., 275
tanks, American versus German, 286
Task Force Brewster, 244
Task Force Navajo, 128–130, 155, 173
Taylor, Maxwell, 288
Thompson, James E., 252
Time for Trumpets, A (MacDonald), 3, 18,
    48, 86, 127, 201, 213, 223
time on target, 14
Toland, John, 87, 223, 243, 279
Tomasik, Edmond J., 267–268, 273–276
Tompkins, Francis P., 268–269
Train, William F., 132, 203
Triplet, William S., 211, 252–253, 267–269,
    272, 277, 279, 287, 289, 292

Truman, Harry S., 294
Tucker, John, 178–179

Ultra communications, 31–32
Unknown Dead, The (Schrijvers), 8

Van Tine, Truman Luther, 135–136
Verdun, 16–17
Vogelsgang, Fritz, 63, 68

Wacht am Rhein (Watch on the Rhine), 34
Wagener, Carl, 33, 89, 265
Wagner, Richard, 33
Waldenburg, Siegfried von, 63, 122, 178, 265
Waldrop, Rex E., 278
Walker, Walton H., 295
Warren, Fred M., 109–111, 119, 126, 151,
    155, 214, 296

Watson, Howard, 126
weather, importance of, 5
Weidinger, Otto, 227, 229, 233, 242
Weigley, Russell, 292
Wemple, John P., 111, 118, 151, 155, 174,
    213–214, 231, 256, 268, 272–273,
    277–279, 295
Wessels, Robert R., 37
Whiteman, Joseph V. "Navajo," 128–129,
    137, 150, 168, 246, 249, 251, 287
Whiting, Charles, 44, 171
Wilmot, Chester, 17, 145, 287
Wilson, Charles McMoran, 291
Wilson, Lieutenant, 272–273
Winton, Harold R., 45, 123, 150
withdrawal, 221–224
Woodruff, Owen E., Jr., 94, 107, 296
Woodruff, R., 228

About the Author

Gregory Fontenot is a retired Colonel of the US Army. He is currently a consultant on threat emulation for Army experimentation and a working historian. He was lead author of *On Point: The United States Army in Operation Iraqi Freedom* and is the author of *The 1st Infantry Division and the US Army Transformed: Road to Victory in Desert Storm, 1970–1991* (University of Missouri Press), winner of the 2017 Army Historical Foundation Distinguished Writing Award for Unit History. He lives in Lansing, Kansas.